# CULTURAL HISTORIES OF CINEMA

*This new book series examines the relationship between cinema and culture. It will feature interdisciplinary scholarship that focuses on the national and transnational trajectories of cinema as a network of institutions, representations, practices and technologies. Of primary concern is analysing cinema's expansive role in the complex social, economic and political dynamics of the twentieth and twenty-first centuries.*

### SERIES EDITORS
*Lee Grieveson and Haidee Wasson*

### ALSO PUBLISHED
Cinema Beyond Territory: In-flight Entertainment and
Atmospheres of Globalisation, *Stephen Groening*
Empire and Film, *edited by Lee Grieveson and Colin MacCabe*
Film and the End of Empire, *edited by Lee Grieveson and Colin MacCabe*
Global Mexican Cinema: Its Golden Age, *edited by Robert McKee Irwin and
Maricruz Castro Ricalde*
Making Movies into Art: Picture Craft from the Magic Lantern to Early Hollywood,
*Kaveh Askari*
Shadow Economies of Cinema: Mapping Informal Film Distribution, *Ramon Lobato*

# The Grierson Effect

## Tracing Documentary's International Movement

*Edited by* **Zoë Druick and Deane Williams**

•

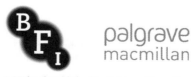

A BFI book published by Palgrave Macmillan

*For Peter Morris, in memoriam* – ZD
*For Ina Bertrand* – DW

First published in 2014 by
PALGRAVE MACMILLAN

on behalf of the

BRITISH FILM INSTITUTE
21 Stephen Street, London W1T 1LN
www.bfi.org.uk

There's more to discover about film and television through the BFI.
Our world-renowned archive, cinemas, festivals, films, publications and learning resources are here to inspire you.

Palgrave Macmillan in the UK is an imprint of Macmillan Publishers Limited, registered in England, company number 785998, of Houndmills, Basingstoke, Hampshire RG21 6XS. Palgrave Macmillan in the US is a division of St Martin's Press LLC, 175 Fifth Avenue, New York, NY 10010. Palgrave Macmillan is the global academic imprint of the above companies and has companies and representatives throughout the world. Palgrave® and Macmillan® are registered trademarks in the United States, the United Kingdom, Europe and other countries.

Cover design: Liron Gilenberg
Cover images: (front) *Where No Vultures Fly* (Harry Watt, 1951), © Ealing Studios; (back) *Man of Aran* (Robert Flaherty, 1934), Gainsborough Pictures; *Fires Were Started* (Humphrey Jennings, 1943), Crown Film Unit; *Man of Africa* (Cyril Frankel, 1954), © Group 3 Limited.
Designed by couch

Set by Cambrian Typesetters, Camberley, Surrey
Printed in China

This book is printed on paper suitable for recycling and made from fully managed and sustained forest sources. Logging, pulping and manufacturing processes are expected to conform to the environmental regulations of the country of origin.

British Library Cataloguing-in-Publication Data
A catalogue record for this book is available from the British Library
A catalog record for this book is available from the Library of Congress

ISBN 978–1–84457–539–8 (pb)
ISBN 978–1–84457–540–4 (hb)

# Contents

# Acknowledgments

The editors would like to acknowledge and thank the BFI Cultural Histories of Cinema series editors, Lee Grieveson and Haidee Wasson, for their unstinting support for this project, as well as everyone else at the press who helped the book along to completion. We also wish to acknowledge the Grierson Archive, Stirling, Scotland, where much of the primary research for this collection was undertaken. Keyan Tomaselli's 'Grierson, Afrikaner Nationalism and South Africa' and Abé Markus Nornes's 'Translating Grierson: Japan' are revised versions of articles that appeared in a special 'After Grierson' issue of the online journal *Screening the Past* edited by Ina Bertrand following the Breaking the Boundaries: The Stirling Documentary Conference held in January 1999.

# Notes on Contributors

IAN AITKEN is Professor of Film Studies in the Academy of Film, Hong Kong Baptist University. He is the author of *Film and Reform: John Grierson and the Documentary Film Movement* (1992), *The Documentary Film Movement: An Anthology* (1998), *Alberto Cavalcanti* (2001), *European Film Theory and Cinema* (2001), *Realist Film Theory and Cinema* (2006) and *Lukacsian Film Theory and Cinema* (2013). He is also the editor of the *Encyclopedia of the Documentary Film* (2006), and *The Concise Encyclopedia of the Documentary Film* (2013) and *Routledge Major Works: Documentary Film* (2012).

IB BONDEBJERG is Professor in the Department of Media, Cognition and Communication, University of Copenhagen and Director of the Centre for Modern European Studies, University of Copenhagen, Denmark. He was the co-director of the European research project *Changing Media – Changing Europe* (2000–5) and the large national research project *Media and Democracy in the Network Society* (2000–6). He served as chairman of the Danish Film Institute (1997–2000). He has published more than 100 articles in national and international journals and books. His most recent single-authored book publications are *Narratives of Reality: History of the Danish TV-Documentary* (2008), *Images of Reality: The Modern Danish Film Documentary* (2011) and *Engaging with Reality: Documentary and Politics* (2014).

STEPHEN CHARBONNEAU is Assistant Professor in the School of Communication and Multimedia Studies at Florida Atlantic University, where he teaches courses in film history, theory and aesthetics. His research interests include the history of documentary film, ethnography, cultural policy and collectivist media practices. He is currently working on a book entitled *Other Americas: Injured Identities, Participatory Media, and the War on Poverty*, a review of state-sponsored uses of film and television as part of Lyndon Johnson's War on Poverty. His work has been published in the *Journal of Popular Film and Television*, *Spectator*, *Challenge for Change/Société nouvelle: The Collection* and *Encyclopedia of Documentary Film*.

CAMILLE DEPREZ is Research Assistant Professor in the Academy of Film of Hong Kong Baptist University. Her initial research areas were the Indian mainstream film – or Bollywood – and television industries. Two single-authored books, *La télévision indienne: Un modèle d'appropriation culturelle* (2006) and *Bollywood: cinéma et mondialisation* (2010), academic articles and book chapters came out of these two long-term research projects. She is currently developing new funded research projects on independent Indian documentary film and French colonial documentary film in Asia. With Judith Pernin, she is the co-editor of the forthcoming book *Post-1990 Documentary: Redefining Independence*.

ZOË DRUICK is Associate Professor in the School of Communication at Simon Fraser University, Canada. Her books include *Allan King's A Married Couple* (2010), *Programming Reality: Perspectives on English-Canadian Television* (2008) and *Projecting Canada: Documentary Film and Government Policy at the National Film Board* (2007). She has also published numerous articles on reality-based and educational media in journals such as *Screen, Television and New Media, Canadian Journal of Communication, Canadian Journal of Film Studies* and *Studies in Documentary*.

MARIANO MESTMAN is Researcher at the National Council of Scientific Research (Argentina) and at the University of Buenos Aires, where he is also Professor in Latin American Cinema. He is author of the book *Del Di Tella a Tucumán Arde: Vanguardia artística y política en el 68 argentino* (2000, in collaboration with Ana Longoni). He has published several articles on cinema and art history in *New Cinemas, Journal of Latin American Cultural Studies, Third Text, Letterature d´America, Secuencias, Film-Historia, Cine Cubano* and *Kilómetro 111*, among others. He was programmer of the Buenos Aires Independent Film Festival between 2005 and 2006.

ABÉ MARKUS NORNES is Professor of Asian Cinema in both the Department of Screen Arts and Cultures, the Department of Asian Languages and Cultures and the School of Art & Design at the University of Michigan. His latest book is *A Research Guide to Japanese Cinema Studies* (2009), which was co-written with Aaron Gerow. His previous books include *Cinema Babel: Translating Global Cinema* (2007). He is also the author of *Forest of Pressure: Ogawa Shinsuke and Postwar Japanese Documentary Film* (2007) and *Japanese Documentary Film: From the Meiji Era to Hiroshima* (2003), as well as many articles in edited volumes and journals such as *Cinema Journal* and *Film Quarterly*.

MARÍA LUISA ORTEGA is Professor of Audiovisual Communication at the Autonoma University of Madrid (Spain). She is co-author of *The Cinema of Latin America* (2003), *Cine documental en América Latina* (2003), *Documental y vanguardia: lenguajes fronterizos* (2005), *Cuba: Cinéma et Révolution* (2006), *De la foto al fotograma. Fotografía y cine documental* (2006), *Cineastas frente al espejo* (2008), *Piedra, papel, tijera: collage en el cine documental* (2009), *Doc. el documental en el siglo XXI* (2010); and editor of *Nada es lo que parece: Falsos documentales, hibridaciones y mestizajes del documental en España* (2005), *Mystère Marker: Pasajes en la obra de Chris Marker* (2006) as well as *Cine directo: Reflexiones en torno a un concepto* (2008); and author of *Espejos Rotos. Aproximaciones al documental norteamericano contemporáneo* (2007). She is member of the editorial board of *Secuencias. Revista de Historia del Cine* and she has been programme advisor of *Cines del Sur* (Granada

International Film Festival) and *Documenta Madrid* (International Madrid Documentary Festival).

SIMON SIGLEY teaches film studies and media practice in the School of Social and Cultural Studies at Massey University, Auckland. His doctoral thesis (2004) was a materialist history of film culture in New Zealand. His research interests are in film and history, reception studies, film aesthetics and the cultural imaginary. He has published on the film-society movement, Jane Campion's reception in France and French film culture's influence in New Zealand. His current major research project is a cultural history of New Zealand's National Film Unit.

MARTIN STOLLERY works part time for the Open University in the UK. He is the author, among other publications, of *Alternative Empires: European Modernist Cinemas and Cultures of Imperialism* (2000). He is currently researching the career of the British film-maker Ian Dalrymple.

KEYAN G. TOMASELLI is Senior Professor and Director of the Centre for Communication, Media and Society, University of KwaZulu-Natal, Durban. He is author of *The Cinema of Apartheid* (1988) and *Encountering Modernity: 20th Century South African Cinemas* (2007), editor of *Critical Arts: South-North Cultural and Media Studies* and co-editor of *Journal of African Cinemas*. He has worked as a documentary film-maker and was co-author of the Film White Paper (1996) and Film Strategy Document (1996) for the South African government.

JULIA VASSILIEVA teaches in film and television studies at Monash University, Melbourne. Her research interests include historical film theory and criticism; Russian classic and contemporary cinema; and Russian art criticism and cultural studies. She has published in the *International Journal of the Humanities, Senses of Cinema, Rouge, Continuum: Journal of Media & Cultural Studies, Screening the Past, Film-Philosophy* and *Cinema Studies*. She is a co-editor of *After Taste: Cultural Value and the Moving Image* (2012).

JERRY WHITE is Canada Research Chair in European Studies at Dalhousie University, Halifax. He is the author of *Revisioning Europe: The Films of John Berger and Alain Tanner* (2011), *The Radio Eye: Cinema in the North Atlantic, 1958–1988* (2009) and *Of This Place and Elsewhere: The Films and Photography of Peter Mettler* (2006). His most recent book is *Two Bicycles: The Work of Jean-Luc Godard and Anne-Marie Miéville* (2013).

DEANE WILLIAMS is Associate Professor in Film and Television Studies, Monash University, Melbourne. His books include *Australian Post-war Documentary Films: An Arc of Mirrors* (2008), with Brian McFarlane, *Michael Winterbottom* (2009) and, with Noel King and Constantine Verevis, the three-volume *Australian Film Theory and Criticism* (2013). He is also editor of the journal *Studies in Documentary Film*.

BRIAN WINSTON has written extensively on the documentary including several books (including *Lies, Damn Lies & Documentaries* [2000] and *Claiming the Real II – Documentary:*

*Grierson and Beyond* [2009]) with a focus on both film history and ethical and legal concerns. Currently he is the Lincoln Professor at the University of Lincoln. He has been a governor of the British Film Institute (and recently edited *The BFI Documentary Film Book* for them), and a Grierson Trustee. A feature-length documentary on Robert Flaherty – *A Boatload of Wild Irishmen* – which he wrote and co-produced was released in 2011.

# Introduction

*Zoë Druick and Deane Williams*

Documentary is cheap: it is, on all considerations of public accountancy, safe. If it fails for the theatres it may, by manipulation, be accommodated non-theatrically in one of half a dozen ways. Moreover, by reason of its cheapness, it permits a maximum amount of production and a maximum amount of directorial training against the future, on a limited sum. It even permits the building of an entire production and distribution machine for the price of a single theatrical. These considerations are of some importance where new experiments in cinema are concerned. With one theatrical film you hit or miss; with a machine, if it is reasonably run, the preliminary results may not be immediately notable or important, but they tend to pile up. Piling up they create a freedom impossible on any other policy.[1]

John Grierson

John Grierson (1898–1972) was a well-known Scottish film critic, theorist and producer who, while not primarily a film-maker himself, was a central player in the establishment of the British documentary movement. His published work on film, education and democracy is essential reading in film history and communication theory and his travels around the world on behalf of the British government helped to establish a range of film production and distribution units globally. Gregarious and charismatic, he was particularly active in the interwar period when social liberalism attempted to negotiate a third way between planned economies and free markets, and during the command economies of wartime.[2] Grierson went away to graduate school in Chicago on a Rockefeller scholarship in the mid-1920s and brought back what he learned in the United States (and not just at university) about film, public relations and sociology to a British civil service seeking to engage new media for the kinds of public communication increasingly required of states. In many ways, Grierson helped to forge the field of documentary as it came to be understood in the postwar world as a technique of citizenship by helping to envision and then justify its institutionalisation. Even more significantly, documentary, devised as a technology for modernisation, was pressed into service for nation-building, for bolstering a mediated public sphere and for conveying in a more compelling and immediate manner the problems and concerns of ordinary people as they related to state projects. It was closely connected to modern educational theories and, depending on the context, was circulated in both theatrical and non-theatrical settings. It ended up being a formative aspect of both classroom media and television documentaries, mainstays of media in everyday life in many parts of the world. In short, without

Grierson, today's media culture and its discursive relationship to the public sphere would in all likelihood not look the same.

However, Grierson was no mere functionary. He synthesised a number of philosophical and theoretical traditions, providing a sophisticated concept of realism (as an expression of ideals) gleaned from Immanuel Kant and other enlightenment thinkers that helped to organise the nascent form of documentary.[3] The representational strategy of types and the use of the story-form were not, in other words, a result of technological immaturities. They were in Grierson's words 'new forms' that stemmed from a belief in the best way to illustrate today's social problems and tomorrow's solutions.[4] As far as political theory went, he was a liberal inspired by American pragmatists. Along with many of his day, Grierson believed in the role of the expert in mediating between the complications of the political and social world and the ordinary voter; the civically minded film-maker could be one such expert. As far as educational theory went, Grierson was similar to many reformers of his day in believing that film could engage students (and other audiences) beyond the cognitive realm, making learning more vital and exciting. The particular pastiche of ideas about technology, education and citizenship that converged on a vision of benevolent leaders and malleable masses was understandably palatable to many different political regimes, especially because it came wrapped up in a moral imperative: it was the responsibility of civil servants of all kinds to convey political ideas to their wards in the most appealing manner possible.

Grierson defined realist documentary as 'a troubled and difficult art' but had a clear view of the instrumental uses it should be made to play: as early as 1933 he said, 'I look upon the cinema as a pulpit and use it as a propagandist.'[5] His enormous influence has turned his name into an adjective commonly paired with lofty terms such as 'legend', 'legacy' and 'tradition'. Very often his name is discussed in conjunction with the British documentary movement, a coterie of progressive film-makers who gathered in the institutional spaces that Grierson helped to establish from the late 1920s to mid-50s (the Empire Marketing Board [EMB], the General Post Office [GPO] Film Unit, the Crown and Colonial Film Units and Group 3 being primary sites). Often this work is connected to the history of British cinema as such. And, even though it has become fairly common to acknowledge the overstatement of his influence and importance, as the centenary of his introduction of the term documentary approaches (first used as an adjective in a 1926 New York *Sun* review of Robert Flaherty's *Moana*), the explanatory and even utopian aspects of film culture that Grierson introduced continue to be an evocative touchstone.[6]

More than the films made by the British documentary film movement, or the crafting of a suggestive definition for documentary, the fact that Grierson affected, through his writings (memoranda, publications and policy papers) as well as the forging of a global network of contacts, the direction of film cultures around the world is the focus here. Rather than contribute to the Grierson legend, then, this collection aims to decentre it. By focusing on the dissemination of his ideas and the ways in which they were materialised in different contexts, we hope to move beyond the freight of the British documentary movement to the many manifestations of film, education and official culture to which Grierson, in various ways, contributed. While at times the focus on Grierson tends to highlight particular stories of national film successes at the expense of other production histories, it is, we maintain, still valuable to consider the ways in which creative work operated within limitations and constraints. It is precisely this tension between individuals and institutions that animates the Grierson effect. This decentring will insist that work done in the colonies and dominions was as important as that done in the imperial centre rather than secondary to it.

To understand the Grierson effect as it has circulated and taken shape worldwide entails reconsidering Grierson himself as a motivating factor for valorising the means of making, circulating and watching documentary cinema. In particular, his emphasis on the connection between film, propaganda, education and citizenship in a democracy was enormously influential. While there have been numerous historical and biographical accounts of Grierson and his ideas, there has been less attention to and examination of the infinitely more intricate and multifarious Grierson effect: how Grierson (the person) and 'Griersonian' (the set of ideas) interacted with local conditions and forces to help bring about legitimising frameworks for documentary and educational film production and circulation.[7] Most fascinatingly, as this volume attests, Griersonian justifications have been enlisted to support projects by people and groups with radically different political orientations – from colonial agents and nationalists to liberation film-makers. Arguably common to them all is a desire to modernise the state and engage its citizens, or at the very least appear to do so. Moving from imperialist to internationalist, from film to television, and maintaining residues of an eclectic philosophical combination of public relations, New Deal socialism, liberal imperialism and Calvinism, it is no wonder, perhaps, that the Grierson effect has been so impressively elastic.

The British strategy to make and use film in the colonies was rooted in a logic of local autonomy under ultimate British authority not dissimilar from other techniques of colonial governance. Through the Empire Marketing Board and the Imperial Relations Trust, the British pushed for a policy that increased the stock of empire films available in every part of the British sphere of influence. Concretely, this meant the organisation of libraries of educational films for schools and non-theatrical circuits. They also innovated in the area of non-theatrical exhibition, both at home and abroad.[8] Nevertheless, it is important to acknowledge the Grierson effect's particular efficacy in creating film infrastructure – the 'machine' referred to in the epigraph to this chapter, including production units and exhibition circuits – that helped to foster spaces for training and engagement with film by locals, usually drawn from elite classes. None of this is taken into account in usual histories of the British documentary film movement, which in the main tend to focus on British film-making, rarely investigating circuits of film distribution, and were certainly never concerned with film-making in the colonies, dominions and elsewhere.[9]

Grierson is perhaps best known for his work with the EMB (1926–33) and the GPO Film Unit (1933–40) in interwar Britain. This institutional and discursive imbrication with discourses of Empire and Commonwealth has meant that his effect has been more recently considered in light of postcolonial cultural histories and film theories.[10] As contributions to this volume by Ian Aitken, Camille Deprez, Martin Stollery and Keyan Tomaselli show, it is because of Grierson's association with British forces of imperialism that his effect has much to tell us about the quality of colonial encounters.

Their chapters provide a nuanced and productive accounting for the multiple ways in which Grierson was engaged in a range of colonial and nationalist formations across the globe in the mid-twentieth century.[11]

As Zoë Druick, Simon Sigley and Deane Williams demonstrate in their contributions, in white settler colonies, such as Canada, New Zealand and Australia, Griersonian ideas were foundational for establishing institutions of film production, archiving and exhibition on a national scale. In other contexts, such as Scandinavia, Latin America and Ireland, contributors Ib Bondebjerg, Mariano Mestman/María Luisa Ortega and Jerry White argue, Griersonian ideas helped to forge visions of independent and even revolutionary cinemas. In Japan, Abé Markus Nornes argues, a set of cultural mistranslations made Griersonian ideas, conveyed through the writings of Paul Rotha, at once central and misunderstood in Japanese film culture.

The consideration of Grierson as, in part, the producer of a set of effects, therefore, has something to offer not only studies of British and Commonwealth cinema, past and present. It also aims to contribute to a new transnational vision of educational and documentary cinema.[12] In many of the cases under consideration, not least Britain, film activity occurred before and after Grierson's influence. It is not the purpose of this book to downplay those other aspects of any national cinema. On the contrary, the hope is that, in tracing a network of influence across the globe, the reader will become more aware of the way in which transnational currents intersect with any given national cinema history, perhaps enlivening new approaches and indicating productive points of contact between previously unconnected national stories.

This project is informed by – and aims to contribute to – a series of recent developments in film studies that are challenging its dominant paradigms and considering films in postnational and extratextual ways. As cinema struggles to recalibrate its new position as a residual medium in the digital age, a new interest has been awakened in accounting for the emergence of the field of cinema studies and reassessing its historically dominant foci. Volumes such as *Uncharted Territory* (1997), *Films of Fact* (2008), *Films That Work* (2009), *Useful Cinema* (2011) and *Learning with the Lights Off* (2012) have illuminated formerly marginal film texts, considering how the discipline of film studies has systematically exscribed and ignored the vast majority of the film material encountered in most people's everyday lives. These include engagements with industrial, documentary, educational, amateur, scientific and governmental films, to name only a few. In addition, these studies have drawn our attention to the importance of moving beyond national paradigms to consider the international ambitions and realities of cinematic circulation. And recent re-examinations of British cinema, such as *Shadows of Progress* (2010), *The Projection of Britain* (2011), *Empire and Film* (2011) and *Film and the End of Empire* (2011), are bringing much needed attention to this corpus of films.

*The Grierson Effect* is offered as a contribution to the project of revitalising film studies through new approaches to film history that emphasise the material cultural conditions of its production and circulation. As already alluded to, one of the most significant results of the Grierson effect was the establishment of institutions dedicated to the production and dissemination of documentary and educational film, including film boards and other agencies, journals and festivals. However, the fact that Grierson advocated for such institutions – or 'machines' – is insufficient, we maintain, to explain their foundation. Rather, a compelling case may be made that Grierson's ideas were taken up and mobilised by a variety of groups and constituents, from governments and industry to film-makers and cultural nationalists. It is precisely the details of how such forces were aggregated and sustained over time that make the story worth investigating.

The contributions follow as closely as possible Grierson's movements chronologically, from the United Kingdom to the United States, back to London and then on to the colonies and dominions, Canada, New Zealand, Australia, India, South Africa, before returning to the UK (Ireland, Scotland) and thence to other realms, such as Latin America. Sometimes, as with Japan, Malaya, Singapore, Hong Kong, Ghana and Scandinavia, Griersonian ideas travelled through published material or the exchange of interested individuals. In the case of Latin America, a context apparently far removed from the British sphere of influence, the Grierson effect was still going strong in the 1950s and 60s.

In this volume, Brian Winston discusses the limits of the British style of documentary film-making. British documentary, he contends, was never really comfortable with either storytelling or film experimentation, and its representations of the working class are famously stilted. Nevertheless, the British documentary movement became an essential aspect of British cinema history, giving its films an unwarranted significance, he argues. One of the reasons we have turned our attention away from the British documentary movement as such and towards the Grierson effect is because of the astonishing international reach of the ideas of film production and circulation that he inspired. If British workingmen and women were stilted on the screen, as Winston claims, so too were the locals depicted in colonial film projects undertaken by the Colonial Film Unit, India's Films Division, Canada's National Film Board, the Hong Kong Film Unit and others. By broadening our scope to consider the relation of all of these film-producing agencies, we are able to go beyond assessments of the calibre of the films themselves, or their place in any one national context, to consider the underlying logics of their production.

When looked at in this way, we see Griersonian ideas involved in a range of projects that Stephen Charbonneau characterises in his chapter as 'managing modernity'; these projects were not limited to the British sphere of influence and nor were they the purview of the British documentary movement alone. In the extant literature, it is not uncommon to find an aesthetic and political distinction – made by some contributors to this volume – that pits a true Griersonianism, meant to signify a more poetically ambitious documentary, against more prosaic and propagandistic forms of official cinema. We argue that whether or not there may be films deemed more successful or politically apposite within this tradition we would be remiss to dismiss the more colonial or propagandistic films out of hand. On the contrary, by doing so we miss the ambiguity of the Grierson effect and risk enacting a wishful revisionism. After all, Grierson himself repeatedly called for propaganda and, at the end of his life, counted educational health films for the developing world among his most precious accomplishments.[13] Rosaleen Smyth reasons that this distinction between poetic and prosaic amounts to one between 'high' and 'low' cultural forms, one which Grierson himself promoted, but that historians and critics need not accept.[14]

As Ib Bondebjerg aptly notes in his contribution, the creative treatment of actuality always takes place in 'compromised conditions'. Indeed, following Abé Markus Nornes, we might say that all translation also involves transformation. In this way, Grierson's ideas have been able to appeal to the entire political spectrum and have manifested an array of aesthetic forms. In each context where the Grierson effect has taken hold, there have been improvised practices and 'selective readings' (Tomaselli). As Mariano Mestman and María Luisa Ortega write, rather than a cinema of protest, Grierson's was a 'cinema with proposals'. It is precisely in attending to what the proposals were in the various locations where his ideas were translated that we are able to see the Grierson effect at work. The creation of networks of individuals and organisations through journals, conferences, film festivals and associations was one of the very concrete effects of such a 'cinema of proposals'.

As Stephen Charbonneau traces in his chapter, in the 1920s, Grierson made a study of American politics and film culture; he also came into contact with revolutionary Russian cinema. In examining the Grierson effect in the United States Charbonneau articulates an issue that is often overlooked in the insistence on Grierson as the father of British documentary, namely the ways in which Grierson influenced and, more importantly here, was influenced: not just by American films and film-making but by American ideals as well. While the ways in which Grierson drew on Walter Lippmann and the Hearst press are well known to Grierson scholars, Charbonneau extends these factors to consider how America, in the form of the initial Rockefeller grant obtained to study in the US, provided a model of internationalism which, as much as anything else, may well have gone on to have a lasting influence on his orientation toward the world.

Upon his return to the United Kingdom, Grierson fell in with the group of film-makers and social activists who made up the London Film Society and the British documentary movement; they became the receiving committee for Soviet cinema in Britain. As Julia Vassilieva shows, their interest in Soviet cinema was almost as strong as their fear of it. Vassilieva's account reverses the notion of influence, utilising the subtitle 'an uneasy dialogue' to account for the way that the Soviet cinema had a broader effect on British documentary than can be accounted for by looking at the influence of Sergei Eisenstein on Grierson's directorial debut *Drifters* (1929). In this way the Soviet concern for the role of cinema in general and documentary realism in particular in shaping society inspired many who attended the lectures and screenings at the Film Society. Grierson himself increasingly dismissed the modernist impulses of the Soviets, paradoxically shadowing the criticisms that arose in the Soviet Union itself that led to a more didactic and less radical role for documentary there in the 1930s.

Abé Markus Nornes traces the influence of Paul Rotha's book, *Documentary Film* (1935), in the Japanese context to invoke the issues of cultural translation often elided in accounts of the Grierson legacy. For Nornes, Rotha's work is the conduit through which Grierson emerges in Japanese film studies, coinciding with particular politicised definitions of documentary film, yet operating in very different ways for different film-makers. Nornes shows how the historical forces at work on Rotha's, and by extension, therefore, Grierson's ideas, led to a peculiar and telling effect in the Japanese context. Ib Bondebjerg's chapter on Scandinavian documentary utilises the figure of Danish film enthusiast Theodor Christensen to map out the inspirational force of Griersonian ideas in the 1930s. He finds a tension between film aesthetics and an 'institutional production culture with very specific assignments for the theme and content of documentaries' in Denmark, Sweden and Norway. Bondebjerg traces this tension between documentary journalism and documentary as a creative art form into the postwar domain of television, a story that has resonance in many of the other cases under examination here as well.

Turning to the colonial work that was such a major part of the Grierson effect, Ian Aitken's chapter argues that there was a divide between the more propagandistic work of the Colonial Film Unit and British poetic documentary aspirations in film work undertaken in Britain's colonies in Southeast Asia: Malaya, Singapore and Hong Kong. The influence of what he calls the 'anti-Griersonian troika' of William Sellers, Tom Hodge and John Lawrence Murray determined the style and production methods of official documentary film across this region until 1973. Nevertheless, in a theme that re-emerges in several chapters, Aitken shows how ultimately compatible the Grierson effect was with the colonial mandate.

The dominions, to which Grierson went next, offer a study in contrasts. There, it was hoped, a countercinema could be forged to resist the Hollywood juggernaut. In her chapter, Zoë Druick pays close attention to the Grierson effect in Canada in order to explore the reasons for the solidity of the Canadian Film Board as the most successful adaptation of the Grierson vision, one that would go on to serve as a model for Australia, New Zealand, South Africa, India and many other countries. Yet, paradoxically, in many ways, the success of the Grierson effect in Canada was somewhat stultifying and came, in some ways, at the cost of diminishing other aspects of Canadian cinema culture and history. In a similar vein, Simon Sigley's chapter considers Grierson's visit to New Zealand and furnishes an account of the Grierson effect in that country, which included the establishment of a National Film Library. Attending to the economic and cultural milieu into which Grierson arrived illuminates the needs Grierson filled for New Zealand's Labour Party, especially in the face of the challenges of World War II.

Deane Williams's contribution echoes Ian Aitken's account of the contradictory impulses of the Grierson effect. In Australia, it was a case of Griersonians, such as Professor Alan Stout, and John Heyer, whose more expansive vision for documentary film was challenged by the continuing influence of the stodgier work of the Department of Information, which had maintained a film unit since the 1920s. Williams argues that this ambivalence was smoothed over by naming the national theatre in Melbourne the Grierson Cinema.

There was considerable activity in the colonies after the war, as national independence became the new political ideal for the colonial world. Camille Deprez describes the storied history of the Films Division in India, which straddled phases of colonialism and independence in that country. The shift from British rule to the government of Nehru saw the maintenance of Griersonian principles for governmental film-making: in this regard, as Deprez observes, 'the Films Division appropriated Grierson's notion of integration and consensus, rather than individualism, to fit in the social context of national heterogeneity of young independent India. The nation was to be placed before the self.' Nevertheless, the legacy of the Films Division has continued to be complex and contested.

In the late 1940s, Grierson lectured in Ireland, proving a surprisingly powerful influence on Irish nationalist film-making, argues Jerry White. Despite the 'steely Scot's' association with colonial masters, and despite anger aroused by his American colleague Robert Flaherty's romantic rendition of Irish folk in *Man of Aran* (1934), Irish film-makers, such as Liam Ó Laoghaire, Louis Marcus and Bob Quinn, were paradoxically inspired by Grierson's consideration of both realism and strategies for small national cinemas. The case of Ireland highlights best, perhaps, the capacious and contradictory aspects of the Grierson effect.

Martin Stollery's chapter examines the case of the Grierson-produced and Cyril Frankel-directed film *Man of Africa* (1953) in relation to a paper delivered by Grierson at a UNESCO-sponsored conference in 1948, The Film in British Colonial Development. These texts are examined in relation to the continued involvement of the British Colonial Office in both the Gold Coast Film Unit and the transition to Ghanaian independence. Stollery takes an insightful look at Grierson's ambivalent vision for film-making in the former African colonies. This theme is continued in Keyan Tomaselli's chapter, which provides a critical accounting of Grierson's engagement with emergent Afrikaner nationalism in South Africa. In 1954, Grierson visited the country, which was undergoing deep political and cultural shifts, and wrote a report on the extant state film services. Although his suggestions were largely rejected by the ascendant Afrikaner nationalist forces, they did go on to establish a state film institution that helped set the scene for the emergence of the apartheid regime.

As the foregoing indicates, Grierson's ideas were affected by and incorporated into a range of political contexts. In a completely different way, the Grierson effect helped manifest a documentary of liberation in Latin America. Mariano Mestman and María Luisa Ortega sketch the continent's emerging film culture in the late 1950s and early 60s, which took 'neorealism and the Griersonian documentary as ... cardinal points'. In seeking to fashion a cinema that would represent real social conditions and experiences, Grierson operated as a local figurehead. For the Latin Americans Grierson's persona, his experiences in bringing film-makers together, of promoting alternate distribution and production systems as well as his links with cine clubs and state bureaucracies, served as a model for thinking about the effect of local circumstances on documentary film production and culture.

Although we are very pleased to gather the discussion of such diverse national and regional contexts in a single volume, realistically not every country touched by the Grierson effect could be included. There is certainly more research to be done about this particular aspect of film culture in South Asia. And, while the British influence in the Middle East no doubt affected film cultures there, definitive research has yet to be published in English. The one notable exception is Iran where, through its use of film for postcolonial nation-building, Hamid Naficy has clearly shown the Grierson effect in operation.[15] Scotland itself is also left out of this selection although, given that Grierson's last post was as the producer of *This Wonderful World* (1957–65), a documentary series for Scottish television, his effect there was inarguably significant.[16]

Despite these inevitable limitations, the volume gathers together records of the host of ways in which the Grierson effect manifested on a global scale. As well as considering the ongoing legacy of Grierson's encounters with a diverse array of film communities, the book provides what we see as a much-needed critical engagement with the multifaceted and often problematic encounters that occurred as part of the Grierson effect. The collection assembles fourteen original essays that, together, offer a global perspective on the Grierson effect. Individual chapters critically examine the influence, in its many forms, of Grierson – as a figurehead, official emissary, representative of British colonialism and British culture, and most importantly, perhaps, as shorthand for a set of ideas – on documentary film-making culture in a number of key countries and regions. It is our hope that this new constellation of international scholarship will open up expanded perspectives on trans/national cinema cultures and histories.

## NOTES

1. John Grierson, 'The EMB Film Unit', in Forsyth Hardy (ed.), *Grierson on Documentary* (London: Faber and Faber, 1966), p. 50.
2. John Grierson, 'Education and the New Order', in Hardy, *Grierson on Documentary*, p. 127; Ian Aitken, *Film and Reform: John Grierson and the Documentary Film Movement* (London: Routledge, 1992).
3. See John Grierson, 'First Principles of Documentary', in Hardy, *Grierson on Documentary*, p. 37.
4. Grierson, 'The Russian Example', in Hardy, *Grierson on Documentary*, p. 23.
5. John Grierson, 'Documentary(2): Symphonies', *Cinema Quarterly* vol. 1 no. 3 (Spring 1933); John Grierson, 'Propaganda: A Problem for Educational Theory and for Cinema', *Sight and Sound* vol. 3 no. 8 (Winter 1933–4), p. 119.
6. Nicolas Pronay, 'John Grierson and the Documentary – 60 Years On', *Historical Journal of Film, Radio and Television* vol. 9 no. 3 (1989), pp. 227–46.
7. Forsyth Hardy, *John Grierson: A Documentary Biography* (London: Faber and Faber, 1979); Joyce Nelson, *The Colonized Eye: Rethinking the Grierson Legend* (Toronto: Between the Lines Press, 1988); Peter Morris, '"Praxis into Process": John Grierson and the National Film Board of Canada', *Historical Journal of Film, Radio and Television* vol. 3 no. 9 (1989), pp. 269–82; Brian Winston, *Claiming the Real: Documentary: Grierson and Beyond* (London: BFI, 1995); Ian Aitken, *The Documentary Film Movement: An Anthology* (Edinburgh: Edinburgh University Press, 1998); Jack C. Ellis, *John Grierson: Life, Contributions, Influence* (Carbondale and Edwardsville: Southern Illinois University Press, 2000); Gary Evans, *John Grierson: Trailblazer of Documentary Film* (Montreal: XYZ Publications, 2005).
8. T. J. Hollins, 'The Conservative Party and Film Propaganda between the Wars', *English Historical Review* vol. 96 no. 379 (April 1981), pp. 359–69; Helen Foreman, 'The Non-theatrical Distribution of Films by the Ministry of Information', in Nicholas Pronay and D. W. Spring (eds), *Propaganda, Politics and Film, 1918–45* (London: Macmillan, 1982), pp. 221–33; Zoë Druick, 'Mobile Cinema in Canada in Relation to British Mobile Film Practices', in Wolfram R. Keller and Gene Walz (eds), *Screening Canadians: Cross-cultural Perspectives on Canadian Film* (Marburg: Universitatsbibliothek, 2008), pp. 13–33.
9. Paul Swann, *The British Documentary Film Movement, 1926–1946* (Cambridge: Cambridge University Press, 1989); Aitken, *Film and Reform*.

10. See Lee Grieveson and Colin MacCabe (eds), *Empire and Film* (London: BFI, 2011); and Lee Grieveson and Colin MacCabe (eds), *Film and the End of Empire* (London: BFI, 2011).
11. See also Anuja Jain, 'The Curious Case of the Films Division', *Velvet Light Trap* (Spring 2013), pp. 15–26.
12. Will Higbee and Song Hwee Lim, 'Concepts of Transnational Cinema: Towards a Critical Transnationalism in Film Studies', *Transnational Cinemas* vol. 1 no. 1 (2010), pp. 7–21.
13. Rosaleen Smyth, 'Grierson, the British Documentary Movement, and Colonial Cinema in British Colonial Africa', *Film History* vol. 25 no. 14 (2013), p. 82.
14. Grierson, 'First Principles of Documentary', p. 35. See also Martin Stollery, *Alternative Empires: European Modernist Cinemas and Cultures of Imperialism* (Exeter: University of Exeter Press, 2000), chapter 6; and Smyth, 'Grierson, the British Documentary Movement, and Colonial Cinema in British Colonial Africa', pp. 82–113.
15. Hamid Naficy, *A Social History of Iranian Cinema, Vol. 2* (Durham, NC: Duke University Press, 2011), pp. 12–15.
16. Jo Fox, 'From Documentary Film to Television Documentaries: John Grierson and *This Wonderful World*', *Journal of British Cinema and Television* vol. 10 no. 3 (2013), pp. 498–523.

## REFERENCES

Aitken, Ian, *Film and Reform: John Grierson and the Documentary Film Movement* (London: Routledge, 1992).

Aitken, Ian, *The Documentary Film Movement: An Anthology* (Edinburgh: Edinburgh University Press, 1998).

Druick, Zoë, 'Mobile Cinema in Canada in Relation to British Mobile Film Practices', in Wolfram R. Keller and Gene Walz (eds), *Screening Canadians: Cross-cultural Perspectives on Canadian Film* (Marburg: Universitatsbibliothek, 2008), pp. 13–33.

Ellis, Jack C., *John Grierson: Life, Contributions, Influence* (Carbondale and Edwardsville: Southern Illinois University Press, 2000).

Evans, Gary, *John Grierson: Trailblazer of Documentary Film* (Montreal: XYZ Publications, 2005).

Foreman, Helen, 'The Non-theatrical Distribution of Films by the Ministry of Information', in Nicholas Pronay and D. W. Spring (eds), *Propaganda, Politics and Film, 1918–45* (London: Macmillan, 1982), pp. 221–33.

Fox, Jo, 'From Documentary Film to Television Documentaries: John Grierson and *This Wonderful World*', *Journal of British Cinema and Television* vol. 10 no. 3 (2013), pp. 498–523.

Grierson, John, 'The EMB Film Unit', in Forsyth Hardy (ed.), *Grierson on Documentary* (London: Faber and Faber, 1966), pp. 47–51.

Grierson, John, 'Education and the New Order', in Forsyth Hardy (ed.), *Grierson on Documentary* (London: Faber and Faber, 1966), pp. 122–32.

Grierson, John, 'First Principles of Documentary', in Forsyth Hardy (ed.), *Grierson on Documentary* (London: Faber and Faber, 1966), pp. 35–46.

Grierson, John, 'The Russian Example', in Forsyth Hardy (ed.), *Grierson on Documentary* (London: Faber and Faber, 1966), pp. 23–8.

Grierson, John, 'Documentary(2): Symphonics', *Cinema Quarterly* (Spring 1933), vol. 1 no. 3.

Grierson, John, 'Propaganda: A Problem for Educational Theory and for Cinema,' *Sight and Sound* vol. 3 no. 8 (Winter 1933–4), pp. 119–21.

Grieveson, Lee and Colin MacCabe (eds), *Empire and Film* (London: BFI, 2011).

Grieveson, Lee and Colin MacCabe (eds), *Film and the End of Empire* (London: BFI, 2011).

Hardy, Forsyth, *John Grierson: A Documentary Biography* (London: Faber and Faber, 1979).

Higbee, Will and Song Hwee Lim, 'Concepts of Transnational Cinema: Towards a Critical Transnationalism in Film Studies', *Transnational Cinemas* vol. 1 no. 1 (2010), pp. 7–21.

Hollins, T. J., 'The Conservative Party and Film Propaganda between the Wars', *English Historical Review* vol. 96 no. 379 (April 1981), pp. 359–69.

Jain, Anuja, 'The Curious Case of the Films Division', *Velvet Light Trap* (Spring 2013), pp. 15–26.

Morris, Peter, '"Praxis into Process": John Grierson and the National Film Board of Canada', *Historical Journal of Film, Radio and Television* vol. 9 no. 3 (1989), pp. 269–82.

Naficy, Hamid, *A Social History of Iranian Cinema, Vol. 2* (Durham, NC: Duke University Press, 2011).

Nelson, Joyce, *The Colonized Eye: Rethinking the Grierson Legend* (Toronto: Between the Lines Press, 1988).

Pronay, Nicolas, 'John Grierson and the Documentary – 60 Years On', *Historical Journal of Film, Radio and Television* vol. 9 no. 3 (1989), pp. 227–46.

Smyth, Rosaleen, 'Grierson, the British Documentary Movement, and Colonial Cinema in British Colonial Africa', *Film History* vol. 25 no. 14 (2013), pp. 82–113.

Stollery, Martin, *Alternative Empires: European Modernist Cinemas and Cultures of Imperialism* (Exeter: University of Exeter Press, 2000).

Swann, Paul, *The British Documentary Film Movement, 1926–1946* (Cambridge: Cambridge University Press, 1989).

Winston, Brian, *Claiming the Real: Documentary: Grierson and Beyond* (London: BFI, 1995).

# 1

# John Grierson and the United States

*Stephen Charbonneau*

John Grierson's status as a uniquely transnational historical figure is evidenced by his synergetic relationship with the United States. Certainly, as often noted, Grierson's particular filmic discourse was forged by his postgraduate years in Chicago, Hollywood and New York. As Jack C. Ellis has recognised, Grierson returned home from the US having solidified three fundamental premises: 'citizenship education was the broad necessity, film the chosen medium, documentary its special form'.[1] Of course, these so-called premises were not strictly speaking the byproduct of American culture. Grierson's time in America afforded him the opportunity to experience contemporary trends in global cinema that included Hollywood, but also encompassed Soviet montage (Sergei Eisenstein's *Battleship Potemkin* [1926]) and romantic ethnography (Robert Flaherty's *Nanook of the North* [1924] and *Moana* [1926]).

At least where the US is concerned, it is best to not speak of *impact* – in which we make a clean, *a priori* detachment of the Griersonian tradition from American institutions and social policies. It would be a mistake to consider this tradition as an entity unto itself, as if it had exerted an influence on American culture from the outside. Instead, it is much more productive to speak of *relation*, of an *interiorisation* in which a Griersonian educational media formation is implicated, shaped and reflected by social developments and institutions in the United States. While much has been written about Grierson's life – and this essay stands on the shoulders of the work of historians and film scholars such as Ellis, Ian Aitken and many others – the hope is that by both adopting a cultural materialist posture and setting our aperture specifically upon the Griersonian tradition and its relationship to the US, that familiar facets of Grierson's legacy will appear anew, more fluid, and more relevant to our contemporary media moment. Certainly, when looked at from this vantage point, one of the critical institutions that moves to the fore is the Rockefeller Foundation and its support for Grierson's studies and work at different stages of his life. Whether the particular type of support under discussion is the fellowship that brought Grierson to the US in the first place, or seed money to initiate a new postwar educational film endeavour, the Rockefeller Foundation is an important benefactor for Grierson.

In each of the three following sections – on the 1920s, 30s and 40s – the Rockefeller Foundation is referred to as either a primary or secondary factor in the development of particular modes of educational cinema. By doing so, our analysis of Grierson's US activities will hopefully support our concern with the dialectical interconnectedness between the Griersonian tradition and broader social forces. In the course of this chapter, I will review Grierson's critical years at the University of Chicago and the well-known influence of the American intellectual, Walter Lippmann; Paul Rotha's visit to the US in the late 1930s against the backdrop of calls for a new educational cinema; and, in a post-World War II era, Grierson's articulation of a particular kind of internationalism in an array of speeches, interviews and proposed projects. As Forsyth Hardy has noted, during the immediate postwar period, 'it was the international idea which dominated [Grierson's] thinking and he felt that the big momentum for the wider international development lay in the United States'.[2] Cutting across all three of these sections is an emphasis on the ways in which the Griersonian tradition develops in tandem with broader modern liberal discourses hailing new instruments of governance to cope with the realities of modernity.

## SOCIAL SCIENCE, CITIZENSHIP AND 'DRAMATIC PATTERNS'

In 1924, John Grierson – a twenty-six-year-old lecturer from Scotland – received a fellowship from the Laura Spelman Rockefeller Memorial to study in the US.[3] This particular event is worth noting not simply for biographical purposes, but also for the way in which it places Grierson's individual history within a broader social context. The memorial was established in 1918 to honour the memory of Laura Spelman Rockefeller, the wife of John D., Sr.[4] The memorial was part of a social formation in the 1920s whose aim was to engender new forms of governance and knowledge. In particular, the Rockefeller Foundation's philanthropic support for education, science technology and the social sciences was grounded in a desire to find 'practical applications of the results of [subsidized] research'.[5] The focus of the fellowship for Grierson, specifically, would turn to the 'role of communication in shaping public opinion'.[6] This instance of private philanthropy registers the influence of American social theory on the management of modern, industrial societies. While itself the byproduct of the concentration of wealth in capitalist society, this private endeavour registers a large-scale, institutional interest in managing modernity.

As has been reviewed extensively, Grierson developed ties to a handful of accomplished social scientists at the University of Chicago, such as Charles Merriam, Robert Park and Harold Lasswell. While Grierson never received a formal degree from the university, he performed graduate research for Merriam on the immigrant population in Chicago. Starting with a specific focus on deviance, Grierson cast a wide net that encompassed 'records of the criminal courts ... members of the I.W.W. [Industrial Workers of the World], alcoholics, and drug addicts'.[7] In reviewing such a broad cross-section of what Ellis calls 'social restiveness' in Chicago, Grierson sought out patterns of behaviour among personal records and biographical details.[8] Ellis notes that a 'common characteristic was discovered – these were people who had been driven from their homes or, at any rate, had lost contact with their families'.[9] We can recognise in this work a desire to tease out explanatory variables which would lend themselves to greater management in this new world. And it was precisely this theme of novelty – the sense that modernity was a 'new', perhaps unruly experience in need of scientific theories and instruments for greater governance – that traversed both the priorities of the memorial and the interests of Grierson. In Grierson's case, novelty arose as a theme through his reduction of social restiveness down to the level of generational differences. Specifically, he focused on the process of Americanisation and a developing 'strain between generations – the parents trying to hang onto the old world; the young attempting to become part of the new ...'.[10] In doing so, the media – specifically the press – came into sharper focus. The reason for this was because Grierson noted a schism in the publics addressed by particular newspapers.[11] As Ellis summarises:

> For the foreign-born there were six thousand foreign-language newspapers in the country at the time. For the first generation there was the Hearst press, like Chicago's *Herald Examiner*, and its imitators ... Grierson noted that, with their headlines and photos, their simplifications and dramatizations, these papers served as informal but nonetheless compelling means of leading young Lithuanians and Poles, Germans and Italians, Irish and Czechs away from their parents and the old country and into an Americanization of one sort or another.[12]

The splintering of immigrant families across generational lines was – it seemed – driven by external factors, by a particular set of social conditions. The mass media, specifically the press, was an instance of modernity producing new subjects, whose disposition was markedly different from their parents or those from the 'old country'. Grierson pushed his analysis further and addressed what he saw as a formal characteristic that distinguished American newspapers from their European counterparts.[13] The way in which the American press organised quotidian events into narrative patterns was – Grierson felt – unique and was an indication of how the 'American mind worked'.[14] A key element was the emphasis placed on action. Ellis writes: 'The active verb was the key: something does something to something; someone does something to someone.'[15] This also resonates with a subject's sensory experience of modernity, including a heightened encounter of kinetic intensities around transportation, production and the mass media. This emphasis on activity, change and the new world is deeply impressed upon the Griersonian tradition and, as Ellis notes, imbued a new documentary practice with a 'dramatic, active strategy'.[16]

The sensationalism and the reliance on narrative Grierson admired in Hearst newspapers dovetailed with lessons learned from Walter Lippmann. Grierson, like many of his political science colleagues at the University of Chicago, was influenced by Lippmann's ideas on the modern society and citizenship as articulated in his book, *Public Opinion* (1922). To review, Lippmann argued that the American democratic process was no longer practical in the wake of dramatic and traumatic changes incurred on the country's path to modernity. In his view, the romantic notion of cultivated and informed voters conducting themselves rationally in the voting booth was untenable given the pace and labyrinthine nature of modern societies, where the application of financial instruments, foreign policy and new production apparatuses rendered the classic democratic, educational model ineffective. What would be needed was, from Grierson and Lippmann's point of view, a new pedagogical framework. Specifically, while the new educational form would address the quotidian world where raw experience begins, it would dare to mobilise this experience into new narrative structures that could give citizens a sense of the real, of the underlying truth to their frenetic lives. Hearst newspapers were a model for Grierson in this regard. In them he claimed to have discerned 'a deeper principle' in which a 'complex world ... could be patterned for all to appreciate if we only got away from the servile accumulation of fact and struck for the story which held the facts in living organic relationship together'.[17] The medium of cinema, Lippmann suggested to Grierson, provided the kind of spectacular 'dramatic patterns' that mass pedagogues might replicate in educational discourses.[18]

Grierson's work in New York City was as influential as his studies in Chicago. As a film critic for the *New York Sun*, he witnessed and learned from film movements that diverged from the Hollywood model. One of his most well-known reviews is of Robert Flaherty's second film, *Moana*, and it was entitled, 'The Moviegoer'.[19] It was in this review that the term 'documentary' was famously coined, although its use was in adjective form: 'Of course, *Moana* being a visual account of events in the daily life of a Polynesian youth, has documentary value.'[20] But for Grierson, this documentary quality was 'secondary to [the film's] value as a soft breath from a sunlit island, washed by a marvelous sea, as warm as the balmy air'.[21] As Ellis notes, the review was both effusive in its praise for the poetic qualities of *Moana* and – at the same time – somewhat restrained in its assessment of the film's relevance to the here and now of modernity.[22] Ellis makes special mention of this comment in particular from the review: '[*Moana*] should be placed on the idyllic shelf that includes all those poems which sing of the loveliness of sea and land and air – and of man when he is part of beautiful surroundings ...'.[23] Specifically, Ellis suggests that this quote implies a 'relegation' of the film, 'as the work of the modern world was gotten on with'.[24] Ellis's insights highlight the consolidation of a core feature of Griersonian thinking, namely the focus on the problems and complexities of modernity and a lack of interest in what he later derisively called 'aestheticky' or poetic film-making on subjects which stray from the challenges of the modern experience.[25]

One of the last major influences on Grierson during this period was Soviet cinema. Grierson actually assisted with the composition of the subtitles for Sergei Eisenstein's *Battleship Potemkin* in preparation for its American premiere in New York at the Biltmore Theatre in 1926.[26] As an indication of how important the film was to Grierson, Ellis reminds us that Grierson later chose to marry the premiere of his first film, *Drifters*, with a screening of *Potemkin*.[27] Grierson was clearly ready to be influenced by Eisenstein's historic film, particularly because the essential elements of Griersonian discourse – as they were taking shape in the late 1920s – share broad characteristics with the writings of Soviet montage theorists. Constructivist tenets – such as the notion that artists are akin to social engineers – underpin ideas of Soviet montage and set up strong points of connection between the Griersonian tradition and Soviet cinema. Whether the theory at hand is Sergei Eisenstein's 'Theory of Dialectical Montage' or Dziga Vertov's 'kino-pravda', the general idea that the cinema – especially through editing – can mobilise a new totality out of the arrangement of individual shots dovetails with Grierson's growing recognition that a new educational form needs to embrace the modernist imbrication of the visceral with the cognitive (see Julia Vassilieva's chapter).

These experiences in the US, preceding Grierson's seminal work with the UK's Empire Marketing Board and – later – the General Post Office, had a profound impact on what became the Griersonian tradition and even go beyond Ellis's triumvirate of citizenship education, the medium of film and the form of documentary. As stated earlier, Grierson's personal story is bound up with broader historical and structural currents during the 1920s. Such currents contribute to a Western cultural formation around the management of modernity and the governance of new subjects experiencing a new world. Zoë Druick has written on the incorporation of documentary film into 'liberal internationalist education and cultural policy' during the 1930s and how – to a substantial degree – this can be seen as a response to anxieties over the ascendancy of Hollywood and the global impact of commercial cinema.[28] Western governments and international organisations, such as the League of Nations, launched initiatives to prop up a pedagogical cinema that would harness the medium's cultural power in order to promote citizenship. The Griersonian tradition is both an agent and a byproduct of this vision of pedagogical cinema. The 1930s were obviously, a seminal decade for documentary film and Grierson's influential work during this decade was an expression of the cultural and historical influences that enveloped him during the 20s.

## PAUL ROTHA, EDUCATIONAL FILM AND PUBLIC SERVICE

Grierson's activity during the 1930s as head of the Empire Marketing Board Film Unit, which later moved to the General Post Office, was both a product of and contributor to the emergence of this particular *épisteme*, a formation of discourses and practices buttressing a new educational cinema. One way in which the Griersonian tradition impacted national cinemas beyond Great Britain during the 1930s included the travels of those who had worked with Grierson, who made films under his supervision. One example of such a visit included Paul Rotha's to the US in 1937, an endeavour underwritten by the Rockefeller Foundation. Paul Rotha was a film-maker and a colleague of John Grierson's at the GPO Film Unit during the mid-1930s; he had also authored an influential work of film history, *The Film till Now* (1930). In his memoir, *Documentary Diary* (1973), Rotha explains how Iris Barry approached him to consider working temporarily for the Museum of Modern Art's (MoMA) Film Library in New York, at which Barry was the curator.[29] The hope, Barry explained, was to elicit financial support for Rotha from the Rockefeller Foundation (which had already contributed to the Film Library) in the form of a fellowship.[30] Barry noted the influence of Rotha's *The Film till Now* in the US and suggested that *Night Mail* (1936) and *Today We Live* (1937) represented a type of documentary film-making that had no parallel in the US.[31] From Barry's point of view the US had 'no counterpart' to the work of the Grierson production team in England.[32]

> She saw now that my proposed visit might be given an added purpose, that of introducing the whole documentary idea of public service using social purpose for progress, to sections of the American public, especially those who might be concerned to promote a documentary movement among American film-makers and imaginative educationists … . In a way, the path had been blazed by Thomas Baird, a specialist in the non-theatrical and educational use of films attached to Film Centre, who had made a short visit at the invitation of the Rockefeller Foundation a little earlier and had met with an encouraging reception.[33]

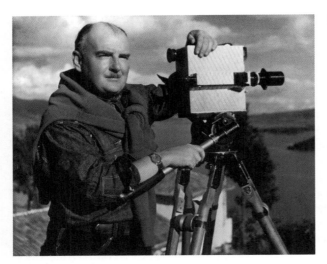

Paul Rotha

Rotha's visit was seen as a chance to advance a particular vision of educational cinema committed to the idea of citizenship and 'service', one that differentiated itself from other forms of US nonfiction film at the time (for a comparison with Paul Rotha's influence in Japan, see Abé Markus Nornes's chapter). Commercially produced newsreels and the work of leftist film collectives, such as the Workers Film and Photo League, did not represent the sort of documentary envisioned here by Barry and Rotha. For Barry, the closest American documentary came to the kind of films made by Grierson and his cohorts was Pare Lorentz's *The Plow That Broke the Plains* (1935), which Rotha dismisses as 'isolated'.[34] John Abbott, director of MoMA's Film Library, reiterated this point during an evening of documentary screenings to a Washington audience of journalists and dignitaries on 10 May 1936.[35] America, he insisted, was falling behind other national cinemas in their embrace of the nonfiction film.[36] Quite pointedly, he maintained that 'the new film of reality is being used today, all over the world, to bring the new world of citizenship before the public imagination'.[37]

These observations indicate that Rotha's visit was part of a broader push to mobilise educational and even propagandistic cinema in the US in the 1930s. In a report entitled 'Rockefeller Support for Non-commercial Film, 1935–1939', Gracia Ramirez reviews the Rockefeller Foundation's work in the 1930s to 'use the motion pictures to influence public taste and to improve educational and recreational films'.[38] While Ramirez notes that one aspect of the foundation's endeavour in this regard included the promotion of film appreciation – producing more critically discerning viewers – the emphasis on bolstering the educational film movement in the US centred on bridging the divide between producers and educational institutions.[39] Specifically, the Rockefeller Foundation Trustees envisioned a 'centralised agency that could direct the efforts from the different interested parties and provide education standards for the nation'.[40]

One of the key figures at the foundation during this time was John Marshall. An assistant director of the Humanities Division from 1933, Marshall's background was

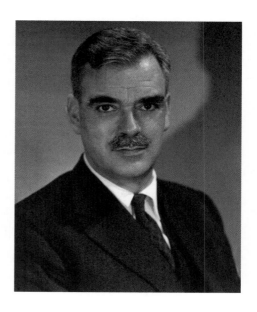

As assistant director of the Rockefeller Foundation Humanities Division, John Marshall drove the foundation to focus on communication (Photo courtesy Rockefeller Archive Center)

academic – a 'medievalist' – whose interests included health education.[41] By 1936 Marshall was encouraging the foundation to commit funds to 'communication-related activities'.[42] While Marshall and David Stevens (respectively assistant director and director of the General Education Board [GEB]) set their sights on deploying radio and film as means of dealing with public-health issues, Brett Gary notes that both eventually broadened 'their interest in the connections between media and education'.[43]

John Marshall was influenced by some of the same debates as Grierson and, as a result, articulated similar concerns about the condition of modern American democracy. Echoing Walter Lippmann and John Grierson, Marshall 'believed that through better uses of mass communication, and in collaboration with men of serious purpose, the Foundation could provide the missing information and insight about public issues that modern democracy required'.[44] While Grierson is historically aligned with Lippmann and Marshall with Dewey, they both absorbed the core assumption of the Lippmann/Dewey debate as outlined by Mark Whipple: that the present state of American democracy is in need of 'prescriptions', of strategies for bolstering civic engagement over the obstacles of modernity.[45]

As an 'administrative catalyst', Marshall drove the foundation to investigate the role of mass communication in shaping public opinion and help project 'academic discipline on the inchoate field [mass communication studies] with which he had found himself involved'.[46] In addition to having established the Film Library at MoMA, the Rockefeller Foundation's GEB – where Marshall was also an officer – supported a number of proposals from the American Council on Education during 1935, including a new network of distribution for educational films in the form of the Association of School Film Libraries, as well as the establishment of the American Film Center (AFC) at Columbia University.[47]

Rotha's visit to the US as a fellow at the Film Library should be seen within the above context, as part of a broader effort to instil a new documentary and pedagogical ethos into the American film scene of the 1930s. It was clearly not the case that Rotha would be 'introducing the whole documentary idea of public service' to American film-makers, researchers and policymakers. However, Rotha's fellowship is indicative of the influence of Griersonian film practice on key players in the US. Rotha's film, *The Face of Britain* (1935) was, in fact, included as part of the MoMA programme of documentary films shown to Washington insiders cited earlier. Barry acquired copies of British documentaries through coordination with Grierson, which included *Night Mail*, *Granton Trawler* (1934), *We Live in Two Worlds* (1937), *Housing Problems* (1935) and *The Smoke Menace* (1937).[48] The Film Library also acquired *Song of Ceylon* (1934) and *Cover to Cover* (1936) through other means.[49]

When Rotha first arrived he met with John Marshall, whom he describes as 'quiet in manner, soft spoken and obviously well informed on most aspects of the educational and documentary film field'.[50] As part of his responsibilities Rotha was to give thirteen lectures at Columbia University to approximately thirty-five students[51] and, in a more informal vein, host private screenings of British documentaries to critics, curators, researchers, etc. The first of such events included the presentation of *Today We Live* and *Night Mail* and elicited the following written response from Eric Knight, a film critic and author.

> I can't tell you how terrifically exciting I found the films. While the excitement came partly from the subjects, it came (I can analyse myself) even more from the remarkable and unbeatably stirring cutting. Visually they were astounding, showing me things I had never seen before ... I swear we have never had in America before any films which, even for a second, showed the remarkable brilliance of cutting that the films revealed throughout their entirety ... [Most notable] was this visual perfection, a hitherto unrevealed flow and contrast and contradiction and rhythm through the cutting, staggering in the first film.[52]

Steeped in hyperbole, Knight's reaction is interesting for the emphasis it places on form, on the particular use of editing. Described as, in itself, 'stirring', Knight's assessment of the editing parallels Grierson's endorsement of *active* representations, of aggressive media representations that forge narrative structures out of what might otherwise be isolated quotidian experiences.

Rotha went on to have meetings with Pare Lorentz (with whom he viewed an early cut of *The River* [1937]) as well as with Ralph Steiner and Willard van Dyke, who had both collaborated with Lorentz on his films.[53] His lectures and screenings were, over the duration of his fellowship, given to a wide array of educational institutions and federal agencies that included the Metropolitan Motion Picture Council, Progressive Education Association, ACE, the Department of Interior and Department of Agriculture.[54] By Rotha's account the term 'documentary' – as a generic label for the *film of fact* – was 'unknown' in the US until 1937–8 when the Griersonian films were introduced and Grierson's own writings began to circulate more widely.[55] While this grand claim should clearly be taken with a grain of salt, Rotha's visit and the heightened interest in the Griersonian documentary during the late 1930s was significant in its contribution to a gathering critical mass of institutional interest in

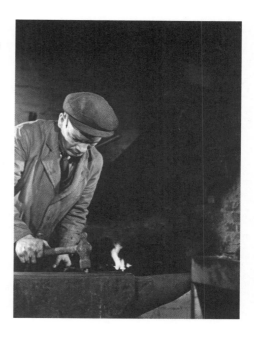

Private screenings of British documentaries like *Today We Live* (1937) drew praise from American critics for their formal innovations

the shaping of public opinion and the use of mass communications. The stakes were only raised as the shadow of a second world war loomed.

## NEW MEDIA, INTERNATIONALISM AND MANAGEMENT

Grierson's departure from the National Film Board of Canada in 1945 (covered in Zoë Druick's chapter) prompted a number of American institutions and companies to solicit his services. Forsyth Hardy notes that there were

> invitations from Hollywood and New York, including the setting up of a political intelligence service for one of the major companies, the control of the *Encyclopaedia Britannica* film venture into American and international education, and the establishment of a film, radio and television set-up for *Newsweek*.[56]

However, the primary focus for Grierson at this time was the consolidation of an international consciousness, of a transnational documentary network that took advantage of the nationalist communication infrastructure that had been developed for the war. Such a vision would need to, in his words, 'be done by functional internationals of our own making – the documentary people of the world if they will get together'.[57]

The US plays a unique role in this postwar globalist discourse for Grierson, because – as mentioned earlier – it is perceived as the country best positioned to initiate new international communications efforts. In an address to the International

Conference of the Junior League at Quebec, Canada on 14 May 1946, Grierson identified the US as the site for one of the most potent ideological forces in the postwar world. For Grierson, this 'great ideological force' is best described as 'the force of the technological revolution emanating from the American heirs of the French Revolution and the liberal democracy of the United States'.[58] And yet the managers of this postwar superpower are, in Grierson's words, 'mixed up' along with the political leaderships of the Soviet Union, the UK and the Catholic Church.[59] In the case of the US, Grierson cites President Truman's contradictory postwar discourse in which he endorses the need for an expanded military while also advocating for a new 'science of human relationships all over the world'.[60] While endorsing Truman's call for this new science, Grierson notes that 'educators and organisers in local communities will need to do what we can and must to mature the higher and not the lower conception which Mr. Truman has articulated'.[61] Ultimately, Grierson argues, the postwar moment is an urgent one. Describing his thought process while preparing this speech, he confessed to the audience ...

> I kept feeling the urgency of the moment, the urgency of basic decisions now, the urgency of the next five years, at the most, in the troubled history of mankind. I cannot apologize for this sense of urgency, for I tell you coldly as one who lived through the decisions that led to Munich and the war, that the cold sweat we had in these decisive days was warm and gentle and kind compared with the cold sweat that should now be rolling down our backs as we think of what the next war will unleash.[62]

Towards the end of the speech he reiterated the five-year window ('five years in which to bring the public mind to a sense of the realities ...'), and this discourse of the now resonates with the Griersonian traits of the active narrative and of the motion picture's unique preparedness for the demands of the moment.[63]

Two months after this speech, Grierson spoke to the American Library Association Conference in Buffalo, New York under the heading, 'The Library in an International World'. Here the urgency of the postwar moment is reiterated and channelled towards the mass media, specifically cinema and radio. The intensity of the moment for Grierson, however, leads him to reiterate the core principles of a Griersonian tradition, hammered out in discourse and practice over the previous twenty years. Alongside his emphasis on the 'urgency of the moment' is the ever familiar accent on the new, the sense of a new world encroaching on the present.

> With all respect, I suggest to you that the old library outlook is over and done with. It served its day ... . But the new problems involve new methods and the worldwide scale of our problems involves new and highly dramatic methods ... I do not say that the day of the books is over, but the day of the books only is certainly over. It is not information that is needed today; in fact, it is not information that is sought. It is enlightenment and that is a very different thing involving as it does the dramatic process of sparking the mind and the heart into new hope, new vision, new realization and new efforts in citizenship.[64]

Continuing to stake out the claim, 'Lippmann was right', Grierson insisted to his audience of American librarians that the 'cold' nature of information was in need of being brought to life, of being dynamised by what he calls the 'bright new media'.[65] While the range of media mentioned includes television, radio and 'traveling exhibits', cinema is still the privileged medium for Grierson due to its 'dramatic nature'.[66] The postwar world, then, receives a familiar diagnosis. The dizzying pace of technological change, political realignment and economic reconstruction reinforces the core tenets of the Griersonian tradition as they became concretised over twenty years. A new modern world continues to outpace our traditional educational institutions and a full embrace of a complementary new media landscape is necessary for the attainment of the 'simplicity and understanding of the elemental interests which unify all men ...'.[67]

Nevertheless, a new emphasis is placed here on a specifically international framework. Whereas Griersonian discourses traditionally generate nationalist associations as they are aligned with an era when documentary was seen as a means of constituting a national imaginary, here he is bringing to the fore an internationalist discourse that had been evolving for the previous decade.[68] The statements cited above in which Grierson characterises the US as a kind of base of operations for this new challenge underscore some of the tensions and contradictions inherent in this new appeal. The gravitational pull of the preeminent global superpower in the immediate postwar period is reflected by the lure of its institutions. In fact the Rockefeller Foundation comes to the fore again as a sponsor of one of Grierson's major endeavours in the late 1940s, The World Today, Inc. The foundation subsidised Grierson's early efforts to accumulate personnel and office space in New York City for the new project.[69] United Artists (UA) struck a four-year deal with Grierson's new company to distribute educational films. UA had 'decided to develop a new policy in the matter of short films and to use its world-wide organization to distribute films of a dramatic nature which will describe and discuss the international scene'.[70] With a production mandate, The World Today expected to organise its documentaries into three different series, 'Worldwise', 'Wonderfact' and 'Venture'; these would respectively cover international events, science/technology and athletics/outdoor recreation.[71]

While the organisation's plans eventually failed due to a number of factors – including a rising culture of red-baiting and the emergence of television – the Griersonian legacy was far from over in the US. While Hardy notes that '[s]hort films on current affairs were no longer as attractive to cinema exhibitors or audiences as they had been during the war', a new era of private institutional sponsorship for countless training, health, safety, human relations, educational and mental hygiene films resonated with the Griersonian tradition. The deployment of short pedagogical films exhibited in non-commercial spaces such as prisons, classrooms, gymnasiums, factories, offices and libraries registered a continuation of a modern liberal discourse invested in managing modernity and the psychic disposition of modern subjects. However, this postwar period also rewired this familiar discourse around new social theories of human management and co-ordination that drew on experiences from the recently concluded war as well as on lessons learned from the labour struggles of the 1930s. As Heide Solbrig has shown, during this time 'corporations commissioned [human relations training] films in the hope of shaping the emotional lives of managers and workers for the sake of influencing their social behavior and class identifications both in and out of the workplace'.[72] The Griersonian triad of film, documentary and citizenship education was embraced by the state during World War II and went on to be incorporated into a new postwar corporate culture, imported under the guise of an apolitical functional address to viewers. This discourse was steeped in scientific modes of expression and helped turn, for instance, 'sociological *theories* of worker-management interaction [into] material *practices* through the narratives and exercises of industrial media products' (author's emphasis).[73] Such uses of pedagogical film during the late 1940s, 50s and beyond may not have satisfied Grierson's personal vision of social change. However, the key point is that the Griersonian tradition is larger than the person with whom it is associated, and it is clear – when looked at from the vantage point of the US – that this body of thought on cultural production is an expression of broader modern liberal currents of regulation and stabilisation.

## CONCLUSION

By the 1960s, Grierson was able to return to the United States as the influence of McCarthyism waned. During this time he frequently noted new trends in *cinema vérité* and the value of, as he put it, 'decentralizing the means of production, taking the myth out of it … and making the documentary film a living tool for people at the grass roots'.[74] These statements reflected a new participatory formation, one still centrally concerned with themes of citizenship and filmic communication, yet rewired to – in theory – uphold the agency of oppressed subjects. New forms of observational and participatory film production to an extent shared a critique of Griersonian form, preferring to adopt more inductive postures in relation to subjects and viewers (in theory). Yet Grierson's openness to these new *vérité* practices suggests a more complex relationship between them and the Griersonian tradition. For instance, the Griersonian emphasis on citizenship, on deploying film as a means of communication between the state and the subject was fluid and flexible enough to both enable and be influenced by this shift to more participatory approaches. Specifically, the Griersonian tradition possessed its own unique internal contradictions around the awkward, unidirectional quality of cinema and an investment in the ideal of communication. This ideal held within itself a notion of 'voice', of expression, that would – sooner or later – unravel expository values, or at least retool them to accommodate a participatory ethos in which the individualised voices of subjects would be brought to the fore. In this sense, the Griersonian approach possessed the seeds of its own unravelling.

Furthermore, as Aitken notes, Griersonian discourse was insistent on the compatibility of 'documentary naturalism and dramatic montage'.[75] Grierson's 'neo-Hegelian and neo-Kantian' influences enabled his thought to accommodate both formalist and realist impulses, recognising the limited but important value of the 'phenomenal' in gaining access to the 'real' by virtue of filmic techniques.[76] With the participatory turn, the yearning for access to the real as a totality falters. The privileging of subject's voices yields a more inductive and fractured whole, nudging the documentary project that much closer to the phenomenal side of the spectrum. This epistemic break suggests a more modest and less confident documentary endeavour that parallels cracks in modern liberalism in the 1960s and eventually engenders heightened reflexive sensitivities on the part of film diarists, essayists and ethnographers. And yet, while this may suggest a fading of the Griersonian tradition, Grierson's assertion of the synchronous relationship between formalist and realist aesthetics is difficult to transcend or cast aside. Many contemporary documentarians speak eloquently about the unique ways in which their films express this complementary view of stylistic techniques and indexical purpose. Present-day discourses of the new similarly rearticulate Grierson's embrace of change and the allure of 'bright new media', with some even echoing the refrain that the 'day of the books only is certainly over'.

## NOTES

1.  Jack C. Ellis, *John Grierson: Life, Contributions, Influence* (Carbondale and Edwardsville: Southern Illinois University Press, 2000), p. 21.
2.  Forsyth Hardy, *John Grierson: A Documentary Biography* (London: Faber and Faber, 1979), p. 150.
3.  Ian Aitken, *Film and Reform: John Grierson and the Documentary Film Movement* (London: Routledge, 1992), p. 2.
4.  'Rockefeller Related Organizations', *Rockefeller Archive Center*, July 2011.
5.  Ibid.
6.  Ellis, *John Grierson*, p. 19.
7.  Ibid., p. 20.
8.  Ibid.
9.  Ibid.
10. Ibid.
11. Ibid.
12. Ibid., pp. 20–1.
13. Ibid.
14. Ibid., p. 21.
15. Ibid.
16. Ibid.
17. Grierson quoted in ibid., p. 22.
18. Ibid.
19. Ellis, *John Grierson*, p. 27.
20. Grierson quoted in ibid., p. 28.
21. Ibid.
22. Ibid.
23. Ibid.
24. Ellis, *John Grierson*, p. 28.
25. Jack C. Ellis and Betsy McLane, *A New History of Documentary Film* (New York: Continuum, 2006), p. 127.
26. Ellis, *John Grierson*, p. 29.
27. Ibid.
28. Zoë Druick, ' "Reaching the Multimillions": Liberal Internationalism and the Establishment of Documentary Film', in Lee Grieveson and Haidee Wasson (eds), *Inventing Film Studies* (Durham, NC and London: Duke University Press, 2008), pp. 66–92 (69).

29. Paul Rotha, *Documentary Diary: An Informal History of the British Documentary Film, 1928–1939* (London: Secker & Warburg, 1973), p. 171.
30. Ibid.
31. Ibid.
32. Ibid.
33. Ibid., pp. 171–2.
34. Ibid., p. 171.
35. Peter Decherney, *Hollywood and the Culture Elite: How the Movies Became American* (New York: Columbia University Press, 2005), p. 134.
36. Ibid.
37. John Abbott quoted in ibid., p. 134.
38. Gracia Ramirez, 'Rockefeller Support for Non-commercial Film, 1935–1939', *Rockefeller Archive Center*, 2009, www.rockarch.org/publications/resrep/gramirez.pdf.
39. Ibid.
40. Ibid.
41. Brett Gary, 'Communication Research, the Rockefeller Foundation, and Mobilization for the War on Words, 1938–1944', *Journal of Communication* vol. 46 no. 3 (1996), p. 130; Decherney, Peter, *Hollywood and the Culture Elite*, p. 149.
42. Gary, 'Communication Research, the Rockefeller Foundation, and Mobilization for the War on Words, 1938–1944', p. 130.
43. Ibid.
44. Ibid., p. 131.
45. Mark Whipple, 'The Dewey–Lippmann Debate Today: Communication Distortions, Reflective Agency, and Participatory Democracy', *Sociological Theory* vol. 23 no. 2 (2005), p. 159.
46. Gary, 'Communication Research, the Rockefeller Foundation, and Mobilization for the War on Words, 1938–1944', p. 130.
47. Ramirez, 'Rockefeller Support for Non-commercial Film, 1935–1939', p. 8; Decherney, *Hollywood and the Culture Elite*, p. 147.
48. Rotha, *Documentary Diary*, p. 172.
49. Ibid.
50. Ibid., p. 176.
51. Ibid., p. 177.
52. Eric Knight quoted in ibid., p. 180.
53. Rotha, *Documentary Diary*, p. 181.
54. Ibid., p. 195.
55. Ibid., p. 184.
56. Hardy, *John Grierson*, p. 150.
57. Grierson quoted in ibid., pp. 150–1.
58. Grierson, John, 'The Political, Economic and Educational Implications of the Atomic Bomb', 14 May 1946, G5.10. 1–6, pp. 1–15, John Grierson Archive, University of Stirling, Stirling, p. 1.
59. Ibid., p. 12.
60. Ibid.
61. Ibid.
62. Ibid.
63. Ibid.

64. Grierson, John, 'The Library in an International World', 17 June 1946, G5.10.7–10, pp. 1–16, John Grierson Archive, University of Stirling, Stirling, p. 12.
65. Grierson, 'The Library in an International World', pp. 13, 16.
66. Ibid., pp. 13, 15.
67. Ibid., p. 15.
68. Ellis, *John Grierson*, p. 153.
69. Hardy, *John Grierson*, pp. 152–3.
70. Grierson quoted in ibid., p. 153.
71. Hardy, *John Grierson*, p. 153.
72. Heide Solbrig, 'Henry Strauss and the Human Relations Film: Social Science Media and Interactivity in the Workplace', *Moving Image* vol. 7 no. 1 (2007), p. 28.
73. Ibid.
74. Elizabeth Sussex, *The Rise and Fall of British Documentary: The Story of the Film Movement Founded by John Grierson* (Berkeley: University of California Press, 1976), p. 196.
75. Aitken, *Film and Reform*, p. 12.
76. Ibid.

## REFERENCES

Aitken, Ian, *Film and Reform: John Grierson and the Documentary Film Movement* (London: Routledge, 1992).
Decherney, Peter, *Hollywood and the Culture Elite: How the Movies Became American* (New York: Columbia University Press, 2005).
Druick, Zoë, '"Reaching the Multimillions": Liberal Internationalism and the Establishment of Documentary Film', in Lee Grieveson and Haidee Wasson (eds), *Inventing Film Studies* (Durham, NC and London: Duke University Press, 2008), pp. 66–92.
Druick, Zoë and Jonathan Kahana, 'New Deal Documentary and the North Atlantic Welfare State', in Brian Winston (ed.), *The Documentary Film Book* (London: BFI, 2013), pp. 153–8.
Ellis, Jack C., *John Grierson: Life, Contributions, Influence* (Carbondale and Edwardsville: Southern Illinois University Press, 2000).
Ellis, Jack C. and Betsy McLane, *A New History of Documentary Film* (New York: Continuum, 2006).
Gary, Brett, 'Communication Research, the Rockefeller Foundation, and Mobilization for the War on Words, 1938–1944', *Journal of Communication* vol. 46 no. 3 (1996), pp. 124–48.
Grierson, John, 'The Political, Economic and Educational Implications of the Atomic Bomb', 14 May 1946, G5.10.1–6, pp. 1–15, John Grierson Archive, University of Stirling, Stirling.
Grierson, John, 'The Library in an International World', 17 June 1946, G5.10.7–10, pp. 1–16, John Grierson Archive, University of Stirling, Stirling.
Hardy, Forsyth, *John Grierson: A Documentary Biography* (London: Faber and Faber, 1979).
Ramirez, Gracia, 'Rockefeller Support for Non-commercial Film, 1935–1939', *Rockefeller Archive Center*, 2009, 15 July 2011, www.rockarch.org/publications/resrep/gramirez.pdf.
'Rockefeller Related Organizations', *Rockefeller Archive Center*, n.d., 1 July 2011, http://www.rockarch.org/collections/rockorgs/lsrmadd.php.
Rotha, Paul, *Documentary Diary: An Informal History of the British Documentary Film, 1928–1939* (London: Secker & Warburg, 1973).

Solbrig, Heide, 'Henry Strauss and the Human Relations Film: Social Science Media and Interactivity in the Workplace', *Moving Image* vol. 7 no. 1 (2007), pp. 27–50.

Sussex, Elizabeth, *The Rise and Fall of British Documentary: The Story of the Film Movement Founded by John Grierson* (Berkeley: University of California Press, 1976).

Whipple, Mark, 'The Dewey–Lippmann Debate Today: Communication Distortions, Reflective Agency, and Participatory Democracy', *Sociological Theory* vol. 23. no. 2 (2005), pp. 156–78.

## 2

# John Grierson and Russian Cinema: An Uneasy Dialogue

*Julia Vassilieva*

John Grierson's effect, as this volume demonstrates, emanates from his promotion of the theory and practice of documentary cinema, his critical role in the founding of the British and Canadian documentary movements, and his important contribution to the forging of a realist approach in cinema. However, film historians in both Russia and the West stress that Grierson's earlier development as a director and as a theorist was influenced significantly by the example of Russian cinema. The argument prominent in the 1930s in the British film industry that 'the British documentary movement was born from the last reel of *Potemkin*' was endorsed by Jay Leyda[1] and reiterated more recently by Jack C. Ellis[2] in his biography of Grierson, while Richard Taylor and Ian Christie highlight that Grierson's early career 'owed much to the fact that he happened to be working in New York when the task of preparing an American release of *Potemkin* came his way in 1926'.[3] However, apart from the seminal encounter of the future father of British documentary and Sergei Eisenstein's revolutionary classic, little scholarly attention has been directed to unpacking the relationship between Grierson's theoretical and practical work and that of his Russian counterparts. This chapter examines the historical context of the dialogue between Grierson and his collaborators on the one hand and the key masters of Russian cinema on the other, and further traces the engagement with Grierson's legacy by film criticism and audiences in Russia through the twentieth and early twenty-first century.

Grierson's first experience of Russian cinema occurred during his stay in the US during 1924–7, while he was conducting his broad sociological research into public educational media and began to realise the potential of the new medium of cinema, which prompted the beginning of his film reviewing for the *New York Sun* (see Stephen Charbonneau's chapter). During this period Grierson developed a close relationship with Robert Flaherty who, towards the end of 1926, became instrumental in launching the first Soviet masterpiece in America, *Battleship Potemkin*. The print was brought by Douglas Fairbanks from his recent trip to Russia, and Grierson and Jack Cohen, the film critic for the *New York Sun*, did the titles for the film's American release. Grierson later described the events leading to his assignment as follows:

> Douglas Fairbanks came back from a triumphant tour of the Soviet Union, and with him came the first print of a film that was to change a good many concepts of film-making. ... Somehow the rumour of this great new experiment in the dialectics of imagery reached us in New York, and somehow we found ourselves called upon to take it apart and put it together again for the American market.[4]

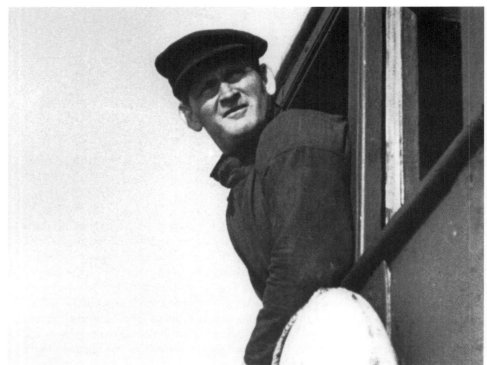

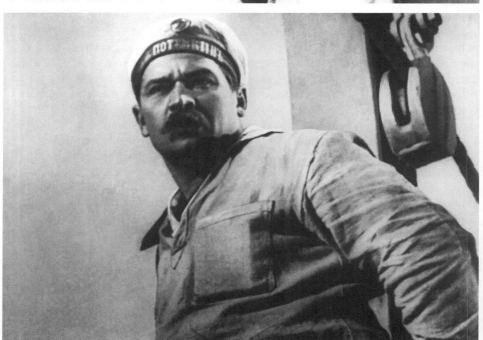

These two shots – from *Drifters* (1929) and *Battleship Potemkin* (1925) – demonstrate striking similarities between Grierson and Eisenstein's cinematography. They also reveal a crucial difference – while Eisenstein presents the solitary male figure as a hero of the Revolution, Grierson imbues his protagonist with more mundane working-class qualities

As a result, as Grierson claimed, he came to know the film 'foot by foot and cut by cut'.[5] Informed by this, one of the received views is that, when Grierson came to direct his first film *Drifters*, the result was a stylistic blend of *Moana* and *Potemkin*. However, as Taylor and Christie point out, *Drifters* now shows little direct influence of *Potemkin*, except in its maritime subject and modest emulation of montage style.[6] The greater significance of the encounter between Grierson and Russian cinema might thus lie in the broader dialogue that was established between the British documentary movement and early Russian cinematic theory.

The years between 1929 and 1934, when Grierson moved from sociological research and freelance journalism to the realisation of his vision of a cinema of 'public affairs' through the Empire Marketing Board and GPO film units, were also marked by close contact between Russian film-makers and Grierson and his collaborators. Grierson met Sergei Eisenstein personally in 1929 when *Drifters* premiered in a double bill with the first English showing of *Potemkin* at the London Film Society, almost exactly three years after the latter's New York opening on 10 November 1926. Two other Russian directors, Vsevolod Pudovkin and Dziga Vertov, had also travelled to London to present their films at the Film Society, including *The Man with the Movie Camera* (1929) and *The End of St Petersburg* (1927). Whereas no more than forty Soviet features were in distribution in Britain before World War II, during the period between 1928 and 1939 the Film Society showed thirty Soviet films, an indication of the intense interest in the Russian experiment displayed by Grierson and his followers. The Russian film-makers' visits provided not only opportunities for Film Society members (who included future film-makers, independent distributors and curators, such as Thorold Dickinson, Basil Wright, Charles Cooper, Tom Brandon, Iris Barry and Ernest Lindgren) to discuss screenings with Russian directors, but also a stimulus to address the broader issue of what cinema should be.

The debates regarding the role and functions of the new medium loomed large in Russia during the decade after the Revolution of 1917, with specific attention to the issue of how history – and indeed 'truth' – should be presented cinematically to the masses. Towards the end of the 1920s a number of films dedicated to the tenth anniversary of the Revolution were released: Dziga Vertov's 1926 newsreel about Lenin – one of a series which went under Vertov's banner of *Kinopravda* – and his more direct contribution to the celebrations in the form of the newsreel *The Eleventh Year* (1928), while in 1927 Efsir Shub's documentary *The Fall of the Romanov Dynasty* and Sergei Eisenstein's docudrama *October* followed, both also significant in this respect. These films fuelled the debate among directors, theoreticians and Party officials as to the most appropriate methods by which the Revolution's course should be captured on screen, the best way to represent 'fact', the construction of the argument versus 'catching life unaware' and the distinction between 'played' and 'unplayed' films as means of representing history. At stake in these debates was the issue that shaped theorisation of documentary as a specific mode of film-making, that of the real and its representation. It was inevitable that some echo of these debates, which so fundamentally informed the epoch, were brought by the Russian directors to their London lectures. At the same time, the 'Russian example' offered Western intellectuals committed to the idea of social and aesthetic change a broader model of how to mobilise cinema to see the world in a new and objective way. As Taylor and Christie note,

Cinema as a new mode of vision, a new means of social representation, a new definition of popular art, embodying new relations of production and consumption – all these aspirations found confirmation in the films and declarations of Eisenstein, Pudovkin and Vertov.[7]

Basil Wright recalled the powerful and challenging effect Eisenstein's lectures had on their audience at the Film Society in November 1929. Wright recorded the following statements from the presentation, which addressed film as 'a science grounded on philosophical and higher mathematical knowledge':

We have now reached a stage in our Theoretical and practical work at which we are in a position to work out a Theoretical basis for film.

Only recently have we begun to feel the real type of purely filmic film which is to come. So far films moving in this direction have been purely experimental (intellectual film). But now the historical moment has come at which we are to find *the synthesis of art and science in an entirely new form of picturization.*[8]

Marie Seton argues that

The impact of Eisenstein's lecture ... produced what Sergei Mikhailovich would have termed a creative explosion in the minds of quite a number of the Film Society Study Group. They were given a stimulus towards making of films based on real life – the realities of British life which had not found expression in the trite story films and ponderous historical pictures made by British studios.[9]

Grierson clearly saw the Russian example as an inspiration and a point of comparison for his work, both directorial and organisational, in Britain. For example, he wrote that 'to produce anything comparable with the Russian films', there would need to be in Britain 'a similar grouping of directors ... and a grouping of dramatic loyalties', while also acknowledging that 'it would take a giant in such circumstances' to achieve work of the same calibre.[10] However, despite Grierson's deep admiration of the Russian experiment in cinema, throughout the 1930s he grew progressively more ambiguous towards its direction. Following the screening of *The Man with the Movie Camera* and Vertov's visit to London, Grierson commented:

The Vertov method of film-making is based on a supremely sound idea, and one which must be a preliminary to any movie method at all. He has observed that there are things of the every-day which achieve a new value, leap to a more vigorous life, the moment they get into a movie camera or an intimately cut sequence. It is a point where we all begin; and, backing our eye with the world, we try to pick the leapers. [...]

Vertov, however, has pushed the argument to a point at which it becomes ridiculous. The camera observes in its own bright way and he is prepared to give it his head. The man is with the camera, not the camera with the man. Organization of things observed, brain control, imagination or fancy control of all things observed: these other rather necessary activities in the making of art are forgotten. *The Man with the Movie Camera* is in consequence not a film at all: it is a snapshot album.[11]

Grierson's verdict on Vertov's *Enthusiasm* (1930) was no less harsh, with him declaring that 'body of thought or body of construction it had none'.[12] On the other hand, Grierson felt compelled to admit that 'It is so full of ingenuities that practitioners like myself will be feeding on its carcase years from now.'[13]

Evidently, Grierson was more drawn to the lyricism, poetry and more pronounced narrative organisation of Pudovkin and Dovzenko's films. He described *Earth* (1930) as 'one of the great films' among few 'responsible for the same renewal of cinematic energy'.[14] He praised Pudovkin's *The End of St Petersburg* and his *Deserter* (1933) even more, saying of the latter: 'no film or novel or poem or drama has sketched so largely the essential story and the essential unhappiness of our time, or brought them so deeply to the mind'.[15] But the only truly hopeful example at the time for Grierson was Victor A. Turin's *Turksib* (1929), a documentary charting the building of the Turkestan–Siberian railway, which Grierson prepared for its British release and which arguably served as inspiration for *Night Mail*:

> There is, I believe, only Turin and *Turksib* which, for all its patches of really bad articulation is the single job that takes us into the future. *Turksib* is an affair of economics, which is the only sort of affair worth one's time or patience.[16]

Throughout the 1930s Grierson's criticism of the Soviet modernist directors became more punishing and rejecting. Grierson judged Eisenstein's *The General Line* (1934) to be a fundamental failure, as 'Eisenstein does not get inside the Russian peasants, not, with true affection, inside the problem of co-operating them'[17] and argued that 'the Russians, I know, will take my point'.[18] Neither, according to Grierson, did Pudovkin and Dovzenko rise to the challenges of the new demands of industrialisation and collectivisation. The imperatives of revolutionary documentary, 'the common problems of everyday life', were only adequately addressed in the mid-1930s in Fridrikh Ermler's *Counterplan* (1932) and in Aleksandr Macheret's *Men and Jobs* (1933).[19] Grierson's criticism of Russian modernist works from the point of view of social politics went hand in hand with his critique of their avant-garde stylistics. The key issue in this debate was, as Bill Nichols shows, broader modernist fragmentation that proposed alternative subjects and subjectivities, not easily conjoined for specific government agendas. As Nichols explains:

> The appearance of documentary involves the combination of three preexisting elements – photographic realism, narrative structure, and modernist fragmentation – along with a new emphasis on the rhetoric of social persuasion. This combination of elements itself became a source of contention. The most dangerous element, the one with the greatest disruptive potential – modernist fragmentation – required the most careful treatment. Grierson was greatly concerned by its linkage to the radical shifts in subjectivity promoted by the European avant-garde and to the radical shifts in political power promoted by the constructivist artists and Soviet film-makers. He, in short, adapted film's radical potential to far less disturbing ends.[20]

Grierson's final verdict on Russian experiment was that 'the Russian talent faded' by 1935. The reasons were explained as follows:

Russian directors are too bound up – too aesthetically vain – in what they call their 'play films' to contribute to Russia's instructional cinema. They have, indeed, suffered greatly from the freedom given to artists in the first uncritical moment of revolutionary enthusiasm, for they have tended to isolate themselves more and more in private impression and private performance. [...] For the future, one may safely leave them to the consideration of the Central Committee. One's impression is that when some of the art and all of the Bohemian self-indulgence have been knocked out of them, the Russian cinema will fulfil its high promise of the late twenties. [...] The revolutionary will almost certainly 'liquidate', as they put it, this romantic perspective.[21]

Similar criticism of avant-garde film-making was growing within Soviet Russia as well, both on aesthetic and political grounds, culminating in the decisive change of direction of Russian cinema initiated in 1935 by the Moscow Conference of Cinema Workers. The conference adopted the new doctrine of Socialist Realism that had been introduced a year before at the First All Union Congress of Soviet Writers:

Socialist realism demands truthfulness (*pravdivost'*) from the artist and an historically concrete portrayal of reality in its revolutionary development. Under these conditions, truthfulness and historical concreteness of artistic portrayal ought to be combined with the task of the ideological remaking and education of laboring people in the spirit of socialism.[22]

It is true that the old theory of rupture or overhaul of the previous avant-garde freedom by the Socialist Realism dogma is currently debated, with positions on the topic ranging from Taylor and Christie's[23] modest call to acknowledge fighting between various artistic Russian groups to Boris Groys's[24] more radical proposal that, rather than being a mortal enemy of totalitarian aesthetics and politics, Russian modernism set the stage for the development of Socialist Realism in art and a state of total control in politics. Nevertheless, the fact remains that from 1934 onwards Socialist Realism became a dominant – indeed exclusive – aesthetic for Soviet artists, composers, cinematographers and writers.

The adoption of the doctrine of Socialist Realism was part of a 'cultural revolution' through which the Party would exercise tight control over cultural affairs, including artistic expression. Socialist Realism was based on the tripartite principles of accessibility (*dostupnost'*), the spirit of the people (*narodnost'*) and the spirit of the Party (*partiinost'*). For cinema, this entailed moving away from the split between the avant-garde and mainstream cinema evident in the late 1920s towards a film style that would be legible to a broad audience. The montage aesthetics of Eisenstein, Kuleshov, Vertov and Dovzenko were liable to the charge of Formalism, which was deemed a great political as well as aesthetic mistake. Instead, the director of Soyuzkino and chief policy officer for the film industry from 1931 to 1938, Boris Shumiatsky urged the creation of a 'cinema for the millions', which would use clear, linear narration based on the model of continuity editing.[25] Various guidelines were then developed to specify content and themes of cinematic production: narratives should feature positive heroes to act as role models for viewers; the storylines should deliver lessons in good citizenship for spectators to follow; and ideologically the films should be informed by the policy decisions of the Communist Party.

Paradoxically for the development that allegedly strived for 'realism', the balance between documentary and fiction cinema, which, as Taylor and Christie observe, had already been stacked in favour of the latter, moved even further in this direction.[26] Discussion in the Soviet press is indicative of this development. In February 1932 *Proletarskoe kino* insisted on the need 'for a ruthless exposure of film theories that were hostile to Marxism'.[27] For the proponents of Socialist Realism, documentarism represented one such theory, 'illiterate, presumptuous and excessively pretentious'.[28] They called for the total eradication of documentarism in Soviet cinema: 'We stand on the position of implacable struggle against documentarism, we have set ourselves the task of destroying it completely.'[29] Consequently, over the 1930s in the Soviet state nonfiction production became totally subordinated to the aim of influencing attitudes and public opinion to justify specific policies of the period within the broader Marxist and Leninist ideological framework. This development led to, as Graham Roberts puts it in his monograph *Forward Soviet!*, 'the not so strange death of Soviet Documentary'.[30] Roberts observes that, beginning in the mid-1930s, 'Documentary cinema was presenting a fantasy world where all was well in the Soviet bloc, and the working class, condemned to reside in the rest of the world, craved the same Utopia.'[31] Although a massive amount of documentaries and newsreels was produced each year up until the postwar period, the continued quantity could not disguise the utter lack of quality.

Towards the end of the 1930s, Stalin's grip on power tightened, the national terror became widespread, and government control over art was consolidated. This period also saw the emergence of the themes of patriotism, Russian nationalism and xenophobia on the ideological agenda. Dmitry and Vladimir Shlapentokh demonstrate in their ideological analysis of Soviet cinema that 'During this time foreigners (regardless of their social status) [...] were treated as enemies of Soviet Russia.'[32] From 1931 the import of foreign films into Soviet Russia was stopped, leading to the interruption of the interaction with the cinemas of other counties – the Iron Curtain fell. As Taylor and Christie observe, these developments led to the general stagnation, if not outright elimination, of aesthetic and theoretical debates on cinema:

> In the shadow of Stalin's 'personality cult' and the accompanying purges the atmosphere was becoming increasingly difficult and public discussion of aesthetic issues increasingly restricted. The film press was moving towards political exhortation rather than aesthetic debate. Open debate was becoming more guarded and hence also more coded and fragmented.[33]

The dialogue with Grierson's theory and practice by the Soviet film-makers, scholars and general public inevitably ground to a halt in this context. However, while personal contacts between Soviet film-makers and Grierson and his collaborators ceased to exist, the emergence of the doctrine of Socialist Realism brought into sharp relief both similarities and differences between Grierson's position and the masters of Russian cinema both before and after 1934. These concerned political philosophy, particularly views on Marxism, the role of the working class, the role of the state and the functions of ideological propaganda.

The first parallel at the level of subject matter is Grierson's dedication to 'the documentary of work and workers'. Grierson's British films, and his Canadian films after them, feature predominantly images of industrial workers involved in collective labour processes contributing towards the common good. As Peter Morris remarks, one is reminded that one of Grierson's early essays was titled 'The Worker as Hero' and of the way the notion of 'hail the hero workers' reverberates powerfully through his work.[34]

Socialist Realism similarly positioned workers and peasants as primary protagonists and privileged everyday subject matter. However, Grierson's decisive difference with it in this respect was that he did not understand the working class to be the driving and most progressive force in history, as Socialist Realism did, in accordance with Marxist historical narrative. By contrast, as Ian Aitken notes, Grierson rejected the Marxist idea that fundamental divisions exist within society, and particularly that class struggle and class conflict are inevitable. Instead, Grierson understood social life as imbedded within 'a matrix of inter-dependent relations' and argued that societies and institutions characterised by higher integration were superior to those with less. As a result Grierson came to believe in the powerful beneficial role of the state in the process of achieving and maintaining social unity.[35] A similar analysis has previously been proposed by Morris, who supported his claims with the following quotation from Grierson's letter written after World War II:

> My personal view is that such total planning by the state is an absolute good and not simply a relative good ... I do not myself think of the attitude I take as deriving from Marx – though this undoubtedly will be suggested – but from Fichte and Hegel. My view of the State, as you know, is that it is only through the State that the person and the will of the person can be greatly expressed. Here I am in sufficiently good academic company not to have particular qualms about attack.[36]

This understanding of the relationship between individual and state had two important consequences for Grierson. One concerned the overriding framework of unity as allowing for resolution of any contradictions, and the second related to the formative role of art and constructivist function of artist/propagandist.

The very privileged position that Grierson accorded to documentary stemmed from his conviction that documentary was ideally suited to representing the interconnected nature of social relationships because it was 'the medium of all media born to express the living nature of inter-dependency ... [it] ... outlined the patterns of interdependency more distinctly and more deliberately than any other medium whatsoever'.[37] Furthermore, while acknowledging that problems exist within this network of interdependency, Grierson believed they are always solvable – usually by the state but sometimes by some abstract entity of 'collectivity'. This attitude resonates with the emphasis that was placed within Socialist Realism's approach on the idea of unity and total sublation of contradictions in society. However, if for Grierson achievement of this unity does not require change of the existing form of the neo-liberal conservative state, the unity implied by Socialist Realism was predicated on the assumption that Marxist ideology will eventually lead to the eradication of contradictions between labour and capital, workers and managers, industrialisation and nature, family and society, in the process of establishing the Communist state.

Grierson's position with regard to the role of the state led to his view on the function of art. He believed art should not reflect but rather shape and mould not only a particular representation of reality but also of human consciousness and action.

> They tell us that art is a mirror – a mirror held up to nature. I think this is a false image … . In a society like ours, art is not a mirror but a hammer. It is a weapon in our hands to see and say what is right and good and beautiful, and hammer it out as the mould and pattern of men's actions.[38]

As a corollary to this, Grierson emphasised the role of the artist as one of 'social constructiveness':

> The oblique paradox of propaganda is that the lie in the throat becomes, by repetition, the truth in the heart. And, consequently, the art of propaganda or public information becomes one of the most powerful forms of directive statesmanship. The place of the educator and the artist in society changes entirely to one of definite social constructiveness.[39]

This statement resonates powerfully with the similar constructivist assumptions prevalent among Russian avant-garde artists and expressed most clearly by Eisenstein in his late work *Method*:

> For me art has never represented 'art for art's sake'. It has never been a project to create something dissimilar to the existing world – 'my own world'. Just as well I have never tried to 'reflect' the existing world. My aim has always been – using art's means – to impact on thoughts and feelings, impact on psyche and through this impact mould the viewer's consciousness in a desirable, needed, selected direction.[40]

However, while for Eisenstein this constructivist agenda had a broader meaning – to create a new man of a new society – for Grierson it was about educating in the direction of the 'right and good and beautiful'. As Nichols comments:

> The principle of citizenship as self-realization, frequently invoked by contructivists and film-makers in the Soviet Union in relation to the creation of a 'new man', became the singular *raison d'être* for Grierson's conception of the documentary, not to foment revolution but to preserve the status quo.[41]

It is in the context of these considerations that the respective positions on realism implied by Grierson's theory and practice and Russian cinema can be compared. The shift from avant-garde practices to the doctrine of Socialist Realism that took place in Russian cinema in the mid-1930s saw the reorientation of concerns from the modernist search, articulated by the pioneers of Russian cinema, for new ways of seeing and depicting the world, and as such grasping reality as it unfolds, to the reinstatement of the nineteenth-century naturalist aesthetics and an overriding preoccupation with state-produced propagandist 'realism'. As Aitken suggests, Grierson's theory of realism similarly underwent a decisive change around 1936, when his earlier focus on philosophical aesthetics was 'replaced by a more functionalist discourse based around issues of propaganda and instrumental "civic education"'.[42] Furthermore, in his revisionist account Morris argued that Grierson's traditionally celebrated organic approach was informed by authoritarian and totalitarian tendencies, not unlike those that shaped the Russian approach to cinema under Communism. However, from within Soviet Russia in its darkest ideological decades of the 1930s and 40s, the differences far outweighed the similarities, with the decisive factor being Grierson's rejection of Marxism. Grierson's position on the relationship between classes, power and the role of the state contributed to partial and cautious engagement with his output in the Soviet Union at precisely the time when he was 'at the peak of his influence'[43] in the West.

Only after the death of Stalin in 1953 did some engagement with masters of foreign cinema become possible again in Russian scholarship. The period known as Khrushchev's thaw, which brought about a reexamination and critique of Stalin's era, ushered in greater artistic freedom and a renewal of dialogue with the West. The period saw some rejuvenation of documentary practices and more broad-ranging engagement with theoretical work from around the world. Following the translation of such important works on the history of cinema as Ernest Lindgren's *The Art of the Film*[44] in 1956 and Georges Sadoul's *Histoire de l'art du cinéma des origines a nos jours*[45] in 1957, Soviet film criticism produced an interpretation of Grierson's work that reconciled his views with Soviet ideology, emphasising similarities and downplaying differences.[46] Numerous entries on Grierson from the time (such as for example that in the *Dictionary of Cinema* [1966]) acknowledged him as a figure responsible for the emergence of the British documentary movement, while stressing that he was influenced by the work of Eisenstein and Pudovkin.[47] Soviet film historians at the time praised Grierson for 'poetic, loving and respectful representation of ordinary people and workers', particularly emphasising the British documentary movement's attention to social problems: unemployment, housing, working conditions.[48] It can thus be seen that while the reception of Grierson's theory and films during this period was overwhelmingly positive, it was still extensively informed by class politics. When a translation of Grierson's 'First Principles of Documentary' was published in the edited collection of translated essays *The Truth of Cinema and Cinema-Truth* in 1967, the editors stressed in their introduction that the British documentary movement was governed by two principles: 'the creative treatment of actuality' and human labour as the primary source of poetry on the screen.[49] The translator also took certain liberties with Grierson's original text, inserting statements that brought Grierson's political position more closely in line with Soviet ideology.

It would take more than thirty years for Russian scholarship and popular perception to come to engage with Grierson's legacy in a less politicised way. This occurred in the wake of the broad-ranging political reforms initiated by Mikhail Gorbachev that became known as *perestroika*. As a result of this, a significant change towards a new outlook on film history as part of broader aesthetic, cultural, social and political processes has taken place in Russia over the last twenty-five years, and it was in this context that a renewed interest in Grierson's heritage emerged at the beginning of the twenty-first century, evident in new translations,[50] broadcasts of his documentaries on TV channel Culture and a continuous stream of screenings of his films by film societies in various places in Russia. These screenings and broadcasts covered a number of important films directed by Grierson and made with his creative involvement, specifically focusing on the early, more pronounced modernist works: *The Drifters*, *Night Mail*, *The Coming of Dial* (1933), *Granton Trawler*, *6.30 Collection* (1934), *Song of Ceylon*, *A Colour Box* (1935), *Coal Face* (1935), *Sixpenny Telegram* (1935). Furthermore, Grierson and the British documentary movement have come to feature prominently in the curricula of cinema studies courses taught in Russian universities.

Overall, the critical shift in the reassessment of Grierson's heritage during the last twenty-five years indicates a move away from the emphasis on the 'documentaries of work and workers' towards reconsideration of Grierson as a major figure in the European modernist movement. From this point of view, Grierson's aesthetic strategies, such as visual composition and rhythmic structure, become the focus of attention, while his focus on industrialisation is reinterpreted as a more general modernist fascination with mechanisation as a distinct feature of the twentieth century.[51]

Recent years have also seen the reinvigoration of broad public interest in Grierson's output.[52] While films made by Grierson and the British documentary movement have never appeared in a VHS or DVD format with Russian subtitles, cine buffs circulate these films with amateur subtitles on the internet. The vivid exchange in the Russian cinephile blogosphere attests to the interest on the part of the wider community in all aspects of Grierson's documentaries – from their empirical content to aesthetics and historical context. As such, this movement mobilises the potential of documentary to forge a connection between 'history and (social) memory', as pointed out by Michael Chanan. Chanan writes,

> the film as such becomes a strange new form of historical past embedded in what is always already a partial perspective on it: a veridical social and historical world as interpreted by the film-maker just a moment before it becomes historical.[53]

As such, for the present generation of Russians, Grierson's theory and practice of documentary became an important fragment in the rich tapestry of political, philosophical and aesthetic movements of the twentieth century, contributing to a vision of the past as a more sophisticated and at the same time nuanced totality.

## NOTES

1. Jay Leyda, *Kino: A History of the Russian and Soviet Film* (Princeton, NJ: Princeton University Press, 1983), p. 195.
2. Jack C. Ellis, *John Grierson: Life, Contributions, Influences* (Carbondale and Edwardsville: Southern Illinois University Press, 2000), p. 29.
3. Richard Taylor and Ian Christie, *The Film Factory: Russian and Soviet Cinema in Documents* (Cambridge, MA: Harvard University Press, 1988), pp. 7–8.
4. John Grierson, *Eisenstein, 1898–1948*, Publication of a spoken tribute following Eisenstein's death given on 2 May 1948, by Grierson, Paul Rotha, Ivor Montagu, Marie Seton and Herbert Marshall (London: Film Section of the Society for Cultural Relations with the USSR, 1948).

5. Taylor and Christie, *The Film Factory*, p. 8.
6. Ibid., p. 410.
7. Ibid., p. 8.
8. Sergei Eisenstein, London Lectures on Film Theory, Précis Notes Taken by Basil Wright, November–December 1929, in Marie Seton, *Sergei M. Eisenstein: A Biography*, rev. edn (London: Dobson, 1978), pp. 482–5.
9. Seton, *Sergei M. Eisenstein*, p. 144.
10. Forsyth Hardy (ed.), *Grierson on Documentary* (London: Faber and Faber, 1966), p. 123.
11. Ibid., p. 127.
12. Forsyth Hardy (ed.), *Grierson on the Movies* (London: Faber and Faber, 1981), p. 141.
13. Ibid., p. 142.
14. Hardy, *Grierson on Documentary*, p. 123.
15. Ibid., p. 130.
16. Ibid., p. 122.
17. Co-operating' refers to the process of creation of collective economy as an antithesis to individual or family farming by the Soviet government in the 1920s. A collective farm, or *kolkhoz*, was legally organised as a production co-operative.
18. Hardy, *Grierson on Documentary*, p. 122.
19. Ibid., p. 183.
20. Bill Nichols, 'Documentary Film and the Modernist Avant-garde', *Critical Inquiry* vol. 27 no. 4 (2001), p. 582.
21. Hardy, *Grierson on Documentary*, pp. 183–4.
22. *Pravda*, 5 June 1934.
23. Taylor and Christie, *The Film Factory*.
24. Boris Groys, *Iskusstvo Utopii/The Art of Utopia* (Moskva: Znak, 1993).
25. Boris Shumiatsky, *Cinematography Millionov/Cinema for the Millions* (Moscow: Kinofotoizdat, 1935).
26. Taylor and Christie, *The Film Factory*, p. 8.
27. Ibid., p. 321.
28. Ibid.
29. Ibid., pp. 321–2.
30. Graham Roberts, *Forward Soviet! History and Non-fiction Film in the USSR* (London and New York: I. B.Tauris, 1999), p. 139.
31. Ibid.
32. Dmitry Shlapentokh and Vladimir Shlapentokh, *Soviet Cinematography 1918–1991: Ideological Conflicts and Social Reality* (New York: Aldine de Gruyter, 1993), p. 98.
33. Taylor and Christie, *The Film Factory,* p. 371.
34. Peter Morris, in Pierre Veronneau, Michael Dorland and Seth Feldman (eds), 'Rethinking Grierson: The Ideology of John Grierson', *Dialogue: Canadian and Quebec Cinema*, *Canadian Film Studies*, vol. 3 (1987), pp. 21–56.
35. Ian Aitken, *European Film Theory and Cinema* (Edinburgh: Edinburgh University Press, 2001).
36. Quoted in Peter Morris, '"Praxis into Process": John Grierson and the National Film Board of Canada', *Historical Journal of Film, Radio and Television* vol. 9 no. 3 (1989), p. 274.
37. Quoted in Aitken, *European Film Theory and Cinema*, p. 165.
38. Quoted in Morris, 'Re-thinking Grierson', pp. 21–56.

39. Ibid.
40. Sergei M. Eisenstein, *Method* (Moscow: Museum of Cinema, Eisenstein-Centre, 2002), p. 46.
41. Nichols, 'Documentary Film and the Modernist Avant-garde', p. 600.
42. Aitken, *European Film Theory and Cinema*, p. 167.
43. Morris, 'Re-thinking Grierson', p. 26.
44. Ernest Lindgren, *The Art of the Film* (Moscow: Iskusstvo, 1956).
45. Georges Sadoul, *Histoire de l'art du cinéma des origines à nos jours* (Moscow: Izdatelstvo Inostrannoi Literatury, 1957).
46. Sergei Drobashenko (ed.), *The Screen and Life* [Ekran i jizn] (Moscow: Iskusstvo, 1962).
47. *Dictionary of Cinema*, vol. 1 (Moscow: Sovetskay Encyclopedia, 1966), p. 390.
48. Sergei Drobashenko (ed.), *The Truth of Cinema and Cinema-Truth* [Pravda kino ikinopravda] (Moscow: Iskusstvo, 1967), p. 12.
49. John Grierson, 'First Principles of Documentary', trans. B. Dvorman, in Drobashenko, *The Truth of Cinema and Cinema-Truth*, pp. 305–15.
50. See, for example, selected translations from Grierson's American period of film journalism in *Kinovedcheskie Zapiski*, the leading journal of film history and theory in Russia, vol. 84, 2007.
51. See, for example, an entry in the online *Encyclopedia of Culture and Education* 'Krugosvet': http://www.krugosvet.ru/enc/kultura_i_obrazovanie/teatr_i_kino/DOKUMENTALNOE_KINO.html?page=0,3.
52. See, for example, a discussion of a screening of Grierson's films at the Moscow Club of Documentary Cinema: http://doc-kino-club.livejournal.com/97579.html.
53. Michael Chanan, 'Documentary, History, Social Memory', *Journal of British Cinema and Television* vol. 1. no. 1 (2004), p. 62.

## REFERENCES

Aitken, Ian, *European Film Theory and Cinema* (Edinburgh: Edinburgh University Press, 2001).
Chanan, Michael, 'Documentary, History, Social Memory', *Journal of British Cinema and Television* vol. 1 no. 1 (2004), pp. 61–77.
*Dictionary of Cinema,* vol. 1 (Moscow: Sovetskay Encyclopedia, 1966).
Drobashenko, Sergei, *Ekran i jizn/The Screen and Life* (Moscow: Iskusstvo, 1962).
Drobashenko, Sergei (ed.), *Pravda kino ikinopravda/The Truth of Cinema and Cinema-Truth* (Moscow: Iskusstvo, 1967).
Eisenstein, Sergei M., 'London Lectures on Film Theory, Précis Notes Taken by Basil Wright, November–December 1929', in Marie Seton, *Sergei M. Eisenstein: A Biography*, rev. edn (London: Dobson, 1978), pp. 482–5.
Eisenstein, Sergei M., *Method* (Moscow: Museum of Cinema, Eisenstein-Centre, 2002).
Ellis, Jack C., *John Grierson: Life, Contributions, Influences* (Carbondale and Edwardsville: Southern Illinois University Press, 2000).
Grierson, John, *Eisenstein, 1898–1948*, Publication of a spoken tribute following Eisenstein's death given on 2 May 1948, by Grierson, Paul Rotha, Ivor Montagu, Marie Seton and Herbert Marshall (London: Film Section of the Society for Cultural Relations with the USSR, 1948).
Groys, Boris, *Iskusstvo Utopii/The Art of Utopia* (Moskva: Znak, 1993).

Hardy, Forsyth (ed.), *Grierson on Documentary* (London: Faber and Faber, 1966).

Hardy, Forsyth (ed.), *Grierson on the Movies* (London: Faber and Faber, 1981).

Leyda, Jay, *Kino: A History of the Russian and Soviet Film* (Princeton, NJ: Princeton University Press, 1983).

Lindgren, Ernest, *The Art of the Film* (Moscow: Iskusstvo, 1956).

Morris, Peter, 'Rethinking Grierson: The Ideology of John Grierson', in Pierre Veronneau, Michael Dorland and Seth Feldman (eds), *Dialogue: Canadian and Quebec Cinema, Canadian Film Studies*, Montreal: Médiatexte Publications and La Cinémathèque Québécoise, vol. 3 (1987), pp. 21–56.

Morris, Peter, '"Praxis into Process": John Grierson and the National Film Board of Canada', *Historical Journal of Film, Radio and Television* vol. 9 no. 3 (1989), pp. 269–82.

Nichols, Bill, 'Documentary Film and the Modernist Avant-garde', *Critical Inquiry* vol. 27 no. 4 (2001), pp. 580–610.

*Pravda*, 5 June 1934.

Roberts, Graham, *Forward Soviet! History and Non-fiction Film in the USSR* (London and New York: I. B. Tauris, 1999).

Sadoul, Georges, *Histoire de l'art du cinéma des origines à nos jours* (Moscow: Izdatelstvo Inostrannoi Literatury, 1957).

Seton, Marie, *Sergei M. Eisenstein: A Biography* (rev. edn) (London: Dobson, 1978).

Shlapentokh, Dmitry and Vladimir Shlapentokh, *Soviet Cinematography 1918–1991: Ideological Conflicts and Social Reality* (New York: Aldine de Gruyter, 1993).

Shumiatsky, Boris, *Cinematography Millionov/Cinema for the Millions* (Moscow: Kinofotoizdat, 1935).

Taylor, Richard and Ian Christie, *The Film Factory: Russian and Soviet Cinema in Documents* (Cambridge, MA: Harvard University Press, 1988).

# 3

# To Play The Part That Was in Fact His/Her Own

*Brian Winston*

*In* The Savings of Bill Blewitt – *a proto-drama documentary directed by Harry Watt in 1936 – there is scarcely a frame which suggests that anything of ordinary behaviour has been captured by the camera. The film was made to sell Post Office savings accounts. In it, Bill Blewitt, a somewhat feckless Cornish fisherman, looses his smack because of a degree of carelessness which makes his name peculiarly apposite. A crucial scene has Bill asking his wife to look up how much he has managed to put by in the Post Office. Clearly embarrassed by being on camera, she fishes the savings book out of her bag and announces: '£24/14/9d'. Bill wants to know because a replacement boat might be on the market but it is likely to be sold to some wealthier stranger, much to Bill's distress. All he can manage to indicate this emotion is a muttered laconic aside describing his rival as 'some yachtsman fellah'. A neighbour pops her head round the door with more news, a message delivered in a sing-song Cornish burr with all the human conviction of an animated puppet. She leaves, bobbing: 'No, can't stay, me dears. Gotta go. Gotta go.'*

One of the more paradoxical aspects of Grierson's legacy is a certain tolerance, to be found in the reception of the classic films produced by the documentary movement, for stilted, 'unnatural' (as it might be) performances by the people featured on the screen. The quality of the 'acting', especially in the synch sequences of the 1930s films, was almost unremarked upon at the time and has scarcely figured in any discussion of the authenticity of the Griersonian archive since.

That we now understand all (off-screen) behaviour as a species of 'performance of a social role'[1] does not remove the question of the authenticity of the performances of such roles on screen in the context of documentary. In this context, 'performativity' speaks to the 'distinct tension between performance and document' noted by Bill Nichols in his initial application of that term to documentary film; that is, the tension 'between the personal and the typical, the embodied and the disembodied, between, in short, history and science'.[2] This 'tension' can – and, I will argue in the case of the Griersonian archive, does – produce inauthentic performances in the older sense of theatricality: in other words, of 'acting' – in fact, poor acting, as conventionally judged. Performativity is not a synonym for performance and treating it so obfuscates the significance of Grierson's legacy in this regard. In the case of documentary, to claim automatic authenticity because all behaviour is 'performative' does not remove consideration of it as performance. The claim on the real demands that performance in the documentary in the older sense of 'acting' be judged against the representational codes reflecting such behaviour as 'real' or 'natural' on the screen.

In Erving Goffman's *locus classicus* for considering all behaviour as performance (*The Presentation of Self in Everyday Life*, 1959), the essential objective for any individual is held to be to 'stage a character' successfully in the public sphere. The reception of this 'staging' – social interaction – teeters, Goffman suggested, between 'cynicism and sincerity';[3] and it is this that conditions what Jane Roscoe has called the 'flicker of authenticity' in the audience's reception of such presentations made by the documentary 'actor'.[4] This flicker acts not unlike a miners' safety lamp. It indicates when the 'gas', as it might be – the 'gas' of acting in the specific thespic sense – is present.

Annette Hill, in her contemporary audience research on reality TV, has found that the question of 'acting' does contribute to what she calls 'the chain of distrust' in the minds of her interviewees, the audience.[5] The 'chain' runs from news and current affairs to the formatted documentary shows. The audience distrust these last most when they think that the participants are acting as in a play – 'acting up' is how they characterise it. For them, this clearly vitiates any claim on the real such programming makes.[6] To say of a documentary subject that they were 'acting', then as now, is to dispute the documentary value of the image, if not to discard that value altogether. Acting, then, extinguishes the 'flicker'. It speaks to the heart of what Annette Hill has called (borrowing from data science) documentary's 'referential integrity'.[7] What is endangered here when the flicker goes out, according to John Corner's analysis, is the pleasure which he suggests we derive from documentary footage as we attempt 'to establish people's "real" character from the clues and the slips provided by the on-screen performance of speech and action' – a process he calls 'selving'.[8]

My contention is that this 'selving' can only be limited when watching the people filmed by the Griersonians. This is not only true for today's audience encountering the archive, wherein the people filmed are figures from the other country we call the historic past; it was also true at the time. And, moreover, one could suggest that this extinguished authenticity in performances, exacerbated as it was by documentary's claim on the real, contributed to the limited audience success the films enjoyed in their day. This does more than impact on the films' reception. The process of 'selving' is not only potentially pleasurable. It also involves the audience mechanism for testing for authenticity – for evaluating the claim on the real. 'Selving' is of a piece, as a concept, with Umberto Eco's image of the metaphorical 'inferential walk', which must be taken to decode any text.[9] Specifically, without taking such a walk, the truth claims of any text – a realist documentary, say – cannot be established by the audience. The quality of the acting as a reflection of quotidian behaviour is thus tested and is central to the acceptance of the authenticity of what is being presented on the screen. The silence about it in the debates on classic documentary is therefore more than curious.

After all, the Griersonian project was in no ways at odds with the Vertovian ambition to 'show us [authentically] life'. As with Vertov, that was Grierson's central purpose – revealing society to the audience for the purposes of public enlightenment and education. This agenda suggested that what the films provided was an enhanced understanding of society, giving the citizenry an improved grasp of what was to be done about its problems. Hence the 'preacher' Grierson's view: 'I look upon cinema as a pulpit, and use it as a propagandist.'[10] Within this project, as Harry Watt explained to Elizabeth Sussex, the films' claim to being 'revolutionary' depended on the fact that 'they were putting on the screen for the first time in British films – and very nearly in world films – a workingman's face and a workingman's hands and the way the worker lived and worked'.[11] Leave aside the firstism, the authenticity of the 'way' of the workers presented on screen in the Griersonian films, especially whenever shot in synch, can be easily disputed. This is critical since such representation – 'the way the worker lived' – is central. In the Auerbachian vision of *mimesis* realism is exactly this.[12] It 'is the artistic form that takes the life of the common people with supreme seriousness'.[13] The Griersonian project is a prime example, therefore, of the realist project. It is the realist aesthetic that demands the classic Anglophone documentary be a 'discourse of sobriety'.[14]

That the performances in the films reveal far more self-conscious, artificial behaviour than much of this claimed reality runs counter to Griersonian ambition. It seriously undercuts the project's 'documentary value'. This is no small matter, for all that Grierson's public relations genius marginalised the issue. Clearly, any such discussion would have implicitly queried documentary's fundamental legitimacy, and not just at the level of aesthetic theory. In the event, however, the possibility that the acting on the screen might in any way cast doubt on the classic documentary's claim on the real was virtually ignored. It is part of Grierson's PR legacy that this has never really happened since either.

Watt's work as a director of actors – that is, of the people who appeared before his camera – was exemplified by *The Savings of Bill Blewitt*. In any subset of documentary production, apart from our contemporary understanding of dramadocs (docudramas), this necessarily means people who are anything other than professional actors – unless, of course, the topic of the film is their work as performers.[15] For a documentary, in all other circumstances, to make any sort of claim on the real meant using a non-professional performer who needed to be, in effect (in a phrase of the novelist Anthony Powell), an 'infinitely accomplished actor got up to play the part that was in fact his [or her] own'.[16]

Watt believed such a directorial feat could be accomplished. In fact, he felt that his 'real people' could be 'far better' than professional film actors at authentically representing their reality on the screen.[17] He came to this realisation when directing his first major GPO film, *Night Mail*, in 1936 (with Basil Wright). It required effort to achieve, though. When casting, he said: 'You look for the extraverts, the bullshit merchants, the boring life and soul of the party boys'. But even that was not the end of the matter. He knew that these lively souls were 'natural hams' but not necessarily convincingly realistic before the lens. However: 'if you wheedle and bully them down to some sort of naturalness, they're actors'.[18] In this he was (unwittingly, probably) echoing Oliver Goldsmith's witty view of the great actor David Garrick who had revolutionised eighteenth-century English acting with his supposedly realistic performances:

On the stage he was natural, simple, affecting;
'Twas only that when he was off he was acting.[19]

In the eighteenth-century debate about the nature of acting, a state of 'war' was held to exist between 'sentiment', which today might be called intuition, and 'calculation'.

The professional business of acting, then as now, was/is to turn the later, at will, into the appearance of the former. Tom King, playing 'Fool' to Garrick's 'Lear', remembered him one night reducing the entire Drury Lane house to tears during the storm scene and, turning upstage, cynically remarking, *sotto voce*: 'Damme, Tom, it'll do.' This was calculation pretending to be sentiment in action.[20] Acting in the Western tradition is thus a species of confidence trick, a simulation of behaviour. In documentaries, though, there should be no trickery; but with all performance it is unavoidable. 'What's Hecuba to him or he to Hecuba that he should weep for her?' is the ever-present, never answered question as to the authenticity of acting.

This does not, of itself, vitiate the possibility of documentary. Not all the paradoxes involved in acting are in play. On the stage, there is a continuum from the duplication of quotidian observed behaviour to overtly formalised presentations in the declaratory mode.[21] The intuitive re-presentation, the quotidian (which requires the application of a complex performance code by professional actors seeking to do it) comes – or ought to come – authentically and automatically for performers in documentaries. There is no need for the theatrical search for inner psychological realism or any other Stanislavskian technique for the 'creation of the living world', primarily by reflecting inner emotional truths and capturing imagined realities behind the behaviour.[22] For the documentary actor, all this is already to hand because they are themselves and, as realism demands, their behaviour reflects quotidian realities. However, the matter of authenticity remains. Credibility is critical because the filmed behaviour must be mimetic, if 'a' story about the 'real' world – rather than a story about a fictional world (to use Nichols's definitional distinction between documentary and fiction) – is to be told.[23]

Watt's 'actors' were like Garrick in that in everyday life, off stage (screen), they were extravert, OTT, etc. Unfortunately, though, on screen, they were no Garricks and their acting was far from 'natural', quotidian. For the most part they were stiff, stilted and awkward. Nevertheless, Watt claimed that they were 'simple and affecting' – authentic. As Swann puts it, Watt believed that: 'their very awkwardness in front of the camera was perhaps their greatest asset. It was proof of their bona fides as real people.'[24]

Authenticity in such a context requires that intuition be all. The documentary actors' intuition under the baleful eye of the camera was then to be, authentically, awkward. Watt, in making his claim for this being desirable, was following his master, John Grierson's basic PR approach to sidelining real problems. Just as Grierson developed a rhetoric to justify the limited appeal of the films themselves (as against the attractions of Hollywood) as ignoring and obscuring their greater impact on the few who saw them, so Watt here attempts to turn the inauthenticity of the performances he obtained into an advantage over culturally acceptable (aka 'Hollywood', as it might be) performance norms.

Herein is the clue to the problem. At one level, the authenticity of awkwardness must mean that the behaviour inauthentically represents the reality of the situation when cameras are not present – unless it is also being suggested that people were, in general, awkward in everyday life. If they were not (which is surely the case), then the claim on the real is undercut. On the other hand, if it is accepted that the awkward behaviour is a consequence of the filming, then, again, the claim on the real is

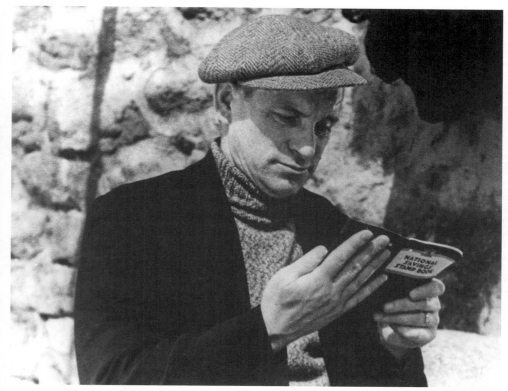

*The Savings of Bill Blewitt* (1936): Bill Blewitt as 'Bill Blewitt'

undercut. Swann acknowledges this implicitly when he writes that the very term 'performance' is itself 'problematic' in this context.[25] Indeed it is. A work's 'documentary value' crucially depends on there being no person appearing in it who 'performs' in the sense of 'to play (a part or character)' (1613, OED); or even more specifically 'to act in a play; to play or sing' (1836, OED). They must all be playing parts – with compelling transparency – that were, in fact, their own. But with these films we do not seem to learn anything of what the player's off-camera behaviour might have been like. The process of 'selving' is thus limited to an empathetic understanding that being filmed is embarrassing if you are not trained up to it.

When he has done with wheedling and bullying, Watt extracts from Bill Blewitt the characterisation of a taciturn, laconic workingman, stoical to the point of paralysis in the face of financial disaster. Other references to Blewitt, though, suggest a different personality altogether. Pat Jackson, who was assistant director on the film, says that Blewitt had the 'mesmeric gift of the gab, glorious Cornish accent, twinkling blue eyes, grin as broad as Popeye and the charismatic charm of the Celt'.[26] Clearly, the Blewitt of *The Savings of Bill Blewitt* was not playing a part that 'was in fact his own'; calculation not intuition was involved. However badly, he was pretending to be somebody else: in short, he was acting, albeit under his own given name. He had not been rechristened by Watt – as might be thought to have been the case, given the appositeness of this name to the character in the film. That Blewitt was no Allakarialluk (rechristened as 'Nanook' by Flaherty) was the truest thing about him in the film. Otherwise, assumptions of truth about 'the' world – that is, 'a' truth of some kind – are hard to discern in it.

This is not to expect Stanislavsky's truth of the 'scenic type' which applies imagination to observed reality.[27] Players in documentary need no such truth because the roles are 'in fact their own'; but they do need to bring a sense of observed reality, drawn from what Stanislavsky terms 'the plane of actual fact'. This is where Watt and Blewitt fall short – in their engagement with 'the plane of actual fact'. The result is an archetypical example of the limitations of performance in the Griersonian documentary.

Nevertheless, Watt used Blewitt again – transported in an unlikely fashion from Cornwall to Aberdeen – on *North Sea* (1938), a documentary about ship-to-shore radio which was the movement's most commercially successful film of the 1930s (albeit that it is still replete with stilted performances). In fact, Blewitt went on to appear in two more documentaries (narrating one) and to have roles in four wartime features. The only substantial difference in his on-screen work between the documentaries and the fictions was that in the former he was either uncredited or appeared under his own name; but in the features his parts were given character names – 'Dick Trehiddle', for example, in *Johnny Frenchman* (1945).

It can, of course, be argued that *The Savings of Bill Blewitt* is a fictional publicity film and its claim to be a documentary rests on the fact that it was produced by the GPO Film Unit and used 'real people' as its actors. Nevertheless, Paul Swann situates this film as marking a crucial advance in documentary, engineered by the augmentation of Grierson's initial vision with Alberto Cavalcanti's dramatic sensitivities when he took over the running of the GPO unit. Given the next three-quarters of a century of documentary development, it is hard to deny that this view holds a certain truth. The advance, though, initially merely highlighted the question of performance in the documentary. This had been there from the start but certainly the arrival of synch filming in 1934/5 exacerbated it. The problem exists even with more purely observational material made in the initial Griersonian mode. Very little in the movement's work treats the main news tropes of the 1930s directly. Neither the rise of fascism nor the economic travails of the Depression figure centrally. The film that comes closest to dealing directly with the unemployed millions of the time, Arthur Elton's 1934 *Workers and Jobs* about the labour exchanges, says nothing to the reality of worklessness – the 'way' of the workers who have no work.

> In one scene, an Exchange manager interacts with a patient group of smartly dressed unemployed. He calls men forward one-by-one to be dispatched to enterprises which might have work for them. A group rises to take tentative steps forward occasioning a testy: 'Do step back now. Give me a chance'; and this is the closest the film (and, indeed, the movement) get to reflecting the stress of unemployment during the Great Depression.

In 1934, a third of all miners, two-thirds of shipbuilders, a quarter of cotton workers, etc., etc. – 3 million insured workers in all – were unemployed. But I am not drawing attention here to the glaring lack of context of this film. Rather am I asking: what picture of behaviour reflecting this stretched social fabric does *Workers and Jobs* provide? 'Do step back now. Give me a chance': this barely registered seconds-long 'surge' towards the exchange manager's counter is the nearest the documentary movement got to filming the despair and anguish of unemployment. I suppose one could say that this almost absurdist representation of the reality of 1930s jobseeking accurately illustrates the hopelessness of the cowed men and the formal coldness of the manager. What it cannot be said to show is any sign of individual human response. Even allowing for the culturally determined reticence of the English in public, all the figures are more like automata than people – never mind desperate people.

The plummy-voiced narrator (let us not forget all the connotations of class that go with accent in Britain) begins by mentioning that there are some 50,000 different types of jobs – not that there are millions on the dole. How could it be otherwise given the realities of sponsorship? (The film was made, by Arthur Elton, for the Ministry of Labour.) The point is that, although documentaries were being presented as uncompromisingly realistic (e.g., see Watt, above), the presentation of self within them worked to support their less-than-realistic, ideologically conditioned reformist, placatory social meaning. After all, running from 'social meaning' (as David Schrire noted in commenting on Grierson's own *Drifters*[28] is central to Grierson's legacy to documentary. The acting in the films of the 1930s and 40s – the ways in which subjects are seen to behave – exactly reflects this flight from social meaning – the basic Griersonian failing. The population is presented as more embarrassed, quiescent and cowed than other evidence suggests it actually was. For the official sponsors who paid for these films, this cannot have been unwelcome. 'Poor' acting (as conventionally judged) and the concomitant concentration on surface appearances without analysis serve their agendas. It is what Grierson bequeathed to the documentary into the era of Direct Cinema and beyond.

So these are not one-off examples, although it must be acknowledged that not all Grierson's 'boys' were equally inept at directing the people they cast. Evelyn Spice (the documentary movement's first – and virtually only – established female director)[29] and Humphrey Jennings (who was never quite one of the 'boys' anyway) made a better fist of directing subjects in their films than did Watt and the others. But even they were not always successful. For example, Spice brilliantly handles the cockney lads apprenticed to the Post Office in *Job in a Million* (1937) but the authority figures – the adult headmaster and a teacher (who sounds like Queen Mary) come over as constipated as ever: 'Truman is not working quite hard enough.' (Quite so.)

Among all the movement's directors, Humphrey Jennings could also sometimes do better than the general run, a significant factor in his enhanced reputation. When he obtained convincing performances, it would seem to have been the result of deploying Wattian wheedling and bullying to a high degree. A major factor involved inducing exhaustion. *Fires Were Started* (1943), the feature-length documentary on the work of the Auxiliary Fire Service (AFS), is where, perhaps, his efforts can be seen to best advantage. He worked fourteen-hour days and 'everybody was frightened of him'; but he was also charming and charismatic, involving cast and crew in the filming process, encouraging informality on the set.[30]

Jennings had a treatment/script containing a lot of dialogue, devised by himself and Maurice Richardson, a novelist who was also at the time an AFS volunteer. Jennings kept this from his actors, though, encouraging them to improvise. However, with his hints and help, in the film on occasion they finished up saying, more or less exactly, the words he and Richardson had heard and noted down during the research phase. Jennings nevertheless somehow convinced them that they had come up with the dialogue themselves.

The assignment was, in propaganda terms, complex – a need to demonstrate that civilian deaths could be expected in the Blitz but that this should not prevent people from staying calm and carrying on. Perhaps this was why a measure of authentic language – not previously permitted – was allowed. The propaganda task was a hard one and to sell it needed as many nuggets of authenticity as possible. This sugaring of the propaganda pill by admitting realistic negatives, such as bad language, can be traced to Shakespeare. In *Henry V*, on the eve of Agincourt, the cockney soldier Bates wishes (to Henry in disguise) that the King 'were in Thames up to his neck and I by him' rather than where they both are – in France waiting for the dawn and the mayhem of battle. Against the King's praying in of patriotism – Wilfred Owen's 'old lie', i.e., *dulce et decorum est pro patria mori* – Bates speaks to a more readily understood and therefore realer emotion. This draws the sting of the lie for the next scene with its great paean of patriotic fervour, Henry's 'St Crispin's Day' speech.

In the same way, the firemen in *Fires Were Started* are allowed 'bloody', 'windy bastards', 'hell', 'Gor blimey' to aid their credibility. Previously swearing, even at this mild level, had not been heard in these images of 'the way the worker lived and worked'. Language had been totally constrained by the mores of the day. All that Watt, for example, could get away with in *North Sea* were distinctly unsalty trawlermen muttering about 'blather'. No wonder that the *Documentary News Letter* thought that in *Fires Were Started* – 'Maybe for the first time we have proper working class dialogue on the screen'.[31]

Although the term 'proper' might be a little strong, propagandists find the admission of negativity almost impossible to sanction, so the sophistications of allowing even this limited degree of realistic dialogue must be admired. Also to be praised is the fact that there is other realistically less-than-perfect behaviour to be seen in *Fires Were Started*:

> One of the firemen, named B.A. for the film, is shown trying to flog a pair of braces. The significance of this is not spelled out – he wants no clothing coupons so the braces are black-market. This would have been fully understood by the original audiences. Elsewhere, people complain about AFS pay-levels undercutting the London Brigade firemen's pay scale; or the firemen are revealed as less than enthusiastic workers. B.A. again: 'We mustn't work too hard, my friends. This job must last till 1.' Hoses get pointed in the wrong direction, sewer covers are mistaken for hydrants, firemen go missing.

All these elements make *Fires Were Started* an exception that proves the rule. One has to look hard to find images of disaffection in the movement's films in the 1930s otherwise. A sorter's fleeting look of faint disdain, given to the back of his supervisor in *Night Mail*, is the only one that comes to mind. Obviously the

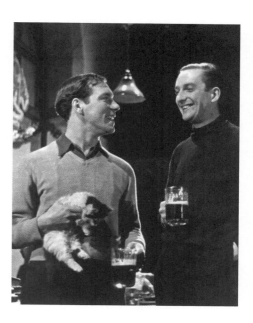

*Fires Were Started* (1943):
Fred Griffiths as 'Johnny
Daniels' and William Sanson
as 'Mike Barratt'

negativities helped the credibility of the firemen's performances in *Fires Were Started* – but Jennings's 'exhaustion technique' (as it might be) was the crucial factor in obtaining them.

Take the scene where the crew gather around the piano prior to the air-raid singing 'One Man Went to Mow'. Jennings had heard people singing the song in a public shelter on a research trip to Liverpool in October 1941 and this was the source for the scene in the film. One of the firemen, Fred Griffiths, recalled the director's working method in a BBC interview in 1970:

> I've started at half past eight in the morning and we go on singing all the way through.
> A break – half an hour, forty minutes for lunch. Start again, at 5 o'clock – cut! He [Jennings]
> comes over to me and says 'I think your voice is going'. I'd been singing for nine hours and he
> said 'Your voice is going'![32]

Unlikely though it seems on face value, the sequence works perfectly in the film. Fred, who was a London taxi driver before volunteering for the AFS, turned out to be exactly the sort of extravert Watt thought essential for synch documentary shooting. As with Blewitt, he was used again. Watt cast him himself as a support player in *Nine Men* (1943), one of the fictional features in which Blewitt also appeared. But Griffiths was far more successful than Blewitt in the long run and his film appearances did not cease at war's end as Bill's did. Fred went on playing loveable cockneys into the late 1970s. The 'actor' became an actor, demonstrating that appearing before the camera could be life-transforming decades before the arrival of reality television. He died, aged eighty-two, in 1994. Even Jennings, though, could put wooden performance moments on the screen.

*In the film, to meet the propaganda brief, one of the firemen, S. A. Horton, renamed in a more stereotypical cockney fashion 'Jacko' for the film,[33] dies on duty. The unit's cockney comic and wide-boy, B. A. (T. P. Smith) relayed the news (after all, untrue as the death was staged) but this required an emotional intensity beyond him: 'He's copped it, I tell you' is not convincing as a reflection of grief. The only domestic scene, between Jacko and his wife, is stilted. Nor is the young woman auxiliary at work in '14 Control' convincing when the building was (supposedly) thrown into chaos by a nearby exploding bomb. (It was actually a studio set.) All the staff dive for cover. The WAFS woman, in the midst of relaying information by phone to District Control, disappears under her desk. She emerges, unruffled –appearing not so much brushed by death as distracted by, say, birdsong: 'Control … Control … Control …. Oh, yes. I am sorry for the interruption, we have another message ….' She is the epitome of staying calm but the incident is deeply unconvincing, not least because when she reappears she has a blatantly fake gash in her forehead.*

I am not here, though, concerned with the unprofessional make-up. The Griersonians always complained about their shoestring budgets: no rocker-set for *Night Mail* train interiors at the Beaconsfield studios in 1936, for example. No effective make-up artist on set in Denham in 1943. Rather, the question is the overall authenticity of the behaviour on the screen. In this case, her actions and speech are authentic as they are vouchsafed by Jennings's own witness. He recorded an incident like this in his research notes as actually having happened; but it requires convincing re-presentation in the film and this is not quite what is on the screen. Indeed, it would take a practised professional to convey suppressed fear and contained discombobulation underlying apparently emotionless 'professional' calm behaviour. This was an acting task beyond the WAFS volunteer.

These limited performances, though, did not affect the claims made for the film at the time or subsequently. *Fires Were Started* – was said by movement insiders to be 'the best handling of people on and off the job that we've seen in any British film'.[34] There is no reason to reject this view. It does, though, speak to the movement's general level of skill at 'handling' people over the previous decade. The failings I am noting here might well have been primarily a consequence of the realities of class. Left-wing the movement's leading lights might well have been but their ability to do this 'handling' of the working class appeared to be somewhat attenuated. The fact is that the best-known Griersonian directors were all privately educated, and – all but Rotha – graduates of Britain's oldest universities. Jennings, for example, was held to have been oblivious to the lower orders until war broke out. Grierson always thought him condescending even then: 'Let's go down' he once said to Denis Forman inviting a visit to the cutting rooms, 'and see Humphrey being nice to the poor people.'[35] And Grierson's sister Ruby's critical role, as a woman and a Scot, in getting the interviews in *Housing Problems*, by assuaging the slum-dwellers' inhibitions in the presence of the gentlemen from the film unit, is well known. Arthur Elton was the film's director. His socialist politics were impeccable but, let us not forget, he was in line to inherit a seventeenth-century baronetcy, which he duly did.

It is no wonder that *Fires Were Started*'s appearance did not herald a breakthrough. Even Jennings seemed capable of tolerating the false, jarring performance.

*Flight Lieutenant Peter Roper, the wounded airman in a later major Jennings film,* Diary for Timothy *(1944–5) sounds so forced that a viewer can be forgiven for not believing him to have actually been wounded. One close-up, though, reveals that his calf has been shot away. The hospital sister in the film is dispassionate to the point of caricature. In fact, synch is usually disastrous if any sort of emotion is on display. In* Diary for Timothy, *Goronwy the miner, delivers an impassioned political speech convincingly but the doctor, a fellow miner and his daughter are frozen with embarrassment for their lines. Jennings, wisely no doubt, cuts the scene when news is brought to the house that 'Goronwy has met with an accident' before his wife is required to react.*

There is a general point about the inevitable distortions, that are part and parcel of all documentaries, which can be made; but omissions at this time were obviously necessary. There was a war on and truth is ever its first casualty. In *Fires Were Started*, Jennings says nothing of the inefficiencies of having independent fire brigades or of the role of women as frontline firefighters. Nor does he show any explicit images of death. There was, of course, an understandable *bilderverbot* on this because of considerations of wartime morale, reinforced by prewar cultural inhibitions. Jacko's end is indicated by flames rising over his boot. Overall, instead of any domestic destruction, we have, say, surreal images of frightened horses being led to safety or a man on crutches hobbling past the fire. Instead of serious indications of wartime stresses and tensions – reported crime, for example, increased by 57 per cent between 1939 and 1945 and 1944 saw the highest number of recorded strikes since records began – we have with what we still live: an uninterrogated myth of miraculously maintained social order. It is a mark of Jennings's genius that he was able to get any whiff of negativity onto the screen.

And it is a mark of Grierson's PR genius – his legacy – that the quality of acting in the documentaries was, and continues to be, overlooked, with possible negative impacts on a film's truth claim being discounted. The movement's tendency to run from 'social meaning' was much reinforced by the general passionless, quiescent stoicism and awkwardness of the 'workingman' on the screen; yet an examination of this remains of minor import in discussions of the films' value.

However, after the war, although some persisted in presenting wooden performances in their films,[36] tolerance for the inauthentic dissipated, albeit slowly. The transference of more authentic records of off-screen behaviour onto film became, in the 1950s, a prime objective. This was embodied by a new level of observationalism which was reflected in an expanded range of topics ('youth', for example) and a fresh tone (journalistic and oppositional). As documentary migrated to television (and society began moving towards the social relaxations of the 1960s), it did not take the stilted with it. Nor did independent film: combating constrained performances was implicit in the rhetoric of the Free Cinema group (i.e., initially, Lindsay Anderson, Tony Richardson, Karel Reisz, Lorenza Mazzetti). Anderson at the time thought (Jennings apart) that: 'British documentaries rarely give the impression of having been made by human beings'; 'the genteel British documentary cinema', the critic Dilys Powell called it.[37] Nor was dissatisfaction limited to Britain. By this time, in America too film-makers were unhappy with the tradition, especially as the fictional techniques of *The Savings of Bill Blewitt* came to be the dominant template for the sponsored synch documentary. 'Real people', Richard Leacock felt, 'were lousy at repeating scripted lines of dialogue' but that had come more and more to be required.[38]

In the UK, the Committee for Free Cinema (with Anderson as its spokesperson) announced that its purpose was to reflect (rather than exclude as the movement, in its view, persisted in doing) 'the rich diversity of tradition and personality' (Committee for Free Cinema, 1957). The result can be seen, say, in Reisz's 1959 *We Are the Lambeth Boys*, an early example of documentary location synch shooting. Reisz filmed in a youth club, capturing a new level of authentic, unstilted talk. For television, Dennis Mitchell – following radio documentarists such as Charles Parker – could essay whole films which depended on recording relaxed talk, e.g., the vivid Liverpudlian voices in his *Morning in the Street* (1959).[39]

Such topics and techniques – and outcomes on the screen – were all new extensions of the documentary tradition. The changes were aided by technological advance. Battery-driven 1/4 inch magnetic tape recorders were available from the early 1950s; flexible 16mm cameras were on hand, their use previously inhibited by their spurious positioning as 'amateur' equipment; and, escaping from the tyranny of artificial 'professional standards', some film-makers were reducing the need for augmented lighting by choosing high-speed Ilford film. At the National Film Board of Canada, in 1958, Michel Brault and Gilles Groul shot *Les Raquetteurs/Snowshoers* exuberantly handholding a specially developed 16mm synch rig. Direct Cinema was waiting to be identified and named. Two years later it was recognised as a distinctive advance and it rapidly acquired a set of production protocols – a *dogme*. Events were to always be more important than was the filming of them. Now the equipment was on hand to enable 'real people' in fact to play the parts that were in fact their own with the film-making so unobtrusive as to not impact on – contaminate (?) – their behaviour. Authenticity of behaviour was guaranteed, vouchsafed by the handheld camera and available sound and the like. 'We don't cheat', Leacock claimed: 'The story, the situation ... is more important than our presence.'[40] He insisted that documentary value could not be obtained in any other way.

With a PR efficiency of the sort previously displayed by Grierson himself, Leacock and the other Direct Cinema practitioners won the argument. They made the expectation of non- or minimal intervention a necessary condition of documentary validity. So much so that within a generation, it was the case that audiences expected that the events seen on the screen 'would have happened, as they happened, even if the filmmaker had not been present'.[41] Zero tolerance developed for traditional methods of documentary film-making. The public – or, better, journalists – became convinced that anything other than the most dogmatic direct cinema was dishonest – never mind that Direct Cinema did not actually deliver on its promises. The impact of this rhetoric on the films in the Griersonian archive has been considerable. Not just dramatised works such as *The Savings of Bill Blewitt* and *Fires Were Started* but even the less reconstructed, more observational films are widely no longer perceived as documentaries at all. (Talk to any teacher of documentary film about the perceptions of their students.)

But, nevertheless, it is part of Grierson's legacy that the possibility of authenticity in performance remains central to the realist documentary's claim on the real. There is still little debate about performances. There is even less examination of the documentary director's skill in obtaining them. The modern observational film-maker's ability to win the trust of the people before her lens (a Kim Longinotto, for example) is as little remarked on as the directorial techniques of her predecessors in the classic sound period (e.g., Humphrey Jennings). That this is so is a persisting consequence of Grierson's conditioning of documentary's reception in the first place. It still seems positively transgressive to raise the matter of the inauthenticity of the performances in those films even now. This is despite the fact that, on its face, the acting (however self-conscious or not) in, say, the Jennings films so perfectly reflects a central propaganda thrust – making the myth of one nation (stiff-upper lip and all) manifest on the screen – their authenticity surely can be queried? But it is hard to do this – to question whether or not, really: 'This is what it was like. This is what we were like – the best of us' (as Lindsay Anderson famously claimed of the Jennings oeuvre in 1954.[42] It is part of Grierson's legacy that Anderson's assertion is not instantly dismissible.

## NOTES

1. I am grateful to Patricia Holland for alerting me to this aspect of the topic in hand and for this formulation.
2. Bill Nichols, *Blurred Boundaries: Questions of Meaning in Contemporary Culture* (Bloomington: Indiana University Press, 1994), p. 97. Stella Bruzzi has pointed out that Nichols's application of the word '"performativity" *complicates terminology slightly* (considering the familiarity of the term "performative" since Judith Butler's *Gender Trouble* was published in 1990', in Stella Bruzzi, 'The Performing Filmmaker and the Acting Subject', in Brian Winston (ed.), *The Documentary Film*, London: BFI/Palgrave, 2013). He does, *en passant*, cite Butler (Nichols, *Blurred Boundaries*, p. 168) but he does not reference Austin, who furnished Butler with the term in the first place. However useful their conceptualisations, neither Butler nor Nichols is concerned with the 'performative' only in J. L. Austin's discrete linguistic sense of 'doing things with words'. (J. L. Austin, *Philosophical Papers* [Oxford: Oxford University Press, 1970], p. 235); e.g. the moment in the British House of Lords when the utterance of the Norman-French phrase 'la Reine le veult' transforms a parliamentary bill into a legal Act; or the fact that, spoken in a specific context, 'I do' will transform a spinster into a wife. Any current confusing synonymy of 'performance' and 'performative' cannot, of course, be laid at Nichols's door.
3. Erving Goffman, *The Presentation of Self in Everyday Life* (New York: Doubleday, 1959), pp. 203, 31.
4. Jane Roscoe, Big Brother Australia: Performing the "Real" Twenty-four-seven', *International Journal of Cultural Studies* vol. 4 no. 1 (2001), p. 473.
5. Annette Hill, *Reality TV Audiences and Popular Factual Television* (London: Routledge, 2005), p. 144.
6. Ibid. and Annette Hill, *Restyling Factual TV: Audiences and News, Documentary and Reality Genres* (London: Routledge, 2007).
7. Hill, *Restyling Factual TV*, p. 139.
8. John Corner, 'A Fiction (Un)like Any Other', *Critical Studies in Television* vol. 1 no. 1 (2006), p. 94.

9. Umberto Eco, *The Role of the Reader: Explorations in the Semiotics of Texts* (Bloomington: Indiana University Press, 1979), p. 33.
10. Paul Rotha, *Documentary Diary: An Informal History of the British Documentary Film, 1928–1939* (New York: Hill & Wang, 1973), p. 42.
11. Elizabeth Sussex, *The Rise and Fall of British Documentary: The Story of the Film Movement Founded by John Grierson* (Berkeley and Los Angeles: University of California Press, 1975), p. 76.
12. Erich Auerbach, *Mimesis: The Representation of Reality in Western Literature* (Princeton, NJ: Princeton University Press, 2003).
13. Terry Eagleton, 'Pork Chops and Pineapples', *London Review of Books* vol. 25 no. 20 (23 October 2003), p. 18.
14. Bill Nichols, *Representing Reality: Issues and Concepts in Documentary* (Bloomington: Indiana University Press, 1991), p. 3.
15. For the purposes of this discussion, the term 'documentary' shall therefore be deemed to exclude dramadocs.
16. Anthony Powell, *At Lady Molly's* (London: Heinemann, 1957), p. 71.
17. Harry Watt, *Don't Look at the Camera* (London: Paul Elek, 1974), p. 55.
18. Ibid., p. 83.
19. Oliver Goldsmith, *Retaliation: A Poem* (London: G. Kearsly, 1774), p. 12.
20. Anon, 'Miscellany', *The Mirror of Taste and Dramatic Censor Vol II* (Philadelphia, PA: Branford and Inskeep, 1810), p. 56.
21. Garrick's revolution was, exactly, to reduce the dominant declamatory element in the stage acting of his day; but no doubt what was left would still seem to us formalistic and false. After all, he had to create 'a living world' before a couple of thousand people in candlelight. He needed to be seen from the gods. The declaratory seems to change slowly over time. Gestural acting's repertoire is culturally determined, limited and time-honoured but the representation of the quotidian is, by contrast, rather dynamic. It marches in reflective lockstep with changes in behaviour in society. Thus, acting to represent the quotidian, or rather what is received as the simulation of realistic quotidian behaviour in any one generation can easily be thought artificial by the next. Even with the intrusive intimacy of the camera this dynamic persists. Think Method: James Dean and Marlon Brando, say, whose representation of everyday behaviour once seemed to be the acme of realistic acting, now seem to have offered codified and dated, calculating and mannered performances.
22. Constantin Stanislavsky, *An Actor Prepares*, trans. Elizabeth Reynolds Hapgood (New York: Theatre Arts Books, 1948).
23. Nichols, *Representing Reality*, p. 109.
24. Swann, *The British Documentary Film Movement, 1926–1946* (Cambridge: Cambridge University Press, 1989), p. 88.
25. Ibid.
26. Pat Jackson, *A Retake Please: Night Mail to Western Approaches* (Liverpool: Liverpool University Press, 1999), p. 40.
27. Stanislavsky, *An Actor Prepares*, pp. 121–2.
28. Rotha, *Documentary Diary*, p. 30.
29. Spice was a Canadian (who married her fellow Canadian and GPO film-maker Lawrence Cherry). Returning to Canada, she played a pioneering role in the development of the National Film Board. Ruby Grierson, one of John's sisters, was the other important woman

involved in the GPO. It was she who found the subjects of *Housing Problems* and coaxed the interviews in that film. Like her sister Marion (there were eight Grierson children), she became a director but was lost at sea during World War II. By 1936, Marion, a journalist, having earned one director's credit, had withdrawn from production.

30. Brian Winston, *Fires Were Started* (London: BFI, 1999), pp. 17–18.
31. Anon, 'Fires Were Started …', *Documentary News Letter*, April 1943.
32. 'The Heart of Britain', *Omnibus* (Robert Vas, t/x 20.9.1970 BBC).
33. He did have an off-screen nickname – 'Johnny' – but that had been assigned to Fred Griffiths, another of the firemen, for the film.
34. Anon, 'Fires Were Started'.
35. Dai Vaughan, *Portrait of an Invisible Man: The Working Life of Stewart McAllister, Film Editor* (London: BFI, 1983), p. 38.
36. Paul Dickson, for example, in *David* (1951) or *The Film That Never Was* (1957).
37. Christopher Dupin, *Free Cinema* (London: BFI, 2006) (booklet to accompany boxed DVD set of same name).
38. Richard Leacock, *The Feeling of Being There* (Paris: Seqeïon, 2011).
39. T/x 25.3.1959 BBC North.
40. André Labarthe and Louis Marcorelles, 'Entretien avec Robert Drew et Richard Leacock', *Cahiers du cinéma* vol. 24 no. 140 (February 1963), p. 26.
41. Jane Roscoe and Craig Hight, *Faking It: Mock-Documentary and the Subversion of Factuality* (Manchester: Manchester University Press, 2002).
42. Lindsay Anderson, '"Only Connect": Some Aspects of the Work of Humphrey Jennings', *Sight and Sound* vol. 23 no. 4 (Spring 1954), pp. 5–8. Reprinted in Winston, *Fires Were Started*, pp. 70–5.

## REFERENCES

Anderson, Lindsay, '"Only Connect": Some Aspects of the Work of Humphrey Jennings', *Sight and Sound* vol. 23 no. 4 (Spring 1954), pp. 5–8.

Anon, 'Miscellany', *The Mirror of Taste and Dramatic Censor Vol II* (Philadelphia, PA: Branford and Inskeep, 1810).

Anon, 'Fires Were Started …', *Documentary News Letter* (April 1943).

Auerbach, Erich, *Mimesis: The Representation of Reality in Western Literature* (Princeton, NJ: Princeton University Press, 2003).

Austin, J. L., *Philosophical Papers* (Oxford: Oxford University Press, 1970).

Bruzzi, Stella, 'The Performing Filmmaker and the Acting Subject', in Brian Winston (ed.), *The Documentary Film Book* (London: BFI/Palgrave, 2013), pp. 48–58.

Corner, John, 'A Fiction (Un)like Any Other', *Critical Studies in Television* vol. 1 no. 1 (2006), pp. 89–96.

Dupin, Christopher, *Free Cinema* (London: BFI, 2006) (booklet to accompany boxed DVD set of same name).

Eagleton, Terry, 'Pork Chops and Pineapples', *London Review of Books* vol. 25 no. 20 (23 October 2003), pp. 17–19.

Eco, Umberto, *The Role of the Reader: Explorations in the Semiotics of Texts* (Bloomington: Indiana University Press, 1979).

Goffman, Erving, *The Presentation of Self in Everyday Life* (New York: Doubleday, 1959).

Goldsmith, Oliver, *Retaliation: A Poem* (London: G. Kearsly, 1774).

Hill, Annette, *Reality TV Audiences and Popular Factual Television* (London: Routledge, 2005).

Hill, Annette, *Restyling Factual TV: Audiences and News, Documentary and Reality Genres* (London: Routledge, 2007).

Jackson, Pat, *A Retake Please: Night Mail to Western Approaches* (Liverpool: Liverpool University Press, 1999).

Labarthe, André and Louis Marcorelles, 'Entretien avec Robert Drew et Richard Leacock', *Cahiers du cinéma* vol. 24 no. 140 (February 1963), pp. 18–27.

Leacock, Richard, *The Feeling of Being There* (Paris: Seqeïon, 2011).

Nichols, Bill, *Representing Reality: Issues and Concepts in Documentary* (Bloomington: Indiana University Press, 1991).

Nichols, Bill, *Blurred Boundaries: Questions of Meaning in Contemporary Culture* (Bloomington: Indiana University Press, 1994).

Powell, Anthony, *At Lady Molly's* (London: Heinemann, 1957).

Roscoe, Jane, 'Big Brother Australia: Performing the "Real" Twenty-Four-Seven', *International Journal of Cultural Studies* vol. 4 no. 1 (2001), pp. 473–88.

Roscoe, Jane and Craig Hight, *Faking It: Mock-Documentary and the Subversion of Factuality* (Manchester: Manchester University Press, 2002).

Rotha, Paul, *Documentary Diary: An Informal History of the British Documentary Film, 1928–1939* (New York: Hill & Wang, 1973).

Stanislavsky, Constantin, *An Actor Prepares*, trans. Elizabeth Reynolds Hapgood (New York: Theatre Arts Books, 1948).

Sussex, Elizabeth, *The Rise and Fall of British Documentary: The Story of the Film Movement Founded by John Grierson* (Berkeley and Los Angeles: University of California Press, 1975).

Swann, Paul, *The British Documentary Film Movement, 1926–1946* (Cambridge: Cambridge University Press, 1989).

Vaughan, Dai, *Portrait of an Invisible Man: The Working Life of Stewart McAllister, Film Editor* (London: BFI, 1983).

Watt, Harry, *Don't Look at the Camera* (London: Paul Elek, 1974).

Winston, Brian, *Fires Were Started* (London: BFI, 1999).

# 4

# Translating Grierson: Japan

*Abé Markus Nornes*

The conception of documentary we associate with John Grierson is arguably, along with Hollywood continuity style, one of the most powerful and fecund approaches to cinema in history. Its global spread from the 1930s on is striking for its speed and eventual ubiquity. Clearly, there are massive forces behind this. The most obvious is, of course, the (pedagogical and military) muscle of the British Empire, with which Grierson's practice was so intimately tied. At the same time, one could argue that Grierson proposed a documentary style that assumed a universal truth that subsumed, sometimes violently, all particularities. This is to say, it was so closely aligned to the epistemology of enlightenment thought that its global proliferation was inevitable. While Griersonian documentary does appear to have engulfed the world by the late 1930s, I would like to point out how it came to *mean* very different things everywhere it went. That is because, despite its universalist pose, Griersonian thought demanded translation in most of the world and any such translingual practice involved transformation as well.

This chapter is devoted to a case study of misprision in the largely monoglottal world of Japan. It tracks the Griersonian idea from England to Japan in the 1930s. Only a privileged few spoke or read English back then, and the translator who seized upon this idea seemed to possess a rather shaky hold on the language. Her translation suffered from many mistakes, which initially remained invisible to her readership. Although the author's idea transformed upon its insertion into the Japanese film world, this did not stop it from inspiring film-makers. Indeed, the latter's inability to access the original actually amplified the translation's transformative power. Its example demonstrates what close analysis of translation practices can reveal about an influential instance of 'cultural translation'.

## PORU RUTA/PAUL ROTHA AND THE PRODUCTIVITY OF MISPRISION

Open any Japanese book on documentary, and the 'theory' of Paul Rotha will be singled out as one of the most influential bodies of thought in the history of Japanese cinema. While there were translations of all the major Western film theorists, from Münsterberg to Eisenstein, it is safe to say that none of their writing was as fiercely contested and discussed as that by Rotha. No other theorist or critic had more impact on actual film practice or underwent as much 'processing'.

Rotha's influence in Japan may astonish the Western film scholar, and the reader may find this essay surprising in a volume dedicated to John Grierson. On its release Rotha's *Documentary Film* (1935) was widely read throughout Europe and America, particularly within the educational film movement. However, it was seen largely as a promotion of British documentary at the time – hardly a theoretical 'Bible'.[1] His place in (our) history is basically as one of the central film-makers of the British school, as a writer and as occasional antagonist of Grierson. Despite Euro-American film studies' renewed interest in documentary, one rarely if ever hears Rotha's name invoked. Even book-length histories of the British documentary movement note *Documentary Film* only in passing. This would undoubtedly alarm Japanese film-makers and scholars, as Japanese books about film theory and history mention Rotha's name in the same breath as Eisenstein, Balazs, Pudovkin, Arnheim, Münsterberg, Moholy-Nagy and Vertov. They rarely cite Grierson. It is through Rotha's adaptation and elaboration of Grierson's approach that documentary was discovered and 'understood'.

Imamura Taihei's 1952 overview of film theory puts Rotha in the privileged position of his final chapter – the author posed with *Documentary Film* for his portrait – and Rotha's prestige has hardly diminished in the intervening years.[2] Thus, in 1960 translator Atsugi Taka offered a completely revised translation of Rotha's 1952 expanded version. This in turn was reprinted in 1976 and 1995.[3] Ironically enough, judging from his papers, Rotha himself appears to have had no idea how powerful he was in Japan. This indicates that while we may speak of Rotha's 'influence', something was happening in Japan that was quite disconnected from larger traffic in film theorisation.[4]

This apparent imbalance may be partially explained by returning to the time when Rotha's book arrived in Japan in the latter half of the 1930s, an opportune moment if ever there was one. Japan was escalating its invasion of China, especially with the 1937 China Incident. On the home front, the government ensured the war reached into the daily lives of citizens everywhere, drawing on young men for cannon fodder and increasingly controlling 'appropriate' behaviour. Police pressure, including mass arrests, imprisonment and occasional torture, had shut down the noisy left by mid-decade. Many progressive intellectuals underwent ideological conversion to a rabid nationalism and an often racist nativism. Those who refused this course quietly retreated underground or disguised their thoughts in carefully chosen language when in public. At the very same time, the government placed elaborate strictures on film-making, ranging from intricate censorship mechanisms to nationalising entire sectors of the industry. This culminated with the 1939 Film Law which mandated the forced screening of nonfiction films, or the so-called *bunka eiga* [culture film].

Along with the pressures of continental warfare, this legislation propelled documentary to a level of prestige comparable to the fiction film. Film journals were filled with articles attempting to theorise a documentary practice appropriate for the times, and included essays by intellectuals as disparate as Hasegawa Nyozekan, Tosaka Jun, Kamei Katsuichiro and Nakai Masakazu. In this atmosphere, the appearance of Rotha's *Documentary Film* – especially its 1938 translation – electrified the film world, and was greeted with the respect afforded the most authoritative of theoretical systems. This intense interest eventually filtered into film-making itself, allowing

Rotha to leave a mark on the history of Japanese cinema that few theorists ever achieve anywhere, any time.

But why Rotha? And by extension, what did his writing mean in wartime Japan? A hint at the answer lies in the title itself – 'Documentary Film'. The manner in which this was translated immediately alerts us to the political ramifications of the translation act, and suggests the exceeding complexity of these questions. A variety of words were circulating in the Japanese film world to designate nonfiction film-making: *jissha eiga*, *kiroku eiga*, *nyusu eiga*, *dokyumentarii eiga* and the like. However, the 1938 edition appeared with language on the cover that may or may not be a mistranslation: 'Bunka Eiga-ron', or 'On Culture Film'. First, the suffix *ron* [argument, discourse] appended to the title could also render a reverse translation as *Documentary Film Theory*. This may have given Rotha's thought a heft we do not feel when reading the original English text. Second, an intertext for the *bunka eiga* is the *kulturfilm* of Universal Filmaktiengesellschaft (UFA) in Germany. These were primarily science films but, upon their successful Japanese release, some critics began using the term for a variety of nonfiction films by Japanese film-makers. The word begins to appear in Japanese texts as early as 1933, and all documentary came under the rubric of *bunka eiga* with the 1939 Film Law. Although most readers knew the term *dokyumentarii eiga* [documentary film], the translator chose to use *ubunka eiga*, which was strongly connected to propaganda film-making by the time Rotha's book appeared. Many of Rotha's contemporary critics pointed out the ambiguity of the film genre to which this title points. Few, however, noted that it firmly inserted Rotha's thought into the discourse raging around the terms of the new Film Law. The translation of Rotha roughly coincided with the announcement of plans for these detailed government regulations over the film industry and, amid the fervent discussion about the new meaning and direction for nonfiction film, Rotha's cheerleading for the documentary found an enthusiastic audience. In one sense, this would appear to sell Rotha out to a radically opposed politics; however, I argue it could also be seen as an attempt on the part of the translator to quietly shift the terms of the Japanese documentary debate in a certain direction. Thus, the short answer to the question above is that Rotha's book meant many things indeed.

The long answer is that because of this slipperiness, a curious situation arose in which Rotha's book appealed equally to the entire political spectrum, with all debate participants claiming Rotha's thought to different ends. The rest of this chapter will examine precisely this struggle over meaning at multiple levels. However, to root out the most important issues underlying this discourse we must look to an arena less obvious than the film magazines, that is, the media through which Rotha's thought came to be known: translation.

Consider this relatively obvious example: the 1938 edition mistranslates 'workers' revolution' with the more innocuous '*rodosha katsudo*', or 'workers' activities' to return the term to English.[5] Only in the postwar revision did the proper translation appear: '*rodosha kakumei*'.[6] The reason is unambiguous; this was a dangerous term in 1939, and a text containing it would never pass censorship review. Authors, translators and publishers had been deflecting such trouble with authorities for nearly a decade by printing obvious synonyms and even substituting problematic words with XX's (called *fuseji*). Readers knew the protocol; when they came across *fuseji* or ambiguous words, they could read past them to the original meanings. The first edition of *Documentary Film* is sprinkled with many examples such as this, but analysis of such simple instances of intentional mistranslation will only get us so far. This is because, first, as the example above suggests, there were entire communities of readers who were forced to conceal their true relationship to the book, and second, everyone knew the translator's command of English was dubious at best because it became one of the issues raised in the debates.[7]

We must dig far deeper into the issue of translation to appreciate the complexity of the highly politicised discourses circulating around Rotha's original text upon its insertion into the Japanese linguistic world. After all, this is the medium through which Rotha came to be known in Japan; very few film-makers and critics could read English well enough to follow the original. Furthermore, shifting our analysis from simplistic notions of (one-way) 'influence' to the site of translation brings an array of larger issues into focus. For example, as suggested above, looking at the sheer volume of translation reveals much about the relationship between cultures (it follows that a lack of translation activity indicates a discourse stuck in an unhealthy short-circuit of desire). When changing texts from one language to another the translator's approach to language and meaning is inseparable from larger historical and ideological currents in the target language. This new linguistic and cultural context often impinges upon the translation, while having little to do with the original text itself. In this situation, where competing translations circulated among overlapping readerships, a struggle over authority occurs – after all, can there be a more powerful position over cross-cultural discourse than that of the translator? We must look at the qualities of a given translation, and ask who the translator is, what her relationship is with the original text, the author and the larger communities of readers. These are all key factors in the relationship to the other. From this perspective the difference between translation theory and documentary film theory is very slim indeed, as both fields involve representations weighed by a debt to an 'original', whether it be the source text or the world.

## DOCUMENTARY FILM ENTERS THE (JAPANESE LANGUAGE) FILM WORLD

Originally, Rotha's book was read by Japan's preeminent prewar film theorist, Imamura Taihei, who passed it on to Domei Tsushin's Kuwano Shigeru. From there, the book surged into the film community.[8] At one point, it came into the hands of Atsugi Taka, one of the first female film-makers in Japanese cinema. Atsugi originally came to film-making as a leading member of the Nippon Puroretaria Eiga Domei [Proletarian Film League of Japan], or Prokino for short. After the breakup of Prokino under police pressure in 1934, Atsugi began writing film criticism and translating foreign film theory. She was also one of the members of a collective producing the early film theory journal *Eiga Sozo*, along with other former Prokino members. This gave her concrete links to Yuibutsu Kenkyukai [Materialism Study Society, or Yuiken], a group of leftist intellectuals organised by philosopher Tosaka Jun.[9]

Atsugi even wrote a review article of Rotha's book in their *Yuibutsuron Kenkyu*, probably the first mention of *Documentary Film* in print. In the late 1930s, Atsugi

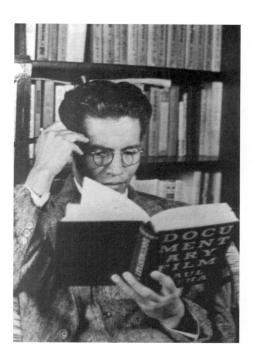

Imamura Taihei posing with an original copy of Rotha's book

began a long career in documentary screenwriting, working for PCL, Toho and Geijutsu Eigasha [Art Film Company, or GES]. This afforded her the chance to bring Rotha's theory into practice. Above and beyond her own film-making activities, Atsugi's most influential project was a translation of Paul Rotha's *Documentary Film*, which she took on at the request of her PCL supervisor; he was moving to JO Studios to become head of production, and wanted the work as a textbook for study groups. Atsugi had been reading the English original, and was glad to use the translation as an excuse to finish the book. She published the first edition in the fall of 1938.[10]

The translation had an enormous impact, and went into second and third printings within a year.[11] The book's influence spread in the late 1930s as critics debated Rotha's terms and their implications for documentary film-making, often offering their own translations of the original in their quotations. Soon an alternative translation by Ueno Ichiro appeared in *Eiga Kenkyu*, a film studies series put out by the magazine *Eiga Hyoron*.[12] There were study groups devoted to Rotha's book in the production companies and film studios. Toho's staff called it the documentary film-maker's 'Bible', and their Kyoto studio actually circulated its own handwritten, mimeographed translation within the company.[13] Before Atsugi's translation appeared the original English-language book was even used for English practice at JO Studios.[14]

About the same time, the original text reached Omura Einosuke and Ishimoto Tokichi, and their reading of the book had a great impact on the formation of GES. Thanks to Rotha's ideas, the company's early films, such as *Yukiguni/Snow Country* (1939) and *Kikansha C57/Train C57* (1940), strove to surpass the usual public-relations film and bring documentary to a new, independent level.[15] Geijutsu Eigasha's own film journal, *Bunka Eiga*, published enthusiastic debates about Rotha's book, as did most of the other serious film publications.

One of the major responses to the Rotha translation involved a knee-jerk reaction to his disdain for the 'story-film', which 'threatens to stifle all other methods of cinema' and 'tends to become an anesthetic instead of a stimulant'.[16] The most vociferous of these critics displayed a near uncontrollable anger. For example, in his book-length, bibliographic survey of film literature, Okuda Shinkichi passes Rotha off with a flourish:

> I – and others – can only recognize [*The Documentary Film*] as a little like drawing water for one's own field [i.e., self-serving]. Above all, his rejection of the feature film, and explanation making documentary the main path for cinema is clearly ridiculous; even as a theory of art, it never exceeds shallow abstraction.[17]

The most scathing attack on Rotha came from Tsumura Hideo, who sarcastically wrote,

> Put a different way, Rotha's book is extremely heroic and vigorous. He praises documentary based on materialist socialism as the most valuable cinema of tomorrow. In contrast to that, it pulverizes the fiction film into dust, with writing like vicious gossip. The way it attacked fiction film was extremely rough with ideological tricks. I confess that this is one of the reasons I had the courage to criticize Paul Rotha.[18]

This now famous attack provoked a response from Takagiba Tsutomu, who ran Toho's Shinjuku News Film Theatre and was a frequent essayist on documentary film. Takagiba humorously rewrote Tsumura's article, substituting 'Tsumura' for 'Rotha' to turn the attack back on the Japanese critic.[19]

However well this strategy neutralised Tsumura's critique, it did not address the key issues: that Rotha's definition of 'fiction' in documentary was less than clear, and that the book was less a theory of documentary film than a specious promotion of government cultural policy. There is a grain of truth to the charges against Rotha – his arrogance, his self-promotion of the English documentary and faith in government sponsorship – but the critical debate that actually affected Japanese film-making practice revolved around the problem of 'fiction' in documentary.

The most tempered discussion of this issue was offered by Kubota Tatsuo in *Bunka Eiga no Hohoron/The Methodology of the Culture Film* (1940). This was one of the more serious attempts to explore the phenomenon of the *bunka eiga*. Although he came out of production (Shochiku's Kyoto studios), Kubota was very well read. He draws on the writings of Münsterberg, Arnheim, Balazs, Eisenstein and most other major theorists. But the book is ultimately a disappointment. Kubota's aesthetic agenda centred on expunging any influence of the avant-garde from documentary, positioning the *bunka eiga* with a hard and fast opposition between fiction film/'sensitivity'/*kansai* versus science film/'intellect'/*chisei*.[20] Unfortunately, this colours his discussion of Rotha as well. Kubota had originally intended to structure his entire book around *Documentary Film*, a measure of Rotha's prestige and influence over the very conception of nonfiction film-making. In the end, he wisely saved the discussion of Rotha for the final chapter. After his careful discussion of the avant-garde, Kubota warns readers that, while Rotha has his good points, his vague definition of 'dramatization', bolstered as it is by questionable examples such as Pabst's *Kameradschaft/Friendship* (1931), could lead documentary to stray too completely into the world of fiction.

This represents one typical brand of discussion that was occurring in all sectors of the Japanese documentary world. In actuality, the relatively innocent-looking debates about Rotha's conceptions of 'fictionality' and 'actuality' veiled struggles over documentary's function in Japanese society. The written record on this score is decidedly one-sided. Rotha proposed a nationally sponsored documentary film committed to the enlightenment and unification of the citizenry, precisely the kind of cinema necessary for a country deeply imbricated in foreign warfare. However, under the restrictive circumstances of 1930s Japan, many other important perspectives went unrecorded. This aspect of Rotha's appeal – especially his apparent sympathies for socialism – necessarily had to be concealed from the public sphere; restricted to private discussion, this body of discourse never appeared in the written record, posing a battery of problems for the historian. There are, however, traces remaining which provide access to these hidden spaces, and in the remaining sections of this chapter we will explore their furthest reaches.

## BATTLE OF THE TRANSLATORS

Like many other (underground) leftists in the documentary film world, Atsugi found Rotha's writing inspirational. Here was a film-maker committed to social change, someone who saw cinema as a medium for critiquing everything from class discrimination to totalitarian political systems. Having spent the last decade immersed in Marxism and committing her life to demonstrating its relevance to film-making, criticism and translation, Atsugi found a true compatriot in Paul Rotha. *Documentary Film* became the 'hidden sacred book' of film-makers like Atsugi who opposed the direction their nation and film industry were taking. Only after the war was over, however, could they reveal their views publicly.

One can feel Atsugi's intense relationship with Rotha's book by scanning her personal copies, which she donated to the National Film Centre of Japan just before her death. Opening their pages provides both a thrill and challenge to the historian. Her 1976 Miraisha version appeared brand new and unopened. Her 1960 Misuzu copy contained only a few pencilled-in notes and an inscription inside the cover: 'To Takeshi, the husband I love.'

Her first editions – Rotha's and her own translation – are far more intriguing. One can quickly detect a pattern in the highlighted sections. For example, in this time of stricture, she singled out the following sentence with a scratch of a pencil: 'There is little within reason and little within the limits of censorship that documentary cannot bring before an audience to state an argument.'[21] While there can be no doubt why she liked such a sentence, the pages are also filled with more obscure checks, question marks, circles and exclamation points. Strange symbols and many 'M.B.'s lie mute in the margins. Bookmarks sit in curious passages – did *she* leave them there? We will never know their significance, but three marks stand out among them all for their powerful evocation of what this book meant at the height of the China War. Apparently, Atsugi read her own translation over the space of several weeks in 1939, because she left dates next to three paragraphs. Scratched on the pages at a time when the government was taking steps to convert all documentary into propaganda in support of the emperor's war, a time when brilliant film-makers were subverting these efforts with clever editing and when open resistance meant persecution (Kamei Fumio's *Tatakau heitai/Fighting Soldiers* [1939] had just been suppressed and he would be in prison within a matter of months), these three passages make Atsugi's cathexis with Rotha's text palpable. For this they are worth quoting in full, with Atsugi Taka's notes rendered in bold:

> Relative freedom of expression for the views of the documentalist [sic] will obviously vary with the production forces he serves and the political system in power. In countries still maintaining a parliamentary system, discussion and projection of his beliefs within certain limits will be permitted only so long as they do not seriously oppose powerful vested interests, which most often happen to be the forces controlling production. Under an authoritarian system, freedom is permissible provided his opinions are in accord with those of the State for social and political advance, until presumably such a time shall arrive when the foundations of the State are strong enough to withstand criticism. Ultimately, of course, you will appreciate that you can neither make films on themes of your own choice, nor apply treatments to accepted themes, unless they are in sympathy with the aims of the dominant system. And in view of the mechanical and hence expensive materials of cinema, it will be foolish of the documentalist if his sympathies do not lie, or at least appear to lie, with those who can make production a possibility.[22] **[6.28.1939]**

The following is a critque of Flaherty's apolitical approach:

> In every location which he has chosen there have existed social problems that demanded expression. Exploitation of native labour, the practises of the white man against the native, the landlords of Aran, these have been the vital stories, but from them Flaherty has turned away … . Idyllic documentary is documentary without significant purpose. It takes romanticism as its banner. It ignores social analysis. It takes ideas instead of facts. It marks a reactionary return to the worship of the heroic, to an admiration of the barbaric, to a setting up of 'The Leader'. [23] **[7.6.1939]**

Finally, there is a Pudovkin quote on the power of montage:

> I found the way to build up a dialogue in which the transition of the actor from one emotional state to another … had never taken place in actuality before the camera. I shot the actor at different times, glum and then smiling, and only on my editing table did these two separate moods co-ordinate with the third – the man who made the joke.[24] **[7.20.1939]**

Atsugi's handwritten dates – these curt pencil scratches – convert this translation from the public domain to something quite new and contradictory. They act as conduits allowing those resistant discourses retained safely in hidden spaces to leak from between the lines. But this is only half the story, because the criticism and debate surrounding Paul Rotha's *Documentary Film* is an instance of oppositional discourses being coded into public view, camouflaged to deflect the threat of reprisals. To render this complicated discourse visible, we must return to the problem of translation. On the one hand, Atsugi weaved her point of view into the very fabric of her translation, both in conscious and unconscious ways. At the very same time, intellectuals with far different perspectives engaged her in a veritable battle of the translators.

In the course of researching the subject of prewar Japanese documentary for a previous book, I occasionally ran across copies of Atsugi's translation in secondhand bookstores. Taking one of these volumes in hand, one can come to a material appreciation for the respect with which Rotha was viewed through the high quality of the printing, binding and paper, as well as the book's beautiful slipcase adorned with elegant handmade rice paper. Every time I found a copy of the Rotha translation, I pulled it off the shelf to take a peek inside and see if it belonged to anyone I knew from my research. One of these dusty first editions contained quite a surprise: every single page carried detailed annotations. Between every single line of the book – cover to cover – someone had diligently scrawled corrections to Atsugi's translation in pencil. Inside the cover, this anonymous editor wrote a message:

> This is a surprising book. She can't understand English. Japanese is pretty bad. Even Ms. Atsugi cannot argue with this. I don't understand how this person had the guts to translate it. This caused the chaos in this country's *bunka eiga* discourse. I'm sorry these corrections are a year late.

The original owner who requested this involved translation check was unclear; apart from this message, there was only an illegible scrawl across the page. (Hereafter, I will refer to this copy of *Documentary Film* as the *teiseiban* [corrected version].)[25]

The first edition of the Atsugi translation came out in September 1938, and whoever pored over Atsugi's work left us only with the message that the translation was so bad that its revision took the better part of a year. Actually, the existence of this *teiseiban* slipped quietly into public view in January 1940 – fourteen months after the original publication of the book – in a programme passed out at Takagiba Tsutomu's Shinjuku News Film Theatre. In addition to flashy advertising for the week's film slate, these pamphlets often turned grey with in-depth essays printed in tiny type. The 18 January 1940 issue contained an article by Sekino Yoshio asserting that the controversies over Rotha spring primarily from the inexperience of the person who had translated him. Sekino wrote, 'Below, let us pick out two or three parts of interest from a corrected text pretty much black with corrections.'[26] He proceeded to compare passages from Atsugi's translation with corrections from the *teiseiban*. (With this in mind the cryptic pencil slash inside the cover clearly reads 'Seki' in hiragana with a long tail.) In the following months, Sekino drew on the *teiseiban* for a series of lengthy articles in which he attempted to clear up the controversy surrounding Rotha's book.[27] These also became the basis for a book entitled *Eiga Kyoiku no Riron/Theory of Film Education* (1942).[28]

The main issues for Sekino revolved around the translation of words like 'story-film' and 'the dramatization of actuality'. He attempted to contextualise Rotha's thoughts on documentary in terms of his development as a critic – the differences between *The Film till Now* and *Documentary Film* – as well as the vast changes in English society itself. His success in reorienting the debate is difficult to judge, although it appears to have mostly influenced Sekino's reputation as an authority over the topic. There is a good reason for this. In this series of high-profile articles, Sekino positioned himself less as a critic than as the translator. He gives a discreet nod to the help of the *teiseiban*, but the substance of his articles is unusual. Rather than provide his own interpretation of *Documentary Film*, Sekino all but retranslates the book! These articles were basically strings of extended quotes from the *teiseiban* with short passages of paraphrase inserted in-between. Thanks to the corrections by Sekino's anonymous colleague, the new translations are quite good – for the most part, they are better than Ueno's or Toho's, and certainly better than Atsugi's. The *teiseiban* itself, with its rows of exclamation-point annotations, remains by far the best translation. However, Sekino ultimately does not offer an actual translation as such, because significant portions of the book are paraphrased or deleted. To be more specific, they are suppressed. Here is a typical, and relatively innocuous, example from Rotha with Sekino's deletions scored through:

> ~~Art, like religion or morals, cannot be considered apart from the materialist orderings of society.~~ Hence it is surely fatal for an artist to attempt to divorce himself from the community and retire into a private world where he can create merely for his own pleasure or for that of a limited minority. He is, ~~after all, as much a member of the common herd as a riveter or a glass-blower,~~ and of necessity must recognize his obligations to the community into which he is born. His peculiar powers of creation must be used to greater purpose than mere personal satisfaction.[29]

Sekino's reading, or more properly his selective translation, evacuates Rotha's left-leaning politics and aligns *Documentary Film* with the dominant ideology of wartime Japan. He effortlessly converts the passage above into an attack on individualism and a call for artists to serve the mission of the national polity. Elsewhere, extremely long series of extended quotations often skip a sentence or two in the middle when Rotha brings in the subject of class or Marxism. The segment of Rotha's audience to which Sekino belonged was probably enthralled with the Englishman's high moral tone and sense of 'mission'.

Sekino himself was far more than a film critic. After studying art at Tokyo University, he worked in the social education section of the Tokyo metropolitan government. In this capacity he promoted the use of film for education through publications, lectures, study groups like STS[30] and regular *Jido Eigahi* [children's film days].[31] In the latter stages of World War II, Sekino worked at Nichiei as the vice president in charge of *bunka eiga* production. Through the sum of these activities, Sekino became a prominent theorist in the education film movement throughout the war; 'theorist' in this context meant that the writer was not in the classroom trenches where the real teaching was going on. With his articles on the Rotha controversy, Sekino moved beyond pedagogical issues of the educational front and claimed a position of authority over the Rotha text, and therefore over Japanese documentary film.

A page from the *teiseiban*, with corrections to nearly every sentence

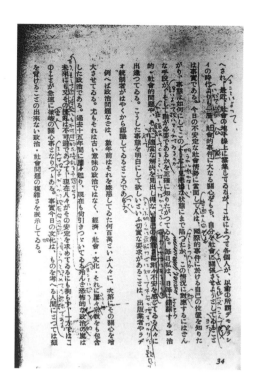

The Rotha we encounter through Sekino's articles speaks of responsible citizenship and the central role of cinema in educating the nation's populace. Sekino's Rotha heightens the stakes of these ideas by drawing the readers' attention to the worldwide sense of crisis – that theme so central to pre-Pearl Harbor Japan – but the English film-maker's calls for peaceful settlement of conflict, disarmament and intelligent social critique are suppressed from Sekino's blow-by-blow 'translation=correction' of Rotha's book. With these themes purged from the text, one is left with a discourse on propaganda and the necessity for state support of documentary to the end of enlightening its citizenry. It is no wonder that Rotha was attractive to Sekino and the new leadership emerging with the Film Law. A further example of this political reinscription of Rotha is *Eiga Kokusaku no Zenshin/The Progress of National Film Policy*, a 1940 book outlining the national film policies of all the major Western nations. The latter half of this book covers the situation in Japan, and offers essays on the implications of the new Film Law for various segments of the film industry. Its chapter on the deployment of film as an instrument of state propaganda cites Rotha as the international authority, proposing the English film-maker's innovations as the proper course for a nationalised film industry.[32]

While Sekino performed an intentional mistranslation of *Documentary Film* in a manner analogous to Atsugi before him, the differences between their actual texts are even more revealing. *Documentary Film* inhabited the space between publicly acceptable discourses and those kept hidden for fear of retaliation. The multiplicity of readings implied by this position was built into all of the published translations. The following example reveals how the differences between Atsugi and Sekino play out in their translations. This is one of Rotha's numerous digs at the powers that be, followed by its extant translations (for the relevant page from the *teiseiban*, see the photograph on p. 69; I will only translate back the key phrases, which are italicised and discussed below):

**Rotha:** Every day I come across persons who manifest increasing anxiety not only at the growing complexity of political and social problems, but at the patent inability of *those in power* to find adequate solutions.[33]

**Atsugi:** Mainichi ni sakuso suru seijiteki, shakaiteki mondai ya, sore ni tekito na kaiketsu o miidashi enai *jiko no munosa* ni kokkoku fuan o kanjite iru hitobito ni deatte iru.[34]

**Ueno:** Mainichi watashi no au hitobito ga seijimondai ya shakai mondai no shinkokuka suru fukuzatsusa ni tsuite fuan o kataru bakari de wa naku, *jibunra* ni tadashii kaiketsu o miidasu *noryoku no nai koto* o gaitan suru no de aru.[35]

**Sekino:** Taezu watashi wa, seijiteki, shakaiteki na jyaku mondai ga masumasu fukuzatsusa o mashite kuru koto ni taishite nominarazu, *toro no hitobito* ga sore e no tekito na kaiketsu o miidashi enai to iu meihaku na muryokuburi ni taishite mo, fuan ga kuwaete iku bakari da to tansaku suru hitotachi ni ikiatte iru.[36]

**Teiseiban:** Mainichi watashi wa, seijiteki, shakaiteki mondai ga masumasu sakuso suru shite kuru koto ni tai shite bakari de naku, *kenryoku no chii ni aru mono* ga, sore ni taishite tekito na kaiketsu o miidashi enai to iu akiraka ni munoryokusa ni taishite masu bakari da to tansaku suru hitobito ni deatte iru.

Rotha's original text sets up a relatively straightforward contrast between, on the one hand, common people who find themselves bewildered by the complexity of the world on the verge of war and, on the other hand, those in power who seem too incompetent to deal with the situation. Here Rotha's critical spirit comes out in force, but he is writing things that landed Japanese in prison in 1939. All of the translators seem to deal with this problem of potential censorship or reprisals in their own ways; everything from vocabulary choices to mistakes reveal the ideological undergirding of their respective translations. The *teiseiban* provides the best, most straightforward, translation of the quotation's most problematic phrase, 'those in power': *kenryoku no chii ni aru mono* [people in positions of (political) power]. However, Sekino strays from the guidance of his *teiseiban* and substitutes this with the rather vague *toro no hitobito* [authorities, intellectuals], deflecting the criticism into ambiguous territory. His other decisions further weaken Rotha's criticism, as a rendering of this phrase back into English reveals: 'but at the clear powerlessness of authorities/intellectuals in finding appropriate solutions'.

Both Atsugi and Ueno completely erase 'those in power' from the sentence. The effect is to create a single group of common people who feel anxiety about the world's complexity and their inability to affect change. We might assume that the translators expunged Rotha's attack on the powerful to preempt punishment by their own authorities. Without more documentation, the case of Ueno is difficult to judge; however, Atsugi produced a postwar version of *Documentary Film* when threats of reprisal were no longer an issue. In the 1960 translation she significantly revises the text with the help of two young scholars[37] and, while this sentence was completely rewritten, Atsugi retains the mistake. Even the 1995 'refurbished edition' [shinsoban] remains unchanged. In other words, Atsugi simply did not understand the meaning in the first place.[38]

At the same time, Atsugi's word choice is still significant. Ueno's exasperated, anonymous masses are literally the people Rotha has met on the street ('jibunra ni tadashii kaiketsu o miidasu noryoku no nai koto o gaitan suru no de aru'), but the Marxist Atsugi does not shirk social responsibility and opts for the much stronger language of 'jiko no munosa', which places the burden of history on herself and the reader – it is the difference between 'their own inability' and 'our own incompetence'. Atsugi's misprision circulates in a grey area between Rotha's original English text and its dim representation in Japanese – the latter reflects a conception of documentary combining Rotha's thinking with that of Atsugi's own film-making community of leftist film-makers who restrict their politics to hidden spaces in the teeth of power.[39] Rotha himself said, 'I came nearest to becoming a Socialist in my Documentary Book.'[40] This was not lost on the film-makers who found themselves subject to censorship and the whims of political power. Many of them had recently spent time in the so-called 'pig box' (butabako or 'slammer') for their film-making activities in Prokino. For some film-makers, Rotha's book simply confirmed the direction they were already taking nonfiction film in in the late 1930s, and knowing that someone outside Japan thought the same way gave them a measure of confidence.[41] However, many others had a far deeper, hidden relationship to Documentary Film. Kuwano Shigeru worked at Domei Tsushin's film unit before becoming the section head in charge of Nippon News at Nichiei. He was probably the second person in Japan to read Documentary Film, having received it from Imamura Taihei, himself a Marxist critic. In a 1973 book on documentary, he reminisced about his own wartime encounter with Rotha:

> This book, for me, was a shock. He was choosing his words extremely carefully, but this is clearly what Paul Rotha was saying: The duty of documentary filmmakers was to somehow replace today's rotting capitalist society and construct a new socialist society, and indicate the clear, social scientific analysis of it (capitalist society) by the emergent classes – the proletariat and the farmers. There was no question that the so-called documentary, which started out as the news film, would become a strong weapon of the movement for social revolution. This has been evidenced by the Soviets. Even in Japan, which was under the violent oppression of a militarist government, each and every cut of the news film preserved a fragmentary 'truth'. Therefore, if we consciously shoot that at the location, and if we edit these scenes purposefully, the 'truth' of modern-day Japanese society – the anguish of the people, the necessity of collapse because of those contradictions – we could precisely indicate this to the people of the emergent classes of Japanese society. However, even though we can do this, what are we Japanese documentary film producers – no, what am I doing right now?![42]

As a film-maker working in what were basically semi-governmental agencies (Domei Tsushin and Nichiei), Kuwano was extremely limited by the form of the newsreel. He did try to include subversive moments in his films to influence spectatorial readings in directions against the grain. For example, he recalls inserting a funeral pyre of some fallen soldiers with melodramatic narration such as 'Even now, the soldiers' souls return to their hometowns, where wives and children quietly wait.' However, this was inevitably snipped by the censors, leaving Kuwano clinging to the hope that his documentary images of the fighting retained some grain of truth.[43]

Film-makers in the budding field of *bunka eiga* had far more latitude in coding multiple readings into their films. This is the issue running quietly behind many of the debates over the fictive qualities of nonfiction film between 1939 and 1942. Film-makers were working out the nature of this new brand of fictionality. Rotha was, in the end, exceedingly vague on this point; Japanese film-makers, on the other hand, were looking for prescription. Shirai Shigeru spoke of Rotha's influence on documentary production, but had he not seen six or seven of the British school films at the Education Ministry (including *Drifters* and *Night Mail*) he would have had no idea what Rotha meant by 'dramatization of actuality'.[44]

Certainly the film-makers who did not attend those screenings were handicapped in their reading of *Documentary Film* and the massive discourse it generated. Many articles discussed the definitions of Rotha's terminology and its translation,[45] but the bulk of the writing was a continuation (and vulgarisation) of earlier Yuiken debates concerning the epistemology of cinema – 'Documentary as art' or 'Documentary as science'.[46] This itself, as Ueno Kozo has suggested, was a structural continuation of earlier struggles over whether film was art; the aesthetic domain simply migrated from 'Cinema as art' to 'Talkie as art' to 'Documentary as art'.[47] However, in one of Atsugi's best articles responding to her critics, we find the best hint at the core issue:

> In order for documentary film to have a meaningful existence as art, we must correctly recognize the essential meaning of this 'fiction'. This is what I want to state over and over again. To this same end . . . filmmakers' efforts must be more than the turning of the camera as it has been up to today. There needs to be more care for 'working' on works, more intensity, more like throwing one's entire soul into the hardships of a novelist.
>
> 'Poetry is more philosophical than history.' – Aristotle.
>
> Today we can find the meaning of this saying if, while native born to the turbulent breath of history, we seek in documentary film the possibility of finding poetry (fiction) in the very center of that history (actuality).[48]

In the midst of the spectacular war films of the day, a new kind of documentary emerged from this group. While other film-makers were locating their practice at the sites of greatest power – the military, the bureaucracy – these film-makers were endeavouring to produce a new documentary film that (indirectly) pointed to the backwardness of the nation, and to the sheer poverty and suffering in everyday life.[49] For their producers, these films were the finest examples of documentary being made. Ishimoto Tokichi set the pattern with *Snow Country*, spending nearly three years recording the fight between Yamagata villagers and their fierce winters. *Snow Country* was unusual for its long-term study, foreshadowing the Yamagata films by the most important postwar documentarist, Ogawa Shinsuke; historian

Tanikawa Yoshio goes so far as to say that it marked the start of Japanese documentary film.[50]

Other films include Atsumi Teruo's *Sumiyaku hitobito/People Burning Coal* (1940/1) and *Ishi no inai mura/Village without a Doctor* (1939). The latter, Ito Sueo's first film, highlights the terrible conditions in village Japan, and the government's obvious inability to provide adequate health care for all its people. Kyogoku Takahide's *Ishi no mura/Village of Stone* (1941) shows the severe manual labour at a rock quarry, and his *Homensen/Field Diagnosis Boat* (1939) follows a medical group travelling the Sumida river to treat river workers. Imaizumi Yoshitama turned his camera to the rough life of train workers in *Train C57*. Ueno Kozo's *Wagu no ama/The Ama of Wagu* (1941) contrasts the hardships of life for female shell divers (including steep pay inequities in comparison to men) with stunning underwater sequences that aestheticise the work itself. Atsugi's *Aru hobo no kiroku/Record of a Nursery* (1942) shows the co-operative efforts between working mothers and nursery schoolteachers to raise healthy, educated children. This impressive body of work arose from the competing claims over the significance of Paul Rotha's *Documentary Film*.

Although Rotha inspired them all, these film-makers took varying positions vis-à-vis the use of reenactment and screenwriting in documentary. What they hold in common is a striking exclusion of the war hysteria and its rhetoric and a focus on the difficult life of Japanese citizens, a socially conscious documentary that resisted the temptations of explosions and exotic locales. In this way, the film-makers encode to various degrees the discontent usually restricted to hidden spaces into their very public media. The film-makers perceived their efforts to be interconnected and raising documentary to an unprecedented level of excellence. While they never gave themselves a collective name or identity, they did consider their combined efforts to be akin to a 'documentary movement'.[51] Their films constitute the finest of the prewar documentary cinema, and an instance of 'cultural translation' where theory and practice were finely tuned and brought into thorough interaction through the mediation of translators – even incompetent, if enthusiastic, translators.

## NOTES

1. See Iris Barry, 'Review of *Documentary Film*', *Saturday Review*, 12 August 1939, which discusses people's anxieties about Rotha's politics and his immodest pontification; also Frank Evans, 'How the Film Can Help Democracy', *Evening Chronicle* (Newcastle on Tyne), 12 May 1939, a book review that examines only documentary's social function (nothing on style); Elizabeth Laine, 'About Documentary Films', *Transcript* (Boston), 10 June 1939; 'Documentary Film', *The Times*, 11 August 1939; 'Documentary Film', *Lady*, 3 August 1939.
2. Imamura's postwar *Introduction to Film Theory* contains the best Japanese overview of Rotha. In contrast to the wartime debates, its reasoned critique reveals how narrowly the discussion was focused in 1940. This suggests how other issues were at stake besides the one explicitly on the table in 1938. See Imamura Taihei, *Eiga Riron Nyumon* (Tokyo: Itagaki Shoten, 1952), p. 184.
3. Paul Rotha, *Dokyumentarii Eiga*, revised and expanded edn, trans. Atsugi Taka (Tokyo: Misuzu Shobo, 1960); Paul Rotha, *Dokyumentarii Eiga*, revised and expanded edn, trans.

Atsugi Taka (Tokyo: Misuzu Shobo, 1976); Paul Rotha, *Dokyumentarii Eiga*, rev edn, trans. Atsugi Taka (Tokyo: Miraisha, 1995). The 1960 edition involved a fairly extensive revision of the translation itself, although this translation has its own problems. The 1995 outing is billed as a 'refurbished edition' [*shinsoban*], but the only apparent difference is a new colour on the jacket.

4. Nothing in his personal files suggests he knew what the Japanese thought of his work. Quite the opposite, he clearly shared fears about the menace Japan posed to the West. In a letter to Eric Knight written at the height of his prestige in Japan, Rotha wrote:

> I agree that the sooner America sees her immediate danger the better and that now more than ever is the time to come into this business . . . . She actually [is] (it sounds) trying to appease the Japs which seems odd after all the examples of appeasement she's had before her [sic]. I agree with all your beliefs about the cementing of the English speaking peoples – at least that would be a beginning basis for reconstruction.
>
> Letter, Paul Rotha to Eric Knight, 28 August 1941, 2001 Box 26,<br>Paul Rotha Collection, UCLA)

After the war (in the 1960s, from the look of the paper and adjacent documents), in a statement to someone in Japan Rotha wrote, 'One day, perhaps, if I am still alive, I will come to visit the land of Hokusai and Kurosawa and Ozu.' (No mention of any Japanese documentarists, let alone his translation by Atsugi.) See Letter, Paul Rotha to unspecified recipient in Japan, ND, 2001 Box 82, Folder 3, Paul Rotha Collection, UCLA.

5. Paul Rotha, *Bunka Eiga-ron*, 1st Japanese edn, trans. Atsugi Taka (Tokyo: Dai'ichi Geibunsha, 1938), p. 108.

6. Rotha, *Dokyumentarii Eiga* (1960), p. 68.

7. In her postwar autobiography, her embarrassment at rushing the translation to print prematurely is clear. See Atsugi Taka, *Josei Dokyumentarisuto no Kaiso* (Tokyo: Domesu Shuppan, 1991), pp. 103–5.

8. Okamoto Masao, *Bunka Eiga Jidai + Jujiya Eigabu no Hitobito* (Tokyo: Unitsushin, 1996), pp. 62–3.

9. Atsugi also married Yuiken philosopher Mori Koichi.

10. Rotha, *Bunka Eigaron* (1938). The original volume is Paul Rotha, *Documentary Film* (London: Faber and Faber, 1935).

11. Paul Rotha, *Bunka Eigaron*, 3rd Japanese edn, trans. Atsugi Taka (Kyoto: Dai'ichi Geibunsha, 1939).

12. Paul Rotha, 'Bunka Eigaron Josetsu', trans. Ueno Ichiro, *Eiga Kenkyu* vol. 1 (1939), pp. 54–84 (covers Chapter I in Rotha's *Documentary Film*); Paul Rotha, 'Dokyumentarii no Jyakuha to Sono Shiteki Kosatsu', trans. Ueno Ichiro, *Eiga Kenkyu* vol. 2 (1939), pp. 50–85 (covers Rotha's Chapter II). While there were many reports on the British documentary movement, Ueno probably wrote the best; this study certainly contributed to his translation: Ueno Ichiro, 'Eikoku no Bunka Eiga', *Eiga Kenkyu* vol. 1 (1939), pp. 146–61.

13. Paul Rotha, 'Bunka Eiga-ron', *Chosa Shiryo* vol. 4 (Kyoto: Toho Kyoto Satsueijo, undated) (Makino Mamoru collection). This mimeographed publication completes the Ueno translation, covering the final Chapter IV.

14. Makino Mamoru, 'Kiroku Eiga no Rironteki Doko o Otte 41', *Unitsushin*, 19 June 1978.

15. Tanikawa Yoshio, *Dokyumentarii Eiga no Genten – Sono Shiso to Hoho*, 3rd edn (Tokyo: Futosha, 1990), pp. 194–5.
16. Rotha, *Documentary Film* (1935), p. 70.
17. Okuda Shinkichi, *Eiga Bunkenshi* (Tokyo: Dai Nippon Eiga Kyokai, 1943), p. 39.
18. Tsumura Hideo, 'Poru Ruta no Eigaron Hihan – Sono Cho "Documentary Film" ni Tsuite', *Shineiga* vol. 9 no. 12 (November 1939), p. 17.
19. Takagiba Tsutomu, 'Kyoko no Riron – Tsumura Hideo-shi no "Poru Ruta Hihan" o Yomu', *Bunka Eiga Kenkyu* vol. 3 no. 1 (January 1940), pp. 525–8.
20. Kubota Tatsuo, *Bunka Eiga no Hohoron* (Kyoto: Dai'ichi Geibunsha, 1940).
21. Rotha, *Documentary Film* (1935), p. 156.
22. Atsugi Taka's personal copy of Rotha, *Bunka Eiga-ron* (1938), pp. 150–2, Atsugi Taka Collection, National Film Centre of the National Museum of Modern Art, Tokyo. Original text is Rotha, *Documentary Film* (1935), pp. 135–6.
23. Ibid., p. 132. Original text is Rotha, *Documentary Film* (1935), p. 108.
24. Ibid., p. 198. Original text is Rotha, *Documentary Film* (1935), p. 143.
25. I have deposited this book in the Makino Collection.
26. Sekino Yoshio, 'Tadashiki "Documentary" Riron no Ninshiki no Tame Ni', *Bunka Nyusu Weekly* vol. 110 (18 January 1940), p. 1 (Makino Collection).
27. Sekino Yoshio, 'Kyo Made no Eiga to Ashita no Eiga (1)', *Bunka Eiga Kenkyu* vol. 3 no. 2 (February 1940), pp. 8–11; Sekino Yoshio, 'Kyo Made no Eiga to Ashita no Eiga (2)', *Bunka Eiga Kenkyu* vol. 3 no. 3 (March 1940), pp. 58–60; Sekino Yoshio, 'Kyo Made no Eiga to Ashita no Eiga (3)', *Bunka Eiga Kenkyu* vol. 3 no. 4 (April 1940), pp. 109–12; Sekino Yoshio, 'Kyo Made no Eiga to Ashita no Eiga (4)', *Bunka Eiga Kenkyu* vol. 3 no. 5 (May 1940), pp. 176–9; Sekino Yoshio, 'Dokyumentariiron Kento no Tame Ni (1)', *Bunka Eiga Kenkyu* vol. 3 no. 6 (June 1940), pp. 236–9; Sekino Yoshio, 'Dokyumentariiron Kento no Tame Ni (2)', *Bunka Eiga Kenkyu* vol. 3 no. 7 (July 1940), pp. 304–7; Sekino Yoshio, 'Dokyumentariiron Kento no Tame Ni (3)', *Bunka Eiga Kenkyu* vol. 3 no. 10 (October 1940), pp. 563–7. The other major series of articles by Sekino is Sekino Yoshio, 'Poru Rosa: Dokyumentarii Eiga no Sonogo no Shinten 1', *Nihon Eiga* vol. 5 no. 7 (July 1940), pp. 22–9; Sekino Yoshio, 'Poru Rosa: Dokyumentarii Eiga no Sonogo no Shinten 2', *Nihon Eiga* vol. 5. no. 8 (August 1940), pp. 68–73, 120; Sekino Yoshio, 'Poru Rosa: Dokyumentarii Eiga no Sonogo no Shinten 3', *Nihon Eiga* vol. 5 no. 10 (October 1940), pp. 72–7, 14.
28. Sekino Yoshio, *Eiga Kyoiku no Riron* (Tokyo: Shogakkan, 1942).
29. Rotha, *Documentary Film* (1935), p. 66; Sekino, *Eiga Kyoiku no Riron*, p. 163. By way of contrast, Ueno Ichiro's translation is complete and correct in Rotha, 'Bunka Eigaron Josetsu', trans. Ueno, p. 79.
30. STS, or the 'Square Table Society', was an influential study group composed of a variety of intellectuals interested in film education. They published their own independent journal: *Eiga Zehi* and *Eiga Dai-issen*. For a history, see Makino Mamoru's column in *Unitsushin* between 26 September and 21 November 1977.
31. For an extensive discussion of Sekino's children's film days, see Gonda Yasunosuke, *Minshugorakuron* (Tokyo: Ganshodo Shoten, 1931), especially pp. 309–28.
32. Yamada Hideyoshi, *Eiga Kokusaku no Zenshin* (Tokyo: Koseisho, 1940), p. 216.
33. Rotha, *Documentary Film* (1935), p. 48.
34. Rotha, *Bunka Eigaron*, trans. Atsugi (1938), p. 34.
35. Rotha, 'Bunka Eigaron Josetsu', trans. Ueno, p. 56.

36. Sekino, *Eiga Kyoiku no Riron*, p. 136.
37. One was Asanuma Keiji, who is Japan's best-known film semiotician.
38. Further evidence that Atsugi did not recognise the mistranslation may be found in the various copies she deposited at the Film Centre. None of them contains any corrections here, although she did underline the *adjacent* sentence in her 1960 edition.
39. This is not the only place where Atsugi's misprision reveals the nature of her (mis)reading of Rotha. Her translation provides many examples. Most critics refer only to how 'bad' it is. For example, in the afterward to his *Eiga Riron Nyumon*, Imamura Taihei points out how thankful we should be for the work of translators like Iijima Tadashi, Sasaki Norio and Atsugi Taka. He also warns the readers to be cautious when it comes to trusting translation; ultimately, they must refer to the original, as Imamura has. He cites one example of misprision, and he singles out Atsugi: Rotha refers to some 'modern authorities' who call dialectical materialism 'out-of-date', but Atsugi translates this *saishin*/'latest' or 'newest'. While Imamura picks a good example of mistranslation he – like everyone else – does not ask what factors led to this particular misreading. It does seem rather obvious. See Rotha, *Documentary Film* (1935), p. 182; Rotha, *Documentary Film*, trans. Atsugi (1938), p. 270; Imamura, *Eiga Riron Nyumon*, p. 184.
40. Letter, Paul Rotha to Eric Knight, 8 November 1938, Paul Rotha Collection, 2001 Box 26; UCLA.
41. This is how the great documentarist Kamei Fumio described his own relationship to Rotha's book. Various people had criticised *Fighting Soldiers* by claiming that Kamei was Rotha's disciple. However, Akimoto Takeshi introduced the original book to Toho studios when Kamei was in China shooting the film. Rotha was less a guidebook than simple inspiration, especially for the second half of the book on practical matters (this was the section translated and circulated within Toho). See Kamei Fumio, Akimoto Takeshi, Ueno Kozo, Ishimoto Tokichi, Tanaka Yoshiji, 'Nihon Bunka Eiga no Shoki Kara Kyo o Kataru Zadankai', *Bunka Eiga Kenkyu* vol. 3 no. 2 (February 1940), pp. 16–27.
42. Kuwano Shigeru, *Dokyumentarii no Sekai – Sozoryoku to Hohoron* (Tokyo: Simul Shuppankai, 1973), pp. 201–2.
43. Ibid., p. 201.
44. Shirai Shigeru and Kano Ryuichi, 'Kameraman Jinsei', in Iwamoto Kenji and Saiki Tomonori (eds), *Kinema Seishun* (Tokyo: Libroport, 1988), p. 73.
45. See Takagiba Tsutomu, '*Dokyumentarii Firumu* no Oboegaki', *Bunka Eiga Kenkyu* vol. 3 no. 4 (April 1940), pp. 112–13; Atsugi Taka, 'Story-film no Yakugo ni Tsuite', *Bunka Eiga Kenkyu* vol. 3 no. 4 (April 1940), pp. 118–19; Takagiba Tsutomu, 'Eiga no Honshitsu ni Kan Suru Ronmo', *Bunka Eiga Kenkyu* vol. 3 no. 10 (October 1940), pp. 577–80; Kubota Tatsuo, 'Gekiteki Yoso to Kirokuteki Yoso', *Bunka Eiga Kenkyu* vol. 3 no. 10 (October 1940), pp. 575–6.
46. See, for example, Ueno Kozo, 'Eiga ni Okeru Geijutsu to Kagaku – Bunka Eigaron no Kisoteki Mondai 1', *Nihon Eiga* vol. 5 no. 2 (February 1940), pp. 24–35; Ueno Kozo, 'Eiga ni Okeru Geijutsu to Kagaku – Bunka Eigaron no Kisoteki Mondai 2', *Nihon Eiga* vol. 5 no. 3 (March 1940), pp. 25–35.
47. Ueno Kozo, 'Eiga ni Okeru Geijutsu to Kagaku – Bunka Eigaron no Kisoteki Mondai 1', *Nihon Eiga* vol. 5 no. 2 (February 1940), p. 33.
48. Atsugi Taka, 'Kiroku Eiga no Kyoko – "Jijitsu" wa Sono Mama "Shinjitsu" de wa Nai', *Nihon Eiga* vol. 5 no. 2 (November 1940), p. 82.

49. Atsugi discusses this phenomenon in her translator's afterward to the 1960 edition of *Documentary Film*: Atsugi Taka, 'Yakusha no Atogaki', in Rotha, *Dokyumentarii Eiga*, trans. Atsugi (1960), pp. 329–34.
50. Tanikawa, *Dokyumentarii Eiga no Genten*, p. 195.
51. See Kamei Fumio, 'Bunka Eiga Geppyo',' *Nihon Eiga* vol. 5 no. 12 (December 1940), pp. 24–6; Kamei *et al.*, 'Nihon Bunka Eiga no Shoki Kara Kyo o Kataru Zadankai', pp. 16–27.

## REFERENCES

Atsugi Taka, 'Story-film no Yakugo ni Tsuite', *Bunka Eiga Kenkyu* vol. 3 no. 4 (April 1940), pp. 118–19.
Atsugi Taka, 'Kiroku Eiga no Kyoko – "Jijitsu" wa Sono Mama "Shinjitsu" de wa Nai', *Nihon Eiga* vol. 5 no. 2 (November 1940), p. 82.
Atsugi Taka, 'Yakusha no Atogaki', in Paul Rotha, *Dokyumentarii Eiga*, trans. Atsugi, 1960, pp. 329–34.
Atsugi Taka, *Josei Dokyumentarisuto no Kaiso* (Tokyo: Domesu Shuppan, 1991).
Barry, Iris, 'Review of Documentary Film', *Saturday Review*, 12 August 1939.
'Documentary Film', *The Times*, 11 August 1939.
'Documentary Film', *Lady*, 3 August 1939.
Evans, Frank, 'How the Film Can Help Democracy', *Evening Chronicle* (Newcastle on Tyne), 12 May 1939.
Gonda Yasunosuke, *Minshugorakuron* (Tokyo: Ganshodo Shoten, 1931).
Imamura Taihei, *Eiga Riron Nyumon* (Tokyo: Itagaki Shoten, 1952).
Kamei Fumio, 'Bunka Eiga Geppyo', *Nihon Eiga* vol. 5 no. 12 (December 1940), pp. 24–6.
Kamei Fumio, Akimoto Takeshi, Ueno Kozo, Ishimoto Tokichi, Tanaka Yoshiji, 'Nihon Bunka Eiga no Shoki Kara Kyo o Kataru Zadankai', *Bunka Eiga Kenkyu* vol. 3 no. 2 (February 1940), pp. 16–27.
Kubota Tatsuo, *Bunka Eiga no Hohoron* (Kyoto: Dai'ichi Geibunsha, 1940).
Kubota Tatsuo, 'Gekiteki Yoso to Kirokuteki Yoso', *Bunka Eiga Kenkyu* vol. 3 no. 10 (October 1940), pp. 575–6.
Kuwano Shigeru, *Dokyumentarii no Sekai – Sozoryoku to Hohoron* (Tokyo: Simul Shuppankai, 1973).
Laine, Elizabeth, 'About Documentary Films', *Transcript* (Boston), 10 June 1939.
Makino Mamoru, 'Kiroku Eiga no Riron teki Doko o Otte 41', *Unitsushin*, 19 June 1978, n p.
Okamoto Masao, *Bunka Eiga Jidai + Jujiya Eigabu no Hitobito* (Tokyo: Unitsushin, 1996).
Okuda Shinkichi, *Eiga Bunkenshi* (Tokyo: Dai Nippon Eiga Kyokai, 1943).
Rotha, Paul, 'Bunka Eiga-ron', *Chosa Shiryo* vol. 4 (Kyoto: Toho Kyoto Satsueijo, undated) (Makino Mamoru collection).
Rotha, Paul, Letter to unspecified recipient in Japan, ND (2001 Box 82, Folder 3; Paul Rotha Collection, UCLA).
Rotha, Paul, *Documentary Film* (London: Faber and Faber, 1935).
Rotha, Paul, 'Letter to Eric Knight, 8 November, 1938 (2001 Box 26; Paul Rotha Collection, UCLA).
Rotha, Paul, *Bunka Eiga-ron*, 1st Japanese edn, trans. Atsugi Taka (Tokyo: Dai'ichi Geibunsha, 1938).

Rotha, Paul, *Bunka Eigaron*, 3rd Japanese edn, trans. Atsugi Taka (Kyoto: Dai'ichi Geibunsha, 1939).

Rotha, Paul, Letter to Eric Knight, 28 August 1941 (2001 Box 26; Paul Rotha Collection, UCLA).

Rotha, Paul, *Dokyumentarii Eiga*, revised and expanded edn, trans. Atsugi Taka (Tokyo: Misuzu Shobo, 1960).

Rotha, Paul, *Dokyumentarii Eiga*, revised and expanded edn, trans. Atsugi Taka (Tokyo: Misuzu Shobo, 1976).

Rotha, Paul, *Dokyumentarii Eiga*, refurbished edn, trans. Atsugi Taka (Tokyo: Miraisha, 1995).

Sekino Yoshio, 'Tadashiki "Documentary" Riron no Ninshiki no Tame Ni', *Bunka Nyusu Weekly* vol. 110 (18 January 1940), p. 1 (Makino collection).

Sekino Yoshio, '*Kyo Made no Eiga* to Ashita no Eiga (1)', *Bunka Eiga Kenkyu* vol. 3 no. 2 (February 1940), pp. 8–11.

Sekino Yoshio, '*Kyo Made no Eiga* to Ashita no Eiga (2)', *Bunka Eiga Kenkyu* vol. 3 no. 2 (March 1940), pp. 58–60.

Sekino Yoshio, '*Kyo Made no Eiga* to Ashita no Eiga (3)', *Bunka Eiga Kenkyu* vol 3. no. 4 (April 1940), pp. 109–12.

Sekino Yoshio, '*Kyo Made no Eiga* to Ashita no Eiga (4)', *Bunka Eiga Kenkyu* vol. 3 no. 5 (May 1940), pp. 176–9.

Sekino Yoshio, 'Dokyumentariiron Kento no Tame Ni (1)', *Bunka Eiga Kenkyu* vol. 3 no. 6 (June 1940), pp. 236–9.

Sekino Yoshio, 'Dokyumentariiron Kento no Tame Ni (2)', *Bunka Eiga Kenkyu* vol. 3 no. 7 (July 1940), pp. 304–7.

Sekino Yoshio, 'Dokyumentariiron Kento no Tame Ni (3)', *Bunka Eiga Kenkyu* vol. 3 no. 10 (October 1940), pp. 563–7.

Sekino Yoshio, 'Poru Rosa: Dokyumentarii Eiga no Sonogo no Shinten 1', *Nihon Eiga* vol. 5 no 7 (July 1940), pp. 22–9.

Sekino Yoshio, 'Poru Rosa: Dokyumentarii Eiga no Sonogo no Shinten 2', *Nihon Eiga* vol. 5 no 8 (August 1940), pp. 68–73, 120.

Sekino Yoshio, 'Poru Rosa: Dokyumentarii Eiga no Sonogo no Shinten 3', *Nihon Eiga* vol. 5 no. 10 (October 1940), pp. 72–7, 14.

Sekino Yoshio, *Eiga Kyoiku no Riron* (Tokyo: Shogakkan, 1942).

Shirai Shigeru and Kano Ryuichi, 'Kameraman Jinsei', in Iwamoto Kenji and Saiki Tomonori (eds), *Kinema Seishun* (Tokyo: Libroport, 1988), p. 73.

Takagiba Tsutomu, 'Kyoko no Riron – Tsumura Hideo-shi no "Poru Ruta Hihan" o Yomu', *Bunka Eiga Kenkyu* vol. 3 no. 1 (January 1940), pp. 525–8.

Takagiba Tsutomu, '*Dokyumentarii Firumu* no Oboegaki', *Bunka Eiga Kenkyu* vol. 3 no. 4 (April 1940), pp. 112–13.

Takagiba Tsutomu, 'Eiga no Honshitsu ni Kan Suru Ronmo', *Bunka Eiga Kenkyu* vol. 3 no. 10 (October 1940), pp. 577–80.

Tanikawa Yoshio, *Dokyumentarii Eiga no Genten – Sono Shiso to Hoho*, 3rd edn (Tokyo: Futosha, 1990).

Tsumura Hideo, 'Poru Ruta no Eigaron Hihan – Sono Cho "Documentary Film" ni Tsuite', *Shineiga* vol. 9 no. 12 (November 1939), p. 17.

Ueno Ichiro, 'Eikoku no Bunka Eiga', *Eiga Kenkyu* vol. 1 (1939), pp. 146–61.

Ueno Kozo, 'Eiga ni Okeru Geijutsu to Kagaku – Bunka Eigaron no Kisoteki Mondai 1', *Nihon Eiga* vol. 5 no. 2 (February 1940), pp. 24–35.

Yamada Hideyoshi, *Eiga Kokusaku no Zenshin* (Tokyo: Koseisho, 1940).

# 5

# A Social Poetics of Documentary: Grierson and the Scandinavian Documentary Tradition

*Ib Bondebjerg*

We know for certain that the Grierson influence on Scandinavian documentary was not just the result of inspiration from a distance, but of direct contact. In Denmark the main theoretician and director of documentary film, Theodor Christensen (1914–67), found inspiration both in the Russian montage theories and film traditions and in the British documentary movement, paying tribute to both traditions in his more theoretical writings. But a piece of historical film footage from around 1935 also shows some of the leading Danish documentary directors waving goodbye to Christensen as he departs on a mission to London to seek inspiration and bring back films from the British documentary movement.[1] In an interview after the war, Christensen explains how carefully he studied the films, the style and editing, and how he shared the grand social vision of films to promote civic and democratic ideals, transmit information and build opinion.[2]

Grierson's influence on the Danish documentary movement of the 1930s and onward is repeated in the other Scandinavian countries, all sharing an early pre-television public-service philosophy of documentary film production and distribution. Whereas the years before 1930 were dominated by very actuality-oriented documentary formats or the anthropological travel documentary, from the 1930s on the actuality tradition merged with more dramatic and poetic styles. But even though similarities can be found between the British and Scandinavian development in the years 1930–60, the Danish connection seems to be the most direct. The social dimension of Danish documentary was perhaps more in line with the Grierson tradition than the Norwegian and Swedish, where the travel films and Flaherty's influence are stronger.[3]

But the institutionalisation of the early documentary film tradition in Scandinavia and in the UK has strong similarities, just as both countries later developed a strong public-service ethos, which clearly continued many of the tendencies and genres initiated in the film movement. In Denmark the support for documentary film was rooted in two institutional frameworks: on the one hand, the public education system and a public–private interest in cultural and informational films; on the other, a direct interest from both private companies and the government in dispensing information to citizens and consumers. The inauguration of Dansk Kulturfilm [Danish Cultural Film Board] in 1932 and Statens Filmcentral [the National Film Board] in 1938 falls within the first framework, whereas the formation of ministerial film boards in the 1940s lies in the other category. But, as in the UK, documentary film-makers in this period had to rely on private or government financing for ventures with very specific

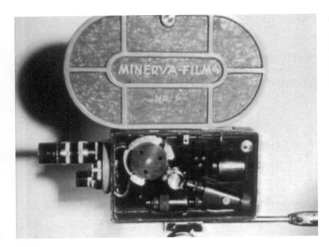

Camera used in the late
1930s and 40s by the leading
Danish production company
for documentary film
(*Den levende virkelighed 1–3*
[Jørgen Roos, 1989], Jørgen
Roos Film/Statens
Filmcentral)

themes and missions, whereas in the modern period after 1960, film-makers had a
better chance of defining their project more freely. The institutional trends in Danish
documentary film culture can also be seen in both Norway and Sweden, although
with a different time schedule and slight national variations. In Norway, for instance,
a public system did not develop until the late 1940s (National Film Board, 1948; Norsk
Kulturfilm, 1946), with private institutions and social movements playing a strong
role before that.[4]

## A POETIC AND A SOCIAL VISION

In one of his first articles from 1938, Theodor Christensen defines the mission of
the Danish documentary film movement in terms inspired by Grierson: 'a realism,
dramatizing modern life ... symbolic sounds, acoustic realism, contrasts between music
and images ... reality, creatively arranged reality, reality in images, words, sound,
music, creating together a narrative, a drama'.[5] Just as Grierson's phrase, 'creative
treatment of actuality' points towards a poetics of documentary in direct opposition
to the dominant tendency of the educational and informational film of those days,
Christensen is clearly rejecting the established, dominant concept of documentary as
a transparent representation of reality or an objective, factual film. The creative
dramatisation of reality with a strong anchoring of the film in a modern world and
with a clear civic mission are the key words. But in actuality the documentary genre
until around 1960 was still very much dominated by films commissioned by public
authorities or private companies, making poetic freedom and critical distance difficult.
Also Scandinavian documentary film-makers between 1930 and 1960 were caught
between a rock and a hard place when it came to artistic freedom, but they used the
little space they had with great creativity. Short films with seemingly very dull content
and themes from everyday life were vibrant with poetry, irony, creative montage and
use of sound and music.

*The Grierson Effect*

In Denmark and the rest of Scandinavia we see similar patterns of inspiration and controversies, and the creative treatment of actuality defined by Grierson certainly had its limits. The history and aesthetics of early Scandinavian documentary is inscribed in this context and the conflict between, on the one hand, a certain aesthetic, creative freedom and, on the other hand, an institutional production culture with very specific assignments for theme and content. In the late 1950s documentary film production gradually became much more independent, and the establishment of public funding for film enabled the development of both new film genres and a much stronger critical tradition, just as the breakthrough of public-service television created a new platform for documentaries with instant access to a mass audience.

When Danish television started in 1951 one of the key figures was the later first Minister for Culture, the Labour politician, Julius Bomholt, and in the *Yearbook of Television* from 1953, he pointed to the documentary genre as a building stone for modern democracy:

> The visual reportage can contribute to the development of our Danish democracy. Pictures from the reality of our whole working society, the industry, crafts, commerce, agriculture, etc., the social life, life in parliament and common national events and social reportage can create a much more intimate connection between the elite and the general public.[6]

We know from Ian Aitken's thorough study of Grierson's ideological background that he was inspired by early theories of public opinion, of the public sphere and of montage and visual communication.[7] The quotations from Christensen and Bomholt point towards a similar line of thought in Denmark, where documentary genres play a crucial role in forming this public space, debate and imagination.

The arrival of television in Scandinavia (Denmark, 1951; Sweden ,1956; and Norway, 1960) was both a challenge and a boost for documentary film-making, and the relation between TV documentaries and more independent film documentaries created conflict from time to time. In the 1950s the film documentary was beginning to free itself from the more restricted and commissioned forms of documentary, but the strong factual and journalistic demands of television could be seen as a new kind of restriction. On the other hand, the distribution patterns of early documentary film through cinema, the educational system and private and public organisations were not nearly as efficient as television. The vision of civic education through poetic, social documentaries in the Grierson tradition seemed almost made for television. But the relationship between documentary film and television historically developed very differently in the three Scandinavian countries.

In Denmark the managing directors of TV did not see film directors as natural coalition partners and, even though a number of documentary films were shown on television, the people developing TV documentary forms did not come from film but were either radio or newspaper journalists. A certain tension between film documentaries and journalism was thus established and can still be identified in the contemporary Danish media culture.[8] In Sweden relations were the complete opposite: people from radio and press did have an important impact on early TV documentary production, but the establishment of a documentary film section on SVT in 1956 headed by the open-minded Lennart Ehrenborg made all the difference.

He intentionally worked on a profile for SVT where independent documentary film directors and journalists worked within the same framework.[9] Institutionally this meant that SVT continued and expanded the Grierson heritage into the new media culture in the sense that the merging of creativity, factuality and journalism was encouraged. Already in the late 1950s we find a strong blend of different documentary genres on SVT and we find people with very different backgrounds working for television. The Grierson tradition is taken to a new critical level in Karl-Axel Sjöblom and Lars Ag's famous documentary series *Strövtåg/Ramble* (1958), a social reportage about ordinary people caught up in the system. Here are the early roots of what later became the investigative television documentary, in form very far from the Grierson tradition, but nevertheless thematically and ideologically related.

## THE TENSION BETWEEN CREATIVITY AND FACTUAL JOURNALISM

The historical tension between film and television documentary found in different forms in Scandinavia can hardly be connected to Grierson, since, according to his biographer Forsyth Hardy, Grierson himself saw the British Broadcasting Corporation (BBC) as a natural heir to his film movement.[10] The connecting line from film to television was furthermore in reality and symbolically confirmed by the fact that Grierson was actually offered a post at the BBC as head of documentary, a post then given to one of his collaborators, Paul Rotha. In 1954 Rotha clearly stated that, despite the controversies within the BBC between different strands of documentary and between journalism and film, he saw television as the modern platform for Grierson's documentary idea: 'To those who still believe that documentary has a specific social job to do, this mass access to audiences and quick answer is of paramount importance. It is something new in the documentary experience.'[11] The fact that Rotha saw modern television as the social medium for documentary, a fact soon proven by developments, did not minimise the tension within the documentary movement between factual journalism and the more independent, creative documentary, which Grierson had pioneered.

The strong institutional tension we see in Denmark and the more open collaboration in Sweden takes a slightly different form in Norway, where television was established much later than in the UK and the other two Scandinavian countries. As Jan Anders Diesen has pointed out in his book on the Norwegian television documentary,[12] Norwegian television (as was the case in the rest of Scandinavia) was directly inspired by and built on principles from the BBC, but it benefited from drawing on a longer experience. The Norwegian channel, Norsk rikskringkasting AS (NRK), very much wanted its documentary profile to build on the independent film production. However, it soon had to develop its own inhouse production. Key to this transformation from film to television documentary in Norway was Carsten E. Munch, who made TV films with a combination of aesthetic creativity and factual social documentation.[13] As Diesen points out, the first ten years of NRK documentary production allowed for a certain artistic freedom, a freedom that was gradually restricted with the later professionalisation and commercialisation of public-service television. One might say that the combination of paternalistic information and creative documentary found in the early Grierson film movement was to a large degree reproduced in the first long period of public-service broadcasting in Norway.

But behind the institutional tensions and the actual collaboration between film and television or the lack thereof, the uneasy conflict between documentary as journalism and documentary as more creative art was just as important. In his book on the Swedish television documentary Leif Furhammer quotes both Lennart Ehrenborg's and Ivar Ivres's (both leading characters in factual and documentary programming) distinction between journalistic reportage with its more objective and less aesthetic approach and the more personal and aesthetic approach of documentary.[14] In Ehrenborg's case the distinction was made to open up for both types of factual programming, whereas Ivres was more normative in his tendency to reject the creative documentary on television. One might argue, with reference to the Grierson legacy, that documentaries in general, film or television, all pay tribute to the notion of public information in the broadest sense of the term. But public information comes in many forms, from the most direct factual statements to the more poetic social forms. However, it is clear that the historical tension between film and television exists despite this common ground and historical heritage.

There is no reason to distinguish between film and television when it comes to the basic formats of documentary genres. The four most basic forms, authoritative, observational, dramatised and poetic[15] are independent of media platforms. The special combination of the authoritative and the poetic of the original Grierson tradition can be found in both modern film and television. But around 1950, when Scandinavian cinema and television began their twisted collaboration on the development of documentary films and programmes, with the Grierson legacy a strong influence on both, the partly separate development of support systems for film and television created not just a natural competition and tension, but also a certain division of labour. Many of the factual and informational functions of documentary were taken over by a journalistic tradition in television, and the documentary film movement became stronger and more focused on the other formats.

## THE DANISH GRIERSON: THEODOR CHRISTENSEN

As already indicated, Theodor Christensen is a key figure in the classical period of Danish documentary film, a kind of Danish Grierson and both a theoretician of film and a productive film director. In 1936 he wrote, together with another important Danish documentary film director, Karl Roos, the first serious theoretical book in Denmark on film, *Film*, a book with references to many of the leading European theorists on film, among them Grierson, Balazs, Arnheim, Spottiswoode, Pudovkin and Eisenstein. Christensen, like Grierson, clearly combines a sociological and aesthetic approach, and his background in a socialist political position very much defines his notion of documentary. The discussion in *Film* of documentary film refers to both Grierson and Spottiswoode. Christensen does not define documentary as a specific form and style, instead pointing to the distinction between fiction and documentary as a difference in 'the way in which the raw material is selected'.[16]

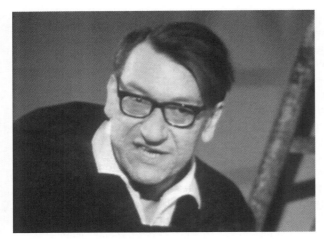

Theodor Christensen
(1914–67), the leading
theoretician, organiser and
director of documentary film
in Denmark from the 1930s.
Here filmed around 1963
(*Den levende virkelighed 1–3*
[Jørgen Roos, 1989], Jørgen
Roos Film/Statens
Filmcentral)

Following modern cognitive film theory,[17] Christensen and Roos thus actually point towards the film's relation to reality and the way it positions the spectator as the crucial distinctive element in documentary film. In their discussion of documentary genres Christensen and Roos quote Grierson's concept of the creative treatment of actuality, which they deem important but somewhat vague, and then move on to a Spottiswoode quote: 'The documentary film is in subject and approach a dramatised presentation of man's relation to his institutional life, whether industrial, social or political; and in technique a subordination of form to content.'[18] But in their discussion of this definition of documentary they judge this to be a bit too much a reflection of just the British, Grierson tradition, rejecting the notion that form can be subordinated to content. They support the idea of dramatisation and Grierson's creativity dimension as a critical distancing of the new documentary from the traditional educational and informational film, but arrive at the conclusion that form is just as important for the sociological mission of documentary as the reality content presented.

Grierson's lasting contribution to the documentary tradition is among other things a historical transformation of the traditional notion of documentary as a kind of transparent, objective and factual representation of reality. Christensen's theory and practice points in the same direction, and they both stressed the creative dimensions of the treatment of the real world. In one of his early articles on documentary, *Er det muligt i Danmark?/Is This Possible in Denmark?* (1937) he argues that the true documentary film is much more than the traditional factual and informational film, that it is about activating the imagination of the spectator through dramatisation, montage and narration, but with a strong anchoring in live, contemporary reality.[19] One of his examples is Paul Rotha and his film *Shipyard* (1935), which is praised for telling the story of the building of a concrete ship with a form and approach that activated the audience and had a wider relevance than the mere incident of construction: a universalistic human approach to social reality.[20]

Christensen's status as the Danish Grierson is reinforced by his important article, 'Documentary – hvad er det?'/'Documentary – What Is That?' (1938), in which

Grierson's notion of the creative treatment of actuality is fleshed out as a programmatic statement about documentary. He takes us from the influence of Russian montage, past the German realism of modernity (Walter Ruttmann) to the crucial breakthrough of the British documentary:

the best (British documentaries) are the most representative documentaries of our time … they can take credit for having discovered and practised a more creative style … exactly because a documentary film is naturalistic it must use the creative possibilities of film art. Reality is its material, but the role of modern documentary is to present it in an authentic and convincing way.[21]

Interestingly enough in this article Christensen also argues that documentary should use the narrative techniques of the fiction film, situating characters in a narrative flow, as long as a fundamental respect for the documentary material is maintained. Christensen's viewpoint on documentary here is not just completely in line with the Grierson tradition but also extremely modern.

As already indicated, the Grierson era in Scandinavian documentary was challenged in the postwar period, especially from around 1948 on, partly due to the advent of television and to other institutional changes in the documentary film culture itself. In 1948 Christensen wrote an article, 'Dokumentarfilmens krise'/'The Crisis of Documentary Film', where he reflects on the situation both nationally and internationally. His starting point is again the leading role of British documentary and Grierson: 'Without Grierson the rise to fame of documentary film would not have been possible. With inspiring slogans, hundreds of articles, analytical and critical work on actual directors, with personal advice and influence he inspired the breakthrough of documentary.'[22] But Christensen sees a certain waning of the Grierson movement internationally and a need for further experiments and new developments.

In 1948 no one could foresee the breakthrough of Free Cinema in the UK in the late 1950s or similar more observational documentary forms in which the voice and form of the Grierson cinema were dramatically changed, while the relation between documentary and contemporary social life continued. But Christensen's critical questioning of the documentary of the 1930s and 40s, a tradition in many ways heavily handicapped by the fact that films were commissioned by the state or corporations, was reflected in the world community of documentary film-makers. The debate was not least about the issue of creative freedom, a strong desire emerging to make not just commissioned films but also those whose topics and ideas were decided more freely by the director. Eventually this led to new forms of support for more independent films, thus paving the way for the new documentary of the late 1950s and 60s. Christensen again played an important role in this transition, not just through his own films, but by formulating doctrines for documentary freedom that were successfully negotiated with SFC – the National Film Board – in 1949. His 'Resolution on Film Freedom' (1948) defined this freedom as: freedom of topic, speech and work method, as well as economic freedom.[23]

These freedoms were however, not secured in terms of public funding and film legislation until the mid-1960s in Denmark. Film laws of 1964 and 1972 based support systems for documentary films on Christensen's four types of freedom, with funding no longer tied to specific topics. Documentary films finally became both creative and informational in ways decided by the director, who got final cut. But the fight for this freedom waged all through the 1950s and the Cold War and the continued domination of commissioned films often created problems. A key example were the so-called Marshall films made in 1950–1, financed partly by the American Marshall money given to Denmark after the war. The idea behind these was completely in line with the Grierson heritage: the films were meant to promote to the general public creative images of the rebuilding and development of modern Denmark and its most important industries. But the films were often made under heavy public scrutiny with debate and interference from the government, along with certain reservations about some of the directors reputed to have left-wing sympathies and critical attitudes. But six films were made, among them Theodor Christensen's own fifteen-minute-long *Alle mine skibe/All My Ships* (1951), demonstrating creative use of the little mermaid and the welder, Christensen's work in building Danish ships after the war and his experiences of the war and postwar period.

## GENRES AND THE SCANDINAVIAN SOCIAL DOCUMENTARY

It would be wrong to pigeonhole the British Grierson tradition and the films it produced in a particular genre. All belonged to the more authoritative form of documentary with an informational intention and a rhetorical structure based on a lecturing kind of voiceover, far from the later observational forms based in reality where characters speak out of their own world. But the Grierson tradition was clearly inspired by forms of cinema with a more poetic, dramatic tone and institutionalised a new form of montage with use of sound and images from a much more experimental vein than usual for informational documentaries. The early European and American forms of poetic documentary incorporated a committed social agenda, which was also deeply embedded in the Scandinavian tradition from 1930 on, a tradition connected to the establishment of a welfare state. The Scandinavian documentary film movement was heavily dominated by films with a social agenda, throwing the spotlight on the lower classes and social inequality. But, as already indicated in connection with the Danish Grierson, Theodor Christensen, this social agenda was directly connected to an aesthetic understanding of documentary opposed to the traditional forms of factual films.

In Norway there was a particularly strong travel and nature emphasis in the early period of documentary, but we also see the growth of two important traditions with links to similar trends in the UK. On the one hand, we have the Norway films and later on the so-called Oslo films and on the other hand, we have the workers' films.[24] Both the Norway and the Oslo films, initiated by Norsk Kulturfilm (established 1946) display a mixture of realism and national romanticism in the depiction of places, people and everyday life in Norway. The Norway films in particular feature a mixture of this nationalist view of the country's wonders alongside a more neutral portrayal of modern everyday life. But there is a link to the Grierson films in the sense that they deal with the building of a common, national identity, a link in much stronger evidence in the Oslo documentaries. The key person behind the Oslo films in the 1940s,

Kristoffer Aamot, had a vision of one film or a series of films portraying everyday life in contemporary Norway. He saw the series as both an educational film project treating culture and knowledge in all aspects of modern life, from an Oslo perspective, but he also envisioned it as a historical archive, documenting life, which could be updated every twenty-five years.[25]

Although with a clear national leaning, both these two Norwegian traditions have strong similarities with the Grierson films. But perhaps the so-called workers' films produced by the Norwegian working-class movement between 1928–40 are even closer to forms and rhetorical elements in the Grierson vein. The difference is of course that propaganda films promote a particular political and social movement while public-information documentaries carry an embedded social message. But some of these films clearly experimented with montage and dramatic and rhetorical structures, often also present in social documentaries without the same very specific ideological and political propaganda purpose. In Norway, as in the rest of Scandinavia, a new freer, social documentary did not develop until the 1960s, a key film in this regard being Erik Borge's *Nedfall/Fall-out* (1964), dealing with environmental problems. Free from the informational and educational tone of earlier social documentaries, the film demonstrated how a social critique and agenda could be set, with a much more understated and indirect argument in images and sounds.[26]

In Sweden the influence of Grierson and Flaherty, both poetic and social, was also clearly present in the work of one of the earliest and most internationally famous of the early documentary directors, Arne Sucksdorff. Sucksdorff did not subscribe to the romantic notion of nature and people outside civilisation, so that his films both on modern life in the cities and on nature were more realistic. A poetic observer of everyday life, Sucksdorff did not have the social agenda of the Grierson tradition either and we find strong links to the European city symphonies and poetic film tradition.[27] In one of his most famous early films *Människor i stad/People in the City* (1947), which won an Oscar, the realism and social focus involved in its careful portrait of Stockholm and its different people are evident. The film has the classical voiceover of the authoritative documentary and the Grierson tradition, while the poetic use of images, the montage of situations and sequences build an imaginative picture of reality. A much earlier film featuring a quite Griersonian social focus, along with experimental montage is Stig Almquist's (and others) *Gamla Stan* (1931), also on Stockholm. The poetic realism in Sucksdorff's films is even more pronounced in the more nature-oriented *Augustirapsodi/August Rhapsody* (1940) or *Vinden och floden/The Wind and the River* (1950). Even though Grierson's influence can be seen in Sucksdorff's films, they also clearly resemble the early Joris Ivens films.[28]

As already indicated, the early start of television in Sweden, and the rather open collaboration between the documentary film culture and that of television meant that the social documentary was more common on television. But, as in the rest of Scandinavia and Europe, the 'free' documentary and the observational format changed the generic scene in the late 1950s. Two of the most prolific documentary film-makers in Sweden in this period were Peter Weiss and Stefan Jarl. Both take the social documentary in Sweden to a whole new level, and completely transform the Grierson legacy and dominance in this genre. Very early on Weiss develops a pre-Direct Cinema format in his films dealing with social groups on the margins of society, films like

*Ansikten i skugga/Faces in Shadow* (1956), about the social outcasts in Stockholm or *Enligt lag/According to the Law* (1957) on young criminals or *Bag de ens facader/Behind the Monotonous Facades* (1960), looking at life in modern housing areas. Weiss's films were a great inspiration for Stefan Jarl in his youth sociology documentaries, for instance, his *Modstrilogi* (*Dom kallar oss mods/They Call Us Misfits* (1968), *Ett anständigt liv/A Respectable Life* (1979) and *Det sociala arvet/From Misfits to Yuppies* (1993). Here the social documentary moves from authoritative, poetic propaganda to an extended documentation and narrative of lives as they unfold.

## A CRITICAL DANISH TRADITION

Left-wing views were dominant among many writers, artists and film-makers in Denmark in the 1930s. In 1930 the Ministry for Foreign Affairs and a group of industrial representatives decided to commission a film about Denmark to represent the country to foreigners. Strangely enough they chose one of the most controversial cultural luminaries, Poul Henningsen, to make the film. Henningsen had a very modern and international outlook, was clearly inspired by Grierson and Russian montage, and certainly not inclined to reproduce the traditional image of the nation. Basically, he made a road movie to swinging jazz rhythms, and his montage of images from all over Denmark were meant to present an updated version of a modern nation on its way forward, often with a slightly ironic tone. Focusing on modern technology rather than tourist sites, he stressed communication, collaboration and industrial elements, with Hans Christian Andersen's fairytale image of the nation nowhere to be seen. Public outcry at the premiere in 1935 led to the film – now considered a classical masterpiece in the Danish Grierson tradition – being banned until 1960, when it finally re-premiered.[29]

This example shows how controversial a modern film form can be and just how tightly the dominant discourse is tied to a certain national hegemony. But the historical dilemma is, just as with Grierson in the UK, that it was the state and private enterprises that first used film for information and propaganda purposes, thus also encouraging the development of a more social and critical tone. Between 1930–60 the hands of documentary film-makers may have been tied to a large degree, but they still tried to speak up and develop a creative and critical space within their confined and defined territory. A number of films in this period featured a creative use of style and technique, increasingly so from the 1940s on, but establishing an independent, critical voice and treating social issues were more problematic. Many of the films made even during the occupation of Denmark largely consisted of information from the authorities or the companies for the general public. Such films could, however, have a social agenda, as we see in Carl Th. Dreyer's *Mødrehjælpen/Maternal Help* (1942), a film clearly made in the Grierson tradition, engaging a case story to help people identify with young mothers and prevent prejudice against children born outside marriage, a very sensitive issue in those days. But critical films could be stopped, as happened to another Dreyer documentary, *Vandet på landet/The Water in the Countryside* (1946). Centring on the problems of getting clean water in the countryside, the film identifies the agricultural sector as one of the main culprits.

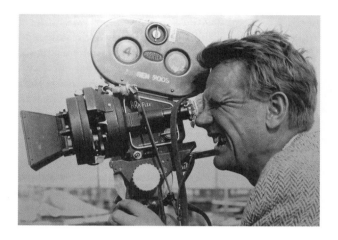

Danish film director Jørgen
Roos filming *Støj/Noise* in
1967. Production: Minerva
Film & Statens Film Central
(*Den levende virkelighed 1–3*
[Jørgen Roos, 1989], Jørgen
Roos Film/Statens
Filmcentral)

Following opposition from those criticised, the film was shelved and has never been
shown in public.[30]

Despite the many restrictions in early documentary production, many of the
official films grew out of a social agenda, which in itself had a certain democratic
dimension. At the same time some different films, with a much more outspoken
critical voice, began to develop by the 1940s. One very famous example during the
occupation of Denmark was Theodor Christensen's and a collective of directors'
film *Det gælder din frihed/It Concerns Your Freedom* (1946), shot illegally by people
belonging to the resistance movement and made in direct opposition to the official
collaboration with the German occupation force, which held sway until 1943. The
subject of intense debate in 1946 after its first public screening, the film in many
ways heralds a new independent documentary. Not until 1955, when an expanded
version was made based on the same original with some additional material, was the
film finally accepted as an authentic documentation of Denmark from the resistance
movement perspective.

So from the 1950s on film in Denmark and in the rest of Scandinavia began to
move in more independent and critical directions from those in the Grierson tradition.
Both Theodor Christensen and another important director, Jørgen Roos, continued a
double track of social films in this period. On the one hand, they made films on social
issues with a more neutral informational discourse, but often in a creative style. Two
examples are Jørgen Roos's *Sølv/Silver* (1956), made for the famous Danish company
Georg Jensen, its subject portrayed in a very elegant and creative way, or Theodor
Christensen's *Her er banerne/Here Are the Railroads* (1948), a presentation showcasing
the public Danish railway company but with imaginative use of montage, sound and
music, clearly inspired by the Grierson tradition.

But a much more critical, social agenda can be found in work by both Roos and
Christensen at this time, either in the form of films addressing more general social
problems and challenges, as in Jørgen Roos's *Slum* (1952), concerning slum districts in
the big cities, or in Theodor Christensen's even more impressive and much earlier
*Mennesker i et hus/People in a House* (1943) on the same theme, with its progressive use

of case studies and witnesses telling their own stories. In many ways the films of Roos and Christensen in the 1950s and early 60s clearly represented and gave voice to the lower social classes, to the young generations trying to find a place in the new society after the war and to women in their quest for equality. Christensen's *I kø foran livet/In Queue for Life* (1958) or *Bare en pige/Just a Girl* (1959) are both examples of this.

But a decisive move towards a more general social critique of the newly affluent society and tendencies within it comes in the early 1960s, at the same time as a freer and more observational cinema emerges. Christensen's *Enden på legen/The End of the Game* (1960) criticises the way society is developing by focusing on the rise of professional sport and entertainment, engaging a rapid and aggressive montage format. In a similar vein, Jørgen Roos's *Vi hænger i en tråd/We're Hanging by a Thread* (1961) represents one of the first films criticising overproduction, pollution and exploitation of people both in the national domain and the third world. The style and form are dominated by the ironic, critical voiceover, the aggressive montage of images contrasting the affluence of Danish society with global problems that pose a threat to this way of life, unless some kind of solidarity in action is achieved.

Although a line can be traced back to the social documentaries started by Grierson in the UK in the 1930s, which advocated social cohesion and solidarity, there is a wide gap between these more official and informational films, and the aggressive and critical voice of modern documentaries.[31] By 1960 Scandinavian documentary film moves in new directions and the Grierson heritage is consigned to history.

## NOTES

1. See Jørgen Roos, *Den levende virkelighed – historien om dansk dokumentarfilm 1–3/Living Reality – The History of Danish Documentary Film*, film series made for DR and SFC, 1989.
2. Roos, *Den levende virkelighed*.
3. Søren Birkvad and Jan Anders Diesen, *Autentiske inntrykk. Møte med ni skandinaviske dokumentarfilmskaparar/Authentic Impressions: Meeting with Nine Scandinavian Documentary Film Directors* (Oslo: Samlaget, 1994), pp. 21ff.
4. Sara Brinch and Gunnar Iversen, *Virkelighetsbilder. Norsk dokumentarfilm gjenom hundre år/ Reality Images: One Hundred Years of Documentary Film* (Oslo: Universitetsforlaget, 2001).
5. Christensen, 1938, quoted in John Ernst (ed.), *Theodor Christensen – en handling af billeder/Theodor Christensen – and Action in Images* (Copenhagen: Rhodos, 1974), pp. 80f (my translation).
6. Julius Bomholt, 'Foran fjernsynet'/'In Front of Television', *Danmarks Radios Årbog* (1953–4), pp. 1–3 (my translation)
7. Ian Aitken, *Film and Reform: John Grierson and the Documentary Film Movement* (London: Routledge, 1990).
8. See Ib Bondebjerg, *Virkelighedens fortællinger. Den danske tv-dokumentarismes historie/ Narratives of Reality: History of the Danish TV-Documentary* (Frederiksberg: Forlaget Samfundslitteratur, 2008); and Ib Bondebjerg, *Virkelighedsbilleder. Den moderne danske dokumentarfilm/Reality Images: The Modern Danish Documentary Film* (Frederiksberg: Forlaget Samfundslitteratur, 2012).

9. Leif Furhammer, *Med TV i verkligheten. SVT och de dokumentära genrerna/With TV in Reality: SVT and the Documentary Genres* (Stockholm: Stiftelsen Etermedierna i Sverige, 1995), pp. 18ff.

10. Forsyth Hardy (ed.), *Grierson on Documentary* (London: Faber and Faber, 1966), p. 258.

11. Paul Rotha, 1954, cited in Elaine Bell, 'The Origins of British Television Documentary', in John Corner (ed.), *Documentary and the Mass Media* (London: Edward Arnold, 1986), p. 71.

12. Jan Anders Diesen, *Fakta i forandring. Fjernsynsdokumentaren i NRK 1960–2000/Factual Genres in Transition: TV-Documentaries in NRK 1960–2000* (Kristianssand: Ij-forlaget, 2005), pp. 42ff.

13. Ibid., pp. 53f.

14. Furhammer, *Med TV i verkligheten*, pp. 7f.

15. See Carl Plantinga, *Rhetoric and Representation in Non-fiction Film* (Cambridge: Cambridge University Press, 1997); Bondebjerg, *Virkelighedens fortællinger;* and Bondebjerg, *Engaging with Reality: Documentary and Globalization* (Bristol/Chicago, IL: Intellect/Chicago University Press, 2013).

16. Christensen and Roos, 1936, quoted in Ernst, *Theodor Christensen*, p. 48.

17. Plantinga, *Rhetoric and Representation in Non-fiction Film*; and Bondebjerg, *Virkelighedens fortællinger*.

18. Christensen and Roos, 1936, quoted in Ernst, *Theodor Christensen*, p. 48.

19. Christensen, 1937, *Er det muligt i Danmark?/Is This Possible in Denmark?*, quoted in Ernst, *Theodor Christensen*, pp. 74f

20. Ibid., p. 75.

21. Christensen, 1938, quoted in ibid., pp. 80–1 (my translation).

22. Chistensen, 1948, quoted in ibid., p. 90.

23. Christensen, 1948a, quoted in Carl Nørrested and Christian Alsted (eds), *Kortfilmen og staten/The Short Film and the State*) (Copenhagen: Forlaget Eventus, 1987).

24. Brinch and Iversen, *Virkelighetsbilder*, pp. 51ff.

25. Ibid., pp. 79f.

26. Ibid., p. 96.

27. Ingrid Esping, *Dokumentärfilmen som tidsresa* – Modstrilogien/*The Documentary as Time Travel – The Mods Trilogy*, Dissertation: Lunds University, 2007, pp. 53f; and Bjørn Sørensen, *Å fange virkeligheten. Dokumentarfilmens århundre/To Catch Reality: A Century of Documentary* (Oslo: Universitetsforlaget, 2001), p. 173.

28. Ibid., p. 174.

29. See Bondebjerg, *Virkelighedens fortellinger*; and Sørensen, *Å fange virkeligheten*.

30. Nørrested and Alsted, *Kortfilmen og staten*, p. 271.

31. Ib Bondebjerg, 'Between War and Welfare: Danish Documentaries in the 1950s,' *Aura* vol. 2 no. 3 (1996), pp. 30–56.

## REFERENCES

Aitken, Ian, *Film and Reform: John Grierson and the Documentary Film Movement* (London: Routledge, 1990).

Bell, Elaine, 'The Origins of British Television Documentary', in John Corner (ed.), *Documentary and the Mass Media* (London: Edward Arnold, 1986).

Birkvad, Søren and Jan Anders Diesen, *Autentiske inntrykk. Møte med ni skandinaviske dokumentarfilmskaparar/Authentic Impressions: Meeting with Nine Scandinavian Documentary Film Directors* (Oslo: Samlaget, 1994).

Bomholt, Julius, 'Foran fjernsynet'/'In Front of television', *Danmarks Radios Årbog* (1953–4), pp. 1–3.

Bondebjerg, Ib, 'Narratives of Reality: Documentary Film and Television in a Cognitive and Pragmatic Perspective', *Nordicom Review* vol. 1 (1994), pp. 65–87.

Bondebjerg, Ib, 'Between War and Welfare: Danish Documentaries in the 1950s', *Aura* vol. II no. 3 (1996), pp. 30–56.

Bondebjerg, Ib, *Virkelighedens fortællinger. Den danske tv-dokumentarismes historie/Narratives of Reality: History of the Danish TV-Documentary* (Frederiksberg: Forlaget Samfundslitteratur, 2008.

Bondebjerg, Ib, *Virkelighedsbilleder. Den moderne danske dokumentarfilm/Reality Images: The Modern Danish Documentary Film)* (Frederiksberg: Forlaget Samfundslitteratur, 2012).

Bondebjerg, Ib, *Engaging with Reality: Documentary and Globalization* (Bristol/Chicago, IL: Intellect/Chicago University Press, 2013).

Brinch, Sara and Gunnar Iversen, *Virkelighetsbilder. Norsk dokumentarfilm gjenom hundre år/ Reality Images: One Hundred Years of Documentary Film* (Oslo: Universitetsforlaget, 2001).

Diesen, Jan Anders, *Fakta i forandring. Fjernsynsdokumentaren i NRK 1960–2000/Factual Genres in Transition: TV-Documentaries in NRK 1960–2000* (Kristianssand: Ij-forlaget, 2005).

Ernst, John, *Theodor Christensen – en handling af billeder/Theodor Christensen – and Action in Images* (Copenhagen: Rhodos, 1974).

Esping, Ingrid, *Dokumentärfilmen som tidsresa* – Modstrilogien/*The Documentary as Time Travel – The Mods Trilogy*, Dissertation: Lunds University, 2007.

Furhammar, Leif, *Med TV i verkligheten. SVT och de dokumentära genrerna/With TV in Reality: SVT and the Documentary Genres* (Stockholm: Stiftelsen Etermedierna i Sverige, 1995).

Furhammar, Leif, 'From Affluence to Poverty: The Early Swedish TV Documentary', in Monica Djerf-Pierre and Mats Ekström (eds), *Swedish Broadcasting: Communicative Ethos, Genres and Institutional Change* (Göteborg: Nordicom, 2013), pp. 241–61.

Hardy, Forsyth (ed.), *Grierson on Documentary* (London: Faber and Faber, 1966).

Nørrested, Carl and Christian Alsted (eds), *Kortfilmen og staten/The Short Film and the State* (Copenhagen: Forlaget Eventus, 1987).

Plantinga, Carl, *Rhetoric and Representation in Non-fiction Film* (Cambridge: Cambridge University Press, 1997).

Roos, Jørgen, *Den levende virkelighed – historien om dansk dokumentarfilm 1–3/Living Reality – The History of Danish Documentary Film*, film series made for DR and SFC, 1989.

Sørensen, Bjørn, *Å fange virkeligheten. Dokumentarfilmens århundre/To Catch Reality: A Century of Documentary* (Oslo: Universitetsforlaget, 2001).

Sørensen, Jørgen, *Danmarksfilmen og Danske billeder/The Denmark Film and Danish Images* (Copenhagen: Gyldendal, 1980).

# 6

# The Griersonian Influence and Its Challenges: Malaya, Singapore, Hong Kong (1939–73)

*Ian Aitken*

The development of official British film-making in Malaysia, Singapore and Hong Kong after 1939 was influenced by a division which emerged between a 'Colonial Office' (CO) and a 'Griersonian' approach to such endeavours. The phrase 'CO approach' refers to a practice of official film-making adopted by civil servants within the CO and Foreign Office (FO); while the phrase 'Griersonian approach' indicates that developed by individuals associated with the British documentary film movement. I am not, therefore, employing the latter phrase in a narrow way, to denote ideas or individuals especially closely associated with the figure of John Grierson, but in this more expansive sense. For present, introductory purposes, the 'Griersonian approach' to official film-making can be defined here as far-reaching in aspiration, scope and authorial intervention, while the 'CO approach' can be characterised as quite the contrary.

On 20 September 1939 the then British government inaugurated a Ministry of Information (MoI) charged with overseeing the production of wartime propaganda. However, the CO was uncomfortable with the MoI because the latter organisation was staffed to a considerable extent by personnel from outside the traditional civil service. This was also particularly the case for the Films Division of the MoI, which, in addition to employing a 'glittering array of intellectuals', also eventually housed the Crown Film Unit, staffed by Griersonians (some close to Grierson, others less so) long mistrusted by civil servants.[1] Shortly after the MoI came into being the CO, in reflexive response, also sought to establish a Colonial Film Unit (CFU), with a mandate to promote Britain and the war effort within the colonies. However, because the MoI was the sovereign body charged with overseeing wartime propaganda production, and against the innermost wishes of the CO, the CFU had to be established within the MoI rather than the CO. Thereafter, the CFU worked under the twofold command of Films Division and the CO, an awkward arrangement which led to difficulties; difficulties which became heightened when the Griersonians within the GPO Film Unit became more actively involved within the MoI, and, in particular, when the GPO Film Unit was transformed into the Crown Film Unit in December 1940. As the central government official film unit, Crown now had, or was perceived to have, the upper hand.

More rifts now developed within Films Division, between Griersonians and their allies, and more conservative figures associated with the CO and CFU. Differences came to the fore, and, at meetings of Films Division, arguments between these two camps broke out recurrently. The picture which emerges here is one of sizeable

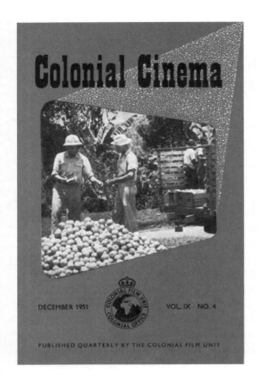

**Colonial Cinema**

DECEMBER 1951     VOL. IX   NO. 4

PUBLISHED QUARTERLY BY THE COLONIAL FILM UNIT

antipathy.[2] Typically, that antipathy was, as mentioned earlier, centred upon the different types of film the Griersonians and the CO-CFU wished to make. The frequently posited 'conservative' position – exemplified by the films of the CFU – was that MoI films should be cost-efficient, and have limited, directly achievable objectives. However, more ambitious members of the documentary film movement believed that such an approach was insufficient. So, for example, Paul Rotha complained that the conservative policy of producing '5-minute shorts', 'just so many crumbs at the table', was a betrayal of the 'documentary idea'.[3] This conflict between the two camps continued after the war, and influenced the diffusion of the British official film into the colonies and dominions of the British Commonwealth up to the late 1960s. As part of that diffusion, and for a variety of reasons, the Griersonians tended to end up in the larger territories, the CO-CFU in the smaller. While, therefore, the Griersonian 'documentary idea' nourished substantial 'growing points' in the dominions of Canada, Australia and New Zealand, no such strong and long-lasting Griersonian sustenance took root in the colonies of Hong Kong, Malaya and Singapore, within which, and in contrast, it was the CO-CFU tradition which prevailed.[4] However, that is not to say that *no* Griersonian encroachment occurred in these colonies. That was not the case, and this chapter will seek to set out what incursion did occur; how that intrusion was challenged by conservative forces, including those of the CO-CFU; and how Griersonism somehow managed to endure within the unpropitious colonial waters of the region.

That endurance was, initially at least, strongest in the colony of Malaya, a colony whose natural resources were of crucial importance for the ailing British economy during the postwar period. However, that very importance was also eventually to deal an ultimate blow to the Griersonian presence there. Malaya was simply too imperative a place for control of official film-making to be left in the hands of idealistic, but also unrealistic, Griersonians. However, the Griersonians were certainly there at the beginning of things, and in number. The Malayan Film Unit (MFU) was established in October 1946, and was the most important official film unit in the southeast Asia region, operating in Malaya, Singapore, British North Borneo and Sarawak; and with links to Hong Kong. There is a straight line to the Crown Film Unit and Griersonian tradition here. In 1938, Alexander Shaw, Ralph Keene and George Noble, then working for the Strand Film Unit, led by Paul Rotha, made *Five Faces of Malaya* for the Malayan

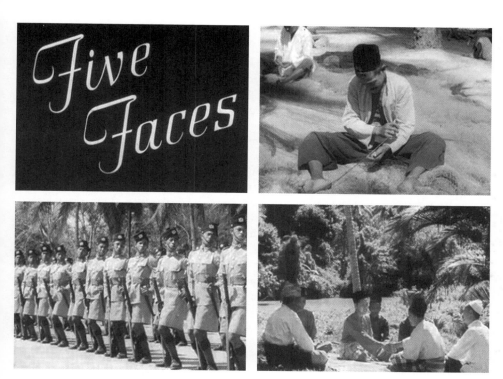

*Five Faces of Malaya* (1938)

government. In 1945 a group of film-makers from the Crown Film Unit also entered Malaya as part of the British Army Film Unit, remaining there until October 1946.[5] Over this period of around one year these film-makers, headed by the Griersonian Ralph Elton, trained up to nine locals in the hope that a permanent film unit could eventually be established. In what would also become the model of choice adopted in Singapore and Hong Kong, Elton hoped that a 'European' film-maker, a 'single knowledgeable man', would preside over such locals.[6] When the Army Film Unit disbanded in October 1946, and the Crown film-makers returned home, the group trained by Elton and the others formed the nucleus of the MFU. The unit was, therefore, initially staffed by people schooled in the documentary film movement ideal. However, this was not to last for long, as, to quote Max Weber, the 'iron cage of modernity' and 'instrumental rationality' quickly took hold in the colony, under the pressure of sectarian, and anticolonial Cold War conflict.

It was the 'Malayan Emergency' of 1948–60 which largely put paid to the Griersonian influence in the MFU. This was a period in which Cold War conflict with the Communist world was being fought throughout Southeast Asia, and, in Malaya, this clash took the form of a struggle between the colonial Malayan government and Chinese Communist insurgents. As mentioned earlier, the Malayan economy was extremely important to postwar Britain, and, because of this, Britain committed significant security resources in order to protect it. As part of this, official film-making was also turned into a weapon of the state. In March 1950 Stanley Hawes, then producer-in-chief of the Australian National Film Board, was commissioned to write a report on the future 'purpose and role' of the MFU in the context of the deteriorating military situation. Hawes had Griersonian connections, having worked with Paul Rotha at the Strand Film Unit during the 1930s, and with John Grierson himself at the National Film Board of Canada, between 1940 and 1946. However, Hawes certainly did not adopt a 'liberal' Griersonian approach in his report on the future of official film-making in Malaya. His view, similar, admittedly, to that adopted by Grierson in Canada during the war years, was that the official film now had to play a more effective and directive role. Production at the MFU would have to be greatly increased, and the remit of the films produced become more functional. Broad-based authorial articulations of the democratic 'documentary idea' were no longer considered appropriate.[7]

In September 1950, five months after the appearance of the Hawes Report, Hugh Carleton Greene arrived in Malaya to head the newly established Emergency Information Services (EIS), a body focusing on the production and dissemination of anti-Communist propaganda.[8] Although the MFU was not directly under the control of EIS, but part of the less instrumental Department of Information, Greene nevertheless intervened directly in the affairs of the unit from the off, insisting that it take on a more purposive role.[9] Neither Greene, nor other senior figures within the colonial government, liked what they saw coming out of the early 'Griersonian' MFU. The first head of the unit, H. W. Govan, had been a combat cameraman with the Army Film and Photographic Unit. He had also had substantial contact with Elton and the Crown film-makers during the early days of the unit. Govan displayed a propensity for making 'social-realist' films with a liberal edge. The colonial government disapproved of this, and his contract was cancelled in late 1950.[10] However, Govan's replacement, B. H. Hipkins, continued in the same vein, and he too was eventually sacked, in 1952.

Hipkins was personally removed by Sir Gerald Templer, who arrived in Malaya in February 1952, having been appointed by Winston Churchill as both high commissioner and director of operations under the Emergency, an unusual dual civilian-military command in a British colony, and one which reflected the felt severity of the crisis.[11] Like Greene, Templer also felt that the information services required rationalisation, and, in August 1952, he received a report from an A. D. C. Peterson, in which it was argued that what was needed was 'an extremely vigorous propaganda effort, carried out in accordance with a coherent plan, by all departments and levels of Government'.[12] In October 1952 Peterson was appointed director-general information services, and one of his first acts was to amalgamate the EIS and Department of Information, thus also bringing the MFU into the systematic campaigns of propaganda soon to be unleashed.[13] It is also at this point that an important figure for this chapter arrives on the scene. In the same month that the Peterson Report appeared Templer both sacked Hipkins, and appointed a Tom Hodge to the posts of director of Films Division and film advisor to the MFU. When he arrived in September, Hodge's primary responsibility was to ensure that, thereafter, official film-making would play a more focused role in helping shape 'the information services of this country into a single and more effective weapon against communism'.[14] Hodge went on to develop a reputation as a thoroughly pragmatic leader-producer, and, also one of the key players in the development of the British colonial official film in Malaya, Singapore and Hong Kong.

What effectively happened in Malaya between 1950 and 1957, when Malaysian personnel took over the MFU against the context of Malayan independence, was that a CO tradition replaced a Griersonian one. The key agent in this changeover, Hodge, had virtually no contact with the Griersonian tradition, but considerable contact with the CO-CFU tradition. Hodge joined the FO in 1939, and was part of the wave of new appointments at the beginning of the war to support the war effort. He first worked at the MoI between 1939 and 1942, helping to make unspecified 'educational films'. From 1942 to 1943 he was at the MoI in Chicago, and, between 1944 and December 1951, was director of films and publications at the British Information Service in New York, where he co-ordinated the making of 'public information' films aimed at the US audience.[15] After 1942, therefore, Hodge worked completely outside of any Griersonian tradition at all. His first appointment in Southeast Asia was as film advisor to the Commissioner General's Office Singapore in December 1951, on the basis of his background as a film propaganda co-ordinator, and against the context of further deteriorating military situations in Singapore and Malaya.

While all these events were taking place in Southeast Asia, back in London the CFU was struggling to survive against a context of budget cuts, and an expected cessation of all funding in 1955. The head of the CFU, from 1939 until the unit's demise in 1955, was William Sellers, an individual who had suffered at the hands of the Griersonians during the war, and who, consequently, bore them no great love during the postwar period. Hodge became close to Sellers from at least as early as 1950, and corresponded with him frequently over the 1951–60 period. As a consequence of this, and also his background in the FO, Hodge came to both associate himself with the CO-CFU stance on official film-making, and distance himself from the early 'Griersonian' camp that he had found at the MFU when appointed in Singapore in 1951. However, the Sellers–Hodge alliance was also to be reinforced by a third major player, at more or less the same time, when a John Lawrence Murray was appointed head of the Hong Kong Public Relations Office, in September 1950. From 1950 to the mid-60s Hodge would come to dominate the development of the official film in Malaya/Malaysia and Singapore, with Murray doing the same in Hong Kong. And behind both figures was Sellers, as a constant reference point and mentor. This exceptionally anti-Griersonian troika then proceeded to shape the progress of the British official film in the region up till at least the mid-1960s.

Murray had been a Fleet Street journalist who, like Hodge, joined the Foreign Office around the outbreak of the war. Murray went on to work as an FO press attaché in China. In 1944–5 he was stationed in Chongqing, central China, where the Chinese government had relocated following the Japanese invasion of 1937. In Chongqing Murray ran a 'largish film strip production unit'.[16] He did, therefore, have some experience with basic forms of official film-making. However, he was not overly sensitive towards the medium, being essentially a newspaperman. The film strips he would have made at that time – on the frontline of the Sino-Japanese conflict – would also have been highly tendentious and functional in character. Between 1945 and 1949–50 Murray was situated at the FO's Guangdong office, on the southern Chinese border with Hong Kong. He then became acting public relations officer in Hong Kong following the resignation of the permanent officer in the summer of 1950.

Once this position was made permanent in September, Murray immediately looked into the possibility of starting up an official film-making unit in Hong Kong. However, he did not seek the MFU's guidance in this because he had already fallen under the influence of Sellers. Even before he gained this post, civil servants at the CO in London had been in touch with Murray about how to develop the official film in Hong Kong; and, from late 1950 onwards, Sellers himself was in regular contact with him concerning this issue. Initially, Murray had thought that Hong Kong might look to the MFU for help. However, he was strongly persuaded against such a course of action by Sellers and the CO. As far as the latter was concerned, the MFU had been established completely outside the CO-CFU system, and by Griersonians; and, in 1950, neither the CO, nor Sellers, wanted official film-making in Hong Kong to fall into Griersonian hands. Murray quickly fell in with this point of view, writing, in 1951, that he now accepted the 'CO dictum' that involvement with the MFU would be a mistake.[17] Murray went on to correspond with Sellers and others at the CO throughout 1951, and what becomes clear from this correspondence is that Sellers and the CO tried hard to direct Murray away from the MFU, and towards the CO-CFU. However, Murray did not require much persuasion. In February 1952 Murray also came into contact with Hodge for the first time. While he was still in Singapore, and just weeks before taking over control of the Griersonian MFU, Hodge visited Murray in Hong Kong. At this meeting Hodge indicated that he had considerable respect for Sellers and the CFU.[18] Hodge and Murray struck up an immediate rapport, Murray finding Hodge 'refreshingly realistic'.[19] The term 'realistic' is significant here, and Murray's understanding of Hodge's position as 'realistic', would come to shape the development of the official film in Hong Kong. Hodge's 'refreshing realism' came with a health warning:

> His warning was in effect: Beware that you don't employ some bright young director or producer who is more interested in making a name for himself than in producing the kind of film that you want in Hong Kong ... who will want to produce one prize-winning documentary once a year in preference to a number of little films, none of them perhaps in the great cinema class, but which will do the job you want done ... . Hodge was full of praise for Sellers and the integrity of the CFU, but discouraging about the likelihood of recruiting an expert – particularly from the defunct Crown – who would put the job before his own career.[20]

So, Hodge warned Murray against appointing someone from Crown, and this reinforced the messages which Murray had been receiving from Sellers, and others at the CO since 1950. Murray now fully agreed that official film-making in Hong Kong should take the form of 'little films ... which will do the job'. Beyond this, though, Hodge's denigration of 'bright young directors' and Crown also led the bureaucratic Murray to the conviction that, unlike Crown and the MFU, film-making in Hong Kong should be controllably small in scale. In March 1952 Murray was offered a large sum of money by the World Health Organisation (WHO) to establish Hong Kong as a regional hub for health-based documentary film-making. But, by then, and under the influence of Sellers, Hodge and the CO, Murray had come to the firm conclusion that such a large-scale enterprise, which might come to resemble Crown and the MFU, was to be avoided. Writing in March 1952, shortly after meeting Hodge, Murray expostulated that he 'could see us being saddled with a young Crown Film Unit (or, perhaps worse still, Malayan F.U.) of our own ... . So I dug my heels in more firmly than ever.'[21] Murray did not want a large film unit staffed by experienced film-makers – possibly even recruited from Crown. By 1952, when it was disbanded, the Crown Film Unit had established a strong reputation among liberal-progressive circles, and many within those circles disapproved of its abolition. However, Crown had always been viewed with suspicion by the generality of civil servants. The tribulations which Sellers had encountered at the hands of Crown personnel during the war would also have been communicated to Murray. Because of all this, Murray turned down the WHO, and the opportunity to develop Hong Kong into a major international centre of documentary film-making was lost.

From 1952 onwards Murray continued to keep in close touch with both Hodge and Sellers. In 1955 he also noted the closure of the CFU and broached the idea of whether someone might be seconded from the unit to start up official film-making in Hong Kong, perhaps even 'Sellers himself'.[22] However, Sellers was re-employed within the CO as advisor on overseas film production, and Murray's chance to align himself formally with his mentor had passed.[23] Despite this setback, Murray continued his efforts to establish a film unit in Hong Kong, with these finally coming to fruition in 1959, when a small-scale Hong Kong Film Unit (HKFU) was eventually formed. However, it was a unit very much in the image of the Murray–Sellers–Hodge troika, and the CO-CFU tradition. This is made clear by Murray, writing to the CO in January 1955, reasserting views on the type of person required as films officer, views indistinguishable from those expressed by Hodge in 1952:

> I don't, above all, want a bright young arty Director who thinks he is going to make a little annual gem for the Venice or Edinburgh Festivals and lets the rest go hang. I want a real worker interested in films as a medium of propaganda and teaching who is prepared to make simple straight-forward documentary and educational films. And plenty of them! [24]

That 'real worker' turned out to be Ben Hart, who had previously worked as a film director with the Federal Information Service Film Unit in Lagos. Sellers had initially pointed Hart out to Murray, and, true to his guru, Murray also came to the conclusion that Hart 'was ideally suited for our particular job'.[25]

Murray's original vision for the HKFU had involved, among the making of many 'little films', the occasional production of what he termed 'prestige' projects. These would 'promote' Hong Kong in a more general way, and would be aimed at an international, as well as Hong Kong audience. Murray also imagined that these films would be outsourced, rather than made by his small-scale unit. In 1961 Murray had the opportunity to put this strategy into effect when the first of the unit's prestige films: *This Is Hong Kong* (1961), appeared. *This Is Hong Kong* was made in Hong Kong by the Hong Kong branch of Cathay Film Services, whose base was in Singapore; and the producer of the film was Hodge. Hodge had left the MFU in June 1957 in some acrimony as the unit 'Malayanised', and, later that year, he took up employment in the Cathay organisation, where he was appointed as director of both the feature-film arm Cathay-Keris and the documentary film arm Cathay Film Services. It was, perhaps, inevitable, then, that, in 1960, Murray would turn to Hodge, now ensconced in this senior commercial position, in order to initiate discussions about *This Is Hong Kong*.

*This Is Hong Kong*, does, however, suffer from the fact that it was outsourced. Largely made by people from outside Hong Kong, the film relies on a number of well-worn stereotypes of the city (the mix of ancient and modern, East and West, etc.). While one of the film's main themes is that of the fast-growing population, remarkably, no mention is made of the cause of that problem: refugees escaping from Communist China. Neither Murray nor Hodge had any desire to include such a controversial political subject in their film. The outsourcing also leads to a certain distance between the filmic narrative and the ordinary Chinese people depicted. In other parts of the film a rather condescending, superior attitude to the locals also comes through. However, the film does manage to attain a degree of human focus sometimes, and this may be put down to the intervention of its scriptwriter and director, Noni Wright. Wright (no relation to Basil Wright) was a New Zealander who had worked at the BBC in London during the war. She joined the MFU in 1953, shortly after Hodge, and left the MFU shortly after him, in 1958, to continue working under him at Cathay Film Services and Cathay-Keris. She died prematurely in a plane crash in 1964. *This Is Hong Kong* was probably Wright's most important film. However, and despite her input, the resulting film clearly bears the overall imprint of the Hodge–Murray model. *This Is Hong Kong* marked the apotheosis of that model within the HKFU, but an apotheosis which quickly faded away.

When Murray retired in 1963 he was replaced by Nigel Watt, a civil servant of whom little is known, other than that he had been Murray's deputy since at least 1960. Few developments of note happened over the next few years. However, in 1965 a potentially Griersonian space opened up when Ben Hart left the HKFU, and was replaced by Brian Salt. Salt had a much wider background in film than Hart, and had been connected to Gaumont British Instructional Film in the early 1950s, directing two films shot in Singapore: *Citizen of Singapore* (1950) and *Study of a Port* (1951). These films were shot in indirect association with the MFU during a period in which the unit still retained a Griersonian character. In the early to mid-1950s Salt was also appointed at the National Film Board (NFB) of Canada, in an attempt to improve technical standards there, particularly in the field of animation.[26] However, while there appears to be a Griersonian connection here, it seems that Salt was not particularly close to the Griersonians who then worked in the NFB.[27] All of this indicates familiarity with the nonfiction film, and, also, a potential Griersonian affiliation. However, this was not borne out in practice later, in Hong Kong. Salt also seems to have turned more towards fiction film-making as his career developed. In 1958, for example, he made the drama-documentary children's film *Toto and the Poachers*, which won a prize at the Venice Film Festival of that year; and, just before coming to Hong Kong, he was employed as a director on the British television Scotland Yard police series *Gideon's Way* (1964).

Salt's first major production at the HKFU, *The Magic Stone: A Legend from Hong Kong* (1965), was an exercise in drama-documentary. Designed to be another HKFU 'prestige' film, *Magic Stone* was a twenty-four-minute colour film which could be compared in style to some of the 'story documentaries' produced by the GPO Film Unit and Crown Film Unit during the 1930s and 40s. However, the comparison ends there and, with its use of quaint local legends, the film had no social, and very little aesthetic significance. Salt only stayed at the HKFU until 1968, and his departure may have been hastened by the furore that broke out over *Magic Stone*, which was not only panned by local critics as a 'flop' and an 'embarrassment', but also managed to recoup only $5,000 of its $400,000 production cost.[28] This was a huge loss for a British colonial official film, and created a considerable scandal, leading to both Watt and Salt coming under substantial criticism.[29] Nevertheless, during his period in charge of the HKFU, Salt did manage to steer the style of the HKFU significantly away from Murray's Hodge-influenced approach.

After Salt left, local cameraman Charles Wang became head of the HKFU, though he stayed for only a few months more, before leaving to work in the private sector. Despite this, though, Wang was an important figure and his cinematography distinguishes some of the most affecting films to emerge from the HKFU. A case in point here is the 1965 *A Race against People*, which deals with the problems of population growth, and house construction. While the narrative is relatively prosaic, the quality of the photography in *A Race against People* is of a high order, and many individual shots seem to have the detailed organised quality associated with still photographs. Clearly, given the fact that none of the scenes were rehearsed, Wang must have waited a while to obtain the image he wanted. A particular kind of compositional structure also emerges in these shots and sequences. The shot and sequence are often divided (by the wall of a building, or such), and have close-ups in the extreme foreground, and lines of direction leading to small areas of light and sky at the very back of the image. In addition to such composed photography, Wang is also able to capture the rhythms of movement well, as he waits for striking rhythms to emerge from people passing before the camera, rhythms which generate effective pictorial patterns. All of this is also reinforced by Wang's use of colour, which is both subtle and organised. At the level of narrative and plot, *A Race against People* may have been about what the commentary refers to as the 'gigantic project' of the rehousing scheme, but Wang also focuses on the lesser, more human-oriented details of the Cantonese culture. Many shots, for example, show children, playing or sleeping; and many others show women caring for these children, while carrying out everyday tasks. Here, it could also be argued, the imagery does not really support the narrative in the way that the film's sponsors would have expected. Wang is clearly an individual whose work merits closer study, and, in many ways, *A Race against People* could be said to be superior to the supposed flagship signature film of the HKFU, *This Is Hong Kong*.

The final period of the HKFU dates from the point that Wang's successor, Albert Young, took over its leadership in late 1968, to its demise, some time in 1973. It also seems that it was in this period, when the unit went into decline, that Griersonian moments become more evident. It is almost as though, as television loomed on the horizon, the unit became simultaneously less important to government officials, and more autonomous in terms of its film-making practice. Much praise here has to go to Nigel Watt, who both protected his film-makers when they were criticised, and gave them a longish leash. This was very different from the Murray era. During this final period a few more significant films were made, and, like Wang, Albert Young also figures as perhaps one of the most important film-makers to emerge from the HKFU. This was not the view of government officials at the time, however, who felt that Young had played his part in the unit's failure.[30] However, looking at the films produced under Young reveals that it was their Griersonian qualities that these officials disliked most, as becomes clear when a comparison is made between two of the last films to emerge from the HKFU: the outsourced *Port of Hong Kong* (1972), and the more 'Griersonian', and film unit-produced, *The Sea and the Sky* (1972).

*Port of Hong Kong* suffers from many of the problems which afflict outsourced official films. Made by a London-based company with no intimate understanding of Hong Kong, it is forced to rely on stereotypical conceptions of the colony. The result is verbose generalisation about 'British pragmatism', 'Chinese common sense', etc. Lack of a close knowledge of the subject also forces the film to rely heavily on statistics, while the jarring soundtrack, which can only be described as a sort of 'rock-Chinese', is generally inappropriate. *The Sea and the Sky*, however, is another matter. The original press briefing suggests that the film was expected to delineate 'the changes that have taken place in the fishing industry in Hong Kong since the end of the Second World War'.[31] What comes to mind here, in terms of this expectation, is John Grierson's 1929 film *Drifters*, and the comparison with *Drifters* is also apposite in other respects too. As with *Drifters*, the officials who commissioned *The Sea and the Sky* were expecting a standard account. In both cases, those officials got nothing of the kind. *The Sea and the Sky* is, actually, strongly reminiscent of *Drifters*, and follows the same narrative model of Grierson's iconic film. As in *Drifters*, the focus is not on the fishing industry, but on *one* trawler. We also see the various stages of the process of fishing, from catching, to selling at market, and later distribution of the product. Like *Drifters*, *The Sea and the Sky* also concentrates on a few individuals, in this case, one family, and its montage sequences of the ship's engines and machinery are similar to those in *Drifters*. *The Sea and the Sky* is definitely not an example of 'decline', though it is obvious why it would have disappointed government officials. Young's film does not really 'promote' anything very clearly, and is actually an exercise in *film-making*, rather than promotion, and one which drifts well away from its remit. This is an intimate study, showing a sensitivity for the fishermen and the natural environment. These film-makers are clearly *familiar* with Hong Kong, and this makes a difference. *The Sea and the Sky* was a considerable achievement for the HKFU as late as 1972, only a year before it ceased operations.

This chapter clearly shows that the development of the official film in Malaya, Singapore and Hong Kong was directly affected by the rivalry which broke out between the Griersonian and CO-CFU traditions during World War II. It is equally evident that, in these colonies, it was the CO-CFU tradition which prevailed. As Malaya and Singapore gained independence in the late 1950s and early 60s, the British official film also faded away from these places, as decolonisation ushered in a localisation which affected production. However, as Britain's 'last colony', the British official film continued in Hong Kong long after it disappeared from Malaya and Singapore. Ironically, though, it was not the expatriates who finally introduced an effective Griersonian element into the HKFU, but the locals: Wang and Young. As the HKFU faded away, that element was also carried on into the field of the television documentaries produced by the Hong Kong public broadcasting organisations which appeared in the late 1960s and early 70s. Here, Rotha's 'documentary idea' finally took root, as critical, investigative documentary films began to appear on subjects such as poverty, drug-taking and social inequality.

# NOTES

1.  Nicholas Pronay and Jeremy Croft, 'British Film Censorship and Propaganda Policy during the Second World War', in James Curran and Vincent Porter (eds), *British Cinema History* (London: Weidenfeld and Nicolson, 1983), p. 153.
2.  Jo Fox, 'John Grierson, His "Documentary Boys" and the British Ministry of Information, 1939–42', *Historical Journal of Film, Radio and Television* vol. 25 no. 3 (2005), p. 357.
3.  Ibid., p. 360.
4.  Ibid., p. 364.
5.  Hassan Abdul Muthalib, 'End of Empire: The Films of the Malayan Film Unit in 1950s British Malaya', in Lee Grieveson and Colin MacCabe (eds), *Film and the End of Empire* (London: BFI, 2011), p. 178.
6.  Ralph Elton, Letter to Basil Wright, January 1946 (BFI Special Collections, London). Quoted in Tom Rice, 'Voices of Malaya', February 2010, *Colonial Film Website*, www.colonialfilm.org.uk.
7.  Muthalib, 'End of Empire', p. 181.
8.  Hugh Carleton Greene, brother of novelist Graham Greene, was associated with the British documentary film movement during the 1930s and 40s. An ex-journalist, he was appointed head of the BBC German Service in 1940, dealing with political propaganda and covert intelligence. In 1945, he became head of the BBC East European Service. He arrived in Malaya in September 1950 as head of the Emergency information services before returning to Britain and the BBC in the mid-1950s. He was appointed director-general of the BBC in 1960.
9.  Muthalib, 'End of Empire', p. 184.
10. Ibid.
11. Peter Lowe, *Contending with Nationalism and Communism: British Policy towards South-East Asia* (London and New York: Palgrave Macmillan, 2009), p. 48.
12. A. D. C. Peterson, quoted in Kumar Ramakrishna, '"Transmogrifying" Malaya: The Impact of Sir Gerald Templer (1952–4)', *Journal of Southeast Asian Studies* vol. 32 no. 1 (2001), p. 87.
13. Ramakrishna, '"Transmogrifying" Malaya', p. 86.
14. 'Child-Prodigy Gets an Expert', *Straits Times* vol. 6 no. 10 (6 October 1952), p. 9.
15. Editorial commentary for Tom Hodge, 'Eleven Years of the Malayan Film Unit: A Record of Solid Achievement', *Educational Screen and Audio Visual Guide* vol. 36 no. 10 (1957), p. 538.
16. Hong Kong Records Service (HKRS) PRO/204, Murray, Letter to Carstairs, 19 March 1952, para. 12.
17. HKRS IS 8/576/51, Murray, Memo to Hon. Colonial Secretary, 19 March 1951, para. 2.
18. HKRS PRO 204, 6/516/52, Murray, Letter to Carstairs, 19 March 1952, para. 15.
19. Ibid.
20. Ibid., paras 16–17.
21. Ibid., para. 7.
22. HKRS 160/1/23, Reorganisation of the Public Relations Office, PRO 1/2, Murray, Letter to S. H. Evans, CO, London, 19 March 1955, paras 10–11.
23. Rosaleen Smyth, 'The Post-war Career of the Colonial Film Unit in Africa, 1946–1955', *Historical Journal of Film, Radio and Television* vol. 12 no. 2 (1992), p. 175.
24. HKRS 160/1/23, para. 9.
25. Ibid.; 'Post of Film and Photographic Officer', PRO 5/7/30, Memo, Murray to Hon. Colonial Secretary, 21 August 1957, para. 8.

26. Gerald G. Graham, *Canadian Film Technology 1896–1986* (Newark, NJ: University of Delaware Press, 1989), p. 114.
27. Ibid.
28. *China Mail*, 28 April 1969.
29. Peter Moss, *No Babylon: A Hong Kong Scrapbook* (Lincoln, NE: iUniverse, 2006), p. 38.
30. Ibid., p. 41.
31. HKRS 70-6–580 (1) 1961–73, Government Information Services Press Briefing on *The Sea and the Sky* (1972), 30 September 1971.

## REFERENCES

'Child-Prodigy Gets an Expert', *Straits Times*, 6 October 1952, p. 9.

*China Mail*, 28 April 1969.

Elton, Ralph, Letter to Basil Wright, January 1946 (BFI Special Collections, London). Quoted in Tom Rice, 'Voices of Malaya', February 2010, *Colonial Film Website*, www.colonialfilm.org.uk.

Fox, Jo, 'John Grierson, His "Documentary Boys" and the British Ministry of Information, 1939–42', *Historical Journal of Film, Radio and Television* vol. 25 no. 3 (2005), pp. 345–69.

Graham, Gerald G., *Canadian Film Technology 1896–1986* (Newark, NJ: University of Delaware Press, 1989).

HKRS PRO 204, 6/516/52, Murray, Letter to Carstairs, 19 March 1952.

HKRS 160/1/23, Reorganisation of the Public Relations Office, PRO 1/2, Murray, Letter to S. H. Evans, CO, London, 19 January 1955.

HKRS 160/1/2/3, Reorganisation of the Public Relations Office, 'Post of Film and Photographic Officer', PRO 5/7/30, Memo, Murray to Hon. Colonial Secretary, 21 August 1957.

HKRS 70-6–580 (1) 1961–73, Government Information Services Press Briefing on *The Sea and the Sky* (1972), 30 September 1971.

Hodge, Tom, 'Eleven Years of the Malayan Film Unit: A Record of Solid Achievement', *Educational Screen and Audio Visual Guide* vol. 6 no. 10 (1957), pp. 538–9.

Hong Kong Records Service [HKRS] IS 8/576/51, Murray, Memo to Hon. Colonial Secretary, 19 March 1951.

Lowe, Peter, *Contending with Nationalism and Communism: British Policy towards South-East Asia* (London and New York: Palgrave Macmillan, 2009).

Moss, Peter, *No Babylon: A Hong Kong Scrapbook* (Lincoln, NE: iUniverse, 2006).

Muthalib, Hassan Abdul, 'End of Empire: The Films of the Malayan Film Unit in 1950s British Malaya', in Lee Grieveson and Colin MacCabe (eds), *Film and the End of Empire* (London: BFI, 2011), pp. 177–98.

Peterson, A. D. C., quoted in Kumar Ramakrishna (2001), '"Transmogrifying" Malaya: The Impact of Sir Gerald Templer (1952–54)', *Journal of Southeast Asian Studies* vol. 32 no. 1 (2001), pp. 79–92.

Pronay, Nicholas and Croft, Jeremy, 'British Film Censorship and Propaganda Policy during the Second World War', in James Curran and Vincent Porter (eds), *British Cinema History* (London: Weidenfeld and Nicolson, 1983), pp. 144–63.

Smyth, Rosaleen, 'The Post-war Career of the Colonial Film Unit in Africa, 1946–1955', *Historical Journal of Film, Radio and Television* vol. 12 no. 2 (1992), p. 175.

# 7

# Grierson in Canada

*Zoë Druick*

There are special reasons why the national use of films should have fitted so quickly and progressively into the Canadian scene. The need to achieve unity in a country of many geographical and psychological distances is only one of them and not the most important. More vital, I think, is the fact that Canada is waking up to her place in the world and is conscious, as few English-speaking countries seem to be, that it is a new sort of place in the world. A medium which tries to explain the shape of events and create loyalties in relation to the developing scene is welcome. I cannot otherwise explain the measure of support we have been given, nor the long-range hopes that have been placed in this school of projection we have set up.[1]

John Grierson

John Grierson's influence on Canada is perhaps the best known of all the stories of the film producer's international work through his long career, although the breadth of the case is rarely considered. Although his time in Britain was plagued by political frustrations, and his influence in other places was piecemeal and spotty, in Canada one may trace a compelling and unequivocal line of influence. From his drafting of the Film Act in 1938 that established the National Film Board (NFB) of Canada the following year, through his serving as the inaugural head of the NFB for the duration of the war (1939–45), to his return as a professor in the late 1960s, in time to influence a new generation of media makers and educators, Grierson's legacy in Canada is both extensive and irrefutable.

But of course the story is not quite so simple. The logics that established documentary as a tool of empire in Britain were congruent with the liberal imperialist perspectives of the ruling elites in Canada and Grierson was accepted into the Canadian fold to do particular kinds of work under clear constraints. If production studies teaches us to consider the structures that organise the creation of media institutions and texts, we might consider Grierson in Canada in such a light: as one actor in a network of relationships that included the new medium of state documentary itself and new communicative infrastructures.[2] Film, especially educational film, was seen to be an expedient way to express international relationships and create national bonds in the tenuously forming new welfare state. The creation of the genre of documentary was an attempt to harness new media to social reorganisation, using technology to support and enhance new models of governance. The new managerial state required publicity, branding and information services. On all three counts, documentary fit the bill.[3] As James Beveridge so aptly put it: 'the time in Canada was ripe for Grierson's idea'.[4]

This chapter on Grierson's effect in Canada is thus subdivided into three sections corresponding to Canadian cinema before, during and after Grierson's involvement. In this way, I hope to emphasise Grierson's role, while also placing it into a larger national and international context.

## CANADIAN CINEMA BEFORE GRIERSON

If Grierson had not existed, Canada, it seems, would have had to invent him. Before Grierson's visits in 1931 and 1938, Canada had already developed one of the most impressive government film services in the world.[5] While the Soviet Union outdid Canada perhaps in terms of the quality of its state-sponsored film-making, the Canadian Government Motion Picture Bureau (CGMPB) holds claim to being the first national film production unit in the world, and was easily the most impressive in the British empire. Established in the final year of World War I (1918), formalising the multifarious strands of government film production that had emerged in different departments during the conflict, thousands of short films and newsreels were produced under the auspices of the CGMPB during its quarter-century lifespan, mainly for international distribution and on topics pertaining to trade, tourism and immigration.[6] However, despite its precocious establishment, the CGMPB was not the first government film organisation in Canada. That honour goes to the Ontario Motion Picture Bureau (1917), carrying out 'educational work for farmers, school children, factory workers, and other classes' in Canada's most populous province.[7] As provinces vied for control of visual education with the federal government and American film suppliers, a number of other provinces followed Ontario's lead.[8]

The CGMPB attempted to make the story a national one in a country defined by its regions. Its most ambitious film project was the seventy-minute feature, *Canada, from Coast to Coast*, made for the Imperial Economic Conference in Ottawa in 1932, representing the apotheosis of a type of film-making developed in relation to national self-presentation at international trade exhibitions.[9] Canada had discovered earlier than most that government-funded film-making was a necessary form of communication in a fledgling modern state, especially one where education was a provincial responsibility. But after 1929, the bureau struggled with the expensive conversion to sound equipment during the austere days of the Depression. More than that, it had lost its vision. By the mid-1930s, Canada's government film production decidedly needed reinvigoration and new rationales for funding.

Beginnings in fiction feature film-making in Canada were thwarted in part by the establishment of a British policy: the screen quota of 1928. According to the terms of this quota, 15 per cent of films shown in British cinema theatres had to be made in Britain or elsewhere in the British empire. This spawned a gold rush of mainly American production companies seeking to make films in Canada that would qualify. These so-called quota quickies were known for their cheap production values and their often salacious B-movie storylines. More often than not they were produced by companies with very short lifespans of only a film or two. Victoria, BC-based Central Films was one of the exceptions, producing twelve films between 1935 and 1937.[10] Although the quota law, which lasted until 1937, failed to produce a thriving

Commonwealth film industry, it did succeed in facilitating a service-oriented Canadian commercial film industry. As with all service-based industries, when the foreign market dried up, so too did the production.

In the mid-1930s, a young film enthusiast named Ross McLean was working as secretary to the Canadian high commissioner Vincent Massey in London. There he heard of the film work being sponsored by Britain's government at the General Post Office, and saw first hand the purposive group that met at the London Film Society. He happened to hear a presentation by John Grierson and was inspired to write a report to Massey, recommending a government film service for Canada that would take into account the documentary work being done in Britain. Massey, a strong supporter of the Canadian arts, forwarded McLean's recommendations on to Ottawa, advocating:

> there should be an independent and exhaustive survey made of our present film publicity activities: the nature of the existing films, the method of their distribution, and suggestions for improvement and extension. I think [for] such a survey to be worth while [it] should be made by an experienced and qualified film expert. There is no one whom I know who could do this better than Mr. John Grierson, probably the leading documentary film producer in the United Kingdom.[11]

Yet, even before this influential report, Grierson had visited Canada and other British dominions in 1931 on behalf of the British government in order to determine how film might be used to cement imperial preference. Britain's Empire Marketing Board, founded in 1926, was tasked with the job of creating imperial sentiment in the colonies and dominions, and had been the first government home of the documentary film movement. Canada, fragmented into regions, sparsely populated for its great size and poised on the border of the US, provided a particularly pressing instance of a nation in need of a healthy mass-media presence that might act as a national cultural bond in the way that the railway had been an attempt to forge an economic one.[12]

Two interests were converging in this area: just as Britain was interested in the strength of Canada's empire sentiments, Canada was interested in the British imperial model because it answered some of the problems facing the federal government. A national film board might be an effective policy instrument to bind together a fragmented, multilingual, multicultural federation in much the same way that the British empire was attempting to overcome its own internal contradictions and divisions, using new media to rebrand itself as the Commonwealth.[13] Moreover Canada was well placed – literally next door to the United States – to open a front in the information war against the US film and newsreel industries for the hearts and minds of British subjects everywhere.

These two forces converged in the pairing of Grierson and Canada. Grierson's own version of the story was as follows:

> In June 1938, I was invited by the Film Committee of the Imperial Relations Trust to make a survey of film developments in Canada. The Imperial Relations Trust had allocated certain limited funds for the encouragement of educational and cultural film services between Great Britain and the Dominions. Its Film Committee required further information on which to

base its recommendations. At the same time, I was invited by the Canadian Government to make a survey of the film activities of the various Government departments and particularly of the operations of the Canadian Government Motion Picture Bureau, with a view to developing the supply of Canadian films to Great Britain and improving the distribution machinery at Canada House.[14]

The emphasis on distribution and exhibition of films in London is noteworthy. Before the film board, the vast majority of Canadian government film production had been for international screens. By the late 1930s, civil servants in the Department of Trade and Commerce were concerned that both South Africa and Australia were producing better film propaganda for distribution in the UK. Upon arriving in Canada in May 1938, Grierson met with representatives of the Department of Trade and Commerce, as well as of Mines and Resources, Fisheries, Post Office, Agriculture, Transport, National Defence, External Affairs, Finance, Justice, Labour, National Revenue, and Pensions and National Health. After assessing the state of Canadian government film production, Grierson pressed for centralisation in a single agency. With his recommendation of the establishment of the film board, Grierson neatly combined the needs of both interested parties. As a convenient panacea to Canada's political problems that also served the needs of imperial cohesion, Grierson recommended 'a central organization which would co-ordinate demands and through which the Canadian Government and British and Dominion film interests could work'. This vision, combining technological efficiency with Canadian nationalism and liberal imperialism was the background to the formation of the National Film Board of Canada by the Department of Trade and Commerce in 1939. In the event, the film board was given the following structure: a dominion film commissioner as CEO, two ministers of the federal government, three senior civil servants and three private individuals with interests in film. Notably, no provincial representatives were officially included. Although both organisations operated simultaneously for a while, in 1941 the NFB successfully absorbed the CGMPB.

With the founding of the film board, Canada's previous attempts at government film-making, as well as its role as a location for British and American narrative feature films, not to mention many forms of amateur, industrial, educational and other forms of non-theatrical film-making, distribution and exhibition, were seemingly struck from the story of national cinema history. For instance, at the moment of the NFB's formation the two largest distributors of non-theatrical film in Canada were General Films Ltd and Associated Screen News, neither of which have yet received the historical analysis they deserve. On the international scene, national cinema had come to mean distinctive commercial feature films or a state film project and, once Canada had adopted the latter, the histories of diverse cinema production and circulation in Canada were submerged, some unable to re-emerge into view for many decades to come.[15]


## THE GRIERSON YEARS

By all accounts Grierson did not particularly wish to become stuck in Canada for six years during the war. However, with no competing offers from Britain, he didn't have many options.[16] He brought with him to Canada for varying lengths of time a number of well-known British and international film-makers, including Arthur Elton, Stanley Hawes (who went on to head the film production unit in Australia), Stuart Legg and Norman McLaren. Luminaries Robert Flaherty, Joris Ivens, Boris Kaufman and Basil Wright all made brief appearances. Along with additional local film-makers hastily hired, Grierson proceeded to establish a thriving, bilingual film organisation, producing two theatrical newsreels, *Canada Carries On* (1940–59) and *World in Action* (1942–5), as well as hundreds of stand-alone short films.[17] A producer of mainly short subject documentaries and animations, the NFB quickly became a force on Canadian and international film screens, both theatrical and non-theatrical.[18] (Remarkably, during the war, Grierson was able to negotiate space in American-owned theatre chains, a feat never accomplished in Canada before or since.) Although war became a dominant topic in NFB films, many others aimed to 'show Canada to Canadians', in the words of the Film Act, highlighting stories about Canadians and government agencies in different parts of the country. As early as 1943, a plan to prepare Canada for the reconstruction of peacetime meant numerous films emphasising cultural cohesion and good citizenship in the face of Canada's different languages, religions and regions.

Prior to national broadcasting, national media distribution was one of Canada's great challenges. Most Canadians lived close to the American border and were receiving broadcast signals from their southern neighbours. It was one thing to reach Canadians through cinemas, but how could the majority of the population who lived in rural locations be included in a national project? Grierson's answer was to develop non-theatrical distribution infrastructure. Travelling cinemas were not new to Canada. The earliest commercial cinema distribution in Canada had been accomplished by cinema entrepreneurs tracing geographically manageable circuits at the turn of the century.[19] And educational film circuits were established in the early twentieth century by the extension departments of universities. One early adopter, the University of Alberta, established its division of visual instruction in 1914 and within a decade its reach had become so extensive that by 1926, over 50 per cent of the province, approximately 300,000 people, was being reached in this way.[20] These large audiences were brought into contact with films at screenings held in farming associations, churches and schools. In addition, the department ran a number of film circuits in the mid-1920s, predating by two decades the National Film Board circuits. The Film Board nationalised this pre-existing regional infrastructure, relying heavily on the model developed by the university extension programmes.[21] Donald Buchanan, a founder of the National Film Society, designed the distribution plan for the NFB with direct reference to the University of Alberta.[22]

A relevant sidebar to this story concerns the assignment of the position of film commissioner. Edward (Ned) Corbett, director of the University of Alberta's wide-reaching extension programme from 1928–36 and executive member of the National Film Society, was lured away from Alberta in 1935 to become the inaugural head of the Canadian Association of Adult Education, an important lobby group that would go on to forge an alliance with the NFB. When Grierson and others suggested that a Canadian be offered the inaugural post of film commissioner, the consensus was that it should be Corbett. Only when he declined was the position actually offered to John Grierson.

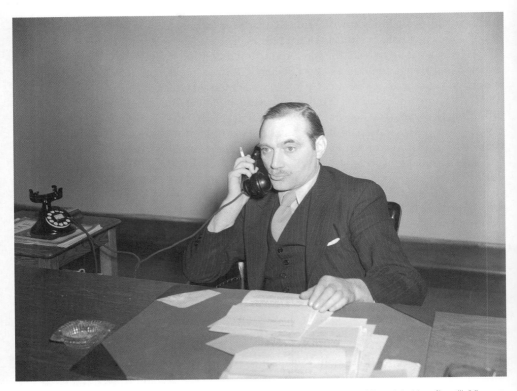

Grierson during his stint as Canadian government film commissioner, 1943 (Visual and Sound Archives film stills/Library and Archives Canada/PA-169782)

Under Grierson, the NFB adopted non-theatrical methods used in Alberta and elsewhere in the British empire, travelling with government films and electricity generators to remote locations.[23] Scaling up the provincial experiments, between 1942 and 1946, the NFB ran an impressive slate of film forums targeting immigrants in rural schools, churches, community centres as well as workers at factories and trade-union halls. Itinerant projectionists, known as field men, drove film equipment and electric generators around circuits in each of the provinces. In January 1942, thirty rural circuits, each consisting of twenty rural communities, began monthly screenings reaching approximately 250,000 Canadians.[24] Films were employed to stimulate and monitor political discussion and to inform citizens about modernisation projects, such as new agricultural methods and the electrification of farms. Just as they were in other parts of the British empire, film programmes were composed of a set of short films about agricultural improvement, profiles of various 'peoples of Canada', propaganda and amusing morality tales. Sometimes the educational films preceded a Hollywood narrative feature. As with colonial film circuits, projectionists sent monthly reports back to the film board detailing the screenings.[25]

Midway through 1942, the NFB began trade-union circuits, sponsored in part by the Workers' Education Association and Labour Congresses of Canada, which were accompanied by trailers meant to spark debate on issues such as absenteeism at the workplace and the role of the worker in wartime production.[26] Discussion trailers were included with all the trade-union circuits as well. Customised for the purpose of engaging viewers with government policies were a series of fifteen trailers made under the series title, 'Getting the Most out of a Film'. Tailored for each programme and social issue with which they dealt, and only a few minutes long, the trailers showed audiences at film screenings debating the ideas presented in the films with a panel of experts. At the end, the moderator turned to the camera in order to address the viewing audience with the injunction to continue the discussion after the screening. These trailers were notable attempts to provide audiences with examples of how engaged audiences might begin discussing the issues posed by a film.

Starting in 1943, the same year that, under Grierson's leadership, the National Film Board combined forces with the Wartime Information Board, the NFB instituted industrial circuits. Established to reach people working in munitions plants and other industrial settings, by 1944 there were 385,000 viewers per month with 3,000 screenings.[27] Statistics for 1944, at the height of the circuits, show that there were thirty-seven full-time NFB operators. Over a quarter of a million people were reached by 1,574 shows in January of that year alone.[28] Worker screenings were carefully managed to try to offset unrest and channel it into patriotic productivity. Screenings were also the site of observation and surveillance, with audience tastes and reactions monitored and reported upon.

In sum, making newsreels from a Canadian perspective and films about Canada and its role in the conflict of World War II was an important addition to the nation's cinema culture. But no less important was the mode of circulation. Bringing films to Canadians in their workplaces, churches and community centres across the country was a concerted effort to consolidate a national infrastructure for non-theatrical distribution, in many ways as important as screenings in cinemas. This commitment was successful in bringing Canadian *content* to Canadian screens (not always the case in provincial film circuits), and a triumphant way to overcome provincial powers in the regulation of education and cinema screens alike.

But, despite the energetic output, the Grierson years were in some ways an ambivalent time for Canadian film-makers. As a rule, wartime NFB films contained no credits. The corporate identity of the board and the public service it was providing were thought by Grierson to be of more importance than individual recognition (although he himself received a great deal). This means that many film-makers who worked at the board have been left out of stories about Canadian cinema: in many cases, it requires dedicated archival work to discover who actually worked on particular films. One compelling perspective on this conundrum comes from Graham McInnes (1912–70), who wrote a memoir of his stint at the wartime film board. McInnes's account holds some surprises, which challenge the value of non-theatrical cinema promoted by Grierson. Take, for example, this admission of ambivalence about Grierson's watchword, non-theatrical documentary film:

> Though Grierson was himself a born teacher and evangelist, and though it was an article of
> faith with him that film, documentary film, was the great teaching and information medium
> of the future, he could never get *us* really excited over non-t[heatrical].[29]

The film-makers at the board often wished to make theatrical films, and contained their ambitions within officially sanctioned parameters.[30] Some exceptional film-makers, like Norman McLaren, were able to leave an authorial mark on government work. Many others laboured in relative obscurity.

## AFTER GRIERSON

Perhaps because of his passion for state propaganda and his involvement with trade-union and immigrant education, not to mention his implication in international networks, after the war Grierson was swept up in a wave of anti-Communist hysteria and was forced out of Canada under a cloud of political paranoia. In 1945, Soviet cipher clerk Igor Gouzenko went to Canadian police with evidence of spying in Ottawa. Among papers examined by the investigators was the cryptic message, 'Freda to the Professor through Grierson'. The professor was thought to be Dr Raymond Boyer, the chair of the Canadian Association of Scientific Workers (CAScW) and Freda was the name of Grierson's secretary at the NFB. Prime Minister Mackenzie King declared the War Measures Act, suspending civil rights, and appointed a royal commission to investigate the many people accused of being Communist agents or sympathisers.[31]

In the aftermath, the film board's supposed access to sensitive government information rendered it a 'vulnerable agency,' a surprising categorisation which put the board in the same security category as the Prime Minister's Office, the Privy Council, External Affairs, Defence and the Royal Canadian Mounted Police (RCMP); every employee was required to pass security clearance.[32] After being called up in front of a tribunal, Grierson's contract was not renewed and over the next few years, until the official RCMP investigation began, untold numbers of NFB employees, most on temporary three-month contracts, were quietly let go. Personal gatherings were infiltrated and monitored; some NFB employees were placed under surveillance.[33]

The Gouzenko Affair has the distinction of being the first Communist witch hunt of the Cold War. The paranoia and surveillance it provoked would not exhaust itself until Grierson's successor, Ross McLean (a supporter since prewar London), was unceremoniously replaced by *Maclean's* editor Arthur Irwin in 1950. The NFB was subjected to a management review, and then thoroughly investigated and exonerated by a multi-party parliamentary committee in 1952.[34]

This political intrigue coincided with striking of the Royal Commission on National Development in the Arts, Letters and Sciences in 1949 and its two years of hearings. This commission was chaired by the same Vincent Massey who had played a part in the early history of the NFB. Many thought that this assessment of the arts in Canada would sound the death knell for the board, but even before the commission reported, a revised Film Act was passed in 1950. Over the previous decade, the NFB had done valuable work consolidating Canadian nonfiction film production *and* circulation and to lose it now would mean relinquishing a significant aspect of cinema culture in the nation. For the short term at least, Canada had sunk all its ambitions for cinema into its state projects.

In part the NFB was saved because its initiatives in film and citizenship melded well with the postwar institutionalisation of citizenship education as advocated by the

UN through its cultural agency UNESCO. Film was given exemplary status in UNESCO discussions as its educational applications extended from demonstrations of practical skills through the circulation of information about national ways of life to the documentation of national cultural production. In this way, we can see that Grierson was just one actor in the complex field in which the National Film Board took shape. Even the discrediting of its leader and the board's subsequent vulnerability did not spell its demise.[35]

With the rural, school, industrial and trade-union circuits of the war period, the NFB had centralised and institutionalised the concept of non-theatrical film screenings. At the end of the war, as film circuit funding dried up, local film councils were established across Canada with the sponsorship and participation of the National Film Board, the bulk of their showings comprised of NFB films. Prints of film board films also circulated widely through public and school lending libraries.[36] While before the war there had been fifteen film libraries in Canada, mostly run by provincial departments of education and university extension programmes; by war's end the number had increased more than fourfold to seventy-three, with more than a third in public libraries.[37]

After being let go from the film board (and put on a US blacklist), Grierson decamped for Paris, where he was invited to become UNESCO's director of mass communications and public information.[38] At the first UNESCO meeting on mass media and international culture, Grierson gave an address in which he linked strong mass-media infrastructure to national reconstruction and development.[39] Echoing and updating the strategy of empire communication for non-commercial and non-theatrical film, the film subcommission recommended that UNESCO should act as an international clearing house of information: 'UNESCO could only act efficiently as an International Clearing House if each country has a national film information centre or national film committee.'[40] The exemplar of this kind of instrumental national film organisation had been achieved in Canada and, even as it served as an example for the rest of the world, Canada continued to build its national film policy around regional cohesion and its international film policy around international understanding.


## CONCLUSIONS

In the last years of his life, from 1969–71, Grierson gave classes at McGill University (sometimes held in his hotel room). His popular classes on film and mass communication ranged widely from discussions about classical philosophies of knowledge to the social responsibility of media-producers.[41] This teaching coincided with the establishment of a new programme at the NFB headed by American George Stoney, the Challenge for Change/Societé nouvelle (1967–80). Associated with media activism of the student and civil rights movements, the programme emphasised the use of process-based film-making to help bring about progressive social change. Perhaps its best-known productions were associated with the conflict surrounding a government plan to relocate a small community of Newfoundlanders from their home on Fogo Island. The Fogo process, as it came to be known, has become a well-regarded approach to using cameras in communities to help participants develop consensus on solutions to collective problems (and harking back to pre-NFB film circuits, it was connected with Newfoundland's Memorial University extension programme). Other films addressed issues of poverty and social inequality in cities and towns across Canada.[42] And, although the programme itself stressed its connection with the Grierson legacy, Grierson himself reportedly had a 'love–hate relationship' with it.[43]

In a screening of one of the Fogo films to Grierson's class at McGill, Colin Low recalls Grierson's condemnation:

> So the film-maker is nothing but a tool, a camera operator or projectionist in the formulation of these problems and solutions. What about the intelligence, world experience, expensive education that could be brought to these people? If you have no opinions, no ideas, no commitments, nothing to say, why further burden these poor folks, whose lives are difficult enough, with manipulative nonsense?[44]

However, with a typical eye to posterity, in a published assessment Grierson was kinder to the programme, lauding its grassroots sensibilities. 'Its local portraits are better than any I know, and its use of the film to ease and give order to local discussion is important.'[45]

It is perhaps no coincidence that Grierson ended his career in Montreal, near to the NFB headquarters, which are also based in that city. Indeed, the invitation had been initiated by Hugo McPherson, NFB film commissioner at the time. This is consistent with Jack Ellis's observation that the NFB chairmen continued to reach out to Grierson for advice and consultation in the decades after he had left the country.[46] And, indeed, while in Montreal, he was sought out by others as well, such as the newly formed Canadian Radio and Television Commission, for his views on information and by McGill University, for his views on technology in the university.[47] Grierson's ideas continued to shape Canadian perspectives and policies on technology and society.

It is a paradox of the Grierson effect that perhaps only in a marginal nation and former dominion was Grierson able to establish the British vision for liberal imperialism, albeit with local inflections. Not only were its films widely distributed and admired, the Canadian Film Board example was used extensively throughout first British and later UNESCO film information to show how film could be engaged for public service. For instance, *The Factual Film*, a British report from 1947, carries an appendix on the National Film Board of Canada which includes the Canadian Film Act in its entirety, as well as a concise history of the institution and its programmes of theatrical and non-theatrical films.[48] Until at least the 1960s, numerous UNESCO mission reports on film in developing countries took the Canadian film board as their model. In an interview with James Beveridge, Grierson pointed this out:

> the greatest export of the Film Board has been the Film Act itself. It's been translated into many languages, it's become the model of serious intention by the cinema in the service of government, all over the world. The success of the Film Board has been in its helping [the Department of] External Affairs to present the Canadian capabilities. The Film Board has been important in saying to countries of very different kinds, all over the world, that the film is an instrument of great importance in establishing the patterns of the national imagination.[49]

Yet the very prominence and prestige of the National Film Board has had the paradoxical effect of sidelining other film activity undertaken in Canada before, during and after the heyday of the NFB, an oversight only just beginning to be addressed more than seven decades after Grierson's arrival in Ottawa. Although successful feature films have been few and far between, industrial and educational film production thrived in Canada, as did a range of experimental, amateur, small-gauge and other kinds of non-theatrical production. Other documentary traditions, some born of the broadcasting model, some more experimental, blossomed.[50] Indeed, part of the film board's legacy was the training of hundreds of aspiring film-makers in public service and the idiom of state documentary, even if they would go on to inflect it in different ways. Grierson's legacy is so bound up with accomplishments in Canadian cinema, particularly those of a documentary and educational nature, that to tease them apart is all but impossible. Yet the field of production studies teaches us to consider the structural aspects of media production, beyond the famous individuals. Media institutions and texts alike are created in complex semantic and material fields, where co-operating and competing interests vie to create logics of emergence and sustenance. If Grierson himself had a somewhat rocky experience in Canada (albeit with a triumphant ending), his ideas about mass communication took root at a pivotal time in Canadian policy formation and have made themselves into an inextricable part of the evolution of Canadian national cinema and its histories.

## NOTES

1. John Grierson, 'The Documentary Idea: 1942', in Forsyth Hardy (ed.), *Grierson on Documentary* (London: Faber and Faber, 1979), p. 248.
2. Vicki Mayer, Miranda Banks and John Caldwell, 'Introduction: Production Studies: Roots and Routes', in Vicki Mayer, Miranda Banks and John Caldwell (eds), *Production Studies: Cultural Studies of Media Industries* (New York: Routledge, 2009), pp. 1–12.
3. See Zoë Druick, *Projecting Canada: Government Policy and Documentary Film at the National Film Board* (Montreal and Kingston: McGill-Queen's University Press, 2007); Scott Anthony and James Mansell (eds), *The Projection of Britain: A History of the GPO Film Unit* (London: BFI, 2011).
4. James Beveridge, 'Grierson and Distribution', in *John Grierson and the NFB*, proceedings of a conference held at McGill University, 29–31 October 1981 (Toronto: ECW Press, 1984), p. 29.
5. Other British delegates had visited Canada in the 1920s, although details are murky. See Beveridge, 'Grierson and Distribution', 30.
6. Charles Backhouse, *Canadian Government Motion Picture Bureau, 1917–1941* (Ottawa: Canadian Film Institute, 1974); Peter Morris, *Embattled Shadows: A History of Canadian Cinema 1895–1939* (Montreal: McGill-Queen's University Press, 1978), p. 133.
7. Ibid., p. 138.
8. Other active provinces were BC, Manitoba, Saskatchewan and Nova Scotia. The Ontario Film Bureau was closed in 1934. See Morris, *Embattled Shadows*, pp. 149, 152.
9. Ibid., p. 167.
10. Peter Morris and Andrew McIntosh, 'Quota Quickies', in *The Canadian Film Encyclopedia*, http://tiff.net/CANADIANFILMENCYCLOPEDIA/Browse/bysubject/quota-quickies.

11. Library Archives Canada RG 20, Vol. 578, p. 169, A-581 pt 1, Vincent Massey to Secretary of State for External Affairs, 18 November 1937, p. 2.

12. Maurice Charland, 'Technological Nationalism', *Canadian Journal of Political and Social Theory* vol. 10 no. 1 (1986), pp. 196–220.

13. Lee Grieveson and Colin McCabe (eds), *Empire and Film* (London: BFI, 2011).

14. John Grierson Archive, G4:4:10, 'Canadian Film Activities', 3 July 1939, p. 1.

15. The exception is Peter Morris's indispensable *Embattled Shadows*. Inspired by the Orphan Film Symposium, a new collection addresses these missing stories in Canadian cinema history. See Zoë Druick and Gerda Cammaer (eds), *Cinephemera: Archives, Ephemeral Cinema and New Screen Histories in Canada* (Montreal: McGill-Queen's University Press, 2014). See also the Canadian Educational, Sponsored and Industrial Film Archive, screenculture.org/cesif.

16. He did visit the UK at least twice, in 1941 and 1944, as well as convalescing in Florida after a heart attack in 1942. See Jack Ellis, 'John Grierson's Relation with British Documentary during World War Two', in *John Grierson and the NFB*, pp. 63–4; H. Forsyth Hardy, 'Democracy as a Fighting Faith', in *John Grierson and the NFB*, pp. 89–90. See also Nicholas Pronay, 'John Grierson and the Documentary – 60 Years On', *Historical Journal of Film, Radio and Television* vol. 9 no. 3 (1989), pp. 227–46; and Jo Fox, 'John Grierson, His "Documentary Boys" and the British Ministry of Information, 1939–1942', *Historical Journal of Film, Radio and Television* vol. 25 no. 3 (August 2005), pp. 345–69.

17. *World in Action* films were shown in India, South Africa, Latin America and the US, fulfilling to some degree the empire dream of decentralised information services to rival American news. See D. B. Jones, *Movies and Memoranda: An Interpretive History of the National Film Board of Canada* (Ottawa: Canadian Film Institute, 1981), p. 36.

18. Graham McInnes, *One Man's Documentary: A Memoir of the Early Days of the National Film Board* (Winnipeg: University of Manitoba Press, 2004).

19. Paul Moore, 'Mapping the Mass Circulation of Early Cinema: Film Debuts Coast-to-Coast in Canada in 1896 and 1897', *Canadian Journal of Film Studies* vol. 21 no. 1 (Spring 2012), pp. 58–80.

20. Ralph Clark, *A History of the Department of Extension at the University of Alberta, 1912–1956*, Dissertation, University of Toronto, 1985, p. 100.

21. Involved universities included the University of British Columbia, Alberta, Manitoba, Prince Edward Island, New Brunswick and Laval. See also C. W. Gray, *Movies for the People: The Story of the National Film Board's Unique Distribution System* (Ottawa: National Film Board of Canada, 1977), p. 219.

22. Beveridge, 'Grierson and Distribution', p. 34.

23. It had been concluded at the Imperial Conference of 1926 that non-theatrical distribution was the way around American dominance of the cinemas of the world. For more see Zoë Druick, 'Mobile Cinema in Canada in Relation to British Mobile Film Practices', in Wolfram R. Keller and Gene Walz (eds), *Screening Canadians: Cross-cultural Perspectives on Canadian Film* (Marburg: Universitatsbibliothek, 2008), pp. 13–33.

24. Dorothy Annesley, 'Films and Canadian Public Libraries', *ALA Bulletin* vol. 40 no. 6 (June 1940), p. 195.

25. There were similarities with the contemporaneous British Mass Observation project. See Michael Pickering and David Chaney, 'Democracy and Communication: Mass Observation 1937–1943', *Journal of Communication* vol. 36 no. 1 (Winter 1986), pp. 41–56; Jeffrey

Richards and Dorothy Sheridan (eds), *Mass-Observation at the Movies* (London: Routledge and Kegan Paul, 1987); John Baxendale and Chris Pawling, 'Representing the People: The Documentary Film Movement and Mass Observation in the Thirties', in *Narrating the Thirties* (London: Macmillan, 1996), pp. 17–45.

26. Gray, *Movies for the People*, p. 52.

27. Yvette Hackett claims 1942, but the NFB Annual Report for 1944–5 states that the circuits were launched in 1943. See Y. Hackett, 'The National Film Society of Canada, 1935–1951: Its Origins and Development', in Gene Walz (ed.), *Flashback: People and Institutions in Canadian Film History* (Montreal: Mediatexte Publications Inc., 1986), p. 149.

28. Library Archives Canada, Ottawa, RG 28 A, Vol. 1/2, file 3-C2-1-3, 'Industrial and Trade Union Circuits Report for January 1944', p. 3.

29. McInnes, *One Man's Documentary*, p. 48, italics in original.

30. See also Zoë Druick, '"Non-theatrical with Dreams of Theatrical": Paradoxes of a Canadian Semi-documentary Film Noir', *Canadian Journal of Film Studies* vol. 12 no. 2 (2004), pp. 46–63.

31. Paul Dufour, '"Eggheads" and Espionage: The Gouzenko Affair in Canada', *Journal of Canadian Studies* vol. 16 (Fall–Winter 1981), p. 190.

32. Reg Whitaker and Gary Marcuse, *Cold War Canada: The Making of a National Insecurity State, 1945–1957* (Toronto: University of Toronto Press, 1994), p. 252.

33. Ibid., p. 248.

34. *National Film Board: Survey of Organization and Business Administration* (Parliamentary Papers, 1950); Special Committee on the National Film Board, *Minutes of Proceedings and Evidence* (Ottawa: Queen's Printer, 1952). Aside from Grierson, known victims of the chill and purge included film-makers Evelyn [Spice] Cherry and Lawrence Cherry and activist Stan Rands, who was attempting to unionise NFB employees; most of the victims never came forward with their stories. See Whitaker and Marcuse, *Cold War Canada*, p. 253; Len Scher, *The Un-Canadians: True Stories of the Blacklist Era* (Toronto: Lester Publishing Ltd, 1992), p. 85. See also Amy Knight, *How the Cold War Began: The Gouzenko Affair and the Hunt for Soviet Spies* (Toronto: McClelland & Stewart, 2005).

35. At time of writing, the board still exists, although its role has largely shifted from a film producer to a film archive. See Zoë Druick 'Sampling Heritage: The NFB's Digital Archive', in Druick and Cammaer, *Cinephemera*.

36. Massey Archives, Toronto, B1987-0082/345 file 04, 2, Ruth Cameron, 'Submission from the Federation of British Columbia Film Councils', n.d. See also Charles Acland, 'Patterns of Cultural Authority: The National Film Society of Canada, 1938–1941', in *Canadian Journal of Film Studies* vol. 10 (Spring 2001), pp. 2–27; James Beveridge, 'Grierson and Distribution', p. 35.

37. Annesley, 'Films and Canadian Public Libraries', p. 195.

38. See Gary Evans, *John Grierson and the National Film Board: The Politics of Wartime Propaganda* (Toronto: University of Toronto Press, 1984), pp. 224–68; Jack Ellis, *John Grierson: Life, Contributions, Influence* (Carbondale and Edwardsville: Southern Illinois University Press, 2000), pp. 229–39.

39. Ibid., p. 229.

40. UNESCO, *Report of the Commission on Technical Needs in Press, Radio, Film, Following the Survey in Twelve War-devastated Countries* (Paris: UNESCO, 1947), p. 38.

41. Colin Low, 'Grierson and "Challenge for Change"', in *John Grierson and the NFB*, p. 96.
42. See Thomas Waugh, Michael Brendan Baker and Ezra Winton (eds), *Challenge for Change: Activist Documentary at the National Film Board of Canada* (Montreal and Kingston: McGill-Queen's University Press, 2010).
43. Low, 'Grierson and "Challenge for Change"', p. 95.
44. Ibid., p. 99.
45. John Grierson, 'Memo to Michelle about Decentralizing the Means of Production', in Waugh et al. (eds), *Challenge for Change*, p. 63.
46. Ellis, *John Grierson*, p. 321.
47. Ibid., p. 324.
48. Arts Enquiry, *The Factual Film* (London: Oxford University Press, 1947), pp. 228–37.
49. Cited in 'John Grierson', in *John Grierson and the NFB*, p. ix.
50. David Hogarth, *Documentary Television in Canada: From National Public Service to Global Marketplace* (Montreal and Kingston: McGill-Queen's University Press, 2002); Zoë Druick, *Allan King's* A Married Couple (Toronto: University of Toronto Press, 2010).

## REFERENCES

Acland, Charles, 'Patterns of Cultural Authority: The National Film Society of Canada, 1938–1941', *Canadian Journal of Film Studies* vol. 10 (Spring 2001), pp. 2–27.

Annesley, Dorothy, 'Films and Canadian Public Libraries', *ALA Bulletin* vol. 40 no. 6 (June 1940), pp. 195–8.

Anthony, Scott and James Mansell (eds), *The Projection of Britain: A History of the GPO Film Unit* (London: BFI, 2011).

Arts Enquiry, *The Factual Film* (London: Oxford University Press, 1947).

Backhouse, Charles, *Canadian Government Motion Picture Bureau, 1917–1941* (Ottawa: Canadian Film Institute, 1974).

Baxendale, John and Chris Pawling, 'Representing the People: The Documentary Film Movement and Mass Observation in the Thirties', in *Narrating the Thirties* (London: Macmillan, 1996), pp. 17–45.

Beveridge, James, 'Grierson and Distribution', in *John Grierson and the NFB*, proceedings of a conference held at McGill University, 29–31 October 1981 (Toronto: ECW Press, 1984), pp. 29–41.

Charland, Maurice, 'Technological Nationalism', *Canadian Journal of Political and Social Theory.* vol. 10 no. 1 (1986), pp. 196–220.

Clark, Ralph, *A History of the Department of Extension at the University of Alberta, 1912–1956*, Dissertation, University of Toronto, 1985.

Druick, Zoë, '"Non-theatrical with Dreams of Theatrical": Paradoxes of a Canadian Semi-documentary Film Noir', *Canadian Journal of Film Studies* vol. 12 no. 2 (2004), pp. 46–63.

Druick, Zoë, *Projecting Canada: Government Policy and Documentary Film at the National Film Board* (Montreal and Kingston: McGill-Queen's University Press, 2007).

Druick, Zoë, 'Mobile Cinema in Canada in Relation to British Mobile Film Practices', in Wolfram R. Keller and Gene Walz (eds), *Screening Canadians: Cross-cultural Perspectives on Canadian Film* (Marburg: Universitatsbibliothek, 2008), pp. 13–33.

Druick, Zoë, *Allan King's* A Married Couple (Toronto: University of Toronto Press, 2010).

Druick, Zoë, 'Sampling Heritage: The NFB's Digital Archive', in Zoë Druick and Gerda Cammaer (eds), *Cinephemera: Archives, Ephemeral Cinema and New Screen Histories in Canada* (Montreal: McGill-Queen's University Press, 2014).

Druick, Zoë and Gerda Cammaer (eds), *Cinephemera: Archives, Ephemeral Cinema and New Screen Histories in Canada* (Montreal: McGill-Queen's University Press, 2014).

Dufour, Paul, '"Eggheads" and Espionage: The Gouzenko Affair in Canada', *Journal of Canadian Studies* vol. 16 (Fall–Winter 1981), pp. 188–98.

Ellis, Jack, 'John Grierson's Relation with British Documentary during World War Two', in *John Grierson and the NFB*, proceedings of a conference held at McGill University, 29–31 October 1981 (Toronto: ECW Press, 1984), pp. 62–76.

Ellis, Jack, *John Grierson: Life, Contributions, Influence* (Carbondale and Edwardsville: Southern Illinois University Press, 2000).

Evans, Gary, *John Grierson and the National Film Board: The Politics of Wartime Propaganda* (Toronto: University of Toronto Press, 1984).

Fox, Jo, 'John Grierson, His "Documentary Boys" and the British Ministry of Information, 1939–1942', *Historical Journal of Film, Radio and Television* vol. 25 no. 3 (August 2005), pp. 345–69.

Gray, C. W., *Movies for the People: The Story of the National Film Board's Unique Distribution System* (Ottawa: National Film Board of Canada, 1977).

Grierson, John, 'The Documentary Idea: 1942', in Forsyth Hardy (ed.), *Grierson on Documentary* (London: Faber and Faber, 1979), pp. 248–58.

Grierson, John, 'Memo to Michelle about Decentralizing the Means of Production', in Thomas Waugh, Michael Brendan Baker and Ezra Winton (eds), *Challenge for Change: Activist Documentary at the National Film Board of Canada* (Montreal and Kingston: McGill-Queen's University Press, 2010), pp. 61–5.

Grieveson, Lee and Colin McCabe (eds), *Empire and Film* (London: BFI, 2011).

Hackett, Yvette, 'The National Film Society of Canada, 1935–1951: Its Origins and Development', in Gene Walz (ed.), *Flashback: People and Institutions in Canadian Film History* (Montreal: Mediatexte Publications Inc., 1986), pp. 135–68.

Hardy, Forsyth, 'Democracy as a Fighting Faith', in *John Grierson and the NFB*, proceedings of a conference held at McGill University, 29–31 October 1981 (Toronto: ECW Press, 1984), pp. 86–94.

Hogarth, David, *Documentary Television in Canada: From National Public Service to Global Marketplace* (Montreal and Kingston: McGill-Queen's University Press, 2002).

Jones, D. B., *Movies and Memoranda: An Interpretive History of the National Film Board of Canada* (Ottawa: Canadian Film Institute, 1981).

Knight, Amy, *How the Cold War Began: The Gouzenko Affair and the Hunt for Soviet Spies* (Toronto: McClelland & Stewart, 2005).

Library Archives Canada RG 20, Vol. 578, p. 169, A-581 pt 1, Vincent Massey to Secretary of State for External Affairs, 18 November 1937, p. 2.

Library Archives Canada, Ottawa, RG 28 A, Vol. 1/2, file 3-C2-1-3, 'Industrial and Trade Union Circuits Report for January 1944', p. 3.

Low, Colin. 'Grierson and "Challenge for Change"', in *John Grierson and the NFB*, proceedings of a conference held at McGill University, 29–31 October 1981 (Toronto: ECW Press, 1984), pp. 95–103.

Massey Archives, Toronto, B1987-0082/345 file 04, 2, Ruth Cameron, 'Submission from the Federation of British Columbia Film Councils', n.d.

Mayer, Vicki, Miranda Banks and John Caldwell, 'Introduction: Production Studies: Roots and Routes', in Vicki Mayer, Miranda Banks and John Caldwell (eds), *Production Studies: Cultural Studies of Media Industries* (New York: Routledge, 2009), pp. 1–12.

McInnes, Graham, *One Man's Documentary: A Memoir of the Early Days of the National Film Board* (Winnipeg: University of Manitoba Press, 2004).

Moore, Paul, 'Mapping the Mass Circulation of Early Cinema: Film Debuts Coast-to-Coast in Canada in 1896 and 1897', *Canadian Journal of Film Studies* vol. 21 no. 1 (2012), pp. 58–80.

Morris, Peter, *Embattled Shadows: A History of Canadian Cinema 1895–1939* (Montreal: McGill-Queen's University Press, 1978).

Morris, Peter and Andrew McIntosh, 'Quota Quickies', in *The Canadian Film Encyclopedia*, http://tiff.net/CANADIANFILMENCYCLOPEDIA/Browse/bysubject/quota-quickies.

*National Film Board: Survey of Organization and Business Administration.* Canadian Parliamentary Papers, 1950.

Pickering, Michael and David Chaney, 'Democracy and Communication: Mass Observation 1937–1943', *Journal of Communication* vol. 36 no. 1 (Winter 1986), pp. 41–56.

Pronay, Nicholas, 'John Grierson and the Documentary – 60 Years On', *Historical Journal of Film, Radio and Television* vol. 9 no. 3 (1989), pp. 227–46.

Richards, Jeffrey and Dorothy Sheridan (eds), *Mass-Observation at the Movies* (London: Routledge and Kegan Paul, 1987).

Scher, Len, *The Un-Canadians: True Stories of the Blacklist Era* (Toronto: Lester Publishing Ltd, 1992).

Special Committee on the National Film Board, *Minutes of Proceedings and Evidence* (Ottawa: Queen's Printer, 1952).

UNESCO, *Report of the Commission on Technical Needs in Press, Radio, Film, Following the Survey in Twelve War-devastated Countries* (Paris: UNESCO, 1947).

Waugh, Thomas, Michael Brendan Baker and Ezra Winton (eds), *Challenge for Change: Activist Documentary at the National Film Board of Canada* (Montreal and Kingston: McGill-Queen's University Press, 2010).

Whitaker, Reg and Gary Marcuse, *Cold War Canada: The Making of a National Insecurity State, 1945–1957* (Toronto: University of Toronto Press, 1994).

# 8

# Imperial Relations with Polynesian Romantics: The John Grierson Effect in New Zealand

*Simon Sigley*

When Gordon Mirams described *New Zealand on the March* (1938) as 'an excellently photographed survey of the progress made on public works in New Zealand',[1] he seemed to be giving substance to a flattering assertion that New Zealand 'led the way in the documentary film movement', inspiring the work of the Empire Marketing Board.[2] *New Zealand on the March* was undoubtedly 'good propaganda for Labour' but it was also 'a very creditable piece of documentary film of real intrinsic interest. The huge modern machines now being used on public works in this country will, I have no doubt, come as a revelation to many people.'[3]

Like the film, this chapter aims to reveal. In the sketchy accounts of John Grierson's visit to New Zealand in early 1940, it is typically assumed that his presence and the report he submitted to the government led straightforwardly to the establishment of the National Film Unit (NFU) in 1941; from which a distinctive documentary tradition developed, informed by concepts of nationhood, democratic citizenship and a progressive political agenda. But Grierson's role in the establishment of the NFU cannot be so neatly packaged; for one thing, the need to inform New Zealanders about World War II and the nation's role both on the battlefield and the home front had already led to changes at the government film studios in Miramar. For another, senior ministers in the Labour administration were not convinced of the need to commit scarce material resources to regular film production in wartime; nor did they properly appreciate what the 'creative treatment of actuality' meant in terms of documentary film. Furthermore, alongside this 'nationalist' agenda, there were unspoken imperial aspects to Grierson's mission in New Zealand.

While Grierson certainly impressed some people, the nature and extent of his influence on public policy, government ministers, high-ranking civil servants and film-makers are not well known. What little we do know draws on unreliable memory, old research and assumed wisdom rather than on evidence.[4] In fact, the mundane, yet significant, details of Grierson's visit, such as when he arrived, whom he saw and what he set out to achieve have not been clearly established in the several brief recycled accounts of his sojourn among those he later affectionately dubbed 'Polynesian romantics'.[5]

Drawing on hitherto undiscovered archival material in New Zealand and Scotland, this chapter documents Grierson's New Zealand visit and the impact he had on his contemporaries; establishes his role in the creation, organisation and production of the NFU; and highlights a neglected component of British 'soft power': the non-theatrical distribution and exhibition of inter-empire documentary films and newsreels – a vital element in maintaining British interests in its former colonies, colonies whose allegiances were being steadily diluted and disputed by the US. While not typically associated with Grierson's visit, the organisation of a network for the non-theatrical distribution and exhibition of British films led to the creation of the National Film Library (NFL) in 1942, a necessary institution in shoring up and extending imperial relations; Grierson knew there was little point in making British films if imperial audiences could not see them.

The notion that New Zealand had once been at the forefront of documentary practice was a discursive gambit probably made by Grierson when he had lunch on 21 April 1939 with Gilbert McAllister, then general manager of the New Zealand Public Relations Council in London.[6] Grierson's introduction to McAllister resulted from a higher-level meeting earlier in April between Sir Stephen Tallents and William Jordan, the New Zealand high commissioner to the UK. Both Tallents and Grierson were working for the Imperial Relations Trust, a body set up in 1937 to strengthen economic, political and cultural connections between the UK, its colonies and the dominions of Australia, Canada, New Zealand and South Africa. According to Grierson, the film committee of the IRT existed primarily 'to aid the flow of films between Great Britain and the Dominions' and disposed of 'certain limited funds' to facilitate the creation of such a network.[7] Securing audiences for British propaganda was thus a primary object of Grierson's work.

Grierson's complimentary gambit was swiftly followed by a more sober assessment of current New Zealand government film in the light of British practice, which had seen 'the documentary film [make] enormous advances both technically and from the propagandist point of view'.[8] It was no longer sufficient to make films that simply highlighted natural splendours or promoted New Zealand butter as 'solid sunshine'. A more directive approach was called for in projecting the nation and its goods overseas, especially in British cinemas. McAllister concurred; he could not recall seeing a New Zealand film in 'a first-class cinema, while the references to New Zealand in newsreels, such as British Movietone News, are most infrequent, and do not begin to compare in number with references to Australia for example'.[9] Grierson also assured McAllister that there were even larger audiences in non-theatrical circuits, comprising various libraries, roadshows run by large corporations, Workers' Educational and Travel Associations, official exhibitions, film societies and schools.

Such an array of publics available for publicity purposes excited the appetites of New Zealand officials, ministers and civil servants, looking for ways to increase sales and boost the country's image. Frank Langstone, Minister of Trade and Publicity, and Walter Nash, Minister of Finance, were both in London in June 1939, with the latter engaged in arduous talks with the British about an urgently needed £16 million loan.[10] Both men were in strong sympathy with the IRT proposal to send Grierson. Indeed, prior to his departure for the UK in April, Nash had talked with J. H. Mason, the general manager of New Zealand Theatres, about increasing the production and distribution of New Zealand films locally and in the UK.[11] Langstone assured McAllister of his department's intention 'to associate itself [with Grierson] in every possible way'. As far as he was concerned, Grierson could 'arrange anything he cared to with "Imperial Relations Trust" which I understand is ready and willing to help in work of this character'.[12]

Prime ministerial sanction for Grierson's visit was given in May 1939[13] but the degree to which this constitutes an 'invitation' by the New Zealand government is moot. Certainly, it was not a local initiative. At best, the New Zealand government accepted an IRT initiative because it saw the need to modernise its use of film as publicity material; at worst, it simply complied with imperial wishes. There were compelling material reasons for such compliance, one of the most pressing being an urgent need to borrow a lot of money from a reluctant British Exchequer so as to avoid a debt crisis and pay for the government's considerable investment in public works and social welfare. British responses to Labour's 'social experiments', e.g., the Social Security Act 1938, ranged from 'impatience to scorn to outright hostility'.[14]

## THE ADVENT OF GRIERSON

Grierson's month-long sojourn began in Auckland on 16 February 1940.[15] He then travelled by rail to Wellington in the company of the acting manager of the government film studios, A. A. Mackenzie, who apprised him of the facilities he later visited, galvanising the much reduced staff and their 'sometimes drooping souls' with his enthusiasm for their work.[16] A ministerial welcome party allowed him to meet many of Wellington's political and cultural elite, most particularly Peter Fraser (deputy prime minister, *inter alia*, and soon to become prime minister upon the death of Michael Savage on 27 March 1940), Sir Thomas Hunter (psychology professor at Victoria University and vice chancellor of the University of New Zealand), J. T. Paul, director of publicity in the prime minister's office, Dr C. E. Beeby (then assistant director of education), and L. J. Schmitt, general manager tourist and publicity.

Grierson was hardly a household name, even in progressive circles, so it was incumbent upon the 'happy few' to advertise his imminent coming along with his views on documentary. In July 1939, *National Education* reprinted a condensed version of Grierson's text on 'The Dramatic Factor in Education', in which the need to engage the viewer's cognitive and affective responses was argued as indispensable in any effective pedagogical practice involving documentary film. 'Films in Schools' took up an emergent nationalist baton by arguing that decolonisation required an attention to the specificities of place and time: 'The Dominion Museum's photographs of New Zealand's Railways, Post Office, waterfronts and productive industries should all be on films.'[17] The widely read *New Zealand Listener* published 'Documentaries for the Dominions: John Grierson, Noted Film Producer, in New Zealand', a week after his arrival. The article explained what documentaries were, why Grierson was there and what he had already recently achieved in Canada with government film (see Zoë Druick's chapter).[18] On 8 March, the same weekly magazine published the transcript of 'Drama on Your Doorstep', Grierson's landmark radio talk, given on 28 February 1940. Strategically, the talk addressed the civic importance of the mass media, specifically radio and documentary, in modernity where it had become impossible for any one person to properly comprehend how complex societies functioned; whence the need for communication intermediaries of the sort Grierson had become. His flattering introduction to the programme (for New Zealand audiences) recalled the advice he had received from Mollie Chilcott of Strand Films in London, who had spoken with Nash and Langstone in 1939: 'I think the best angle from which to approach them is that of putting their [social] experiment on record, encouraging the English working man and generally telling the world the story of their own particular social development.'[19]

Grierson obliged: 'You have done things of tremendous international importance in this country with your social experiments. There are audiences all over the world who would want to see and hear about these things.'[20] Topics of interest to other countries included 'the work of Sir Truby King, your grassland research, your Plunket system, your schools, your housing, your approach to economic problems'.[21] Appealing to his listeners' progressive tendencies and proselytising urges, Grierson's introduction summoned them to act: 'it is your right and your duty – and your urgent need – to show democracy in action by bringing these things to life'.[22] Radio and films offered a method of doing that. 'Both had dramatic quality; both were able to bring things to life quickly; both were able to give people a living sense of the giant organisations which served them.'[23] This was a topic that the Labour government had a particular sensitivity to, given that it was responsible for the creation of 'the most comprehensive system of public health, pensions, and superannuation in the world'.[24]

Grierson's workload during the twenty-eight days he spent in New Zealand was extensive and included long discussions with senior ministers. He wrote a twenty-nine-page report covering the state's varied use of documentary film production, distribution and exhibition, and added a four-page personal memo to Peter Fraser, the real power of the Labour administration: 'National Information Services: Special Problems'.[25] This action plan accentuated three points:

1 *Marketing* involved constructing a series of positive images of the country so that 'New Zealand's contribution to the living whole of the Commonwealth should be brought into the imagination of the United Kingdom';
2 *State managerialism* led to large departments staffed by civil servant 'lifers' who worked lazily. Offsetting this perception involved 'bringing alive to the public the problems and achievements of the organisation', as well as drawing attention to 'the dramatic part communications as a whole … played in modern life';
3 *Nationalism*: films could create a national consciousness of issues that rose above the narrowness of domestic 'bread and butter' politics.

Such considerations may have seemed rather distant with the world at war and, in any case, insofar as selling New Zealand produce to the UK was concerned, there was little urgency, as the British government had already offered on the declaration of war in early September 1939 to buy the country's entire exportable surplus of meat and dairy products.[26] As far as speaking to the nation was concerned, radio was already under government control, having been nationalised in 1935[27] and emergency regulations introduced in September 1939 gave the government great powers of censorship, control of all property, persons and institutions. Moreover, this 'constitutional autocracy' elicited a strong national consensus.[28]

With Fraser's attention captured by more pressing matters (a cancer-ridden prime minister soon to die, ructions among the left-wing of the party and an impending Easter conference), the report produced no immediate action plan for either of

Grierson's twin objectives: government film production and the efficient non-theatrical circulation of inter-empire documentary; but he was hardly expecting one. His longer-term vision anticipated progressive implementation of his recommendations. In a letter to Tom Baird, a British distribution specialist and colleague from his GPO period, Grierson wrote that New Zealand was 'on its way to co-ordinating and developing its Government film activities and producing a really quite creative policy', and forecast that the country would be heard from 'quite effectively in about three years time'.[29] In a letter to his patron, Sir Stephen Tallents, he anticipated that: 'With five years to follow up, periodically, the development of production and distribution services in each Dominion, we can make a living reality of it.'[30]

Moreover, while the spirit in government circles was apparently willing, the necessary 'flesh' (in the form of suitable staff) was not; a very real shortage of competent personnel at the senior executive and administrative levels plagued the civil service. Very careful and detailed planning was required to implement the government's relatively vast (for New Zealand) programme, but 'the public servants (like the ministers) were not, in general, very well educated nor experienced in sophisticated administration'.[31] For Grierson, there was no one who combined the necessary civil-service qualities with effective (far less imaginative) film knowledge.[32] In a lengthy memo penned on the eve of his departure from New Zealand for Australia, he pointed out that he had

> strongly urged that they take the brightest young civil servant they can spare and let me give him an intensive training for six months in Canada, England and the United States. It will be fatal if they take a second rater who has not the necessary imagination, or bring in a technical film man who has not the necessary vision of film as an instrument of the new public information.[33]

In other letters sent to superiors and colleagues in the immediate wake of his New Zealand sojourn, Grierson expressed his confidence that the tasks he had been given by the IRT were well on the way to realisation; this was especially the case with regards to the Advisory Film Council that he expected Sir Thomas Hunter to lead. The council was to administer the non-theatrical circuit of films. Its importance in the overall British scheme of strengthening imperial ties was such that Grierson provided seeding money for the venture, some £1,250, with £500 earmarked for the purchase of hundreds of British films, and £750 held in reserve for future developments.[34]

While finding a suitable film controller was problematic (Grierson's strong preference was for W. B. Sutch, an influential economist and senior policy advisor, but neither Fraser nor Nash were convinced),[35] the situation seemed more promising with regards to the executive officer for the film council. Both Hunter and Beeby were keen for Stanhope Andrews to be appointed. An 'effective choice', Andrews had already 'absorbed much of our theories of education and public information'.[36] Strategically, this position was crucial to the IRT, as the Film Council was the organisation through which

> the New Zealand Government, the United Kingdom and other Empire Governments – reach out to the non-theatrical public of New Zealand. It will tell us what the audiences like or want.

It will use all existing technical agencies for actual exhibition, e.g., Schools, Universities, Museums, Institutes, Educational Sound Films, etc., to secure its national result.[37]

Non-theatrical distribution of British and dominion films was all the more pressing because the usual theatrical release was so haphazard and subject to commercial rather than cultural or political exigencies. There was also the problem that British authorities tended to sign exclusive distribution deals with particular commercial interests. In New Zealand, the deal with British Empire Films meant that British government films were unavailable for other outlets. The celebrated film *Night Mail* was a cause of special regret, as it had

> not been properly promoted in New Zealand and accordingly has only had the most partial distribution. Like all the others tied up in this ineffectual system of circulation, it represents a film wasted, which might have been most valuable to British interests, if more knowledgeably and systematically handled.[38]

Not only would a national non-theatrical distribution and exhibition circuit partially compensate for the screening lacunae already noted in commercial theatres, Grierson insisted on its 'primary importance and influence'. One was 'assured of audiences everywhere, of the greatest value for prestige purposes, so long as circulation is systematized and built up by such agencies as the proposed Advisory Film Council and so long as you have material to give free'.[39] The real battle lay with shaping public perception positively to British interests through building 'an approach to the public which, with all the great National Organizations behind it, gives us the emphasis we seek'.[40]

In his letter to Lord Clarendon, chairman of the IRT, Grierson praised Sir Henry Batterbee's achievements in raising local awareness of British documentary through the many private screenings he hosted in his house, where the cream of Wellington society regularly gathered. In a sign of increasing British concern about its influence, the post of high commissioner to New Zealand was created in July 1938, with Batterbee its first appointment. He was expected to develop 'the system of communication and consultation between His Majesty's Governments', which had been emphasised at successive imperial conferences.[41] To facilitate his mission, Queen Mary had given him a 16mm projector and with

> a none too rich supply of films from England, he has kept the flag flying very effectively at his dinner parties. ... I found that the leaders of most sections of Wellington's ministerial, educational and civic groups already knew a good deal about our work and were very appreciative of the sight of England our films were giving.[42]

The strategic propaganda importance of non-theatrical distribution in developing imperial sentiment was such that Grierson raised the matter again with Peter Fraser (now PM) in a letter sent from Pago Pago in early May 1940 as Grierson steamed from Australia to Canada. He reminded Fraser of the action plan for 'mobilising as much screen space as is reasonable' and the dividend the government could earn both nationally and internationally if the Advisory Film Council was established. Nationally, it facilitated 'an opportunity for local leadership of opinion, as theatre audiences do not', while internationally it opened up 'large non-theatrical audiences in educational and civic circles: particularly in the Dominions and the United States'.[43]

## IN GRIERSON'S WAKE

New Zealand had been a 'good experience', described by Grierson as 'a gracious country', where

> the model of manners provided by a hand-picked British stock on the one hand and by the native Maori, not less, on the other, makes for a very distinctive people. The blessings of Polynesia and the South Seas are on it.[44]

Despite the graciousness of the country, the potential cloying quality of angels was apparent in his letter to Tallents, where he noted a more

> intensive interest there in good works than anywhere I ever saw and for a moment I am almost thankful for the change of Sydney, where good works, if any, are a strict second to horse racing, brilliant beaches, good looks and political manoeuvre.[45]

Grierson did not enjoy the same enthusiastic welcome in Australia as he had in New Zealand. Certainly, the minority-led Menzies government was of a more conservative hue than the Labour government across the Tasman Sea. In his Pago Pago letter to Fraser, Grierson confessed as much, admitting that he found Australia 'difficult to bring into focus on this question of films'.[46]

However, Grierson had good reason to believe in the success of his New Zealand mission. Not only had powerful 'progressive-minded' ministers listened to him, but his zest and zeal also impressed senior civil servants, whose administrative knowledge and control was of paramount importance in furthering the scheme hatched by the IRT and given shape by Grierson. Moreover, his fondness for the New Zealanders was a reciprocal affair, as an anonymous government official writing to the New Zealand high commission in London confirmed:

> Whoever was initially responsible for sending Grierson to this country deserves a high place in heaven. He made a great impression on the town [of Wellington] and I think everyone wished that he could stay and live here forever .... What we would like to see is the realisation of his and our aim for this country.[47]

Although some people in Wellington energetically fanned the fire he lit, its light and warmth were experienced fitfully. Of those he influenced, the most important here were Paul (director of publicity in the PM's office, and, in effect, chief censor); Schmitt (general manager tourist and publicity); Beeby (director of education); and Andrews (editor *National Education*).

In a handwritten letter of thanks to Schmitt, Grierson wrote that he could have done little without his 'progressive spirit and co-operation'; provided direction with regards to seeking 'creative leadership'; and advised against any hasty action in acquiring more film production equipment and staff, as this would 'cause distrust in Treasury' and jeopardise 'the scheme as a whole'.[48] A few weeks later, Schmitt wrote back having spent 'the last 24 hours or so with you in spirit' as a result of reading Paul Rotha's seminal *Documentary Film*. The letter reveals a man fully in sympathy with the objectives proposed in Grierson's report and the underlying ideological orientation informing them. They had a 'great job of work' to do.

> My enthusiasm and keenness has been fired by yours and also by Rotha's last chapter 'Policies and Purposes' in so far as it appeals for action by means of documentary to show to those millions – who unthinkingly enjoy liberty under democratic governments – the reasons why they do enjoy it and to enable them to understand why the democratic policy is best.[49]

Schmitt had evidently 'caught the spirit of documentary properly' and assured Grierson that he would do all he could 'to assist in the production and distribution of this class of film'.[50]

Another zealous disciple was Stanhope Andrews whose editorship of *National Education* gave him a platform from which to proselytise. As part of the media campaign he later orchestrated in his drive to see the government adopt more of Grierson's suggestions, he published 'Home Is What You See in It', an essay by W. B. Sutch, whose several provocations may have cost him the position of national film controller.[51] Sutch argued in favour of making the country better known to New Zealanders by developing a sense of place, one communicated through various media (theatre, film, radio, literature): 'In not one of these fields have the possibilities been exploited of showing New Zealand to itself.'[52] As an emergent cultural nationalist, Sutch may have overstated his case for strategic reasons, as some New Zealand-born writers were already producing a locally grounded literature in the 1930s.

A fortuitous event that reinforced the value of film in promoting the war effort was the return of HMS *Achilles* in February 1940. In the Battle of the River Plate (13 December 1939), the *Achilles* became the first New Zealand unit to fire on the enemy when it engaged the German 'pocket battleship' the *Admiral Graf Spee* in the South Atlantic. Huge crowds turned out in Auckland and Wellington to greet the returning 'heroes' and international newsreel coverage was extensive. Grierson appreciated the felicitous timing of this event. It neatly underpinned a vital component of his scheme – the orderly distribution of British, Canadian and Australian government propaganda films, as well as those (few) made by the New Zealand government's own film studios in Miramar.

The person most likely to advance this strand of Grierson's scheme was Beeby. His ambitions in this regard, however, suffered a setback following his meeting with the prime minister on 16 April. As reported by Grierson, Fraser's initial response to the development of non-theatrical distribution had been enthusiastic, but Fraser made it clear to Beeby 'that he had not given the scheme the full and final approval which Mr. Grierson seemed to imagine'.[53] Ostensibly, Fraser had two main objections: the first was that the government should not provide funding to an organisation (Council of Adult Education) it did not directly control; the second was that the voices of other government departments might not be heard by the council.

These objections were overcome when the education department assumed responsibility for establishing a national organisation for the distribution and exhibition of non-theatrical films. A 'workaround' suited to local conditions had been created. Two events were fundamental: the first was the appointment of Walter Harris to the newly minted position of 'supervisor of teaching aids' – principally visual – in April 1941.[54] The second was the creation of the National Film Library a year later with Harris in charge. Foreign governments now had an official repository and clearing house for their films. More fully convinced of the cultural and educative use of film, the government provided a service that articulated the demand of its diverse non-theatrical audiences, secured the supply of appropriate films and co-ordinated their distribution and exhibition. Grierson's 'advisory film council' was now a fledgling state institution; but what of documentary film production?

## MAINTAINING THE FIRE HE LIT

From various quarters, both internally and internationally, the pressure to do something bold with regards to government production of documentary film steadily accrued. Resorting to a congenial strategy, Andrews launched the *New Zealand Film Letter*, published by the Wellington Film Unit (more an expression of hope than a reality at this stage). Its first issue appeared in November 1940. Announcing that 'more people in New Zealand are influenced by films than by books', but that there had been no film equivalent to literary periodicals, the *Film Letter* clearly signalled change. Andrews's advocacy of government film production was a priority: 'After a year of war, the New Zealand Government's film publicity adds up on the production side to 14 poster films and the release of some first class material about the *Achilles* in the international Fox Newsreel.'[55] Unsurprisingly, however,

> Our lone Government film unit has not yet produced anything of the quality of Harry Watt's GPO film *Squadron 992*, which was made within a few weeks of the first raid on the Forth Bridge, and has just arrived in New Zealand through the United Kingdom High Commissioner, Sir Harry Batterbee. But as policy becomes more clearly defined, and organisation is geared up from the production of scenics to that of documentaries, the Miramar people will be able to give a good account of themselves. There is ample talent and technical skill in this country to produce first-rate film documents of ourselves just as soon as we get round to making use of it.[56]

A polemical piece entitled 'Films for Democracy' asserted the value and importance of using film as a communication medium and recycled Grierson's argument that modern societies were complex, impersonal conglomerations requiring specialists to mediate between state institutions and citizens.

> Some restoration of that person-to-person contact is essential to democracy ... it can be done with the aid of modern machinery of communication if it is used imaginatively. Above all it can be done by the use of films ... . That's ourselves wanting to know each other [and] wondering then why, in the name of democracy, they are still fiddling while London burns.[57]

'They' refers obliquely yet pungently to the two primary government leaders, Fraser and Nash, who together amassed considerable power during the war; the latter found delegation of authority notoriously difficult, which did nothing to make decision making more timely.[58] 'Films for Democracy' was republished by the nationally circulated *New Zealand Listener* on 6 December and may have further indisposed Nash towards Andrews whom he already suspected of engaging more in self-aggrandisement than in advancing the general interest.[59]

The campaign to raise awareness and stimulate action about the value of documentary film continued among the educated when the official bulletin of the New Zealand Library Association devoted the major part of its May 1941 issue of *New Zealand Libraries* to the topic of 'Books and Film'. The Wellington Film Unit had contributed an article entitled 'Film in the Community's Service: Films about Ourselves', which drew comparisons between the cultural value and social influence of books and films, and sought to establish parallels insofar as their distribution was concerned: highly organised with books via the library system; in need of similar institutional treatment with regards to non-commercial films.[60]


## A DREAM COMES TRUE

With Andrews and his associates mounting an effective media campaign and the government in trouble over an ill-considered verbal provocation, the chance to 'walk the talk' was finally given to the small working and production subcommittee of the government film studios. The result was *Country Lads*, a nine and a half-minute film about the departure of New Zealand soldiers, screened to ministers and invited guests in June 1941.

To understand the government's new willingness to engage with the 'maturer processes of film-making'[61] (a documentary mode that arranges, shapes and interprets 'reality'), it is necessary to provide the backstory – the immediate wartime context and its effect on the government's decision making with regards to national information services used to publicise the war effort.

When the Germans took control of Greece in April 1941, the island of Crete became a secondary target; as part of their evacuation from the Greek mainland, the Second New Zealand Expeditionary Force fought a ten-day battle and suffered heavy casualties: there were 671 deaths, 1,455 wounded and 1,692 prisoners on Crete, which was on top of the losses in Greece – 291 killed, 599 wounded and 1,614 prisoners of war.[62] For a small nation like New Zealand, Greece and Crete were military catastrophes.

With Peter Fraser overseas, explaining the losses to the people back home became Walter Nash's thankless task. In a provocative radio talk, broadcast in the first days of June 1941, he complained that fewer than 5 per cent of the New Zealand people understood the seriousness of the war. The following day, an editorial in the *Press*, entitled 'Publicity and the War Effort', took issue with Nash, attributing this colossal ignorance to the government's own unfocused efforts. The censorship and publicity branch in the PM's office had 'the responsibility of seeing that the New Zealand people are kept adequately and correctly informed about the war situation and fully conscious of their own obligation to participate in the war effort to the limits of their ability'.[63] Clearly, the information was not getting through.

In the harsh light of this public-relations mess of its own making, the government gave 'gadfly' Andrews the opportunity he sought. *Country Lads* was the result. Put together to show what film could do to promote the war effort and pull the nation together, it combined footage of New Zealand troops parading around Wellington with footage of them leaving for the Middle East in January, April and August 1940, and wove these images around a narration that pulled the disparate regions of the country into an imagined national community of common endeavour. Very real socioeconomic and ethnic divisions that structured relationships between such formations as employers and workers, Pakeha and Maori, urban and rural, men and women, were healed in the edit, with a commentary that also emphasised the reasons for going to war – the defence of democratic freedoms and common values: 'Canoes and ships brought the New Zealanders here long ago. Fighting New Zealanders. Pioneers looking for elbow room. Men and women who couldn't be shut in against their wish.'[64] Andrews's narration also made the visual communication task and dramatic potential of the medium clear: 'Until now only a handful of us have known what troop departures looked like; how it feels to say *au revoir* to soldier friends and relations at the ship's side; the sorrow and the pride of it.'[65] Here was an instance of documentary 'drama on your doorstep', as discussed by Grierson during his February 1940 radio talk.

Many of the ideas Andrews had developed in his twenty-two-page memo, 'National Publicity and Adult Education in War Time',[66] were on display in the film: the close integration of civilian and soldier, the sight of marching troops, the ordinary associated with the extraordinary, the clear-sighted democratic conviction of the need to fight so far from home and, importantly, the *faces* of New Zealand men and women that filled the screen in tight midshots and close-ups. It was well received by the assembled audience of ministers, MPs, senior civil servants and wives; tears were said to have pearled down glistening cheeks. A chapter in a recent book still claims that Prime Minister Fraser was present, also teary-eyed, at the screening of *Country Lads* in July [sic] 1941, but this was impossible as he was overseas at the time.[67] A short newspaper review of the screening consecrated the endeavour and called for its continuation:

> *Country Lads* expresses the national spirit of the times ... [it] is a simple little film, but it pictures a great moment in the history of this young country, and pictures it competently. More could be done on these lines. Often easily obtainable newsreel shots could be used in a film of emotional force that would bring the screens of New Zealand theatres into their place as a medium of national self-expression.[68]

In late October 1941, 'A Dream Comes True: New Zealand Films for the People by the People', appeared in the *New Zealand Listener*. On either side of the title are headshots of Andrews and Grierson, visually underscoring the close connection between the new entity and its mentor. The text described the origins of documentary film and the intentions of the NFU; the nationalists had carried the day: 'Putting Ourselves on the Screen. Real events, real people', was to be the main business of the NFU.

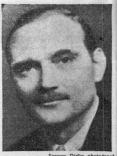

# A DREAM COMES TRUE

### New Zealand Films For The People. By The People

(Written for "The Listener")

*AN official advertisement in the papers, one or two notices of staff appointments—these are all the news the general public has received so far of what may become a very important development of New Zealand's own film industry. This article reports what has happened and suggests what it is hoped will happen.*

S. P. Andrew photograph
**E. S. ANDREWS**
*Producer, National Film Unit*

Spencer Digby photograph
**JOHN GRIERSON**
*His arguments carried weight*

THE story begins back in 1922 when the Internal Affairs Department, followed later by the Government Tourist and Publicity Department, hit upon the idea of using film as an advertising method. This was almost a revolution in itself. In those times, film meant the story picture, very silent, over-dramatic, mostly melodramatic, and, at its best, slapstick. To use film for show-

beneath large hotel porticos at the foot of large mountains or lakes with a dark red filter making sunset scenes at mid-day.

Now, Miramar is setting out to put a new sort of New Zealand into its pictures. The scenically beautiful New Zealand cannot be avoided in the process, and no one would wish that it should be, but the National Film Unit is going to bring the scenery to life by putting people and cities and factories into it, wars, and peace, work as well as play, humanity at large as well as nature run amuck.

### Sources of Inspiration

than either. This was reality, and Flaherty's discovery was the discovery that reality could be made the star turn in romance.

Flaherty's first inspiration was more or less sunk on the rocks of Hollywood's extraordinary prejudice against doing the sensible thing. He influenced the big-business film industry, but only subjectively. He inspired a few directors to make life on the screen look more like life as it really is lived. The direction and photography of *The Iron Horse* or *Grapes of Wrath* were in a similar tradition. But the real job of developing the ideal of these "documentary" films

public how film could be handled. John Grierson is accepted as the leader of this group, which developed into the British G.P.O. Unit, and many of whose members now operate under the British Ministry of Information's control. Grierson and his fellows proved that the romance of reality can be far more effective than the romance of unreality.

The New Zealand public has not often been fortunate enough to see their work

The establishment of the NFU in 1941 and the less heralded NFL a year later was, indeed, a dream come true for both cultural nationalists (such as Andrews) and imperial propagandists (such as Grierson) (*New Zealand Listener*, 24 October, 1941, p. 6)

A year later, 'Propagandists with Good Consciences: National Film Unit's First Year' appeared. Andrews's text celebrated its achievements, described its productions and its relationship with government. The 'propaganda' in the title refers to the interpretive function of documentary practice, as distinct from newsreels, which might describe and expose events but did not 'cut under the merely photogenic surface to the fundamentals of social and economic change, and across national barriers to international understanding'.[69] Here, documentary's deeper purpose was to reveal the suprasensible 'real' that lay beyond or beneath the phenomenal. Simply recording the material world was not the 'maturer form of documentary' in any Griersonian sense. Shaping the phenomenal world was a matter of comprehending underlying 'generative forces'; it took 'artistry' to articulate these using the material world as a kind of dumb matter.

> It was this belief which caused [Grierson] to reject the idea of film as mimesis ... . [He] believed that the cinema articulated contemporary reality through material aesthetic processes intrinsic to itself, and he rejected the view, which was prevalent at the time, that cinema could reproduce external reality.[70]

Andrews understood the selective and interpretive processes that construct the 'truth' of cinematic realism, and would have concurred with Grierson's rejection of a mimetic cinema: 'the movie-camera ... does not show a battlefield, but compels attention upon that small portion of it within the fairly narrow angle of view of the lens'.[71]

# CONCLUSIONS

Although most versions of Grierson's sojourn in New Zealand describe the establishment of the NFU in terms that recall Julius Caesar's pithy *veni, vidi, vici*, and ignore his role in setting up the NFL, this account has sought to demonstrate that the events leading to their formation were more complex. Single-factor explanations based on light research are unable to describe events with complex causations. For example, to simply reprise the notion that the economist and policy advisor W. B. Sutch was a 'key instigator' of Grierson's visit is not enough; such an assertion requires proof.[72] The only evidence adduced for this appears to be a handwritten note by Andrews: 'Don't forget that it was Bill Sutch who persuaded Frank Langstone to get Grierson to New Zealand in the first place. ... It was my report that persuaded PF [Peter Fraser] to set up the Unit.'[73] However, the account of the NFU's genesis described here demonstrates that Andrews's report had no such clearly suasive force. Furthermore, there is no material evidence in the papers that document Grierson's trip (sponsored by the IRT on recommendations emerging from imperial conferences) that show any involvement by Sutch, let alone credit him with being 'a key instigator'.

The establishment of the NFU arose from wartime contingencies beyond Grierson's (and his acolyte Andrews's) control. Having said that, it is clear that Grierson's influence concerning the state bureaucracy's managerial use of film was considerable and enduring. Furthermore, his energy and zeal were inspirational, his contacts multiple and his administrative acumen valuable in negotiating potential pitfalls, e.g., with regard to Treasury's typical objections to increases in government spending. It is also clear that a fundamental component of Grierson's mission has hitherto been ignored in accounts of his stay in New Zealand, namely the founding of the NFL – an institution that not only distributed non-theatrical films but also materially assisted in the creation of audiences for propaganda (as well as 'educative' and cultural) purposes. It was of vital British interest that inter-empire relations be strengthened using various forms of 'soft power' and films were powerful propaganda weapons.[74] It is in this light that Grierson's surprising four-page letter to Fraser from Pago Pago in early May (1940) should be seen. Beeby's meeting with the PM in mid-April taught Grierson that Fraser had reservations concerning the imperial scheme.[75] The letter reminded Fraser of their conversation and Grierson's recommendations for 'mobilising screen space' and the dividend the government could earn if the Advisory Film Council were established.[76]

The so-called 'delay' in developing documentary film production and non-theatrical distribution should not be attributed to personal antipathy (another single-factor explanation);[77] rather there were more mundanely complex reasons, including a shortage of appropriately qualified people, wartime exigencies, central control (Fraser and Nash) and internal political struggle within the Labour Party (suppression of the left wing). It is also worth reiterating that Grierson himself expected no extreme 'makeover' of national publicity services but a gradual development over three to five years (the British were in it for the long haul in their efforts to dilute American economic and cultural power, as well as nascent nationalist sentiment, in what was 'their' sphere of influence). On that time scale, the New Zealanders' ability to establish both the NFU in 1941 and NFL in 1942 was ahead of schedule, albeit slightly askew of empire when national circumstances are factored in.

Entering a land of 'progressive' political ambition, Grierson encountered largely congenial conditions for the reception of his documentary ideals among the Polynesian romantics he assiduously courted. Like some latter-day incarnation of Duncan Gray seducing Maggie, he may have heard Robert Burns's refrain ringing in his ears as he left: 'Ha ha, the wooing o't!'[78]

## ACKNOWLEDGMENTS

I am grateful to Russell Campbell and film historian and archivist Clive Sowry for reading an earlier version of this chapter and helping to improve its accuracy and structure.

## NOTES

1. G. Mirams, 'Propaganda in News Films', *National Education*, 1 July 1938, p. 239. The original title is *New Zealand Marches On*. (My thanks to Clive Sowry for pointing this out.) Mirams was developing a reputation as an independent film critic, a position he consolidated when he became subeditor for the *New Zealand Listener* in 1939.
2. Archives NZ, TO 1 49/11/1 Part 1, 'Memo on Films', 21 April 1939, Gilbert McAllister, New Zealand Public Relations Council.
3. Mirams, 'Propaganda in News Films', p. 239.
4. The following texts construct the standard version of Grierson's New Zealand visit: Jonathan Dennis and Jan Bieringa (eds), *Film in Aotearoa New Zealand* (Wellington: Victoria University Press, 1992, 1996); Margot Fry, 'A Servant of Many Masters: A History of the NFU, 1941 to 1976', MA thesis, Victoria University of Wellington, 1995; John O'Shea, *Don't Let It Get You* (Wellington: Victoria University Press, 1999); Geraldene Peters, 'Political and Alternative Film Making: 1940 to 1950', in *New Zealand Film: An Illustrated History* (Wellington: Te Papa Press, 2011).
5. The expression is in Jack C. Ellis, *John Grierson: Life, Contributions, Influence* (Carbondale and Edwardsville: Southern Illinois University Press, 2000), p. 138.
6. 'New Zealander Had Varied Career in British Film Work', *Dominion*, 31 July 1947 – an interview with Margaret Thomson.
7. Letter from Grierson to McAllister, John Grierson Archive, University of Stirling, G4/5/8 (hereafter Grierson Archive).
8. Ibid. Grierson had already made a similar assessment of Canadian government film.
9. Archives NZ, 'Memo on Films'.
10. Keith Sinclair, *Walter Nash* (Dunedin: Oxford University and Auckland University Presses, 1976), p. 186; and Nancy M. Taylor, *The New Zealand People at War: The Home Front, volume 1* (Wellington: V. R. Ward, 1986), p. 35.
11. G3/15/6, Grierson Archive.
12. G3/15/16, Grierson Archive.
13. Archives NZ, TO 1 49/11/1 Part 1, Letter: Savage to Jordan, 18 May 1939.

14. This was one of the most important single pieces of legislation in New Zealand history. Nash got the loan on very harsh terms, with some UK newspapers calling them 'impossibly onerous; indeed blackmailing'. See Sinclair, *Walter Nash*, p. 176.

15. Grierson travelled first class aboard the Matson liner, *Mariposa*, from San Francisco, and was accompanied by his wife. When he left New Zealand, he was aboard the *Monterey*, another Matson liner, which sailed from Auckland on Friday 15 March 1940, for Sydney. Interestingly, the length of time he spent in New Zealand was influenced by steamship timetables. (My thanks to Clive Sowry for this information.)

16. G4/24/35, Grierson Archive.

17. *National Education*, 2 October 1939, p. 353.

18. *New Zealand Listener*, 23 February 1940.

19. G3/15/44, Grierson Archive.

20. *New Zealand Listener*, 23 February 1940.

21. G4/33/1, Grierson Archive. Truby King was an important health reformer (notably of the mentally ill) and founder of the Plunket Society, credited with significantly reducing infant mortality.

22. Ibid.

23. *New Zealand Listener*, 23 February 1940.

24. Sinclair, *Walter Nash*, p. 166.

25. Archives NZ, TO 1 49/11/1 Part 1.

26. Sinclair, *Walter Nash*, p. 189.

27. Patrick Day, *The Radio Years: A History of Broadcasting in New Zealand* (Auckland: Auckland University Press, 1994), p. 4.

28. Ibid., p. 208.

29. G4/24/71, Grierson Archive.

30. G4/24/66, Grierson Archive.

31. Sinclair, *Walter Nash*, p. 154.

32. G4/5/6, Grierson Archive, Memo to Sir Henry Batterbee.

33. Ibid.

34. Ibid.

35. G4/5/5, Grierson Archive.

36. G4/5/6, Grierson Archive.

37. Ibid.

38. Ibid.

39. Ibid.

40. Ibid.

41. *Gazette*, 13 March 1939, p. 1, http://news.google.com/newspapers?nid=1946&dat= 19390313&id=V4wjAAAAIBAJ&sjid=p5gFAAAAIBAJ&pg=4193,2263959.

42. G4/24/63, Grierson Archive.

43. Archives NZ, TO 1 49/11/1 Part 1.

44. Ibid.

45. G4/24/66, Grierson Archive.

46. Archives NZ, TO 1 49/11/1 Part 1.

47. Ibid., 22 April 1940. An unsigned letter to R. M. Campbell (then official secretary to the New Zealand high commissioner in London). The anonymous writer has an insider's political knowledge; one candidate is W. B. Sutch, then working for the Minister of Finance.

If it were he, this would mean Sutch could have had nothing to do with organising Grierson's visit.

48. Archives NZ, TO 1 49/11/1 Part 1, Letter: Grierson to Schmitt, 13 March 1940.
49. Ibid., Letter: Schmitt to Grierson, 1 April 1940.
50. Ibid.
51. W. B. Sutch, *National Education*, 8 March 1941, p. 61. Grierson discussed Sutch with Nash, who harboured doubts about his suitability for the position. He had been suspected of leaking documents from the Committee of Imperial Defence to a Communist newspaper while in London with Nash in 1937 (Sinclair, *Walter Nash*, p. 148); written a 'Marxist history of the working class' while commissioned to write a survey of New Zealand social services for the 1940 centenary (ibid., p. 208); and made himself unpopular in other ways, notably in a speech that incensed many Roman Catholics because of its strongly anti-papal theme (ibid., p. 209).
52. Sutch, *National Education*, p. 61.
53. Archives NZ, TO 1 49/11/1 Part 1, Letter: Beeby to Minister of Education, 8 August 1940.
54. Harris was a close friend of Beeby's from their university days in Christchurch.
55. *N.Z. Film Letter* vol. 1 no. 1 (November 1940).
56. Ibid.
57. Ibid., p. 2.
58. Sinclair, *Walter Nash*, pp. 258–62. For Michael Bassett, Fraser assumed more decision-making responsibility because his 'Cabinet was light on talent … .' See Michael Bassett and Michael King, *Tomorrow Comes the Song: A Life of Peter Fraser* (Wellington: Penguin, 2000), p. 204.
59. Nash had apparently annotated Andrews's memo on 'National Publicity' with the word 'nebulous' and thought he was primarily self-seeking. Cited in Fry, 'A Servant of Many Masters', p. 27. Although there are many errors in this chapter of the MS, citing of sources seems reliable.
60. *New Zealand Libraries* vol. IV no. 10 (May 1941), p. 113.
61. The expression is Grierson's and excerpted from the letter he wrote to Clarendon (G4/24/63, Grierson Archive).
62. Bassett and King, *Tomorrow Comes the Song*, p. 215.
63. *Press*, 3 June 1941.
64. From part 2 of commentary in *Country Lads* (1941).
65. From opening paragraph in commentary of *Country Lads*.
66. *National Education*, May 1940. The main burden of the memorandum was the construction of a national spirit to further the war effort. In MS-0982/501, Papers relating to War Publicity and Information Services including minutes of the War Publicity Committee, J. T. Paul papers, Hocken Collections Archives and Manuscripts, p. 8.
67. Geraldene Peters, 'Political and Alternative Film Making: 1940 to 1950', in *New Zealand Film: An Illustrated History* (Wellington: Te Papa Press, 2011), p. 105.
68. *Dominion*, 28 June 1941.
69. Ibid.
70. Ian Aitken, *Film and Reform: John Grierson and the Documentary Film Movement* (London and New York: Routledge, 1990), p. 69.
71. MS-0982/487, 21 May 1941. Hocken Collections Archives and Manuscripts.
72. Peters, 'Political and Alternative Film Making', p. 105.

73. Cited in Fry, 'A Servant of Many Masters', p. 18, and reprised by Peters, 'Political and Alternative Film Making', p. 105.
74. The Empire Marketing Board's film unit, set up by Grierson, was one result of the 1926 Imperial Conference. The British government was exploring the cinematic possibilities of using 'film propaganda for peacetime and commercial purposes'. For more on the EMB film unit's propaganda, see Gary Evans, *John Grierson and the National Film Board* (Toronto: University of Toronto Press, 1984), p. 27.
75. I am speculating that Beeby communicated the gist of the meeting to Grierson, which then prompted him to write while in transit.
76. Archives NZ, TO 1 49/11/1 Part 1.
77. This account relies on the uncorroborated personal memory of E. S. Andrews, interviewed informally in 1989, almost fifty years after the events described. In this tale, it is claimed that 'Grierson's directness irritated Prime Minister Peter Fraser, who interpreted his manner in terms of a misplaced sense of superiority.' In Peters, 'Political and Alternative Film Making', p. 104.
78. Robert Burns, 'Duncan Gray', 1792.

## REFERENCES

Aitken, Ian, *Film and Reform: John Grierson and the Documentary Film Movement* (London and New York: Routledge, 1990).
Archives NZ, TO 1 49/11/1 Part 1, 'Memo on Films', 21 April 1939, Gilbert McAllister, New Zealand Public Relations Council.
Archives NZ, TO 1 49/11/1 Part 1, Letter: Savage to Jordan, 18 May 1939.
Archives NZ, TO 1 49/11/1 Part 1, Letter: Grierson to Schmitt, 13 March 1940.
Archives NZ, TO 1 49/11/1 Part 1, Letter: Schmitt to Grierson, 1 April 1940.
Archives NZ, TO 1 49/11/1 Part 1, Letter: Beeby to Minister of Education, 8 August 1940.
Bassett, Michael and Michael King, *Tomorrow Comes the Song: A Life of Peter Fraser* (Wellington: Penguin, 2000).
Burns, Robert, 'Duncan Gray' (1792), http://www.robertburns.org/works/387.shtml.
Day, Patrick, *The Radio Years: A History of Broadcasting in New Zealand* (Auckland: Auckland University Press, 1994).
Dennis, Jonathan and Jan Bieringa (eds), *Film in Aotearoa New Zealand* (Wellington: Victoria University Press, 1992, 1996).
Ellis, Jack C., *John Grierson: Life, Contributions, Influence* (Carbondale and Edwardsville: Southern Illinois University Press, 2000).
Evans, Gary, *John Grierson and the National Film Board* (Toronto: University of Toronto Press, 1984).
Fry, Margot, 'A Servant of Many Masters: A History of the NFU, 1941 to 1976', MA thesis, Victoria University of Wellington, 1995.
*Gazette* [Montreal], 13 March 1939, p. 1, http://news.google.com/newspapers?nid=1946&dat=19390313&id=V4wjAAAAIBAJ&sjid=p5gFAAAAIBAJ&pg=4193,2263959.
G3/15/6, John Grierson Archive (JGA).
G3/15/44, JGA.
G4/5/5, JGA.

G4/5/6, JGA, Memo to Sir Henry Batterbee.

G4/24/35, JGA.

G4/24/63, JGA.

G4/24/66, JGA.

G4/24/71, JGA.

G4/33/1, JGA.

Grierson, John, 'Letter from Grierson to McAllister', ibid., University of Stirling, G4/5/8.

Mirams, G., 'Propaganda in News Films', *National Education*, 1 July 1938, p. 239.

MS-0982/487, 21 May 1941, Hocken Collections Archives and Manuscripts.

*National Education*, 2 October 1939, p. 353.

*National Education*, 8 March 1940, p. 61.

*National Education*, May 1940.

*New Zealand Libraries* vol. IV no. 10 (May 1941), p. 113.

*New Zealand Listener*, 23 February 1940.

'New Zealander Had Varied Career in British Film Work', *Dominion*, 31 July 1947, Clippings from New Zealand Film Archive, NZ Personality, Vertical Files, Thomson, Margaret.

*N.Z. Film Letter* vol. 1 no. 1 (November 1940), p. 1

O'Shea, John, *Don't Let It Get You* (Wellington: Victoria University Press, 1999).

Peters, Geraldene, 'Political and Alternative Film Making: 1940 to 1950', in *New Zealand Film: An Illustrated History* (Wellington: Te Papa Press, 2011), pp. 103–27.

*Press*, 3 June 1941.

Sinclair, Keith, *Walter Nash* (Dunedin: Oxford University and Auckland University Presses, 1976).

Sutch, W. B. *National Education*, 8 March 1941, p. 61.

Taylor, Nancy M., *The New Zealand People at War: The Home Front, volume 1* (Wellington: V. R. Ward, 1986).

# 9
# The Grierson Cinema: Australia

*Deane Williams*

In Australia documentary film history, much has been made of 'the Grierson effect', with the Father of Documentary's visit to this country and Aotearoa/New Zealand (see Simon Sigley's chapter in this book) in 1940 on behalf of the Imperial Relations Trust the originary moment of much scholarship. Elsewhere I have written about the ways in which Grierson's visit has functioned as a 'foundation upon which the discourse of documentary film in this country has been built'.[1] Much of this notion of influence has been connected to the establishment of the Australian National Film Board (ANFB) in 1945, in a mirror image of the Canadian institution similarly attributed to Grierson and his ideals (see Zoë Druick's chapter in this book). At the same time, the establishment of the ANFB has been understood as a key component of the federal government's social reform programme in the immediate postwar years. Yet, the establishment of ANFB, while understood as a landmark initiative, eventuated in an institution that, from its inception, not only failed to live up to the vision for documentary film that Grierson proposed, it also failed to live up to the 'documentary hopes' held by a considerable network of on-the-ground individuals and their institutions who had been agitating for government support for documentary film since the 1930s.[2]
To better provide some sense of how Australian documentary film culture was positioned around the time of Grierson's visit and, following this, the manner in which the Grierson discourse was utilised, this chapter will first, indicate how the emblematic Australian National Film Board failed to live up to Grierson's vision. Second, it will demonstrate how the figure of Grierson and his proposals were relied upon, emblematised in Melbourne's Grierson Cinema, to reinforce the already extant agitation for nationwide co-ordination of documentary film-making; and third, it will indicate how at the state level, using the example of the Melbourne State Film Centre, institutions formed the intricate network which constituted a documentary film culture in immediate postwar Australia.[3]
    In Australia, as Ina Bertrand and Diane Collins tell us, 'most States, and several Commonwealth Government departments, had their own production facilities before the First World War', the primary unit being the federal government's Cinema and Photographic Branch which was established as early as 1921 and continued until World War II.[4] With the commencement of the war, most film-making activity in Australia was pressed into war service, in particular the Department of Information's Film Division established in 1940 as an administrative institution for co-ordinating

film production in the war effort.[5] The division had a small, experienced film unit, its members dispatched to the Middle East more as war correspondents, whose image and sounds were then passed on to the newsreel companies Cinesound and Movietone, the former emphasising the Australian war effort, the latter the international effort.[6]

It is important to understand that the industrial landscape for film production had been cleared during the war years due to the near cessation of narrative feature film production, with most personnel, equipment and facilities enlisted in the production of documentary, newsreel and informational films for the war effort. This brought about what Stuart Cunningham and William D. Routt have described as a 'documentary boom' with 'nearly a hundred films produced for the Department of Information in 1940–45 as well as the weekly newsreels turned out by Cinesound and Movietone'.[7] Albert Moran and Tom O'Regan go further, delineating between two discourses of Australian film, the documentary and the narrative feature. In their distinguishing between these discursive moments, Moran and O'Regan posit that this 'documentary boom' was displaced as 'the quintessential Australian film' by the narrative feature in the 1970s when a groundswell of activism led to government support for the 1970s film revival, and another kind of Australian film industry. By 1943, the Australian government began planning for postwar life. The Department of Post-war Reconstruction was set up, as Albert Moran tells us, in order to

> give expression to a vision of post-War Australia as an improved and reconstructed society.
> During and immediately after the War, Post-War Reconstruction undertook a series
> of broad initiatives towards that goal. In the process it established a series of different
> instrumentalities such as the Commonwealth Universities Commission, the Australian
> National University, the Snowy Mountains Authority and the Australian Broadcasting
> Control Board. The ANFB was such an initiative.[8]

The Australian National Film Board is best understood as an administrative institution, initially envisaged as a manifestation of this new 'vision of post-war Australia' in material terms; as an Australian film industry supported by the federal government. Initially, formulated by important figures such as Dr H. C. Coombs, director-general of Post-War Reconstruction, Colin Dean, secretary to the Minister for Post-War Reconstruction, Professor Alan Stout and esteemed film-maker and film- society activist John Heyer,[9] the ideal ANFB was envisaged as a government institution that was to provide a system for documentary, educational and instructional film production based on the Canadian National Film Board and at variance to the commercial feature film industry.[10] In the war and immediate postwar years, documentary film was envisaged as a key proponent of the vision for postwar reconstruction. Moran and O'Regan tell us:

> It was felt that such a film should help to construct a unified nation by showing one part of
> the country to other parts. It was to focus on the kinds of social problems facing a particular
> part of the nation and would show how these were being overcome. It needed to get away
> from the cliches of 'kangaroos, koala bears and fields of waving wheat' and had instead, to
> focus on elements of Australia and the national experience not usually seen. Such a film was

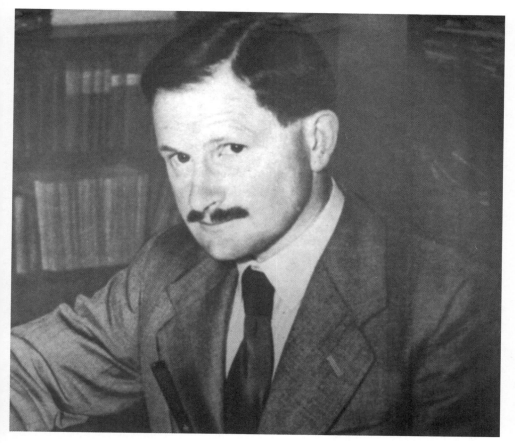

Alan Stout (1900–83), Professor of Moral and Political Philosophy, University of Sydney, Member of the New South Wales Documentary Films Council, Prime Minister's Committee on National Morale and a Griersonian (*Pix* vol. 19 no. 9, 1 March 1947)

not to be imitative of British or American films and if it were to be dramatised, then actors rather than stars were to be used. In any case, the film should not have been studio bound but rather, it was to be shot on location, and of course, had to be documentary.[11]

These distinctly nationalist sentiments are what drove the likes of Coombs, Stout, Heyer and Dean in their imagining and agitation for documentary film in Australia.

A key activist and disseminator of the discourse of documentary in this period was Alan Stout. Stout was an Englishman who taught at the University of Edinburgh before taking up a Professor in Moral and Political Philosophy at the University of Sydney in 1939 and establishing a reputation as a public intellectual.[12] Stout was a member of many government committees including the Prime Minister's Committee on National Morale during World War II, founding president (1963–7) of the New South Wales Council for Civil Liberties, the Council of the Australian Consumers' Association[13] and the New South Wales Documentary Films Committee.[14] In Stout's membership of the

Committee on National Morale, it is possible to see some congruence between his roles in political and moral philosophy, education, documentary film and the role ascribed to it by Grierson. Stout wrote, in words that complement Grierson's ideals, that 'the essence of democracy is "the free activity of all its members co-operating in a wide variety of different and sometimes competing voluntary organizations, independent of the state, for the active furtherance of interests common to their members"'.[15] From the late 1930s Stout was involved with the emerging international film-society movement alongside film-maker John Heyer. In fact Stout had brought to Australia an interest in grassroots film culture through his membership of the Edinburgh Film Guild 'for the 5 years preceding the war'.[16] Both Heyer and Stout were concerned with building audiences for non-Hollywood films of the period, not just documentary, something that they felt could be achieved through state structures for distribution. Stout wrote of his hopes for building documentary audiences in Australia:

> It was the film societies springing up in the 1930s which ensured them faithful and enthusiastic audiences. These societies, which are now even more flourishing than before the war, are composed of ordinary persons drawn from every class and occupation, who are not content with the fare offered by the commercial theatres. ... The film societies also arrange discussions on films, and lectures by well known documentary directors and film critics. The documentary movement in Britain has owed a great deal to these societies. ... I was disappointed to find when I came to Sydney a few months before the war that there was no similar society here, especially as I had read in Rotha's book on documentary film that the Film Society movement had spread to the dominions, including Australia. I should like to see established after the war a Commonwealth-wide Society with branches in the capital cities and larger country towns, drawing on a common stock of films.[17]

In his role Stout was careful to promote a particular kind of documentary film, in distinction to the newsreels and instructional films which dominated Australian screens during the war. Clearly influenced by Grierson's writings, as well as Paul Rotha's, Stout, like Heyer, sought to promote 'the creative treatment of actuality' as the repository of both hope and education for postwar Australia.

> We have seen that documentary films deal with living facts and real life, and that they are not just prosaic descriptions, but dramatic interpretations. That is why neither the newsreel nor the scenic and travel film are documentary, for they merely depict surface events, without going below the surface to explain and interpret. Thus the newsreel shows you the race; but the documentary would get behind it to *racing* as a social force in the lives of the people. The newsreel shows you the opening of a new reservoir or a dam in a hydro-electric scheme; the documentary goes behind the event to the problems of water-supply and electricity, and our dependence on both.[18] (emphasis in original)

Similarly, John Heyer saw the importance of distribution systems, including audience cultivation as key to building an Australian cinema, especially if it were to compete with the might of Hollywood. Drawing on similar sources to Stout, Heyer saw the film-society movement in tandem with government support for documentary film as the best response to commercial cinema. From the early 1930s, Heyer, along with his friend cameraman Damien Parer, was an autodidact in film theory and history, importing and reading *Experimental Cinema* and *Close Up* while attending art-house screenings of films imported into Australia by embassies and the likes of Friends of the Soviet Union.[19] This education encompassed a sound understanding of the importance to an alternative or documentary film culture of film societies such as New York's Film and Photo League in the US and the networks established in the UK such as the [London] Film Society, initiatives he would have been aware of from his reading and from Alan Stout's experiences in Edinburgh. However this vision and the hopes that motivated Coombs, Dean, Stout and Heyer were diminished from the outset.

The ambitious vision for a federally funded and structured system for the production, distribution and exhibition of documentary and educational films was immediately stymied by the perceived threat felt by commercial producers and exhibitors.[20] At the same time the intergovernmental power-plays of the time, fuelled by the territories established during wartime, remained intractable. The Films Division, as John Hughes tells us, was widely criticised by 'some sections of the press and from within other branches of the government and army'.[21] The strongest criticisms, within the confines of government, emanated from the Prime Minister's Committee on National Morale, which included Alan Stout as a key member as well as Alfred Conlon, who headed up the committee.[22] These included 'the DOI's use of American advertising agencies, their lack of strategic thinking, their lack of engagement with modern technologies of public opinion, and the quality of their propaganda efforts'.[23] At the same time John Heyer, although not an official member of the committee, wrote reports disparaging the Film Division's productions and distribution structure, as well as lamenting its approach to documentary as 'being unaware of the potential of the documentary ... something they still regard as dry ... that the audience has to sit out, instead of the vital absorbing documentary it can be'.[24] It is possible to see a groundswell of criticism of the DOI's Film Division aligning with the Grierson-inspired documentary vision embraced by Stout, Heyer and others meant that the Department of Information saw the emergence of agitation for a new kind of administrative structure for governmental film-making, the Australian National Film Board, as threatening, and sought to hold onto the reins.

As John Hughes tells us, in May 1944 Coombs describes his vision for the film authority 'dealing with documentary, educational and instructional films as a preliminary step in any film production and distribution', utilising Great Britain and Canada as models, and opines that this authority should be a departure from the roles played by the Department of Information. Fuelled by the criticisms from Heyer and from sections of the armed services, Coombs sought to reconceptualise government propaganda 'in a post-war world in dire need of information and morale-building'.[25] Eventually, the director-general of information under the leadership of E. G. Bonney, outmanoeuvred Coombs to retain control of film production and distribution.

As Bertrand and Collins point out, the fledgling movement for a federal government-supported documentary film industry faced, in the main, two primary obstacles. First, the attempts to delineate documentary, based on the notion of a classical, creative conception of the form, from newsreel, instructional and educational film, led to a difficulty in conveying the importance of these films to morale without straying into the realms of 'enjoyment' or 'popularity', traditionally the territory of commercial film interests.[26] Second, the difficulty in distinguishing documentary from these associated nonfiction forms meant that the status quo in film production, carefully guarded by the Department of Information, was always going to be difficult to alter. This second obstacle was further complicated by the involvement of the Department of Information, which already had its own Films Division and the Department of Post-war Reconstruction, which sought to engage documentary film in promoting its vision for Australia. Coombs, supported by Dean, Stout and Heyer, looked to the Canadian National Film Board for a model of a government institution that was a departure from the existing arrangements. Important to this discussion is a conference of all interested parties in June 1944 to reach a consensus on the new film authority. While Coombs saw this conference as an opportunity to build consensus and to consolidate his vision for governmental film-making, Bonney, the DOI's director-general, carefully manoeuvred to maintain his department's control over all aspects of documentary film production, signalling issues such as DOI experience, personnel and equipment built up over the war years as well as containing the language of documentary to that already defined by his department; newsreel, educational and instructional film. While it is true that all this led to the formation of the ANFB, it was a lost opportunity and engendered a remarkable division that to some extent remains in place today. Nevertheless, the impetus provided by the likes of Coombs, Stout and Heyer also continued into a particular thread in film-making by Heyer himself, whose directorial efforts in the 1940s and 50s are even today understood as some of the most creative of the period and belonging to a documentary tradition exemplified by the best of the British documentary movement and Robert Flaherty's films, as well as Australian documentary film-makers Colin Dean, R. Maslyn Williams and Catherine Duncan.[27]

In 1948 famed Modernist architect and Chief of the Public Works, Percy Edgar Everett, saw the realisation of his design for the Department of Agriculture Annex at 17 St Andrews Place, Melbourne. As its name suggests, the annex was an extension of the state government's Department of Agriculture after World War II during postwar reconstruction, benefiting from the increased technical support for agriculture. The building incorporated facilities for making films and radio programmes and included, in the basement, the Grierson Cinema. This cinema was, according to Heritage Victoria, 'architecturally notable as the most intact and as one of the most stylish Moderne cinemas' in Victoria with 'its egg-shaped plan, etched ceiling lights, curved stage and intimate scale'.[28] The cinema was initially created for the viewing of inhouse department productions but, in time came to be associated with the Victorian government's State Film Centre.

The State Film Centre was set up in 1946 and housed at 110 Victoria Street, Carlton with screenings held at the Radio School of what was then Melbourne Technical College, now RMITU and at Nicholas Hall, part of the then Methodist Church grounds of the Wesley Church, Lonsdale Street in Melbourne's centre. In late 1969 the State Film Theatre in the same precinct was completed, with screenings commencing in 1970. In the 1970s and 80s the State Film Theatre and the Grierson Cinema became twin premises for public, that is government-funded screenings, often in the form of mini-festivals or events rather than ongoing commercial screenings and the administration of the State Film Centre, including its library, was moved to premises adjacent to the theatre.

The State Film Centre emerged about the same time as John Grierson visited Australia in 1940 on behalf of the Imperial Relations Trust. Grierson, in fact, claims at once to have been responsible for the setting up of the committees as well as reporting that his visit had propelled the formation of the centres in numerous capital cities, writing in his 'Memorandum to the Prime Minister',

> As a result of my recent visits to Sydney, Melbourne, Adelaide and Brisbane, State Film Committees are in process of formation for the specific purpose of developing the use of films in all branches of State education and discussion. No doubt similar committees could easily be initiated in Tasmania and Western Australia. In New South Wales this development has the energetic backing of Mr. Drummond [that State's Minister for Education]. His Committee will represent School, University, University Extension and Agricultural Education, primary and secondary producers, women's organisations, etc. In Melbourne the initiative has been taken by [University of Melbourne] Vice Chancellor Medley with the co-operation of the Director of Education; and similar interests will be represented on his Committee. In Adelaide and Brisbane the proposal is to extend, under the guidance of State Committees, the existing Visual Education services to schools and provide wider film service for all educational and social groups throughout the States. In Adelaide, this development has the backing of Mr. Jeffreys, the Minister of Education, Dr. Fenner and Dr. Portus; in Brisbane of Mr. Cooper, the Treasurer, and the Director of Public Instruction.[29]

As we can glean from the memorandum, in contrast to his experiences with the federal government where he was met with a measured indifference, at the state level Grierson was better received. Bertrand and Collins put this down to a possible 'personal incompatibility of Menzies and Grierson, to lack of interest in the Imperial Relations Trust, and to fear of trespassing on private enterprise'.[30] It may also have been that the just established Films Division, Department of Information was understood by the wartime Menzies government as already performing its role in the production of propaganda for the war effort and didn't appreciate Grierson proposing an ambitious model of federal and state-based production and distribution.[31]

However, Grierson did make successful representations to state governments. As Bertrand and Collins point out, the New South Wales state government responded immediately to Grierson's April 1940 suggestion and within six weeks had established the New South Wales Documentary Films Committee including a £2,000 grant. Grierson himself granted £300 from the Imperial Relations Trust to both the New South Wales Documentary Films Committee and to the University of Melbourne Extension Board, a precursor of the Victorian State Film Centre and £200 to the Canberra Films Council.[32]

Of course it was no surprise that New South Wales took up the mantle Grierson handed them, given the prominence of the figures of Stout and Heyer there. By March 1941 with pressure from the NSW committee, a conference was convened to address the problems faced by the states whose Departments of Education, up until this point, had taken carriage of the use of non-theatrical film. Bertrand and Collins:

The problems which were facing the State bodies were again discussed, particularly the sources of film and the supply of projectors. The thorny issues – the definition of documentary film and hence the selection criteria, the overlapping needs of schools and communities and hence the overlapping functions of State education departments and the new State film councils – were also raised and again left unresolved. However, it was decided that a new Commonwealth Documentary Films Council should be established, as a coordinating body for the State Films Council.[33]

This council meant that Grierson's proposal of a 'single authority with multiple functions' was divided into two with the Documentary Films Council taking carriage of non-theatrical film distribution while a body known as the National Films Council was to liaise between commercial film interests and the Department of Information.[34]

As Grierson suggests, and as we have seen, Victoria's State Film Centre emerged among a host of federal and state government initiatives under the banner of nation-building yet the local Australian imperatives identified by Coombs, Stout, Heyer and others, of a federal system that could serve the states as well, jarred with the imperialist mission represented by Grierson. In Australia, as with most countries, postwar reconstruction was a nationalist affair, at once a retreat from internationalism brought to the fore during the war as well as a concern with desperate, immediate concerns.[35]

Like these initiatives and the increased support for technological assistance for agriculture, the federal government's Department of Post-war Reconstruction was mirrored at a state level with a focus on social reform including housing, social welfare, education and, at the time, its close cousin, the arts. The State Film Centre was at the time just one component in an incredibly complicated system of film acquisition, distribution, screening, production, criticism and reviewing that accumulated over this period yet provided a state-based nexus for these activities.[36]

An instructive link between the State Film Centre and the National Film Board was the Victorian Documentary Film Council, which was the initial advisory board for the State Film Centre and had representation on the Commonwealth Documentary Films Council established in 1941. The Victorian State Film Centre also enjoyed close working connections with a myriad of community groups such as the Federation of Victorian Film Societies, Children's Cinema Council, Community Movement, Australian Teachers' Federation, Police Association, Marriage Guidance Association, Rotary Clubs, the Australian Religious Film Society, Victorian Education Department, Soldier Settlement Commission, as well as RSL branches, parents and teachers associations, church groups and on. The State Film Centre had links with overseas distribution companies, film journals and film critics like Penelope Houston and Roger Manvell. It is in this period that film societies also began to emerge. As Cunningham and Routt tell us,

> In 1944 the Sydney Workers' Educational Association formed a Documentary Film Study Group, and the Australian Film Society (Victorian division) was organized for the same purpose in the same year. The following year film societies in Canberra and Sydney were created, and in successive years after that the Melbourne University Film Society (MUFS) and the Sydney University Film Group.[37]

These initiatives eventuated in the Australian Council of Film Societies (1950), still in existence today and in 1954 gave rise to Australia's first film festival at Olinda, just outside Melbourne, resulting in what is now the Melbourne International Film Festival.

The Grierson Cinema and the State Film Centre were twin institutions engendered by the close alignment of education and the postwar renewal of interest in cinema, with a strong reliance on realist, and mostly documentary, film as their mainstay. The role of the Victorian Documentary Film Council in advising, really overseeing, the State Film Centre and its reporting line to the Minister for Education is instructive in this. When the National Film Board came into being in May 1945, the Victorian government along with other states was invited to form a State Advisory Committee for consultation on film acquisition and production. This occurred in December 1945. This committee's chairman A. H. Ramsay reported to the Victorian government on the establishment of the State Film Centre. It wasn't until 1949 that this State Advisory Committee decided to change its name to the Victorian Documentary Film Council in line with similar names for these committees in South Australia (Documentary Films Committee) and New South Wales (Documentary and Educational Films Council).[38] In New South Wales, as Shirley and Adams tell us, work towards the setting up of a national, government-co-ordinated documentary movement had been begun as early as the 1930s by people such as David Henry Drummond, Alan Stout, John Heyer and Newman Rosenthal, all of this before and around Grierson's visit.

Of course, Alan Stout and John Heyer weren't the only people thinking about documentary's role in postwar Australia. Newman Rosenthal was director of Melbourne University's visual aids department, later TV research programme 1955–66.[39] He was the person mainly responsible for securing the £300 grant from Grierson's Imperial Relations Trust, in order to set up the Victorian counterpart in the state-based film distribution system, the Victorian Documentary Film Council. In 1949 Newman Rosenthal wrote an article for *Meanjin* entitled 'Has the Documentary Film a Future?', in which he called for a continuation of the wartime governmental support for documentary film. Weighing documentary film against both entertainment and propaganda, Rosenthal writes that 'documentary has a future only if governments can be made to appreciate the wider implications and so to finance productions which have no other purpose than the intangibles of information, education and morale'.[40] This 'Has the Documentary Film a Future?' was a published version of the Victorian Documentary Film Council-initiated First Annual John Grierson Lecture delivered by Rosenthal.[41] Rosenthal's article is an example of two things: (1) the close alignment of film and education in this period, where the national good had well and truly turned to documentary film since World War II, in numerous ways, at the same time as John Grierson visited Australia on behalf of the Imperial Relations Trust. This alignment worked its way into the state-level structures of government film administration through the likes of the Victorian Documentary Film Council, running the State Film Centre (with, as we have seen, comparative arrangements in South Australia and NSW) and on to the National Film Board. In other directions the State Film Centre worked out in networks across the state. (2) It is possible in this nascent period to see another factor in Australia's insistence on documentary realism. While Adrian Martin, Ross Gibson and others have addressed the issue of the cultural aesthetics of realism, it may be that in these locations, these structures, these figures, it is possible to see the emergence of the institutional support for the continuation of the moral imperatives documentary film offered, at a local level, at a tangent, yet engaged, with Grierson's ideas. Rosenthal writes:

> The attitude of the democratic governments (in varying degree according as their ideas of freedom varied) seems to have been that a democracy was a community of people who not only had the right, but also the responsibility to think for themselves, that problems had a better chance of solution if the nature of those problems were the more clearly understood; and that, through factual representation which film could give and the wide discussion which it could stimulate, there would come that confidence in communal institutions and communal leadership which was so basic to communal morale and communal stability.[42]

## CONCLUSION

Yet in all this sits the Grierson Cinema, an overarching notion redolent of this country's reliance on an authorising model to understand the structures which resulted from the wartime embracing of newsreel, instructional and educational film for propaganda purposes. Part of this myth is the association of the Australian National Film Board with the agitation for an Australian film industry based on Griersonian principles, and locally, the Grierson Cinema, 'one of the most stylish Moderne cinemas', a figure of both empire and of nascent postwar governmental institutionalisation with the very same principles. In Australia in the postwar period, the Grierson Cinema is not only an authorised centring of film culture, a 'Grierson effect', it is also an anomaly, a misrepresentation of the ongoing groundswell, of the on-the-ground intricate and shifting associations between individuals and their groupings, between creative documentary and newsreel and instructional film, between wartime and postwar reconstruction that constitute Australian postwar film culture.

## NOTES

1. Deane Williams, 'Between Empire and Nation: Grierson in Australia', *Screening the Past* (1991), http://www.latrobe.edu.au/screeningthepast/firstrelease/fr0799/dwfr7e.htm.
2. The snapshot of documentary film culture of this period that Shirley and Adams provide is entitled 'Documentary Hopes' – see Graham Shirley and Brian Adams, *Australian Cinema: The First Eighty Years* (Sydney: Angus and Robinson/Currency Press, 1983), pp. 174–9.
3. In Australia, there are three levels of government, the federal or commonwealth government resulting from the 'federation' of six independent British colonies and two territories. These colonies have also maintained individual state governments: New South Wales (NSW), Queensland (Qld), South Australia (SA), Tasmania (Tas.) Victoria (Vic.) and Western Australia (WA) and two mainland territories, the Northern Territory (NT) and the Australian Capital Territory (ACT). See http://australia.gov.au/about-australia/our-government.

4. Ina Bertrand and Diane Collins, *Government and Film in Australia* (Sydney: Currency Press/Australian Film Institute, 1981), p. 94.
5. Albert Moran, *Projecting Australia: Government Film since 1945* (Sydney: Currency Press, 1991), p. 2.
6. Shirley and Adams, *Australian Cinema*, p. 166.
7. Stuart Cunningham and William D. Routt, '"Fillums Became Films" (1940–56)', in Ina Bertrand (ed.), *Cinema in Australia: A Documentary History* (Kensington: University of New South Wales Press, 1989), p. 181.
8. Moran, *Projecting Australia*, p. 3.
9. John Heyer is, to this day, one of Australia's most highly regarded film-makers. His *The Back of Beyond* (1954) won the 1956 Grand Prix Assoluto at the Venice Biennale Film Festival and is known to generations of Australians. See Deane Williams, 'John Heyer's International Perspective: *The Overlanders, The Valley Is Ours, The Back of Beyond*', in *Australian Post-war Documentary Films: An Arc of Mirrors* (Bristol and Chicago, IL: Intellect, 2008), pp. 83–112.
10. John Hughes, 'After *Indonesia Calling*', PhD (Project) Exegesis, School of Media and Communications, College of Design and Social Context, RMIT University, Melbourne, 2012, pp. 107–9. As Hughes suggests, Coombs uses the term 'Australian film industry' in his strategy for setting up the ANFB, in line with the vision embraced by the Department of Post-war Reconstruction, and against the forces of the Department of Information marshalling to retain control over government film-making.
11. Albert Moran and Tom O'Regan, 'Two Discourses of Australian Film', *Australian Journal of Screen Theory* vol. 15 no. 16 (1983), p. 166.
12. 'Alan Ker Stout', *Australian Dictionary of Biography*, http://adb.anu.edu.au/biography/stout-alan-ker-15921.
13. Ibid.
14. Shirley and Adams, *Australian Cinema*, p. 176.
15. Stout quoted in D. H. Monro, 'Obituary: Alan Ker Stout, 1900–1983', *Australasian Journal of Philosophy* vol. 61 no. 3 (1983), p. 338.
16. A. K. Stout, 'Documentary Films', n.d., p. 14. This document has a subheading –

    revised script of four talks given over the National Network of the A.B.C. [Australian Broadcasting Commission] in December 1943, and January and February 1944. The first three form a connected series under the general title 'Documentary Films in Adult Education'. The fourth is a very brief outline of the historical development of Documentary Films.

17. Ibid.
18. Ibid., p. 5–6.
19. See my *Australian Post-war Documentary Films*, pp. 95–6.
20. Bertrand and Collins, *Government and Film in Australia*, p. 102.
21. Hughes, 'After *Indonesia Calling*', p. 104.
22. Ibid.
23. Ibid.
24. John Heyer, quoted in ibid., p. 106.
25. Bertrand and Collins, *Government and Film in Australia*, p. 103.
26. Ibid., p. 102.

27. See Williams, 'John Heyer's International Perspective' , pp. 83–112.
28. 'Department of Agriculture Annex', *Victorian Heritage Database*, http://vhd.heritage. vic.gov.au/vhd/heritagevic?timeout=yes#detail_places;65614.
29. John Grierson, 'Copy of Memorandum from Mr. John Grierson. Memorandum to the Prime Minister', *After Grierson*, ed. Ina Bertrand. Special edition of *Screening the Past: An International Electronic Journal of Visual Media and History* (uploaded 1 July 1999), http://tlweb.latrobe.edu.au/humanities/screeningthepast/classics/cl0799/jg2cl7a.htm.
30. Bertrand and Collins, *Government and Film in Australia*, p. 98.
31. See Williams, 'Between Empire and Nation'.
32. Bertrand and Collins, *Government and Film in Australia*, p. 98.
33. Ibid., p. 101.
34. Ibid.
35. See Williams, 'Between Empire and Nation'.
36. The State Film Centre evolved into the current Australian Centre for the Moving Image, a large, multi-venue exhibition space at Melbourne's Federation Square, http://www. fedsquare.com/.
37. Cunningham and Routt, '"Fillums Became Films" (1940–1956)', p. 182.
38. A. H. Ramsay, 'Letter to the Hon. T. T. Hollway M.L.A. Premier of Victoria', 31 March 1949.
39. Newman Hirsch Rosenthal also wrote many books including *Films in Our Lives: An Approach to Film Appreciation* (Melbourne: Cheshire, 1953) and *Film in Instruction* (Melbourne: Robertson and Mullers, 1945–7).
40. Newman Rosenthal, 'Has the Documentary Film a Future?', *Meanjin* vol. 8 no. 2 (Winter 1949), p. 110.
41. Other Grierson Lectures include Patricia Edgar, 'Children's Television: The Past, the Present and the Future', 1979; Brian McFarlane, 'From Page to Screen', 1983; Peter Watkins, 'Broken Mirror: The Role of the Audio-visual Media in Today's Society', 1985.
42. Rosenthal, 'Has the Documentary Film a Future?'.

## REFERENCES

'Alan Ker Stout', *Australian Dictionary of Biography*, http://adb.anu.edu.au/biography/stout-alan-ker-15921.
Bertrand, Ina and Diane Collins, *Government and Film in Australia* (Sydney: Currency Press/Australian Film Institute, 1981).
Cunningham, Stuart and William D. Routt, '"Fillums Became Films" (1940–1956)', in Ina Bertrand (ed.), *Cinema in Australia: A Documentary History* (Kensington: University of New South Wales Press, 1989), pp. 179–87.
'Department of Agriculture Annex', *Victorian Heritage Database*, http://vhd.heritage.vic. gov.au/vhd/heritagevic?timeout=yes#detail_places;65614.
Gibson, Ross, 'Formative Landscapes', in Scott Murray (ed.), *Back of Beyond: Discovering Australian Film and Television* (Sydney: Australian Film Commission, 1988), pp. 20–32.
Hardy, Forsyth (ed.), *Grierson on Documentary* (London: Faber and Faber, 1966).
Hughes, John, 'After *Indonesia Calling*', PhD (Project) Exegesis, School of Media and Communications, College of Design and Social Context, RMIT University, Melbourne, 2012.
Jacobs, Lewis (ed.), *The Documentary Tradition*, 2nd edn (New York: W. W. Norton and Co., 1979).

Martin, Adrian, 'Nurturing the Next Wave: What Is Cinema?' in Scott Murray (ed.), *Back of Beyond: Discovering Australian Film and Television* (Sydney: Australian Film Commission, 1988), pp. 90–101.

Martin, Adrian, 'Melbourne Journal: Adrian Martin Measures the Distance of Australia's Rootlessness in Search of a Native Cinema', *Film Comment* vol. 38 no. 4 (July–August 2002), pp. 12–13.

Monro, D. H.,. 'Obituary: Alan Ker Stout, 1900–1983', *Australasian Journal of Philosophy* vol. 61 no. 3 (1983), p. 338.

Moran, Albert, *Projecting Australia: Government Film since 1945* (Sydney: Currency Press, 1991).

Moran, Albert and Tom O'Regan, 'Two Discourses of Australian Film', *Australian Journal of Screen Theory* vol. 15 no. 16 (1983), pp. 163–73.

Ramsay, A. H. 'Letter to the Hon. T. T. Hollway M.L.A. Premier of Victoria', 31 March 1949.

Rosenthal, Newman, 'Has the Documentary Film a Future?', *Meanjin* vol. 8 no. 2 (Winter 1949), p. 110.

Shirley, Graham and Brian Adams, *Australian Cinema: The First Eighty Years* (Sydney: Angus and Robinson/Currency, 1983).

Stout, A. K., 'Documentary Films', n.d., p. 14.

Williams, Deane, 'Between Empire and Nation: Grierson in Australia', *Screening the Past* (1991), http://www.latrobe.edu.au/screeningthepast/firstrelease/fr0799/dwfr7e.htm.

Williams, Deane, *Australian Post-war Documentary Films: An Arc of Mirrors* (Bristol and Chicago, IL: Intellect, 2008).

**1 0**

# John Grierson in India:
# The Films Division under the Influence?

*Camille Deprez*

## INTRODUCTION

This chapter will investigate the influence of the Griersonian documentary film tradition on the origins, objectives and developments of the Films Division of India against the political, economic and social background of the period 1948–64. This timeframe corresponds to the early but crucial years of India's independence and covers the period of Prime Minister Jawaharlal Nehru's leadership, from his creation of Films Division in 1948 until his death in 1964. First, this chapter will determine the exact connections between the British documentary film movement and Films Division of India, in order to better comprehend why, how and the extent to which the latter both overlapped and diverged from the former. Then, it will argue that, despite the strong relations between the Indian official documentary film service and the British movement, and despite the strong British belief in the continuing reality of imperial links somehow or other after India's independence, Films Division of India was more significantly concerned with its national independence and the invention of a national identity in postcolonial times. So, beyond Films Division's role in reinventing India's identity after decades of British colonial rule, this chapter will focus on the limits to the British influence on the Indian public documentary film service, emphasising the divergences between the two traditions.

## THE INFLUENCE OF THE BRITISH ADMINISTRATIVE MODEL AND DOCUMENTARY FILM MOVEMENT

The British legacy to Films Division of India is significant in several respects. In the early 1940s, the British colonial administration, or *Raj*, contributed to the establishment of an Indian documentary and newsreels institution, by setting up the Indian Films of India, the Indian News Parade and the Army Film Centre, at a time when it knew that Indian independence was inevitable. These propaganda films were designed to show that the empire did not fail and that the handover was not won by Indian nationalists, but planned by the British themselves. In his article on these films, Philip Woods states:

> Indians needed to be portrayed in positions of authority ... working for the war effort
> spontaneously and on a self-organizing basis. British officials felt that these views confirmed

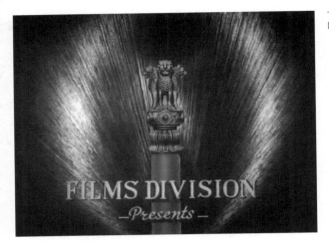

their own optimism about the demand for films about modern India, which could, of course, reflect well on the British contribution to that modernity.[1]

However, Indian nationalist leaders and the local audience appropriated this original objective to serve their own nation-building function. Woods adds that

> The demise of the FAB [Film Advisory Board] in 1943 and its replacement by Information Films of India [IFI], under direct government control, marked a novel phase in the use of film for propaganda in British India. This and the use of compulsory viewing of newsreel and government shorts marked a new level of state intervention in the cinema industry in India. IFI was a much larger production unit than its predecessor and the amount of government expenditure on film production rose dramatically.[2]

Thus, IFI had developed the idea of a public documentary film service before India gained independence. These British film units prepared the foundation for Films Division. In her book on Nehru, Judith M. Brown remarks that the first prime minister of independent India, Jawaharlal Nehru, had inherited the *Raj* and its instruments of governance – with all their limitations – as part of the transfer of power. This smooth transition was also secured by the fact that Nehru shared a number of values with the British rulers, including a belief in the vital role of the state in managing a nation's economic, social and political life, as well as a similar elitist political style. This continuity of style and attitudes enabled him to become a bridge figure between the older colonial world and a new order emerging out of the destruction of the old European empires.[3] Maintaining these instruments and style of governance was also considered a necessity for the stability of the new government and institutions. However, Richard Osborne points out the complex case of India within the British empire:

> In Britain, the Ministry of Information (MOI) was formed as the department responsible for publicity and propaganda [...]; [that] in most empire countries, the MOI assumed

responsibility for the factual films that were destined for overseas audiences, but [that] in India a more complicated situation evolved [...]. [Local] organisations were affiliated to the Government of India, and were responsible for producing films aimed at both domestic and overseas audiences. [However, the MOI] part funded some of the films and was responsible for their distribution in other Allied countries.[4]

This complex situation, mixing some level of local autonomy with British imperial intervention, aroused suspicion among Indian nationalists, causing Information Films of India and the Indian News Parade to cease production of documentaries and newsreels in 1946, after the Indian Legislative Assembly passed a motion to cut the budgetary grant. In 1948, after two years void of official documentary film-making, Nehru created the Films Division of the Ministry of Information to lead the production and distribution of Indian information films. Its set-up and objectives clearly originated from the British colonial film units and Grierson's government-service approach. The objective of this chapter is not to critically assess the achievements of the British documentary film movement – as it is accepted that it did produce variegated works in both the poetic and realist traditions of film-making and used varied methods depending on the local context of the British ruled countries;[5] but to summarise what it stood for in order to better comprehend why, how and the extent to which Films Division of India overlapped and diverged from its British counterparts. In London, the Empire Marketing Board (1926–33), the General Post Office (1933–40) and the Crown (1940–52) film units made films for government departments – the latter was even included within the Ministry of Information – in order to promote British state agencies and empire, and to guarantee national unity, social progress and stability.[6] In this context, these units worked as training schools, in which the collective always took the precedence over individual voices and creativity. Film was perceived as an efficient medium of communication between the state and the general public, and was more specifically used as a means of passing down social and political messages from the elite to the people, thus maintaining a clear hierarchical conception of society. For instance, the Crown Film Unit was created during World War II in order to broadcast official statements about the war and encourage patriotism. The films were crafted to publicise and promote the policies and point of view of the state, in informative, expositional and educational ways. Conceived as tools of social persuasion, they served propagandist and civic educational purposes. British documentaries and newsreels were made to encourage social wholeness, that is to say the unified and interdependent character of society. They also promoted new economic and social developments, and thus regularly featured symbols of modernity, such as trains and other means of transport, and national unity, such as the Post Office services or the infrastructure of the market economy. They tended to be concerned with the content and expressive richness of the actuality image; the interpretive potential of the editing; and the representation of social relationships. This chapter argues that, in the early years of independence, Films Division of India was intended to sustain the new nation's spirit, using similar tools and references. The British documentary film developed at a time when realism was considered an alternative to the success of the illusionary and artificial fiction film, best exemplified by Hollywood, and thus observed people in a mix of real and recreated environments.

John Grierson in India: The Films Division under the Influence?

155

Although Films Division emerged two decades later, it also provided an alternative to the flourishing escapist Bollywood formula. Films on industries and goods were projected on foreign screens, following the 1930s model of the British Empire Marketing Board, whose films were meant to promote trade. Despite this influence, Films Division also established a distance from several aspects of the British tradition. Indian documentaries and newsreels of the late 1940s–early 60s neither specifically focused on the difficult living conditions of the working class, nor did they criticise the position and actions of the state. British documentaries were of two kinds: either promoting government services, official procedures and private industrial activities, or experimenting with the film medium, via new sound, visual, narrative and editing techniques. But this chapter will further demonstrate that Films Division was dominated by public agencies, that in its early days, most of the production served official purposes and that formal experimentation remained occasional. Finally, FD adopted the British tactic of reaching out by dispatching projection vans to India's scattered rural majority. However, unlike the British distribution model, films were mainly shown theatrically, and this chapter will show that this had a contrasting impact on their reception.

So, Nehru adapted the initial war propaganda purpose of information films to the new times of peace and independence, and enlisted documentary cinema for his larger project of nation-building, integration and development. While IFI and INP had functioned as separate units, Films Division was comprised of both units, namely the Documentary Films of India and the Indian Newsreel Review.[7] The new independent government of India maintained the Rule 44A of the Defence of Indian Rules, passed by the British in 1944, whereby exhibitors were compelled to include in every one of their programmes a maximum of 2,000 feet of film approved by the government and for which they had to pay a rental fee. Since Films Division supplied over 6,000 cinemas in the country, this compulsory exhibition assured FD a stable market and regular incomes. FD's administrative apparatus followed to a large extent the organisational model established by John Grierson and the British documentary film movement. In many cases, the personnel recruited for Films Division had previously worked for the British film units of India. So, Ravi Vasudevan notices

a line of continuity rather than discontinuity at the time of decolonisation. While some key institutions, state-run film-making and newsreel units were disbanded, key people and policies continued when the new institutions, such as the Films Division, came into being.[8]

In 1942–3, the British government appointed Alexander Shaw, a disciple of John Grierson, to set up the first Indian film unit. He had trained a small team of technicians and film-makers, who later worked for FD, including Ezra Mir, P. V. Pathy, Bhaskar Rao, Clement Baptista, Hom Sethna and Krishna Gopal. Other new recruits had mainly worked in the Indian feature film industry before joining FD. As in Great Britain in the late 1920s–early 30s, they knew little about documentary film-making at first and were mainly trained by their peers, who themselves had been trained by the British. This situation perpetuated the influence of the British film tradition on FD production. Films Division also shared Grierson's idea of coexistence and collaboration between the public and private sectors, with the public sector being always at the commanding heights. In India, Films Division dominated the documentary scene due to its centralised set-up, established infrastructure, monopoly over the cinemas and weekly film releases. The private sector was represented by 'outside producers', which included various individuals, private companies and partnerships. Some of these, like James Beveridge, were clearly influenced by the British film tradition. Trained by John Grierson in the late 1930s and 40s, Beveridge had left the National Film Board of Canada in 1954 to come to India and work for the private oil company Burma-Shell. Between 1954 and 1958, when the film unit was closed down, Beveridge produced forty films, some of which were purchased by Films Division. This situation helped to infuse the institution with the Griersonian tradition. Beveridge had, for instance, sponsored the documentary *Village in Travancore* (1956), directed by Fali Billimoria, a film-maker trained by Alexander Shaw during World War II. Furthermore, Films Division subscribed to the British top-down administrative system, according to which elite advisers knew what was best for the common people. During the period 1948–64, chief producers Mohan Bhavnani (1948–54), V. Shantaram (1954), Jean Bhownagary (1954–6), Ezra Mir (1956–61) and K. L. Khandpur (1962–8), as well as the film-makers, all belonged to the Indian educated social elite and were closely acquainted with the British culture and style. The new independent government of India also followed the British model by consolidating state control over Films Division in order to develop a strong public documentary service for the country. In her book on Indian postcolonial nationalism, Srirupa Roy analyses the role played by Films Division in shaping the nation-state for the Indian population and argues that 'Films Division enabled the constitution of a distinct identity for the state as an authoritative representative of the Indian nation, an identity that could be recognized both by non-state audiences and by state elites themselves.'[9]

The subjects of the films were in most cases recommended by the various ministries of the government of India and by state governments before the beginning of each financial year. The completed films had to be approved by the Film Advisory Board, which had been appointed by the government in 1949 and consisted mainly of civil servants, and also certified by the Board of Films Censors. These two elitist boards kept a watchful eye on the value of the films for the general public.

Philip Woods asserts that during the colonial era, the Indian film audience was divided into three social groups, which partly overlapped: the Western-educated and English-speaking urban elite; the city audience, which mixed the middle with the working classes; and the rural audiences, who were mainly accessed through mobile vans touring the villages. Films would be made differently according to the target audience, with an assumption, for instance, that films for Indian rural districts would have to be slower in tempo, explain modern things and be adapted to the local culture, a rather tall order in practice.[10] After independence, Films Division continued to target the same groups. Mohan Bhavnani, chief producer of the documentary film section from the creation of FD in 1948 until 1954, later stated that

Modern documentary techniques were more suited to educated audiences, who could understand devices like 'wipes', 'flash backs', 'dissolves', and fast tempo. But the same techniques would rather confuse village and illiterate audiences, the film being still new and rare to many of them. Therefore, technical devices were avoided, the tempo slowed down, and sometimes shots were repeated to stress the main idea of the theme.[11]

This statement confirms the fact that the Indian elite in charge of Films Division reproduced the vision developed by the British to a large extent. This state-sponsored institution also shared the main objectives set by John Grierson for the British documentary film movement.

## THE POSITIVE SOCIAL FUNCTION OF ART

John Grierson's ideological stance was mainly influenced by idealist and positivist philosophy.[12] He believed in the need for social reform and for an efficient modern society, in which elites govern the majority. The context of confused public identities, widespread illiteracy and other problems of underdevelopment, which characterised India during Nehru's leadership, was quite different from that of Great Britain. However, the range of political, social and economic reforms planned for new independent India confirms that Jawaharlal Nehru was both committed to social reform and an idealist. At the instigation of Nehru, Films Division appropriated Grierson's notion of integration and consensus, rather than individualism, to fit in the social context of national heterogeneity of young independent India. The nation was to be placed before the self. Grierson's idea that films should not try to teach the public to 'know everything about everything all the time', but 'instil an understanding of the significant generative forces in society',[13] applies to early Films Division films. These generative forces were mainly of two orders: shaping a common consciousness and establishing an allegiance through nonfiction films about the national project of integration and development. FD productions were not only meant to educate the Indian populace, but also to bring hope to these millions of people who had recently achieved independence and to motivate them to work for a better future. The meaning of that 'better future' was defined by the local elite, as reforms were never initiated by the people they concerned. Grierson's ideas and statements can be found in official documents published by the Indian Ministry of Information from the creation of Films Division to the present day, and these support the conclusion that Grierson had a significant influence on the purpose and objectives of the Indian public documentary film service. For instance, the following quote appears in one of Films Division's publications:

> The film is a creative medium of information, education, persuasion and inspiration. It has a special importance, therefore, as a contributor to the community life of today. It has therefore a very special role in creating the better shapes of the community of tomorrow.[14]

The 1951 Report of the Film Enquiry Committee mentions that the 'documentary section [was] concerned with the production of short films of instructional, cultural and educational value'.[15] This Griersonian concept was adapted to the Indian context and needs, with other official publications mentioning that films were meant to 'establish rapport between the rulers and the ruled, to inform the masses about the meaning of Independence, to acquaint them about the plans and projects being launched, to present them a balance-sheet of progress'; and add that the documentary film was the ideal medium for illiterate people, a majority of the Indian population at

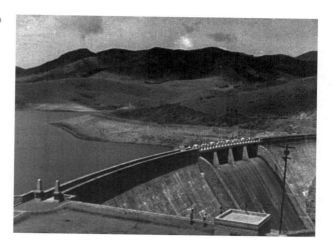

A still from the Films Division documentary *Rivers in Harness* (1949)

that time, and that it 'could weld the people of different castes, communities, religions, regions and languages into a nation'.[16]

Following the model developed by the British movement, FD films emphasised the interrelation of social practices within Indian society. Documentaries on the building of dams such as *Rivers in Harness* (1949) or *Golden River* (1954), illustrated how the resultant infrastructures could improve cultivation (via irrigation) and the comfort of Indian homes, thanks to the installation of electric lighting and appliances. By the same token, films about education programmes such as *Basic Education* (1950) demonstrated how they benefited entire communities and contributed to the nation's economic self-sufficiency. The films also supported the idea of a social elite governing the average people for their own good, a situation that was presented as social consensus. Films always presented political leaders and various experts, like engineers, doctors or teachers, in a positive light and the larger population as obedient contributors to the reforms planned for them by the ruling class. This harmonious picture of the social organisation of India was meant to both reinforce national cohesion and validate state reforms.

The purpose of the films was to stimulate enthusiasm among the Indian general audience in the context of independence and nation-building. Films Division was particularly influenced by Grierson's idea of the positive and negative social function of art, and that the positive representation should always dominate the negative one. This explains why FD film narratives often progressed from a problematic situation (the poor irrigation system, the lack of electricity, the unsatisfactory legal system, etc.) to its resolution. This narrative structure conveyed the notion that the Indian people were always taking action and that India was constantly moving forward and improving negative circumstances. According to Grierson, the positive social function of art involved grabbing the power and energy of modern life, to represent the essence and spirit of things.[17] FD film-makers took this on board, filming engineers and other technical experts at work, but also planes, trains and cars, which they considered symbolic visual representations of modernity. In the same vein as

John Grierson in India: The Films Division under the Influence?

159

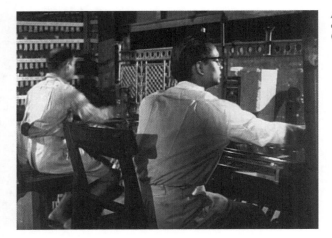

A still from Films Division
documentary *Vigil on Wheels*
(1955)

the realist actuality footage of the railway network in the British documentary *Night Mail*, Films Division produced works such as *The Vital Link* (1951) and *Vigil on Wheels* (1955) to illustrate the state's capacity to conduct large-scale projects for the economic development of India. These films showed the various stages of the construction of new railway tracks and the efficient organisation and training of railway personnel. Dynamic montages of men at work, clocks ticking, racing train wheels, steaming locomotives, powerful sound effects of drums and whistles all conveyed the positive energy of modern change. Each obstacle, be it a train accident or a fallen bridge, was inevitably overcome. The railway network was presented as an unstoppable work in progress, connecting the entire population of India together and contributing to its development by transporting goods and passengers. In order to stimulate audience enthusiasm, films elaborated on the dynamic drive of change by featuring dramatic visuals, such as the raging forces of nature or impressive aerial shots of the country, accompanied by expressive or sometimes lyrical commentaries; and by resonant post-synchronised soundtracks, using instruments such as drums, cymbals or conches, or even the sound of loud crowds. In many cases, commentaries emphasised the race against time, which India would eventually win. This ineluctable move forward would often be visually conveyed through superimposed images of continuous calendar pages. These visual and sound elements were reinforced by fast-paced montage editing, with few transition effects. This combination of various cinematic tools was meant to represent the positive power and energy of change. But unlike *Night Mail*, a sequence which matched the recitation of W. H. Auden's poem with the pace of the train's wheels, breaking new formal ground for the documentary medium, the Indian films avoided any experiments that were too innovative or intellectual. As mentioned earlier, different films would target different audiences. For rural spectators, the focus would be on how to grow potatoes and cotton, on dry farming methods or kitchen gardens. The whys and wherefores would be explained in a straightforward manner, again following the British colonial vision according to which villagers could only understand basic facts and ideas filmed in a simplistic and direct manner. Former film-maker and controller of Films Division, K. L. Khandpur, recalled:

> Usually one central idea [was] emphasized, supported by just a few relevant points. The job of the filmmaker [was] to facilitate the audience in understanding the subject. Films should appeal more to the emotions of the audience than to their intellect.[18]

Thus, FD personnel subscribed to Grierson's vision of the positive and idealist function of art, as well as his call for social consensus, but adapted these concepts to the needs of the new independent India. Therefore, unlike British films, FD documentaries seldom made any critical comment or raised any doubt about state policies, so contributing to the loss of credibility of both Nehru's government and Films Division. This chapter will later demonstrate that FD films of the period 1948–64 failed to serve their social purpose efficiently, since they never established the distance necessary to allow scriptwriters and film-makers to accurately describe and analyse the social issues depicted. Besides, the strong connection between FD films and the Griersonion tradition also engendered ambiguities and restrictions.

## AMBIGUITIES AND LIMITS TO THE BRITISH INFLUENCE

Over the period 1948–64, and even later, India held an ambivalent position toward the British, inherited from a history of colonial resistance to this imperial power. The country's recent colonial past meant that Great Britain was the obvious model for building the political and administrative system of the new Indian nation, including a public documentary film service. However, India also needed to separate itself from the British rulers, in order to create its own independent national identity. This ambiguous position was already noticeable before independence and led to contradictory decisions. For instance, during World War II, the Indian film-maker V. Shantaram, despite his loyalty to the Indian nationalist movement, cooperated with the British rulers to become head of Information Films of India, because he wanted to oppose fascism. And in 1946, Indian nationalists had cut the budget of the IFI, bringing the production activity to a full stop, because the institution was considered a symbol of colonial oppression in times of struggle for independence. But this halt also deprived the Indian people of locally produced official moving images of the birth of independent India, including the handover ceremonies and Nehru's first speech to his free nation.

So, despite the fact that the origins and objectives of Films Division were significantly influenced by John Grierson and the British movement, the Indian public documentary service sought to establish its own identity and thus presented several specificities and differences from its British counterparts. Documentary film-maker and historian B. D. Garga mentions that, in comparison with the British documentary, Films Division started with better technical and financial resources. It had six units for the production of documentaries and a newsreel organisation with ten cameramen posted at important centres. At first, it produced thirty-six documentaries and fifty-two newsreels per year, which were distributed through centres established in the main cities of Bombay, Madras, Calcutta, Lucknow and Nagpur. The compulsory exhibition of their films in every cinema in the country guaranteed a stable market and an assured income.[19] This situation marked a difference with that of Great Britain, where documentary film distribution was not compulsory and mainly non-theatrical. With a production of over 2,700 films in the first twenty years after the creation of Films Division and a weekly paying audience of 20 million, the reach of these official documentaries marked the unique situation of India. The films produced by Films Division had to adapt to India's specific context, and in particular to its largely illiterate and heterogeneous audience, its linguistic diversity and to the challenges of national integration and development. Influenced by the British social elite, English remained the dominant language within FD, at both administrative and production levels. However, in order to reach out to a wider audience, films were quickly dubbed in up to thirteen local languages.

This ambiguous attitude toward the British also led to some inner contradictions. The control of the production and distribution of documentaries by government agencies, including their approval by the Film Advisory Board and the Film Censor Board, was unique among democratic nations and seems quite at odds with democratic processes. The private sector, and more precisely private exhibitors, started to oppose the compulsory exhibition rule very early on. They compared it to the Hollywood blind and block booking strategy and criticised it for restricting their right to free enterprise, which was perceived as undemocratic. Besides, private producers were reluctant to make documentaries, knowing that Films Division would only pay a low rate to purchase what they called 'outside productions'. In addition, the films did not always fulfil the social function claimed by Films Division. The 1951 *Report of the Film Enquiry Committee* remarks that documentaries were often criticised by film professionals and by the general audience for 'being mere travelogues, and those which aimed to instruct were either considered pompous in their approach or too timid to force the obvious conclusion'.[20]

By the late 1950s and early 60s, all commentators agreed upon the fact that FD films had begun to look like one another, despite fresh approaches by some in-house and independent film-makers, including Jean Bhownagary, P. V. Pathy, A. Bhaskar Rao, James Beveridge and Paul Zils. The press and the parliament criticised the documentary film for failing to fulfil its social obligations. With the objective of producing up to 150 documentaries annually, as well as a weekly newsreel in thirteen languages, quantity soon surpassed quality. This was a period of expansion for FD, as various ministries required more and more films as part of their integrated-plan publicity programmes. Although FD's budget and earnings kept increasing over the 1950s and 60s, directors gradually lost the momentum afforded by independence. Their films made no profound and realistic study of the people or situations. Indeed, scripts were written at desks in Delhi and Bombay offices rather than on location. Most film-makers knew only English and Hindi and were unfamiliar with other Indian languages, regions and cultures; and this affected the relevance of the films. A large number of documentaries focused on the common heritage of all Indians and presented different places of interest, monuments, arts, crafts and religious festivals, in order to consolidate India's national identity and highlight its grandeur. This extensive list included *Festival Time* (1950), *Handicrafts of Travancore* (1950), *Our*

*Original Inhabitants* (1953), *Ancient Weavers Today* (1957), *Mandu – The City of Joy* (1959), *Indian Art through the Ages* (1959), *A Century of Indian Archeology* (1960), *Kathakali* (1960), *Folk Dances of India* (1961) and *Dances of Assam* (1963), but all tended to generalise about Indian history and traditions. Also, this objective of national integration generated films like *Festival Time*, in which more importance is given to Hindu festivals compared to other religious traditions, misleading the audience into believing that everyone in India faithfully follows Hindu rituals. The limited duration of the films, often around ten minutes, and the haste in which most were produced, were partly responsible for this lack of accuracy and relevance. Despite an urgent need to create an independent national identity for India, Films Division didn't have the personnel and resources to make radical changes in the structure of the organisation and in the style of the films, reducing its ability to deliver pertinent films.

Most of FD production still referred to the various aspects of the social and economic development of India in positive terms. Srirupa Roy characterises FD films by their 'ponderous and heavy-handed style' and adds that 'for the most part, they lend themselves all too readily to charges of clumsy propaganda and bureaucratic ineptitude'.[21] According to her, 'More than a third of the total output of documentary films in the first two decades after independence, were those that addressed the themes of planned development and various aspects of social and economic modernization.'[22]

Indeed, most FD product continued to deliver official messages of success and control to the mass audience, while giving the impression of an objective report, a strategy inherited from the British documentary film movement. Various cinematic and narrative tools were employed in order to achieve this objective. An affirmative and authoritative voiceover always explained the images, leaving little space for synchronous sound – a technical limitation which helped FD to manipulate real facts – alternative views and thus dissenting audience interpretation. Film-makers preferred straightforward images and few transition effects, in order to give the impression that these recorded images were the exact reproduction of real situations and events. The recurrent pans and static cameras were both the result of the technical limitations of the times and useful tools. Indeed, pans allowed vast areas to be framed and almost matched the human gaze; while static shots allowed people to move around, enter and leave the frame, giving the visual impression that genuine and unstaged situations, places and people were being recorded. Drawings of maps of India were regularly deployed to convey the idea of an objective report of situations and events, although maps can easily be manipulated to support the official point of view on various issues, such as controversial borders with Pakistan, the progress of railway tracks or dam projects. Staged sequences were also common, because they delivered official messages more efficiently than newsreel footage.

However, Roy's remark also suggests that one-third of FD production did not perfectly match official statements and plans for reform. By the mid-1960s, film directors and the general audience were largely disillusioned with Nehru's policies and with his failure to achieve national unity, economic progress and social change. These policies were indeed seriously challenged by political, social and economic unrest, encompassing peacekeeping on the borders with China and Pakistan, rising Hindu extremism, Marxist movements and tribal activism, a persistent caste system, a religious and community-based society, agricultural and industrial failures (including food shortages and delayed construction works), as well as financial difficulties resulting from the Indian rupee currency crisis. So, from the mid-1950s and early 60s on, film-makers including T. A. Abraham, Mohan Whadwani, Clement Baptista, A. Bhaskar Rao, Fali Billimoria and Jean Bhownagary started to raise more independent voices. Their creativity was acknowledged, entitling them to choose their subjects, and as a result they diverged from official themes and statements to venture into experimental explorations. For instance, T. A. Abraham's *Symphony of Life* (1954) offered a lyrical representation of human and natural life in India, by replacing the usual voiceover commentary with music, and by editing sound and image creatively in order to emotionally involve the spectators. This expressive editing reinforced the impact of actual shots of villagers and tribal communities' daily routines, as well as that of images of rivers, waterfalls, monsoon rains and dams, by adding S. V. Shirali's poetic original soundtrack. Some films also started to address persisting problems and obstacles to India's development and modernisation. Some took conventional form, such as *Dry Leaves* (1961), which presents the dowry system as a plague to a harmonious society and makes a straightforward pledge for its abolition. Others were more innovative, such as Debaki Kumar Bose's series of four films, including *Arghya* (1961), on the endurance of the caste system and untouchability, and how to break down caste barriers at community level. Having made several films on Indian literature, Bose based two on poems by Rabindranath Tagore, with a lyrical use of music and literary references to convey his very down-to-earth message. These forerunners, who leaned towards the poetic tradition of the British documentary film movement, contributed to shaping more personal and critical approaches to the documentary film medium within FD's centralised production set-up. Finally, a gap developed between the initial project of Films Division to make socially purposive films and the reality of the films produced. The first documentary chief producer, Mohan Bhavnani, was dismissed from his post in 1954 for clashing with the bureaucrats. His agenda had been to make films cheaply and quickly to reach a heterogeneous audience.[23] But his practical and utilitarian approach interfered with the procedural stance of the state administration. In 1960, Bhavnani declared that:

> Above all, the making of a pure documentary requires a man of vision and idealism, who can dare to face the revealing truths of his subject, no matter how unpalatable these may be to the various sections of society.[24]

However, Films Division could not proceed with this approach, since the central government and state ministries commissioned documentaries to support their official policies, plans and statements. For instance, Nehru believed in decentralising administrative functions to the local level, as a way to encourage self-reliance, and inaugurated the system of *panchayati raj* – or rule of the village council of five – in 1959. Films like *Our Panchayats* (1950) were produced to support this reform and to convince the population that decentralisation was the best option. This entirely staged documentary is presented to the viewers as if the record of real events, mediated by a voice-of-God narration. The film first focuses on village life before the *panchayati raj* was implemented. It shows how villagers struggled to settle their disputes in front of a court and how the process was time- and money-consuming. The film highlighted the villagers' laziness and helplessness, mocking their quarrelsome behaviour by introducing the sound of cackling chickens. In the second part, *panchayat* members are elected; quarrelsome villagers are happily reconciled; and local problems of road infrastructure, health, food supplies and the like are resolved. This is yet another example of a socially purposive film that demonstrates how the negative aspects of the existent local political and legal systems can be overthrown by the positive reform of the *panchayats*, unifying social relationships, in a typical Griersonian way. However, this initial objective of democratic political change effectively failed to come into practice, a situation not reflected in the films. In 1966, the Chanda Committee for broadcasting and information media pointed out the loss of public interest in official documentaries and newsreels:

> because of organisational defects, the documentaries [were] produced mechanically and disinterestedly, making them dull and uninteresting. Their treatment [was] often superficial and the absence of humour and satire [was] a contributory factor. Also, the pattern of documentaries [had] now become so stereotyped [...] it [was] easy to anticipate sequences and conclusions.[25]

In most cases, documentaries clearly deviating from the official state position would not be approved by the Film Advisory Board and Film Censor Board. This consensual position revealed the limitations of Films Division as a production centre for socially purposive documentary films, and this explained why the general audience began to view these films with growing scepticism.


## CONCLUSIONS

Films Division's documentary production of the late 1940s–mid-60s remains an underresearched topic and further archival research is needed to comprehensively understand this period of official documentary film-making. The influence of John Grierson and the British documentary film movement on Films Division of India was crucial in several respects – including that of administrative style and personnel, as well as themes, purpose and aesthetic features – but the historical context in which these documentaries were produced differed from that of Great Britain. India adapted the exercise in national projection, for which the British documentary film movement had first been initiated, to counter the influence of Hollywood, to define and support its own national identity in a largely illiterate, poor and diversified social context. However, important discrepancies started to appear between the ideal project pursued by Nehru's government and reality on the ground. Official FD films did circulate a progressive and reformist opinion but failed to reflect on economic setbacks, social conservatism and rising political opposition. In depicting too positive a picture of India's situation, they failed to confront problems, and therefore could not help to overcome them.

So, once the general post-independence exaltation had passed, film-makers and audiences slowly started to reconsider the status and value of Films Division documentaries. Disenchantment with Films Division came when people realised that

John Grierson in India: The Films Division under the Influence?

165

the promises made by Nehru had not been fulfilled. Official films lost credibility and became associated with propaganda. Since the late 1960s, and more significantly from the 70s and 80s onwards, counter-documentary practices have developed within and outside Films Division, and its monopoly status has been increasingly challenged. This also created new opportunities for film-makers to develop their own style and distance themselves more clearly from the British documentary film tradition.

## NOTES

1. Philip Woods, 'From Shaw to Shantaram: The Film Advisory Board and the Making of British Propaganda Films in India, 1940–1943', *Historical Journal of Film, Radio and Television* vol. 21 no. 3 (2001), p. 300.
2. Ibid., pp. 304–5.
3. Judith M. Brown, *Nehru, Profiles in Power* (Harlow: Pearson Education Limited, 1999), pp. 90, 185.
4. Richard Osborne, 'India on Film, 1939–1947', in Lee Grieveson and Colin MacCabe (eds), *Film and the End of Empire* (London: BFI, 2011), p. 120.
5. For a critical assessment of the British documentary film movement, and more specifically of its imperial ideology and reception, see Martin Stollery, *Alternative Empires: European Modernist Cinemas and Cultures of Imperialism* (Exeter: Exeter University Press, 2000), pp. 140–202.
6. See the entries 'Empire Marketing Board', 'General Post Office', 'Crown Film Unit' and 'John Grierson' in Ian Aitken (ed.), *The Encyclopedia of the Documentary Film*, volume 1 (London: Routledge, 2006).
7. *Report of the Film Enquiry Committee* (New Delhi: Ministry of Information, Government of India Press, 1951), pp. 51–2.
8. Ravi Vasudevan, 'Official and Amateur: Exploring Information Film in India', in Grieveson and MacCabe, *Film and the End of Empire*, p. 74.
9. Srirupa Roy, *Beyond Belief: India and the Politics of Postcolonial Nationalism* (Durham, NC: Duke University Press, 2007), p. 34.
10. Woods, 'From Shaw to Shantaram', p. 299.
11. Mohan Bhavnani, 'The Background of the Short Film in India and Future of Documentary', *Marg* vol. 13 no. 3 (1960), p. 5.
12. See Ian Aitken, 'John Grierson, Idealism and the Inter-war Period', *Historical Journal of Film, Radio and Television* vol. 9 no. 3 (1989), pp. 247–58; Ian Aitken, *Film and Reform: John Grierson and the Documentary Film Movement* (London: Routledge, 1990), pp. 37–47, 184–95; and Ian Aitken (ed.), *The Documentary Film Movement: An Anthology* (Edinburgh: Edinburgh University Press, 1998), pp. 35–44, 76–7.
13. Aitken, *Film and Reform*, p. 191.
14. John Grierson, 'O These Problems, These Priorities', in Jag Mohan (ed.), *Four Times Five* (Bombay: Films Division, Ministry of Information and Broadcasting, 1969), p. 7. References to Grierson also appear in Jag Mohan (ed.), *Two Decades of the Films Division* (Bombay: Ministry of Information and Broadcasting, 1969); Jag Mohan (ed.), *Documentary Films and Indian Awakening* (New Delhi: Publications Division, Ministry of Information and Broadcasting, 1990); and '60 Years of Films Division', *Documentary Today* vol. 1 no. 4 (2008).

15. *Report of the Film Enquiry Committee*, p. 52.
16. Mohan, *Two Decades of the Films Division*, p. 11.
17. Aitken, *Film and Reform*, p. 60.
18. K. L. Khandpur, 'The Technique of Documentary Making in India: Approach to Factual Films', *Marg* vol. 13 no. 3 (1960), pp. 44–5.
19. B. D. Garga, *From Raj to Swaraj: The Non-fiction Film in India* (New Delhi: Penguin Books, 2007), p. 134.
20. *Report of the Film Enquiry Committee*, p. 54.
21. Roy, *Beyond Belief*, p. 34.
22. Ibid., p. 47.
23. Garga, *From Raj to Swaraj*, p. 133.
24. Bhavnani, 'The Background of the Short Film in India', p. 6.
25. Ashok K. Chanda, *Committee Report on Broadcasting and Information Media* (Delhi: Ministry of Information and Broadcasting, 1966).

## REFERENCES

'60 Years of Films Division', *Documentary Today* vol. 1 no. 4 (2008).

Aitken, Ian, 'John Grierson, Idealism and the Inter-war Period', *Historical Journal of Film, Radio and Television* vol. 9 no. 3 (1989), pp. 247–58.

Aitken, Ian, *Film and Reform: John Grierson and the Documentary Film Movement* (London: Routledge, 1990).

Aitken, Ian (ed.), *The Documentary Film Movement: An Anthology* (Edinburgh: Edinburgh University Press, 1998).

Aitken, Ian (ed.), *The Encyclopedia of the Documentary Film*, volume 1 (London: Routledge, 2006).

Bhavnani, Mohan, 'The Background of the Short Film in India and Future of Documentary', *Marg* vol. 13 no. 3 (1960), pp. 4–8.

Brown, Judith M., *Nehru, Profiles in Power* (Harlow: Pearson Education Limited, 1999).

Chanda, Ashok K., *Committee Report on Broadcasting and Information Media* (Delhi: Ministry of Information and Broadcasting, 1966).

Garga, B. D., *From Raj to Swaraj: The Non-fiction Film in India* (New Delhi: Penguin Books, 2007).

Grierson, John, 'O These Problems, These Priorities', in Jag Mohan (ed.), *Four Times Five* (Bombay: Films Division, Ministry of Information and Broadcasting, 1969), pp. 7–8.

Khandpur, K. L., 'The Technique of Documentary Making in India: Approach to Factual Films', *Marg* vol. 13 no. 3 (1960), pp. 44–5.

Mohan, Jag (ed.), *Two Decades of the Films Division* (Bombay: Ministry of Information and Broadcasting, 1969).

Mohan, Jag (ed.), *Documentary Films and Indian Awakening* (New Delhi: Publications Division, Ministry of Information and Broadcasting, 1990).

Osborne, Richard, 'India on Film, 1939–1947', in Lee Grieveson and Colin MacCabe (eds), *Film and the End of Empire* (London: BFI, 2011), pp. 118–49

*Report of the Film Enquiry Committee* (New Delhi: Ministry of Information, Government of India Press, 1951), pp. 9–65.

Roy, Srirupa, *Beyond Belief: India and the Politics of Postcolonial Nationalism* (Durham, NC: Duke University Press, 2007).

Stollery, Martin, *Alternative Empires: European Modernist Cinemas and Cultures of Imperialism* (Exeter: Exeter University Press, 2000), pp. 140–202.

Vasudevan, Ravi, 'Official and Amateur: Exploring Information Film in India', in Lee Grieveson and Colin MacCabe (eds), *Film and the End of Empire* (London: BFI, 2011), pp. 73–94.

Woods, Philip, 'From Shaw to Shantaram: The Film Advisory Board and the Making of British Propaganda Films in India, 1940–1943', *Historical Journal of Film, Radio and Television* vol. 21 no. 3 (2001), pp. 293–308.

# 11
# Grierson in Ireland

*Jerry White*

Ireland is not isolated, but belongs to an internationale. It belongs to the great and powerful internationale of the Catholic church; it belongs to the green internationale of rural countries developing progressive rural cultures; it has common interests on a dozen and one fronts. All this should be considered as Ireland makes its film plans. It means power to exchange films; it means power to produce films co-operatively with other nations; it means power to create, from the films of small nations with similar interests, a common film front to the larger world.[1]

John Grierson

We tend in this country to look to the British Documentary movement as our model, but having seen a great number of British, American and Continental documentary films over a number of years, I feel strongly that our documentary style, if such ever develops, will be much closer to the continental than the British.[2]

Colm Ó Laoghaire

John Grierson's impact in Ireland is, on the one hand, minimal. He gave at talk at a Dublin hotel in 1948, and a Jesuit review published the text of it a few months later. *Et puis, voilà.* It is thus not entirely unreasonable to dismiss his importance, given that Grierson never came back to the Republic of Ireland and showed very little interest in the North during his stints at the EMB, the GPO or the Central Office of Information (COI). And yet, I think the more compelling reading of Irish film history has Grierson as the man in the shadows, the steely Scot offering an example to his cousins across the Irish Sea. This can be seen in Irish cinema's very early days, with *Man of Aran* in 1934. That was made by the most famous Griersonian of them all, Robert Flaherty, and putting Grierson back into the history of that film can actually help us come to a more nuanced view of the conventional wisdom that it is not quite an Irish film. During his 1948 visit to Dublin Grierson was, to some extent, speaking to Irish cinephiles, the most prominent of whom was Liam Ó Laoghaire, a model Griersonian in that he took a great interest in world cinema and worked as a documentary film-maker, making films about 'social or civic or educational interest', to borrow a phrase from Grierson's 'A Film Policy for Canada'.[3] Those were also the kinds of films made by Gael Linn in the 1950s and 60s, and that was just about the only form of genuinely indigenous film-making in the Republic during this era. Gael Linn paved the way for the films of Louis Marcus, one of the only Irish documentarians to be nominated for

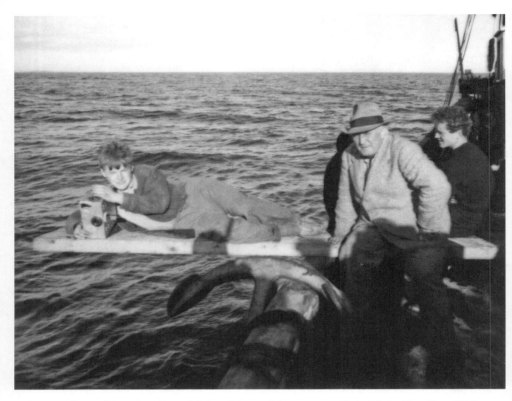

The most famous Griersonian of them all, Robert Flaherty, off the west coast of Ireland filming *Man of Aran* (1934)

an Oscar and Griersonian to the core. Bob Quinn, who came out of the 1960s and 70s Irish-language counterculture is today the closest thing Irish documentary has to a chief dissident, and he is just as Griersonian as Louis Marcus, if not more so. Harvey O'Brien, author of the very comprehensive *The Real Ireland: The Evolution of Ireland in Documentary Film*, is quite sceptical of positions like mine, writing that 'The extent to which Grierson's pronouncements directly affected documentary practice in Ireland is debatable.'[4] I take his point there, and there's no doubt that the explicit influence of the grey eminence is not comparable to his impact on the cinema of Britain, Canada or even New Zealand. But that should not obscure the degree to which Irish film-makers and institutions have sought to direct and mark the national cinema in ways that are defined by a civic/rhetorical rather than commercial/narrative vision of cinema's vocation, in ways that show the unmistakeable impact of the Grierson effect.

## ROBERT FLAHERTY AND *MAN OF ARAN*

Although there had been sporadic film-making efforts in Ireland since the birth of the medium, the production of Flaherty's *Man of Aran* represents a landmark. The film's

*The Grierson Effect*

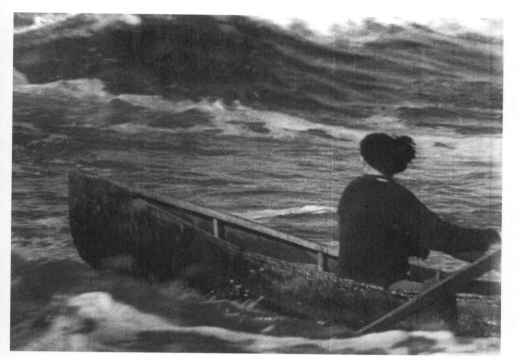

Tiger King, playing the titular role, faces a very serious wave in Flaherty's *Man of Aran*

reception upon its release and its representational legacy is central to the discourse around Irish cinema, and there is no sense in rehearsing that here.[5] The aspect of this history that it is useful to excavate in this context is Flaherty's sometimes difficult connection to Grierson, largely because it illustrates the degree to which Irish film was defined, from the very early days, by the fundamental tension of Griersonianism: between well-thought-out technocratic institutions and the unpredictable actions of individual film-makers.

Grierson's connection to Flaherty is, again, basically canonical; the importance of this for Ireland, though, has relatively little to do with the popularisation of the term 'documentary' via Grierson's review of Flaherty's 1926 film *Moana*. Rather, it has to do with Flaherty's interest in cinema as an escape from modernity, and Grierson's scepticism towards that. O'Brien sees the genesis of *Man of Aran* in terms of his relation to Grierson, writing that '*Man of Aran* was probably the most Rousseauian of all the director's films and was proof of his continuing distance from those whose work he had inspired, including John Grierson.'[6] What O'Brien is alluding to there is the film that Flaherty had made right before *Man of Aran*, *Industrial Britain* (1931), from which Flaherty was famously fired by Grierson because he was unable to keep to a budget (the film was finished by Grierson and Edgar Anstey),[7] but also because he was more interested in small-scale handcrafts than industry. Martin McLoone writes of *Man of Aran* that 'In Ireland, the film arrived just as the de Valera government was reinvigorating the ideals of cultural nationalism and it provided an almost perfect cinematic expression of the ascetic romanticism that lay behind this whole project.'[8] *Man of Aran* thus represents Flaherty turning his back on the British documentary movement and its ideology of technocratic progressivism in favour of something more Rousseauian, in O'Brien's formulation. In so doing, he ended up synchronising with what would become the prevailing forces of Irish cultural politics. The de Valera to whom McLoone alludes is Éamon de Valera, one of the few surviving leaders of the 1916 Easter Rising and prominent figure in the War of Independence, leader of the anti-treaty side during the Civil War, and in 1926 founder of Fianna Fáil, the centre-right party that would go on to dominate Irish politics during the twentieth century. Part of the representational legacy of *Man of Aran* is that it has come to serve as something of a negative example for a later generation of Irish film-makers who have sought to correct its outsider-romanticism with a more detailed and nuanced set of images produced from the inside. But one benefit of looking at Irish cinema through the 'Grierson effect' is to show us that the film-maker Irish radicals (such as Bob Quinn, about whom more later) have reacted against most strongly is also the one whose most celebrated film marked his complete break with the flinty godfather of documentary.

## EARLY CINEPHILES, FIRST DOCUMENTARIES

The early history of film culture in Ireland should sound very familiar to readers of this anthology. The Irish Film Society was founded in 1936, and in 1945, the most cinephilic of its founders, Liam Ó Laoghaire, published a history of world cinema called *Invitation to the Film*. Kevin Rockett writes that with this book, 'he placed himself firmly in the Griersonian context of seeing documentary as a social tool showing people how the democratic system and its institutions operate'.[9] He probably has in mind passages like the one where Ó Laoghaire marvelled how 'The brilliant Scot, John Grierson, made *Drifters* in 1929 and persuaded civil servants into accepting the film as a medium of national propaganda.'[10] But it wouldn't be long before Ó Laoghaire showed himself to be a Griersonian in more than his approach to film history.

A few years after the founding of the Irish Film Society, an ostensibly quite different group came into being, one whose political position seemed dissimilar but whose didactic, nonprofit vision of cinema was actually quite close to that of the Irish Film Society. Harvey O'Brien recounts that the initial government grant to the National Film Institute of £2,000 (awarded in 1943) was to be directed towards

> establishing a library of 'suitable' educational films, including films in Irish, and [the society] was granted a further £250 by the archbishop towards the cost of purchasing three film projectors which would be used to set up mobile exhibition units which would tour parish halls and other approved venues to show them.[11]

What we can see here, I believe, is the emergence in Ireland of a kind of 'Griersonian consensus', a widespread sense that cinema in Ireland is basically a nonprofit affair where both government and documentary would play an important role. Despite the clear political differences between the animators of the Irish Film Society and the National Film Institute, the development of an Irish film *industry* fails to excite the imagination of either. When people attached to these groups turned to film production, the Griersonian quality of Irish film-making became even clearer.

This conflict between the Irish Film Society and National Film Institute views of both Ireland and cinema is embodied by two films: Brendan Stafford's *A Nation Once Again* (1946) and Ó Laoghaire's *Our Country* (1948). *A Nation Once Again* was ostensibly meant to commemorate the 100th anniversary of the death of Thomas Davis, founder of the *Nation* and a hero of the Young Ireland movement. The eighteen-minute film basically tried to show the degree to which many of Davis's hopes for an independent Ireland were now being realised, and it has generally been seen as boisterous propaganda for the ruling party Fianna Fáil (the sense of it being somewhat obnoxiously nationalist is probably fed by the recurring images of Irish military parades and fly-overs). That is the case not only with historians such as Rockett and O'Brien, but also with the film's contemporaries, most importantly Liam Ó Laoghaire. The film he made two years later, the six-minute *Our Country*, could not have seemed more different. This film is dominated by images of children living in urban squalor, and is narrated throughout by an impossibly awkward voiceover relating facts about Ireland's economic underdevelopment, currency devaluation and so on. The film featured three members of Clann na Poblachta, an upstart political party that, having won two seats in a pair of 1947 by-elections, seemed to be the next big thing in Irish politics when *Our Country* was being made. That was indeed the case, as the party ended up as a junior coalition partner when Fianna Fáil lost the 1948 election to rival Fine Gael; O'Brien speculates that '*Our Country* may have given them an additional edge.'[12] What is more important for our purposes here, though, is the degree to which the conflict between these two parties was being played out, in miniature, as a conflict between two didactic, nation-building films with various kinds of connections to the state apparatus. Even when the ruling Fianna Fáil and the insurgent Clann na Poblachta squared off against one another, they were doing so under basically Griersonian conditions.

## A FILM POLICY FOR IRELAND

That election where Fianna Fáil was ejected and Clann na Poblachta entered into coalition took place on 4 February 1948, three months before Grierson's only actual appearance in Ireland, which he made in his capacity as film controller of the Central Office of Information. What he left behind was a manifesto of sorts, an address given at the Gresham Hotel and published in the September 1948 issue of the Jesuit review *Studies*, called 'A Film Policy for Ireland'. The degree to which this affected film-making in Ireland, both North and South, is indeed debatable.

Although their work was supposed to encompass the entire empire, and at the very least the entire United Kingdom, neither the EMB nor the GPO film units were very active in Northern Ireland.[13] Proinsias Ó Conluain's *Scéal na Scannán/Story of Cinema*, a kind of Irish-language counterpoint to Ó Laoghaire's *Invitation to the Film*, writes as rapturously about Grierson as Ó Laoghaire does but also notes that

'Grierson only worked with one Irishman at that time.'[14] That was Norris Davidson, who in addition to working for Flaherty on *Man of Aran* (he produced a short film called *Dancers of Aran* in 1934), worked on two films in County Down (part of Northern Ireland) for the EMB: *Hen Woman* (n.d.) and *Meat for Millions* (n.d.).[15] The situation didn't change much when Grierson returned from Canada to head up the film unit of the UK's Central Office of Information. John Hill recounts the difficulties that seemed inevitable to COI-led film production in the North, some of which had to do with a fear of Irish nationalism and an associated sensitivity about what constituted the regional specificity of Northern Ireland, in his comprehensive survey of film-making there.[16] Indeed, it is striking that Northern Ireland does not come up at all in 'A Film Policy for Ireland', which shows a great deal of enthusiasm for and idealism about what Ireland could do with cinema if its energies were focused in certain ways.

Grierson returns frequently to the example of Canada, which is hardly surprising given that only three years earlier he had resigned as commissioner of the National Film Board there. Only four years earlier, Grierson had published an essay called 'A Film Policy for Canada' in the 15 June 1944 issue of *Canadian Affairs*, and so it is easy to see this as something of a sequel. That essay has a central place in the history of Canadian cinema, if for no other reason than that it advocates Canada focus more attention on non-commercial uses of film, especially documentary, and essentially abandon all hope of competing with Hollywood films. After recounting the difficulties of building a national film industry, Grierson asks (in a section called 'If You Can't Fight Them, Join Them'): 'Are there not other possibilities for the development of Canadian film production? I think there are and far more practical and possible than this dream of a Canadian Hollywood.'[17] In Canada this vision has been the subject of a number of frontal attacks, most famously from Peter Morris and Joyce Nelson,[18] both of whom anticipated Brian Winston's book-length critique of the Griersonian tradition. No comparable influence, either positive or negative, has accrued to 'A Film Policy for Ireland'. I rather suspect that this has to do less with Canada than with the other recurring reference for Grierson, the other job that he had recently departed: UNESCO.

Grierson left Canada in 1945 for New York and, after getting caught up in the investigation of an Ottawa-based spy ring (a secretary at the NFB had been named by the Soviet defector Igor Gouzenko), he decamped to Paris to serve as an advisor to UNESCO during 1947. This was the year before his 'A Film Policy for Ireland' talk, and so it's no wonder that it comes up so much, fresh in his mind as it was. But Grierson was taking the opportunity here not simply to argue for film as a tool of educational, scientific or cultural development, although he was certainly doing that. Rather, he was trying to argue that Ireland needed to start thinking of itself as a 'small country'. Both Morris and Nelson, however, critique Grierson's legacy in no small part because of its implicit hostility towards Canadian self-determination. Nelson, for instance, writes that 'Grierson, ever the Empire man, felt that the film aspirations of a country like Canada were simply muddying the picture, whereas Britain was obviously entitled to "a truly national film industry".'[19] Morris, in his 'Backwards to the Future' essay, slams what he sees as Grierson's circular logic on the desirability of a small-country film industry:

Lost … is any suggestion that other nations did not regard Hollywood's hegemony over their film industries as an inevitable benefit of the new internationalism and that there were indeed policy options – well-known and applied in Europe and Latin America – that might counteract that control.[20]

But when he was speaking in Ireland, rather than speaking in terms of the inevitable defeat that is the lot of small countries living next to big and powerful ones, he tries to rally the troops. Grierson writes in 'A Film Policy for Ireland' that his sense as a *Scotsman* is that

our problems as small nations in close proximity to a larger and richer nation have been in many ways similar. A great part of the struggle has been: not to maintain economic independence, but to preserve what we had of our own traditions, our own culture, our own way of looking at things.[21]

Here the 'new internationalism' that Morris derided has taken a very different form, one closer to what critics such as himself, or Joyce Nelson, would seem to be desiring: co-operation among countries in the name of decentralising power. But only four years had passed between 'A Film Policy for Canada' (which, you will recall, has a section called 'If You Can't Fight Them, Join Them') and 'A Film Policy for Ireland'. What could have happened to Grierson in such a short time to change his rhetoric so radically?

The answer, of course, is that UNESCO happened. Grierson's year at the UN-sponsored organisation was mostly devoted to beginning the work of building a series of international coalitions of film boards and film-makers, some of which was directly related to the work of post-World War II small-state reconstruction. This was very different from what he had been doing at the EMB, GPO or the NFB, in no small part because he was no longer 'the Empire man', to use Joyce Nelson's formulation. He seems to have taken to this new supranational affiliation with zeal, if 'A Film Policy for Ireland' is to be taken as any indication. Recalling his experience at the United Nations Conference on Freedom of Information at Geneva, he writes:

The deep issues there were not, and are not, the issues between the Western Bloc and the Eastern Bloc, between the big issues of the big countries. They are the issues which arise from a real fear on the part of the smaller countries that the big fellows, on both sides, are only too insensitive to the special cultural interests of their smaller neighbours and, in certain cases, are inclined to ignore their quality … . Unesco can, and should be, a powerful ally to the small country developing its film services.[22]

Note that Grierson does not say 'the small country developing its film *industry*'. The overall suggestions that he was making in Dublin are actually not at all far off what he had to say in the pages of *Canadian Affairs*. In Ireland as in Canada, his sense of film policy was that it should support film as a government-sponsored public service, not as an industry.

In Canada this has led to Grierson being seen as a patronising outsider whose indifference to the plight of a small country was a major impediment to building its own film industry; that is the line of both Nelson's *The Colonized Eye* and Morris's 'Backwards to the Future'. His Irish experience, though, gives the opposite sense, that his calls for greater internationalism were simply ignored, despite the interest of a number of key cultural figures writing in both Irish and English. Writing three years before Grierson's Dublin talk, Liam Ó Laoghaire argued that they needed to resist a cinema defined by cheap commercialism and that 'the way to do so seems to me to lie with a National Film Board which would see that cheap sentimental scripts would never reach the production stage, and that a high standard of work would be aimed at'.[23] Proinsias Ó Conluain concludes his 1954 booklet *Ár Scannáin Féin/Our Own Films* with a list of twenty-eight proposals for a national institution that would support film-making in Irish. Number twelve begins: 'That the body have a Director or Controller to manage the production and so on, as John Grierson did, say, with the National Film Board of Canada, or as the head of the state body Cinecittà does in Italy'.[24] I thus have no real argument with Harvey O'Brien's scepticism about Grierson's influence in Ireland; if one is taking the macro-view, it seems clear that the national cinema, including its documentary cinema, evolved along different lines. But the Griersonian model did provide an alternate path for Irish cinema to follow, and those who chose to follow it were by no means marginal parts of that country's cinematic history.


## GAEL LINN

Gael Linn is a language-revival organisation, founded in 1953, and is well known for being the most progressive and forward-looking of its kind. Part of this has to do with its embrace of mass media. Its traditional-music label is of long standing, and shortly after its foundation it presented a series of proposals for the then-nascent Irish television service RTÉ.[25] It has also produced a number of documentary films: the best known of these are the weekly newsreel series *Amharc Éireann/A View of Ireland* (1955–64)[26] and George Morrison's historical compilation films *Mise Éire/I Am Ireland* (1959) and *Saoirse?/Freedom?* (1960). All of these films are narrated in Irish Gaelic and, like all of Gael Linn's films, they were initially distributed in unsubtitled prints (recent DVD issue versions all carry English subtitles). In addition to language what they share is a basically Griersonian sense of cinema, both in terms of aesthetics and institutions. Gael Linn and its film-makers saw their task not as building an Irish film industry, but as using film to both bolster the Irish language and present a renewed vision of Ireland's present and its past. The task was basically pedagogical, and quite consistent with Grierson's sense that 'It is worth recalling that the British documentary group began not so much in affection for film *per se* as in affection for national education.'[27]

*Amharc Éireann*'s producer, Colm Ó Laoghaire, was something of a 'reluctant Griersonian', inasmuch as the films clearly have some pedagogical function, and certainly have a nation-building one via the normalisation of the Irish language. But Ó Laoghaire's reluctance is even more explicit in his 1957 essay about the series, where he argues that the Grierson school is, essentially, too humanist and progressive for Ireland. He writes of the British documentary movement:

All those working in the School were people with definite theories of social progress and looked on documentary as a means of propagating these. Now anyone who is familiar with the films and writings of these people and their circles will know that they tend to be Liberal and Humanist in their outlook.[28]

The suspicion here to my mind, isn't really political; in terms of the function that these films had in the life of the nation, as well as their relationship to the state (Gael Linn was not a state body but has always been state-subsidised), the closeness to a Griersonian sensibility seems to me transparent. The hostility is, just as Ó Laoghaire says, ideological. There is clearly something of the worldly, rationalist Brit to Grierson, a type that would have aroused strong suspicion on the part of the Irish Catholic middle class. In Ireland that 'rationalist Brit' perspective is widely associated with Trinity College Dublin, historically a stronghold of the Protestant elite which Irish Catholics needed a special dispensation from their bishop to attend until the 1970s.[29] British rationalism may have seemed a foreign imposition, and Ó Laoghaire's longing for a continental connection is far from surprising in that context. But I hope the two epigraphs to this essay show, that longing is, ironically, further indication of the Griersonian influence in Ireland; Grierson, following his UNESCO experience, thought Ireland needed to think in more continental terms as well.

George Morrison, director of *Mise Éire* and *Saoirse?*, had a slightly different relationship to that Griersonian influence. Morrison's internationalism had little to do with documentary film-making as such. Instead, he was active in the Fédération International des Archives du Film (FIAF) and wrote an article calling on Ireland to establish an international-standard archive in 1966.[30] What brought him to that cause was the process of making *Mise Éire* and *Saoirse?*, both of which are made up entirely of archival footage. *Mise Éire* narrates the period from 1896 to 1918 (basically up to the outbreak of the War of Independence), and *Saoirse?* takes us to 1922 (basically up to the outbreak of the Civil War); Morrison planned to make a third film, about the Civil War (1922–3), but it never materialised. *Mise Éire* and *Saoirse?* have been controversial in Ireland because of the sometimes strident nationalism of their voiceovers. Both films are 'assembly films' about the fall of one regime and the painful emergence of another and, as O'Brien among others has pointed out, their closest cinematic relation would seem to be Esfir Shub's *Fall of the Romanov Dynasty* (1927). But O'Brien is not convinced, writing that 'The films do not evince a dialectical mode of interpretation or offer cross-correlations between the social strata as Shub did in *Fall of the Romanov Dynasty*.'[31] Of course, that is not far off the way in which Grierson-era films embraced many aspects of the Soviets' approach to editing while also 'softening' their agit-prop qualities and doing so, essentially, in the service of the state. The fragmented jumpiness of *Turksib* (1929) became the gentler and sometimes pastoral rhythms of *Night Mail* in a way very similar to how the fist-raised coup-o-philia of *Fall of the Romanov Dynasty* became the sometimes romantically tragic but basically heroic nationalism of *Mise Éire* and *Saoirse?*. Like his Gael Linn colleague Colm Ó Laoghaire, George Morrision was a kind of unconscious Griersonian, another example of the way in which the effect that gives this collection its title was part of a political consensus about the proper role of documentary, even in places where the dominant ideology may have seemed very different indeed.

## LOUIS MARCUS

Although the number of film-makers involved in work sponsored by Gael Linn was relatively small, their influence was significant. That was especially true of Louis Marcus, who got his start as an assistant editor on *Mise Éire* and *Saoirse?*; spent time in Israel studying both the nascent film industry and the revival of Hebrew (Marcus is Jewish and a very fluent Irish speaker); and went on to produce some of the country's most widely circulated documentaries, such as the Oscar-nominated shorts *Fleá/Festival* (1967) and *Páistí ag Obair/Children at Work* (1973). In addition to his films, though, Marcus's Griersonian sensibilities can be seen in a series of polemical articles that he published in the *Irish Times* in 1967. To continue with this dialectical motif, there is a sense in which the proposals for an indigenous film culture advanced by Liam Ó Laoghaire and Proinsias Ó Conluain were colliding with the nation-building documentary production of Gael Linn to synthesise a kind of 'complete Griersonian' in the form of Louis Marcus.

The late 1960s seemed to be a grim time for Irish film production. Although the fairly wide release accorded to *Mise Éire* and *Saoirse?* had generated some excitement, the cinematic infrastructure in the country remained either underdeveloped or inaccessible. The latter tendency seemed to be embodied by Ardmore Studios, a Wicklow-based facility set up by the Seán Lemass government in 1958 meant to lead to the emergence of a local industry but in fact far too expensive for anyone but British and Hollywood productions to actually use. What he saw as a 'record of neglect' on the part of the government towards Irish cinema led him to write a five-part series of articles for the *Irish Times*, published between 27 March and 1 April 1967; the second in the series bore the title 'The Irrelevance of Ardmore Studios'. Summarising the perspective of those pieces, O'Brien writes that 'Marcus argued, using points startlingly similar to those made by Grierson two decades earlier ... that documentary was uniquely placed to advance the representation of Ireland as a medium of self-exploration as well as self-promotion ...'.[32]

That was especially true of the fourth instalment, titled 'A Dearth of Documentary'. He opened that salvo with a veritable précis of Grierson's position in 'A Film Policy for Canada', insisting that small countries should recognise the need to ensure that 'Specialised films are made on 16mm for showing as educational and promotional aids everywhere from classrooms to conference halls.'[33] Here is Grierson in 'A Film Policy for Canada':

> When you think of this nation's organizations you will readily see how big this new 16mm audience can be ... . Wherever people are gathered together in the name of a specialized professional or social or civic or educational interest, there you have a ready made audience for films which are devoted to their interest.[34]

Indeed, in the last instalment of the series, 'The Way Ahead', Marcus identifies Canada and Holland as the countries to emulate. Although he praises the festival and critical acclaim of the NFB's films, it's the social cohesion by which he is most impressed: 'But the Board's main activities are directed to developing a homogenous and dynamic community out of the many diverse elements in Canadian life – a function which could

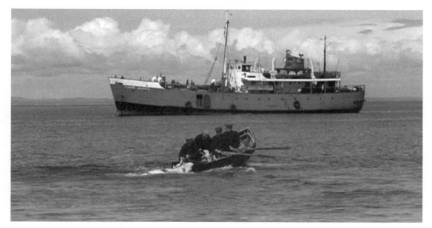

Transporting a cow to a ship waiting offshore ...

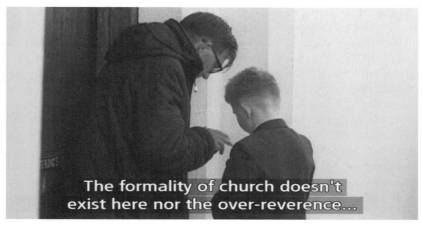

A priest hears a boy's confession at the top of Croagh Patrick ...

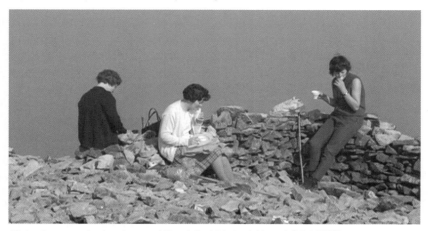

Pilgrims have some lunch at the top of Croagh Patrick in Louis Marcus's *Pobal* (1970)

not be more relevant to Ireland.'[35] To return to his previously quoted formulation, it's worth recalling here that Grierson's affection for film was really an affection for what he called 'national education'. So it was, at least in the pages of the *Irish Times*, for Marcus.

This is not to dismiss the importance of the films that Marcus made. Indeed, there is a real sense in which Marcus's film-making embodies the evolution of a Griersonian sensibility, the way in which it changed over time. So while he is probably better known for films like *Fleá* and *Páistí ag Obair*, his most relevant film for our purposes here is *Pobal/People* (1970). This is a twenty-three-minute exploration of the daily life of Ireland, with sections observing a busy Dublin open-air market; taking us into a farming community just outside the city; cutting between Protestant and Catholic religious services; following pilgrims as they climb Croagh Patrick; watching Aran Islanders as they load cows onto a large ship from their tiny curraghs; and finally at a crowded, noisy hurling match, all connected by an Irish-language voiceover. What Marcus is doing, essentially, is trying to visualise a homogenous and dynamic community (one that is connected by the presence of a single language in the soundtrack: Irish) out of the many diverse elements in Irish life: urbanites, villagers and islanders; Catholics and Protestants; markets and sporting events. The longest section in the film is the one devoted to climbing Croagh Patrick, a very popular religious site in County Mayo with a particularly demanding ascent. Marcus includes footage of priests saying mass and hearing confessions at the summit, but he lingers the longest on images of the pilgrims, with the voiceover saying 'Against the mountain, they resemble a human rosary, all focussed on the summit' (that is over a medium long shot of a single old woman making her way up and an extreme long shot of many pilgrims walking in the same direction with the mountain visible in the distance). The film is very close indeed to the magnum opus of the second generation of Canadian Griersonians, the *Labyrinth* (1967) project. This was a multi-screen installation made for Expo 67 in Montreal by the film-makers attached to the National Film Board of Canada's Unit B. Its single-screen version is called *In the Labyrinth*, and among other topics it moves between images of horses in southern Alberta, an Orthodox wedding in Greece, Soviet cosmonauts in training, Buddhist religious practice and Winston Churchill's state funeral. The work is defined overall by a broad, progressive humanism, a philosophy that does indeed derive from the ideology of which Colm Ó Laoghaire was so suspicious. Today the work is a seminal example of the emergence of a technologically sophisticated, outward-looking and multicultural conceptualisation of Canadian nationalism. *Pobal* is defined by a comparably broad-minded attempt to bring together diverse strands of experience into some shared sense both of the human condition and of Irishness.

## BOB QUINN

Today Louis Marcus is a kind of establishment figure for Irish documentary and for the Irish language. Bob Quinn, on the other hand, has become the country's senior dissident, having also built a career making films in Irish but having done it in the Connemara Gaeltacht, on the western coast where Irish still functions as a community language. Most histories of Irish cinema include some discussion of his work, but generally focus on his feature films such as *Poitín* (1974), which was the first feature to be made entirely in Irish. This obscures the fact that the bulk of his oeuvre is in documentary cinema (and O'Brien's book *The Real Ireland* is an exception there, devoting significant discussion to Quinn's three-part 1983 essay film *Atlantean*), and also obscures the fact that he is just as much of a Griersonian as his long-time friend Marcus. When he gave the keynote address to the Canadian Association for Irish Studies in 2000 (held in Edmonton), he opened by recounting a slight variation on a well-worn tale about Grierson and, to bring this essay full circle, Robert Flaherty:

> The man who knew most about Flaherty and his work was John Grierson. This Scot founded the National Film Board of Canada, drank copiously and ended up presenting (on Scottish TV) *This Wonderful World*, which, along with Godard's *Breathless*, first suggested to me the possibilities of film. In the Thirties, Grierson and Flaherty made the documentary *Industrial Britain*, but his natural inclination was for the exotic. He informed Grierson that he was leaving. Why? I want to film the savages in Samoa, he explained. Grierson responded: Go ahead. I'll stay and film the savages in Birmingham. That's how I felt about staying and filming in Connemara, the most bleakly beautiful part of the west of Ireland.[36]

Quinn began his media work in the area when he bought a portable video rig and began filming local events and then showing those videos in community halls. He called his production company Cinegael, and recalled in Edmonton how 'The NFB's Challenge for Change programme inspired me to set up the first closed-circuit community TV service in Ireland – perhaps in Europe.'

Challenge for Change was a programme set up by the NFB that had two basic goals: regionalisation and collaboration.[37] The second one was probably more of a priority, and the basic principle of Challenge for Change was that film-makers needed to learn to make films with people and communities, rather than merely make films about them. Challenge for Change's flagship initiative was in a community very much like Connemara: Fogo Island, off the northeastern coast of Newfoundland. The 'Newfoundland Project' ended up being thirty-two films altogether, and gave rise to the 'Fogo Process', wherein rushes were shown at community gatherings and everyone present was empowered to have footage removed from a final cut.[38] This means of participatory film-making was enormously influential on Quinn. He encountered it in a serious way when he went to Montreal in 1975 to make a film that eventually showed on RTÉ called *A Film Board for Ireland?*. This is a documentary portrait of the National Film Board of Canada; Challenge for Change, and specifically the Newfoundland Project, have a central place in the film. Quinn features images from Roger Hart's *A Memo from Fogo* (1972), a kind of 'résumé film' that summarised the Fogo experience a few years after the completion of shooting there. He also includes an interview with Dorothy Hénaut (an NFB veteran involved in both Challenge for Change and its French-language sister programme *Société nouvelle*) where she states that Grierson wanted the board to be 'an inch to the left of the government' and that Challenge for Change represented a return to this goal after a period of 'soft' documentaries in the 1950s.

Those familiar with the literature on Challenge for Change will recall that Grierson was famously sceptical of the programme; one important effect of Quinn's *A Film*

*Board for Ireland?* is to remind us that this is more complicated than some historians have presented it. Colin Low, the director of the Fogo films, has recalled in somewhat traumatised tones the dressing-down that Grierson gave him during a screening of his work at McGill University. He remembers him saying

> So the filmmaker is nothing but a tool, a camera operator or projectionist in the formulation of these problems and solutions. What about the intelligence, world experience, expensive education that could be brought to these people? If you have nothing to say, why further burden these people with manipulative nonsense?[39]

But a few years later Grierson would write a memo about what he saw as the possibility of Challenge for Change, and of the changes brought by new technologies such as 8mm film. The memo is fascinating reading. He is his grouchy self in some places – 'I am all for the 8mm revolution, as long as the 8mm mind doesn't go with it'[40] – but elsewhere he is gently open-minded about the possibilities of grassroots engagement offered by Challenge for Change. The key passage that links his lingering scepticism about these possibilities to Quinn's work comes about two-thirds of the way through the memo, when he laments:

> there is not yet a real decentralizing of production. The cinéastes may make their films with the people and in the villages, but they are soon off and away from the people and the villages to their normal metropolitan milieu.[41]

The work of Bob Quinn, especially his Challenge-for-Change-influenced video work, is exactly what Grierson seemed to be longing for. Quinn had left the metropolitan centre *before* embarking on any of this film-making, never to return to it again (he came to Connemara after quitting RTÉ television in a huff over the station's creeping technocratic organisation). He has made films all over the world, but almost all of them, in one way or another, bring his arguments back to the culture of the Connemara Gaeltacht. His efforts at decentralisation, however modest, were substantial inasmuch as he was making films as a part of a production company incorporated in An Cheathrú Rua, Co. Galway and so bringing his world experience and expensive education to Connemara, having permanently relocated and become a fully functioning citizen of that village. Quinn began as a certain kind of Griersonian film-maker: invested in documentary, in search of a form of mass communication that would be genuinely public, etc. He became a very different kind of Griersonian, someone keenly aware of the need to use cinema to redefine the relationship between centre and periphery. Like Marcus, his ideological approach evolved in ways that were, no doubt unwittingly, quite consistent with the evolution of Griersonianism itself.

## CONCLUSION

My effort here has not been to show that the thought of John Grierson has had a clearly visible role in the development of Irish cinema, especially given the relatively superficial engagement that he had with the place. One way to summarise 'the

*The Grierson Effect*

Grierson effect' in Ireland would be to say 'he gave a talk about policy at a hotel in the late 1940s. None of the government people paid his proposals much mind.' And that would be basically correct. Indeed, part of Harvey O'Brien's arguments about Grierson not being very influential have to do with the fact that in some cases 'an alternative (and less demanding) infrastructure already existed'.[42] But much of the infrastructure that did exist in the late 1940s bore the mark of Grierson's sense that cinema, especially cinema in small countries, needed to embrace a civic, non-commercial and non-narrative vocation. Colm Ó Laoghaire's sense that Irish film-makers tended to look to the British model seems to me basically correct, and that tendency has led to a very wide variety of deviations from a capitalist, consumption-driven model of cinema. Seeing Irish cinema through the Grierson effect allows us to see Flaherty finding Rousseau on the Aran Islands and the Frenchman turning out to be closer to Irish political perspectives than most have heretofore thought; Ó Laoghaire and Ó Conluain, Ó Laoghaire and Morrison struggling in widely different ways to link Irish cinema to broader trends in world cinema; Marcus and Quinn embracing the most ambitious of humanist projects and the most detailed of localist ones. The Grierson connection forces us to see Irish cinema as *diverse*, both aesthetically and politically. Seeing that kind of diversity may sometimes seem a stretch and it is never less than a struggle, but it does allow us to see Ireland's cinema not as a pale shadow of British cinema isolated by its failure to sustain a substantial film industry, but rather as part of the internationale of small countries, struggling with some of the fundamental tensions of globalisation.

## NOTES

1. John Grierson, 'A Film Policy for Ireland', *Studies*, September 1948, p. 286.
2. Colm Ó Laoghaire, 'Gael Linn "Vest Pocket" Documentaries', *National Film Quarterly* vol. 1 no. 1 (1957), p. 10.
3. John Grierson, 'A Film Policy for Canada', in Douglas Fetherling (ed.), *Documents in Canadian Film* (Peterborough: Broadview, 1988), pp. 62–3.
4. Harvey O'Brien, *The Real Ireland: The Evolution of Ireland in Documentary Film* (Manchester: Manchester University Press, 2004), p. 57.
5. On the production and legacy of *Man of Aran*, see O'Brien, *The Real Ireland*, pp. 44–51 and Martin McLoone, *Irish Film: The Emergence of a Contemporary Cinema* (London: BFI, 1999), pp. 38–44. On the film's 1930s reception, see Kevin Rockett, Luke Gibbons and John Hill, *Cinema and Ireland* (London: Routledge, 1987), pp. 71–3, 201–3; Lance Pettitt, *Screening Ireland: Film and Television Representation* (Manchester: Manchester University Press, 2000), pp. 77–81; and Ruth Barton, *Irish National Cinema* (London: Routledge, 2004), pp. 47–9.
6. O'Brien, *The Real Ireland*, p. 48.
7. For a summary, see Ian Aitken, *Film and Reform: John Grierson and the Documentary Film Movement* (London: Routledge, 1990), pp. 120–1.
8. McLoone, *Irish Film*, p. 38.
9. Rockett *et al.*, *Cinema and Ireland*, p. 76.
10. Liam Ó Laoghaire, *Invitation to the Film* (Tralee: The Kerryman, 1945), p. 87.
11. O'Brien, *The Real Ireland*, p. 62.

12. Ibid., p. 67.
13. Oddly, that's not true of either the EMB as a whole or the island of Ireland as a whole. For a discussion of the relationship between the EMB and the Irish Free State (which existed from 1922–37), see Mike Cronin, 'Selling Irish Bacon: The Empire Marketing Board and Artists of the Free State', *Éire-Ireland* vol. 39 nos 3–4 (2004), pp. 132–43.
14. Proinsias Ó Conluain, *Scéal na Scannán* (Dublin: Stationery Office, 1953), p. 98.
15. Ó Conluain does not give the dates for either film. Rachel Low's *History of British Film*, volume 5 (London: Allen & Unwin, 1979) lists *Hen Woman* as 1933, and specifies that it was unfinished (p. 217). In his essay 'The EMB Film Unit', however, Grierson writes that 'J.N.G. Davidson made *Hen Woman*, the unit's only story documentary.' See Forsyth Hardy (ed.), *Grierson on Documentary* (New York: Harcourt, Brace and Company, 1947), p. 123.
16. See John Hill, *Cinema and Northern Ireland* (London: BFI, 2006), pp. 114–20.
17. Grierson, 'A Film Policy for Canada', p. 59.
18. See Joyce Nelson, *The Colonized Eye: Rethinking the Grierson Legend* (Toronto: Between the Lines, 1988) and Peter Morris, 'Backwards to the Future: John Grierson's Film Policy for Canada', in Gene Walz (ed.), *Flashback: People and Institutions in Canadian Film History* (Montreal: Médiatexte, 1986), pp. 17–35. See also Peter Morris, 'Re-thinking Grierson: The Ideology of John Grierson', in Pierre Vérnonneau, Michael Dorland and Seth Feldman (eds), *Dialogue: Cinéma canadien et québécois/Canadian and Quebec Cinema* (Montreal: Médiatexte, 1987), pp. 21–56 and Brian Winston, *Claiming the Real: The Documentary Film Revisited* (London: BFI, 1995).
19. Nelson, *The Colonized Eye*, p. 161.
20. Morris, 'Backwards to the Future', p. 20.
21. Grierson, 'A Film Policy for Ireland', p. 285.
22. Ibid.
23. Ó Laoghaire, *Invitation to the Film*, p. 171.
24. Ó Conluain, *Ár Scannán Féin* (Dublin: Foilseacháin Náisiúnta Teoranta, 1954), p. 26.
25. See Robert Savage, *Irish Television: The Political and Social Origins* (Cork: Cork University Press, 1996), pp. 181–90, 193–210. RTÉ stands for Raidió Teilfiís Éireann, which is Ireland's state-owned broadcaster, responsible for both television and radio services. Despite its name it broadcasts mostly in English; the Irish-language television service TG4 and radio service Raidió na Gaeltchta are separate entities but are under RTÉ's institutional umbrella.
26. For a highly detailed discussion of film-making in Irish generally and the work of Gael Linn specifically, see Heather Macdougall, 'Finding a Voice: The Role of Irish-language Film in Irish National Cinema', PhD dissertation, Concordia University, 2012. A very thorough discussion can also be found in B. Mairéad Pratschke, 'A Look at Irish-Ireland: Gael Linn's *Amharc Éireann* Films 1956–64', *New Hibernia Review* vol. 9 no. 3 (2005), pp. 17–38.
27. Hardy, *Grierson on Documentary*, p. 169.
28. Ó Laoghaire, 'Gael Linn "Vest Pocket" Documentaries', p. 9.
29. A good analogy here is the place of the Anglophone and elite McGill University in the life of the majority-francophone city of Montreal. Grierson, of course, was a kind of grey-eminence-in-residence at McGill during the 1960s and 70s, and Quebec film-makers viewed him with a very similar kind of suspicion (even if they were not writing about it in terms like Ó Laoghaire's).
30. See George Morrison, 'An Irish National Film Archive', *Éire-Ireland* vol. 1 no. 4 (1965), pp. 39–62.

31. Harvey O'Brien, 'Projecting the Past: Historical Documentary in Ireland', *Historical Journal of Film, Radio and Television* vol. 20 no. 3 (2000), p. 341.
32. O'Brien, *The Real Ireland*, p. 166.
33. Louis Marcus, 'The Irish Film Industry 4 – A Dearth of Documentary', *Irish Times*, 30 March 1967, p. 10.
34. Grierson, 'A Film Policy for Canada', pp. 61–2.
35. Louis Marcus, 'The Irish Film Industry 6 – The Way Ahead', *Irish Times*, 1 April 1967, p. 9 .
36. This address was eventually published as Bob Quinn, 'Recycled Rants', *Film West* vol. 42 (2002), pp. 26–30. Here I am quoting the transcript of Quinn's talk in Edmonton, as the published version doesn't include the bit about Grierson and Flaherty. That likely-apocryphal chat between them is also recounted in Gary Evans, *John Grierson: Trailblazer of Documentary Film* (Montreal: XYZ, 2005), p. 24.
37. See Thomas Waugh, Michael Brendan Baker and Ezra Winton (eds), *Challenge for Change: Activist Documentary at the National Film Board of Canada* (Montreal/Kingston: McGill-Queen's University Press, 2010) for an incomparably comprehensive survey of the effort, both in English and in French (its sister programme was known as *Société nouvelle*).
38. For a précis of Challenge for Change and the Fogo Process, see Zoë Druick, *Projecting Canada: Government Policy and Documentary Film at the National Film Board of Canada* (Montreal/Kingston: McGill-Queen's University Press, 2007), pp. 144–6.
39. Colin Low, 'Grierson and the Challenge for Change', in Waugh *et al.*, *Challenge for Change*, p. 20.
40. John Grierson, 'Memo to Michelle about Decentralizing the Means of Production', in Waugh *et al.*, *Challenge for Change*, p. 62.
41. Ibid., p. 63.
42. O'Brien, *The Real Ireland*, p. 57.

## REFERENCES

Aitken, Ian, *Film and Reform: John Grierson and the Documentary Film Movement* (London: Routledge, 1990).
Barton, Ruth, *Irish National Cinema* (London: Routledge, 2004).
Cronin, Mike, 'Selling Irish Bacon: The Empire Marketing Board and Artists of the Free State', *Éire-Ireland* vol. 39 nos 3–4 (2004), pp. 132–43.
Druick, Zoë, *Projecting Canada: Government Policy and Documentary Film at the National Film Board of Canada* (Montreal/Kingston: McGill-Queen's University Press, 2007).
Evans, Gary, *John Grierson: Trailblazer of Documentary Film* (Montreal: XYZ, 2005).
Grierson, John, 'A Film Policy for Ireland', *Studies*, September 1948, pp. 283–91.
Grierson, John, 'A Film Policy for Canada', in Douglas Fetherling (ed.), *Documents in Canadian Film* (Peterborough: Broadview, 1988), pp. 51–67.
Grierson, John, 'Memo to Michelle about Decentralizing the Means of Production', in Thomas Waugh, Michael Brendon Barker and Ezra Winton (eds), *Challenge for Change: Activist Documentary at the National Film Board of Canada* (Montreal/Kingston: McGill-Queen's University Press, 2010), pp. 61–5.
Hardy, Forsyth (ed.), *Grierson on Documentary* (New York: Harcourt, Brace and Company, 1947).
Hill, John, *Cinema and Northern Ireland* (London: BFI, 2006).

Low, Colin, 'Grierson and the Challenge for Change', in Thomas Waugh, Michael Brendan Baker and Ezra Winton (eds), *Challenge for Change: Activist Documentary at the National Film Board of Canada* (Montreal/Kingston: McGill-Queen's University Press, 2010), pp. 16–23.

Macdougall, Heather, 'Finding a Voice: The Role of Irish-language Film in Irish National Cinema', PhD dissertation, Concordia University, 2012.

Marcus, Louis, 'The Irish Film Industry 4 – A Dearth of Documentary', *Irish Times*, 30 March 1967, p. 10.

Marcus, Louis, 'The Irish Film Industry 6 – The Way Ahead', *Irish Times*, 1 April 1967, p. 9.

McLoone, Martin, *Irish Film: The Emergence of a Contemporary Cinema* (London: BFI, 1999).

Morris, Peter, 'Backwards to the Future: John Grierson's Film Policy for Canada', in Gene Walz (ed.), *Flashback: People and Institutions in Canadian Film History* (Montreal: Médiatexte, 1986), pp. 17–35.

Morris, Peter, 'Re-thinking Grierson: The Ideology of John Grierson', in Pierre Vérnonneau, Michael Dorland and Seth Feldman (eds), *Dialogue: Cinéma canadienne et québécois/Canadian and Quebec Cinema* (Montreal: Médiatexte, 1987), pp. 21–56.

Morrison, George, 'An Irish National Film Archive', *Éire-Ireland* vol. 1 no. 4 (1965), pp. 39–62.

Nelson, Joyce, *The Colonized Eye: Rethinking the Grierson Legend* (Toronto: Between the Lines, 1988).

O'Brien, Harvey, 'Projecting the Past: Historical Documentary in Ireland', *Historical Journal of Film, Radio and Television* vol. 20 no. 3 (2000), pp. 335–50.

O'Brien, Harvey, *The Real Ireland: The Evolution of Ireland in Documentary Film* (Manchester: Manchester University Press, 2004).

Ó Conluain, Proinsias, *Scéal na Scannán* (Dublin: Stationery Office, 1953).

Ó Conluain, *Ár Scannáin Féin* (Dublin: Foilseacháin Náisiúnta Teoranta, 1954).

Ó Laoghaire, Liam, *Invitation to the Film* (Tralee: The Kerryman, 1945).

Ó Laoghaire, Colm, 'Gael Linn "Vest Pocket" Documentaries', *National Film Quarterly* vol. 1 no. 1 (1957), pp. 9–10.

Pettitt, Lance, *Screening Ireland: Film and Television Representation* (Manchester: Manchester University Press, 2000).

Pratschke, B. Mairéad, 'A Look at Irish-Ireland: Gael Linn's *Amharc Éireann* Films 1956–64', *New Hibernia Review* vol. 9 no. 3 (2005), pp. 17–38.

Quinn, Bob, 'Recycled Rants', *Film West* vol. 42 (2002), pp. 26–30.

Rockett, Kevin, Luke Gibbons and John Hill, *Cinema and Ireland* (London: Routledge, 1987).

Savage, Robert, *Irish Television: The Political and Social Origins* (Cork: Cork University Press, 1996).

Waugh, Thomas, Michael Brendan Baker and Ezra Winton (eds), *Challenge for Change: Activist Documentary at the National Film Board of Canada* (Montreal/Kingston: McGill-Queen's University Press, 2010).

Winston, Brian, *Claiming the Real: The Documentary Film Revisited* (London: BFI, 1995).

# 12

# White Fathers Hear Dark Voices? John Grierson and British Colonial Africa at the End of Empire

*Martin Stollery*

An enduring claim made about pioneering British documentaries such as *Drifters* and *Housing Problems* is that they extended the scope of realist representation within British cinema by eschewing middle-class protagonists and making the working class their primary focus. In the 1950s Grierson and his protégés operated in a very different context, where the British documentary impulse was considered by certain commentators, including some of its original proponents, to be in decline. One continuity between the two periods, however, was a commitment to representing hitherto overlooked or inadequately represented social groups. As Raymond Williams has pointed out, 'social extension' is a common feature of nineteenth- and twentieth-century realist representations.[1] The new frontier for the documentary movement in the 1950s was an international one. For Grierson, British colonial Africa became a privileged site, at least in theory, for extending realist representation during this period.

The immediate impact of John Grierson's initiatives and concepts, like those of other similarly influential figures, was to an extent determined by the degree to which they meshed with or challenged existing or emergent practices and ideas within pertinent fields. For example, Ian Aitken has emphasised the broader context of what historians have described as British 'middle opinion' in the 1930s as an important element in the documentary movement's emergence and acceptance during that decade.[2] This helped to sustain the movement in the face of hostility from the film trade. These general considerations also apply to other phases of Grierson's career and later stages of the movement's development. Two projects arising from or related to Grierson's thinking about film and British colonial Africa during the late 1940s and early 50s provide contrasting examples of acceptance and viability on one side, and rejection on the other. There was a neat fit between some of Grierson's ideas in this area and the emergent work of the Gold Coast Film Unit (GCFU) during the 1950s. By contrast, Grierson's attempt to put some of his ideas into practice within the British feature-film industry revealed a definite incompatibility within that arena, notwithstanding Colonial Office support.

The African projects most closely associated with Grierson were designed to move beyond mainstream British feature films set in contemporary Africa in the 1950s, such as *Where No Vultures Fly* (1951) and *Simba* (1955). These tended to centre on liberal white protagonists. One precedent for these feature films was the Crown Film Unit documentary, *Daybreak in Udi* (1949), which celebrated the progressive leadership of

E. R. Chadwick, a white District Officer in Eastern Nigeria.[3] Grierson was working for the Central Office of Information, which encompassed Crown, when *Daybreak in Udi* was released, but he was not closely involved in its production, and considered 'it ha[d] the curse of talking down upon it'.[4] Grierson's preference during this period was for documentary and feature films about Africa which, as he put it, apparently minimised or eliminated the involvement of the 'White Father', and instead supposedly enabled black Africans to find their own voice.[5]

The pursuit of this aspiration can best be explored by considering Grierson's direct and indirect impact upon two distinct film projects: the GCFU and his Group 3 production *Man of Africa* (1953).[6] Both related to British colonial Africa during a transitional period. Immediately after World War II some British politicians and commentators still believed that, even if India was 'lost', colonies in Africa could play an increasingly vital role within the British imperial economy for the indefinite future. By the mid-1950s decolonisation in British colonial Africa was well advanced, and the Gold Coast/Ghana became the first African colony to gain independence from Britain in 1957. During this period Grierson elaborated his views on films for and about Africa in a paper delivered at a conference on 'The Film in British Colonial Development', convened by the British Film Institute (BFI) and the Colonial Office in January 1948. Grierson's biographers have paid scant attention to this episode in his career, but this paper, later published in *Sight and Sound*, assumes importance for any historian interested in locating his work within imperial, international and transnational as well as national contexts.[7] Grierson's January 1948 paper was a further stage in a development within his thinking that Jo Fox has identified as beginning in earnest during World War II. This involved

> a deeper desire to understand and represent the Dominions and the Empire, integrating them into the British experience, bringing the portrait of imperial life back home and indeed depicting nations in the process of defining their own national identities outside of their 'role' as British 'subjects'.[8]

Fox is correct about this general shift of emphasis in Grierson's thinking, but the extent to which he was willing to envisage African nations as fully independent entities is open to debate.

As Andrew Higson has argued, historians should avoid assuming that Grierson's ideas were automatically or straightforwardly carried through into the film practices of his colleagues, or that he was necessarily the primary influence upon them.[9] GCFU productions may have been consistent with the broad framework of Grierson's ideas about postwar film-making in Africa, but they were shaped by other local factors as well. Similarly, fellow Group 3 executive Michael Balcon was almost as influential as Grierson upon the production of *Man of Africa*, albeit in a constraining as well as enabling capacity. Additionally, as I have argued in more detail elsewhere, Grierson's writing was often crafted to address diverse or even divergent readerships, with deliberate ambiguities or evasions, and the connotations of certain words and phrases mobilised to this effect.[10] Grierson's speeches and writings can therefore be seen as nodal points for contemporary discourses, combining and expressing them with particular acuity, promoting documentary while attempt to negotiate the concerns of different interest groups.

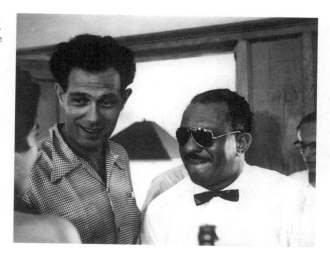

Sean Graham (left) in Ghana in the 1950s (With thanks to Emma Sandon and Catherine Graham)

With these caveats in mind, Grierson's paper on 'The Film in British Colonial Development' can be related to several significant films and film-making projects he was directly or indirectly associated with during the first half of the 1950s. Grierson was coming to the end of his tenure as director of mass communication and public information at UNESCO when he delivered the paper at the beginning of 1948. Its first part focused upon UNESCO's fundamental education projects, which had been formulated with assistance from the Colonial Office, a leading COI client.[11] Later that year Grierson was appointed controller of films at the COI, a post he held until the end of 1950. His last major role within British cinema was as a producer of feature films at Group 3 between 1951 and 1955. The arguments he put forward in 'The Film in British Colonial Development' were therefore attuned to prospective clients and employers and soon carried weight as far as actual film production was concerned.

The same year that he delivered and published 'The Film in British Colonial Development', Grierson appointed Sean Graham to head the newly established GCFU. Grierson was involved in this appointment because the COI was responsible for the Colonial Film Unit (CFU), of which the GCFU was nominally a part, until control of the CFU was transferred to the Colonial Office in 1950. Once Graham was in the Gold Coast/Ghana, other more immediate factors contributed to his development as a director and the nature of the films he directed there. These included Graham's wish to distinguish his work from the primarily educational films produced by the CFU's William Sellers. Graham saw himself, by contrast, as a professional film-maker, whose vocation was to be a 'storyteller'. Yet he also considered himself one of Grierson's followers.[12] Graham periodically returned to London, and worked with Grierson's close colleague Basil Wright. Wright produced Graham's *The Boy Kumasenu* (1952), arguably the GCFU's most accomplished film.[13] At the very least, the ideas Grierson articulated in 'The Film in British Colonial Development' constitute one historically proximate intellectual context for GCFU productions.

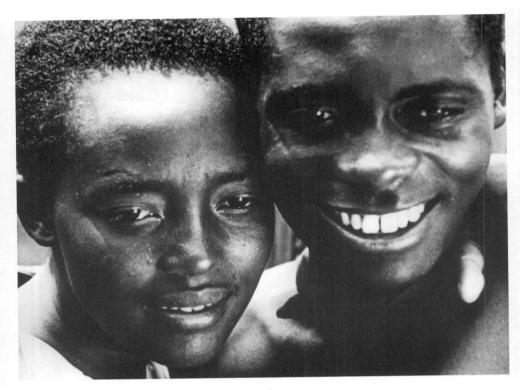

*Man of Africa* (1954): 'the first ambitious, dramatic all-negro film'

*Man of Africa*, produced by Grierson, who worked closely with director Cyril Frankel on what was his first feature film, provided an opportunity to try to achieve an innovative representation of Africa within mainstream, commercial British cinema. Initially conceived as a Crown Film Unit documentary, Grierson and Frankel expanded the project into a feature film for Group 3 after Crown was disbanded in 1952. The film that eventually emerged was fairly ambitious by documentary standards, with a £40,000 production budget, but modest compared to British features. Rank, by comparison, worked to a model of approximately £150,000–200,000 for a feature film around this time.[14] *Man of Africa* dealt with the migration of a group of Bakiga people in Kigezi, Uganda, from overpopulated, soil-eroded highlands to new homes in the lowlands inhabited by Batwa pygmies. The African actors in the film were all non-professionals, from the region in which the film was set, many of whom did not speak English. Like *The Boy Kumasenu*, described in *The Times* as 'the first feature film to be made in Africa ... with an entirely African cast', *Man of Africa* was promoted by Grierson as 'the first ambitious, dramatic all-negro film'.[15] The accuracy of such claims in relation to either film is not the most pertinent issue. More significant is that such claims were being made at this time about films that bore traces of Grierson's influence. The Africanisation of film production was a major preoccupation in 'The Film in British Colonial Development'.

This played out in different ways in the GCFU's film-making practices and in *Man of Africa*'s 'all-negro' narrative.

## A 'TRULY DECENTRALISED … GENUINE AFRICAN UNIT'[16]

For Grierson in his 1948 paper the 'first necessity' in addressing 'the problem of development on the economic, technological, social and cultural levels' was to 'create a body of men who live and work with the African problem, who are the African problem in its creative aspect, knowing it and living with it'.[17] Grierson contrasted this decentralised model to the CFU's practice during World War II of producing films for African audiences from a London base. By 1948, however, Grierson was endorsing an existing trend rather than advocating a new one. Decentralisation had already begun within the CFU, which by 1946 had embedded units in some parts of British colonial Africa.[18] The commitment to decentralisation should be seen within the broader context of nationalist political agitation for independence, and the transfer of financial responsibility for film production from the imperial centre to colonial governments. Africanisation also carried a financial benefit; Africans were cheaper to employ than Europeans. Grierson therefore provided an inspirational gloss to the more prosaic declaration of K. W. Blackburne, the director of information services at the Colonial Office, also a delegate at the 1948 conference, who said his department was 'trying to teach the people of the Colonies to run the show themselves and doing precisely that thing in the film world as in every other field'.[19]

As Tom Rice has argued, Grierson's proposal in 'The Film in British Colonial Development' was 'ambiguous and tentative'.[20] Grierson did not specify the exact nature, extent or timescale of the further Africanisation of film production. He also followed the Colonial Office's line in maintaining a measure of centralisation, for example in postproduction and film processing. None of the speeches published from the conference explicitly advocated Africans being trained up to become film unit heads, producers and directors as soon as possible. A lone, partial exception was A. R. Baëta, an African delegate from the Gold Coast/Ghana, who modestly suggested 'that it will save a lot of labour and uncertainty about the suitability of educational films if Africans were trained to write the script'.[21] Baëta's was the only published contribution to the conference which explicitly referred, with due deference to the 'very great help English people are giving us', to Africans' 'development towards nationhood'.[22] Compared to this, Grierson's formulation was less specific and more gradualist. He recommended 'sending out experts to teach natives, help natives in the technical processes involved'.[23] Baëta's piece politely echoed elements of Ghanaian nationalist rhetoric, which Grierson neither endorsed nor rejected. Grierson's phrasing at the 1948 conference was more consonant with assumptions prevalent at that time within the Colonial Office that internal self-government or full independence for Ghana was some time away, and not, as it turned out, respectively three years and less than a decade in the future.

A similar vagueness about whether or when black Africans could assume greater degrees of authority and responsibility pervaded the GCFU's production practice. White director Graham and cinematographer George Noble formed the GCFU's nucleus, with writers such as Montgomery Tully and Jerrard Tickell contributing to individual films. By contrast, the historian of African cinema, Manthia Diawara, concludes that Africans within the unit 'remained in the background'.[24] Rice notes that Graham saw the GCFU as a local rather than a colonial unit, but that 'local' does not necessarily equate to what we might understand as 'African', but rather to an administration run by Europeans working and living in the colonies'.[25] Certainly, unlike the Indian Film Unit in the years leading up to independence, no African was given the opportunity to direct in nearly ten years of the GCFU's existence. However, the relationships between background and foreground are worth exploring in more detail.

Despite the ambiguities of the 'local', African recruits such as Sam Aryeetey and R. O. Fenuku were eventually given screen credits on some of the unit's later productions, for example as editor and camera operator respectively on *Mr Mensah Builds a House* (1955).[26] More broadly, Peter Bloom and Kate Skinner have hypothesised about the consequences of Graham's practice of 'loose scripting', his relative openness to creative contributions and improvisation from the African crew and the incorporation of dialogue in different African languages. They conclude that in productions such as *The Boy Kumasenu*, this practice 'generated a dense layering of references and associations, some of which were either obscure, or wholly invisible, to the expatriates who commissioned the film'.[27] One example is the orphan motif in *The Boy Kumasenu*, strongly resonant in Ghanaian popular fiction and theatre. Bloom and Skinner reason on this basis that 'audiences in the Gold Coast, in particular, may have been attracted to features of which the film maker and producer were only partially aware'.[28]

Jennifer Blaylock has also highlighted the fact that African members of the unit sometimes challenged cinematographer Noble. They insisted that women in rural areas, in Noble's words, 'wore three times the clothing they usually did', and that children 'with their lovely glistening skins' were fully clothed before he could film them.[29] These interventions by some of the African crew can be seen as part of a broader cultural trend that peaked in the Ghanaian 'anti-nudity' campaigns of the late 1950s and 60s. These campaigns sought to encourage women, especially in certain northern areas of the country, to dress in ways defined by activists as more appropriate to the newly independent, modern Ghanaian nation. One key concern throughout these campaigns was to project a suitably modern image of Ghana to the rest of the world, although in some instances the very existence of the campaigns was seen as potentially drawing negative attention to the 'problem' of nudity.[30] Some GCFU productions such as *Amenu's Child* (1950) and *The Boy Kumasenu* were exhibited in Britain and elsewhere, as well as in the Gold Coast/Ghana. The unit's work therefore raised the same issue of foreign perceptions and the alleged sartorial 'backwardness' of some parts of the country. Discreet intervention by some African crew members during production could resolve this without viewers of the finished films being any the wiser, although this ran the risk of frustrating Noble's search for photogenic black bodies.

Grierson's strategic silence about whether white expatriates or black Africans should lead film-making projects within British colonial Africa, so long as they knew and lived with the African 'problem', raises questions pertinent to Graham's career. Graham was recently described by one former member of the GCFU, Chris Hesse, as a 'rebel' in relation to his immediate employer, the Gold Coast Information Services Department, partly because he 'fell in love with [Ghanaian] culture' and 'created an awareness that oh, our stories could be moulded into film'.[31] The omniscient narrator in Graham's 1964 novel *A Surfeit of Sun* says at one point that 'talk about colour became idiotically irrelevant when you lived in a multi-racial community ... . You liked people, or you did not. Barriers of class, of education and background remained. One ignored pigmentation'.[32] It is tempting to attribute these liberal humanist sentiments to Graham himself during his GCFU period. Conversely, it would be reductive to consider the junior members of the GCFU simply as undifferentiated 'Africans' or Ghanaians. Graham recalls recruiting several of them from Achimota School, an elite institution run along British public-school lines which educated many of the emergent Ghanaian nationalist elite.[33] Educational and other considerations, such as the exclusively male composition of the group, their class and regional identities, would be relevant to any closer analysis of the production of GCFU films.

Historians of colonial film-making in Africa often tend to end their narratives at independence. Yet as Brian Larkin has recently argued in relation to nonfiction film production in Nigeria, continuities between the pre- and post-independence periods also require attention.[34] This is the case with the GCFU, whose impact extended beyond independence in 1957. Graham recalls being offered a post by Kwame Nkrumah, but he declined and returned to Britain in the hope of furthering his career as a film director there. Several African members of the unit, such as Aryeetey and Hesse, later rose to senior positions within the Ghanaian film industry. Some GCFU films also continued to circulate after independence. Cinema-van commentator James Amuah has recalled Ghanaian audiences enjoying screenings of *Progress in Kojokrom* (1953) and *Mr Mensah Builds a House* on mobile projectors long after Ghanaian independence.[35] One reason why some GCFU films remained in circulation is that the specific development objectives they were designed to achieve were approved by post-independence Ghanaian governments. Yet their longevity must also relate to a continuing appeal to post-independence audience sensibilies. After 1957 the GCFU films that remained in circulation entered a new discursive framework located between post-independence government priorities and the local sensibilities of audiences in different parts of Ghana, often mediated by cinema-van commentators.[36]

Grierson's 'main proposition' in 'The Film in British Colonial Development' was that 'it is not a question of films coming from outside but of films being created from the inside by and for the colonial peoples themselves'.[37] The inside/outside opposition is not however a particularly useful distinction in this instance. The GCFU films which endured in Ghana after independence can be better understood as products of what Mary Louise Pratt calls a 'contact zone', a concept which draws attention to the 'interactive, improvisational dimensions of colonial encounters', without losing sight of the fact that these typically occur within 'radically asymmetrical relations of power'.[38] Although it is important to recognise the interactivity and improvisation that occurred during the production of GCFU films, it is also worth reiterating the obvious point that this could never have extended to any fundamental critique of British rule, or explicit support for full political independence. Celebrations of the latter were recorded as a *fait accompli* in one of the last Ghanaian productions in which Graham was involved: *Freedom for Ghana* (1957). The political struggle that led to this outcome could not be explicitly represented in GCFU films. Yet at the same time British colonial authority was barely visible in many of them. As Rice says of *The Boy Kumasenu*, 'the film promotes gradual change', but 'does not promote continued British involvement' in African social issues.[39] Kumasenu finds a foster parent and mentor in an educated African doctor, the type of moderate African leader the British were keen to endorse at that time. The virtual invisibility of British colonial authority is highly pertinent to *Man of Africa* as well.

## 'TIME FOR THE AFRICAN TO SPEAK FOR HIMSELF'

Grierson forcefully expressed the conviction that 'it was time for the African to speak for himself' during the late 1940s and early 50s.[40] In a neat rhetorical move he attempted to exemplify this in his paper on 'The Film in British Colonial Development' by concluding with two extended quotations 'in the dark voice of [African-American writer] Richard Wright, and not in my own white one'.[41] In the early 1930s Grierson had been equally insistent that white British 'workmen on the job' should 'do their own commentary' in documentary films, 'with idiom and accent complete', although this proved difficult to achieve in practice.[42] *The Boy Kumasenu* and *Progress at Kojokrom* featured voiceover commentaries by white English speakers, but there is evidence that the amount of commentary was reduced during the latter's production.[43] GCFU films were, to a certain extent, able to incorporate black African voices, and languages such as Fante and Twi, partly because of their primary orientation towards Gold Coast/Ghanaian audiences. The most important factor, as far as language is concerned, is that these films were often exhibited with live commentary in the African languages with which particular audiences in the Gold Coast/Ghana were most familiar.

Man of Africa, on the other hand, involved negotiating a different set of opportunities, constraints and challenges. Group 3, its production company, was formally established in 1951 through very modest loan funding from the National Film Finance Corporation (NFFC), with the intention of supporting and co-ordinating independent film production, and developing new features directors. This formed part of the postwar Labour government's larger strategy of moving, partly in response to financial crisis, towards a more mixed economy within the film industry, and counterbalancing the dominance of the 'duopoly' of Rank and the Associated British Picture Corporation (ABPC). Grierson was initially an executive producer at Group 3, but illness and a divergence of views between him and production controller John Baxter led to a realignment after August 1952.[44] Grierson concentrated after that time on what Sue Harper and Vincent Porter describe as a small number of 'pet projects', such as *Man of Africa*, and Baxter assumed the new title of managing director.[45] Yet even Grierson's pet projects were pursued within a context where, as Simon Popple points out, Group 3 was 'divorced from other major companies in terms of its production capabilities' but remained 'reliant on established distribution and exhibition networks'.[46]

Grierson had nurtured the idea of an African film project for some time. He tried to involve Richard Wright, writing to him in October 1950: 'I propose to do a film in

Africa next year. I want you with me if you can manage.'[47] This proposed collaboration might have produced interesting results. In addition to evading the question of African independence, which Wright supported, Grierson tended to conflate African-American and African experiences and identities in 'The Film in British Colonial Development'. His paper showed little sensitivity to the complex relationships between the African diaspora and Africa that Wright explored in his 1954 book on Ghana, *Black Power*. Montagu Slater, an old colleague of Grierson's, was eventually employed as *Man of Africa*'s scriptwriter. Although a Communist Party of Great Britain (CPGB) member, Slater was a safer choice than Wright, who also had Communist affiliations, but little film experience. Slater had worked on *Coal Face*, scripted *Daybreak in Udi*, and recently garnered critical acclaim for Group 3 with his script for *The Brave Don't Cry* (1952).

As far as other members of the production team were concerned, the ideal of training African technicians that Grierson articulated in 'The Film in British Colonial Development' was not applied to *Man of Africa*. The crew of film-makers who shot the documentary in Uganda were predominantly white Britons. The only black Africans involved on the production side were porters and the interpreter and adviser Seperiera Mpambara, who received a production assistant credit on the opening titles.[48] The claims made about *Man of Africa* representing black Africans 'with warmth from within' and enabling them to speak for themselves therefore rested primarily upon its exclusively black African cast and use of language.[49] Not only were no white people seen or heard in the finished film, director Frankel also deliberately avoided filming any of the Asian traders who populated the district in which it was set.[50]

Although Slater's track record as *Daybreak in Udi*'s scriptwriter would have helped him to secure the job, Frankel denied that *Man of Africa* was in any way modelled upon this earlier Oscar-winning film.[51] Production documents support this claim; Slater's script notes initially envisaged a somewhat experimental approach to *Man of Africa*. His first draft of the script echoes certain aspects of Soviet film-maker Sergei Eisenstein's theorising, which in turn was influenced by the anthropologist Lucien Lévy-Bruhl. The pertinent Eisenstein concepts were 'image-sensual thinking' and accessing the 'primitive' levels of spectators' psyches. These concepts were by then available in English translation in the books *The Film Sense* (1942) and *Film Form* (1949). Slater wrote in early March 1952:

> There are two special problems, that of native actors and the problem of language. In a sense both are aspects of one problem. It seems likely that the best solution may turn out to be a combination of several methods. Sometimes the story will be told in terms of symbol, mime, action and atmosphere, using native speech often like a sound effect. The native speech will increase the feeling of strangeness: but almost at once we shall want to reverse this process and persuade the audience to become identified with the people in the story. There will be scenes in which we hear both English and native speech, sometimes by the use of an interpreter: sometimes we shall simply dub in English (but not very often): and, finally, we may attempt the novelist's device of interior monologue, though this last device will have to be used sparingly, the language reproducing the directness and simplicity of native thinking, its habit of thinking in images and emotions, always intuitively, not in a logical but an emotional form. Since this is how English audiences think too, the problems, though difficult, ought not to be invincible.[52]

Slater's comments belong to a long tradition, especially prevalent in the silent era, of theorising cinema's potential to perform what Rachel O. Moore describes as 'modern magic', where linguistic boundaries are transcended and powerful, primal emotions are experienced by spectators.[53] Yet invocations of this 'modern magic' frequently involve representations of or assumptions about 'primitives', in this case the 'natives' in *Man of Africa*, who are considered to exist in closer proximity to it than other social groups.[54]

In the world of film practice, rather than theory, African voices became one of the sticking points that eventually convinced Grierson's fellow Group 3 executive, Michael Balcon, that *Man of Africa* was not a viable commercial proposition. Sound recording on location in Kigezi proved challenging, but these technical difficulties were intertwined with and preceded by underlying concerns about the comprehensibility of African voices for British audiences.[55] Even during the script-development phase, one undated memorandum noted that the production team

> welcome and accept the warning of depending too much on dialogue and the danger of indistinct African voices. We aim in the shooting script to ... [use] dialogue only when necessary ... the suggestion of some limited form of narration is at the front of our minds and will be used if necessary.[56]

A further undated memorandum conceded that 'recorded African voices are terribly difficult to understand'.[57] On 1 September 1953, after a screening of the first colour print of the film, Frankel noted that Balcon 'found the dialogue of the African voices lacking in rhythm. He felt ... that we should possibly have an English voice as a narrator.'[58] This comment suggests that at this stage of the production process African voices featured more prominently, albeit speaking dialogue scripted by British film-makers, and within the context of performances directed by Frankel (with Mpambara's assistance). This earlier version might well have been an intriguing historical precursor to later films produced by African film-makers after independence, marked by distinctive modes of orality.[59]

The compromise arrived at in *Man of Africa* involved the African-American actor Gordon Heath voicing some of the African characters' dialogue, as well as interior monologues and commentary on the narrative action. In some respects this was a canny solution; it faintly echoed Slater's initial thoughts about the use of language in *Man of Africa*, and it kept the film 'all-negro'. Heath's voice would have been familiar to some British audiences from his work in British theatre and television, including his lead role in Kenneth Tynan's touring production of *Othello* in 1950, and the BBC television broadcast of the play *Deep Are the Roots* (tx. 7 May 1950). The recourse to Heath parallels Grierson's use of Richard Wright quotations in his paper on 'The Film in British Colonial Development'. In both cases relatively familiar African-Americans were mobilised to speak for anonymous Africans. Yet Heath's casting was contrary to the intention expressed in one of the *Man of Africa* production memoranda, which said that the film would differ from those 'where Africans ... required for leading roles ... have usually been introduced from abroad'.[60] This trend in British feature production can be traced as far back as the 1930s films set in Africa starring Paul Robeson. It continued in two British films produced around the same time as *Man of Africa* that included reasonably substantial roles for black African characters: *Cry, the Beloved Country* (1951) and *The Heart of the Matter* (1953). The former provided an early role for Sidney Poitier as a South African priest. The latter, set in Sierra Leone, featured the Bermudan actor Earl Cameron.[61]

## DEVELOPMENT

In addition to the emphasis upon building up a 'genuine' African unit, and the related conviction that it was 'time for the African to speak for himself', the other key concept in Grierson's paper 'The Film in British Colonial Development' was development itself. This term of course had wider ramifications beyond cinema. Frederick Cooper has argued that in British government circles at that time 'development' referred simultaneously to 'increased output and to increased welfare', and thus was a term that could serve 'multiple political purposes'.[62] The key words 'development', 'develop' and 'developing' featured prominently in Grierson's 1948 paper, in which he described Africa as representing 'an economic potential which is enormous' as well as a location where the 'social progress' achieved over the last twenty-five years in Britain had to be extended.[63] Yet although the dual objectives of increased economic output and increased welfare for 'natives' could be acknowledged in intellectual exchanges, such as those which took place at the Colonial Office/BFI conference in January 1948, it was tempting to emphasise the latter rather than the former when representing colonial development to wider audiences. For example Ernest Bevin, Britain's Foreign Secretary, stated a few months before Grierson delivered his paper

> we must be careful that our plans for the development of our Colonial Dependencies cannot in any way be represented as springing solely from our selfish interests. It is above all important that in their presentation there is no possible suggestion of exploitation of the colonial populations.[64]

This stance resonated in *Man of Africa*. Grierson noted in his feedback on an early version of the script that the motivation for the resettlement scheme needed to be made clear. Various options for achieving greater clarity were explored as the script was developed.[65] Yet even in those versions of the script where the colonial administration's initiation of the scheme was acknowledged, there was never any suggestion that increased economic productivity resulting from the resettlement of the Bakiga people might also be of benefit to the British authorities. All the options considered posited the British colonial authorities as unseen, benign, selfless agents of the state, in accordance with Grierson's philosophical view of the (colonial) state as an essentially neutral entity.[66]

The opening sequence in the extant version of the film briefly signals the official context before moving into the narrative proper. A written title dedicates the film 'to the imaginative colonial servants who organised the original Kigezi trek, gave us the freedom of Uganda and encouraged the making of a picture which does not even mention them'. In the opening shots, an African character reads from a newspaper about the 'local' government's preparation for the scheme. After this brief diegetic reference to colonial governance, subsumed again under the term 'local', the personal narrative focusing exclusively on African characters begins. Two objectives are achieved here. As Tom Rice has argued, the opening dedication 'contextualises the film's action within a rhetoric of colonial development'.[67] In addition, as Grierson explained in a short promotional piece on *Man of Africa*, the Colonial Office supported the project, so some acknowledgment of British officials' role in Uganda was necessary.[68] Dedications, as Gérard Genette points out, implicate a 'person or a thing as a kind of ideal inspirer', which in this case is British colonial authority.[69] The import of this was evident to the American film historian Richard Griffith, who described *Man of Africa*, non-pejoratively, as 'an apology for British colonial administration'.[70] Yet limiting the explicit reference to colonial governance to the opening title enabled Grierson to claim *Man of Africa* as 'the first ambitious, dramatic all-negro film'.

In fact, the resettlement programme in Kigezi was a rather unusual case. Unlike some other resettlement schemes pursued elsewhere in British colonial Africa, the one in Kigezi, for which John Purseglove, district agricultural officer, was officially responsible, could be judged a success. It is therefore unsurprising that the Colonial Office was willing to support a film about it. The Kigezi programme became a showpiece development project because, in this instance, there was little resistance from the Africans involved and it met the objectives defined by the British colonial authorities. A significant factor was that the resettlement scheme closely followed existing migratory patterns within the region.[71] This particular scheme in Kigezi therefore provided ideal material for a film intended to foreground African characters and experiences while nevertheless dovetailing with colonial economic imperatives. Changes to the film's title, however, obscured this particularity and implied the film had a paradigmatic status it was problematic to claim.

Ian Aitken has demonstrated that Grierson's epistemology assumed that 'the abstract and the general (the real) was of greater significance than the empirical and particular (the phenomenal), but ... the empirical and particular constituted the best means of comphrehending the abstract and general'.[72] This striving for the general over the particular can be discerned in deliberations about what to call the film. By May 1953 Grierson was considering abandoning the working title, *The Kigezi Story*, in favour of *The African*, because in his view 'it's maybe the first time anyone ever really saw an African'.[73] By July 1953 James Lawrie and Balcon at Group 3 were informing Grierson that Kigezi should not feature in the title because 'no one ever recommends anyone to go and see a picture if he isn't sure how to pronounce the title'.[74] Grierson apparently suggested *Jonathan the African* and *Song of Africa* as alternatives. Frankel says he eventually settled on *Man of Africa* in the hope of achieving the 'direct communication' with British and American audiences *The Kigezi Story* might preclude.[75] The film's title, initially promising a regionally specific narrative, was aggrandised to a more generalised one. To call a film *Man of Africa* implies that its representation of social progress and development, ostensibly led by Africans yet discreetly credited to colonial officials, is applicable to Africa as a whole.

## 'NORA', TRAVELOGUES AND TELEVISION

A final, instructive contrast can be made between *The Boy Kumasenu*, and *Man of Africa*. The former deals with journeys and connections between the country and the city, and between Ghana and the African diaspora, in a relatively complex manner. Kumasenu (Nortey Engmann) follows his cousin Agboh (Frank Tamakloe) from a small fishing village to the capital, Accra, with the help of his uncle, who gets him a job working for a friend who runs a store just outside the city. The sequence detailing Kumasenu's work in the story includes a telling detail that may have resonated more with the Ghanaians involved in the production of *The Boy Kumasenu*, and with Ghanaian audiences, than with the white members of the GCFU. A lorry driver, who the commentator describes as speaking a 'blend of many languages', asks to hear the famed Trinidadian calypsonian Lord Kitchener's song 'Nora' (1950). This was a major hit of the time in West Africa and Ghana.[76] African experience and cultural traffic therefore extends across the country and the city in this film, as well as beyond national boundaries, rather than being reductively fixed in place. Within *The Boy Kumasenu*'s overarching narrative of confronting juvenile delinquency, the pleasures and dangers of modern African city life, including alcohol, the lure of crime, casual sexual relationships, popular music and dance, are represented or alluded to. All of these factors would most likely have contributed to the film's popularity in the Gold Coast/Ghana, with 40,000 people reportedly seeing it in the first three weeks of its release.[77]

In *Man of Africa* Grierson and his collaborators aspired to produce a film in which the typical African was not represented as a stereotypical 'tribesman with a weird way of life'.[78] Grierson reiterated this point in the early 1960s, challenging viewers' assumptions by stating that after their migration 'the Bakiga didn't really know how to live on this new land on the Congo. Strange as you might think, they didn't even know a thing about wild animals because they had never seen them.'[79] Nevertheless, *Man of Africa* followed a well-established tradition in British films about Africa by unfolding within a predominantly rural setting populated by spectacular wildlife. In British cinema of the 1950s, as Wendy Webster puts it, 'urban African settings were thin on the ground'.[80] *Where No Vultures Fly*, the most commercially successful British film set in Africa prior to *Man of Africa*, was shot in Technicolor. It combined a white liberal protagonist in the *Daybreak in Udi* mould with the travelogue pleasures of an African game-park setting. The liberality of the white colonial protagonist was a relatively new, emergent phenomenon within British film-making; colour cinematography of African wildlife and landscapes was not. *Man of Africa* went beyond this emergent trend in its 'all-negro' casting. As Frankel later put it, films such as *Where No Vultures Fly* 'were not about Africans, but featured British actors with Africans in the background'.[81] Yet *Man of Africa* did not break with precedent as far as visual pleasures were concerned. Frankel said its exotic African rural setting was one reason for shooting the film in Ferraniacolor, a cheaper, more mobile colour technology than Technicolor, but still more expensive than the black-and-white cinematography employed in the majority of low-budget Group 3 productions.[82]

*Man of Africa*'s spectacular aspects were further accentuated when, even after Balcon's concerns about African voices had been addressed, it failed to achieve distribution. Balcon persisted in his view that the film was not suitable for general release. Frankel believed that as a result of this *Man of Africa* was deliberately sidelined during the transition between Associated British Film Distributors (ABFD) and British Lion as Group 3's distributors.[83] The only version of *Man of Africa* to eventually secure commercial distribution in British cinemas in the 1950s was a drastically shortened one, marketed as a travelogue. The trade journal *To-Day's Cinema* approved this version's 'handy length' as a supporting item, and its wildlife sequences involving 'a raiding herd of elephants, and the depredations of baboons', captured by 'visually impressive colour photography'.[84] The *Monthly Film Bulletin* concluded that in its reduced state 'any assessment of the film's original intentions' became 'difficult'.[85] Grierson, Frankel and Slater insisted their names be taken off this version. For the film historian, this outcome serves as a rather brutal reminder of two things. The first is the pressure to conform often exerted upon film projects seen during production as departing too radically, even if only in certain respects, from established or emergent norms. The second is that the boundary between films of empire associated with the British documentary movement, and the travelogue, described by Grierson as one of the 'lower categories' of nonfiction film, was not always clear cut.[86]

Grierson was able to contextualise *Man of Africa* on his own terms when he screened an extract on his television series *This Wonderful World* (episode 141, tx. 26 January 1961). His epistemology of moving from the empirical and particular through to the abstract and general to comprehend an idealist notion of 'the real' can be seen at work here. To invest the extract with topicality, while at the same time divesting it of specificity, Grierson referred to the 'news from the Congo', and the fact that *Man of Africa* was shot 'on the borders of all the present agonies and tribulations'. Grierson continued, more abstractly: 'In a way we foresaw them. We wanted to make a film about the racial and human differences in Africa – but not just between black and white.'[87] The extract showcased what he had previously praised as 'the most poignant moment in the film, when a negro baby is dying and a little pygmy foster-mother is brought in to save its life'.[88] For Grierson this recognition of a common bond of humanity between the Bakiga people and the Batwa pygmies epitomised the transcendence of 'the old trible [sic] prejudices and vanities' which threatened to 'cut across all the high hopes for the future'.[89]

Colonialism's continued presence or legacy in African societies was pushed to the margins of Grierson's remarks, just faintly audible in the passing reference to differences 'between black and white'. This parallels the way that colonial authority is virtually invisible within *Man of Africa*, despite its role as a primary instigator of narrative events. Grierson's 'high hopes' for the African future were a humane alternative to much media coverage of the Congo crisis at that time, which represented a chaotic situation in which African atavism and tribal discord threatened European lives and interests. Yet it is also instructive to compare Grierson's comments with the now famous inaugural speech made by the first Congolese prime minister, Patrice Lumumba, six months earlier. Lumumba articulated a powerful alternative narrative of Congolese identity and high hopes for the future whose circulation was initially restricted, or adversely interpreted, in North American and Western European contexts.[90] Lumumba, like Grierson, urged his compatriots to forget 'hazardous tribal quarrels', but most centrally he envisaged a dynamic new national identity forged out of a shared experience of resistance to colonialism: 'no Congolese worthy of the name will ever forget that independence has been won in struggle'.[91] This was one 'dark voice' Grierson seems not to have heard.

## ACKNOWLEDGMENTS

I am grateful to Patrick Russell at the BFI for helping me to access both *Man of Africa* and its director, and to Cyril Frankel for kindly agreeing to be interviewed. Karl Magee, curator of the John Grierson papers at the University of Stirling, and Nathalie Morris, at BFI Special Collections, provided access to archival material. Emma Sandon, Peter Bloom, Kate Skinner and Tom Rice generously shared their unpublished interview material. Emma Sandon also kindly offered helpful feedback on an earlier draft of this essay. Jo Fox furnished valuable information about *This Wonderful World*.

## NOTES

1. Raymond Williams, 'A Lecture on Realism', *Screen* vol. 18 no. 1 (Spring 1977).
2. Ian Aitken, *Film and Reform: John Grierson and the Documentary Film Movement* (London: Routledge, 1990).
3. This film is available to view at colonialfilm.org.uk.
4. John Grierson, 'Progress and Prospect [1949]', in Forsyth Hardy (ed.), *Grierson on Documentary* (London: Faber and Faber, 1979), p. 199.
5. John Grierson, 'Making *Man of Africa*', *Films and Filming* vol. 1 no. 2 (October 1954), p. 14.
6. The BFI National Archive holds a viewing copy of *Man of Africa*.
7. Forsyth Hardy, *John Grierson: A Documentary Biography* (London: Faber and Faber, 1979) does not mention the paper or conference at all. Jack Ellis, *John Grierson: Life, Contributions, Influence* (Carbondale and Edwardsville: Southern Illinois University Press, 2000), briefly refers to it (p. 236). For further discussion of the British documentary movement, imperialism, internationalism, nationalism and transnationalism, see Martin Stollery, *Alternative Empires: European Modernist Cinemas and Cultures of Imperialism* (Exeter and Chicago, IL: Exeter University Press, 2000); Martin Stollery, 'From *Storm over Asia* to *Dawn over Africa*: Transnationalism and Imperialism in British Intellectual Film Culture of the Late 1920s and 1930s', *Transnational Cinemas* vol. 2 no. 1 (2011); Martin Stollery, 'The Last Roll of the Dice: *Morning, Noon and Night*, Empire and the Historiography of the Crown Film Unit', in Lee Grieveson and Colin MacCabe (eds), *Film and the End of Empire* (London: BFI, 2011).
8. Jo Fox, 'John Grierson, His "Documentary Boys" and the British Ministry of Information, 1939–1942', *Historical Journal of Film, Radio and Television* vol. 25 no. 3 (2005), p. 363.
9. Andrew Higson, 'Review of Ian Aitken, *Film and Reform* and Paul Swann, *The British Documentary Film Movement, 1926–1946*', *Screen* vol. 32 no. 3 (Autumn 1991).
10. Stollery, *Alternative Empires*, pp. 147–8, 154–7, 178–80.
11. See Phillip W. Jones with David Coleman, *The United Nations and Education* (London: Routledge, 2005), p. 30.
12. Emma Sandon, Tom Rice and Peter Bloom, 'Changing the World: Sean Graham', *Journal of British Cinema and Television* vol. 10 no. 3 (2013), p. 526.

13. This film is available to view online at colonialfilm.org.uk.
14. Sue Harper and Vincent Porter, *British Cinema of the 1950s: The Decline of Deference* (London and New York: Oxford University Press, 2003), p. 266.
15. Anon, 'Feature Film from the Gold Coast', *The Times*, 3 January 1952, p. 8; Grierson, 'Making *Man of Africa*', p. 14.
16. John Grierson, 'The Film in British Colonial Development', *Sight and Sound* vol. 17 no. 65 (Spring 1948), p. 4.
17. Ibid., pp. 3–4.
18. See Rosaleen Smyth, 'The Post-war Career of the Colonial Film Unit in Africa; 1946–1955', *Historical Journal of Film, Radio and Television* vol. 12 no. 2 (1992); Tom Rice, 'From the Inside: The Colonial Film Unit and the Beginning of the End', in Grieveson and MacCabe, *Film and the End of Empire*.
19. K. W. Blackburne, 'Financial Problems and Future Policy in British Colonies', *The Film in Colonial Development: A Report of a Conference* (London, 1948), p. 35.
20. Rice, 'From the Inside', p. 145.
21. A. R. Baëta, 'The Two Worlds', *Sight and Sound* vol. 17 no. 65 (Spring 1948), p. 6. Rice, 'From the Inside', correctly points out of the conference that there were 'no "colonials" among its seven invited speakers' (p. 145). However, Baëta's comments were subsequently published in *Sight and Sound*, whereas some of the invited speakers' papers were not.
22. Baëta, 'The Two Worlds', p. 7.
23. Grierson, 'The Film in British Colonial Development', p. 4.
24. Manthia Diawara, *African Cinema: Politics and Culture* (Bloomington: Indiana University Press, 1992), p. 6.
25. Rice, 'From the Inside', p. 147.
26. This film is available to view online at colonialfilm.org.uk.
27. Peter Bloom and Kate Skinner, 'Modernity and Danger: *The Boy Kumasenu* and the Work of the Gold Coast Film Unit', *Ghana Studies* no. 12 (2009), p. 2.
28. Ibid., p. 17.
29. George Noble, 'Cameraman on the Gold Coast', *Colonial Cinema* vol. 10 no. 2 (1952), quoted in Jennifer Blaylock, *African Agency in the Gold Coast Film Unit*, posted 27 October 2010, https://cinemaintransit.wordpress.com/2010/10/27/african-agency-in-the-gold-coast-film-unit/.
30. See Jean Allman, '"Let Your Fashion Be in Line with Our Ghanaian Costume": Nation, Gender, and the Politics of Clothing in Nkrumah's Ghana', in Jean Allman (ed.), *Fashioning Africa: Power and the Politics of Dress* (Bloomington: Indiana University Press, 2004).
31. Chris Hesse, 'Personal Interview with Chris Hesse', conducted by Kate Skinner, Accra, 23 June 2010.
32. Sean Graham, *A Surfeit of Sun* [1964] (London: Panther, 1967), pp. 51–2.
33. Sandon *et al.*, 'Changing the World', p. 532.
34. Brian Larkin, *Signal and Noise: Media, Infrastructure, and Urban Culture in Nigeria* (Durham, NC: Duke University Press, 2008), pp. 102–3, 119–20.
35. Jennifer Blaylock, 'An Interview with a Former Cinema Van Commentator', posted 26 January 2011, https://cinemaintransit.wordpress.com/2011/01/26/an-interview-with-a-former-cinema-van-commentator/. See also the GCFU titles listed in *Catalogue of Films: Ghana Central Film Library 1971–72* (Accra, n.d), http://archive.org/details/CatalogueOfFilmsGhanaCentralFilmLibrary1971-72. *Progress in Kojokrom* and *Mr Mensah Builds a House* are available to view at colonialfilm.org.uk.

36. Rice, 'From the Inside', emphasises the potential for commentators to move 'away from the script and from the official line' (p. 149).
37. Grierson, 'The Film in British Colonial Development', p. 3.
38. Mary Louise Pratt, *Imperial Eyes: Travel Writing and Transculturation* (London: Routledge, 1992), p. 7.
39. Tom Rice, *The Boy Kumasenu*, May 2008, http://www.colonialfilm.org.uk/node/332.
40. Grierson, 'Making *Man of Africa*', p. 14.
41. Grierson, 'The Film in British Colonial Development', p. 4.
42. John Grierson, 'The GPO Gets Sound', *Cinema Quarterly* vol. 2 (1934), p. 216; Martin Stollery, 'Voiceover/Commentary', in Scott Anthony and James Mansell (eds), *The Projection of Britain: A History of the GPO Film Unit* (London: BFI, 2011), pp. 171–2.
43. See Tom Rice, *Progress at Kojokrom*, April 2008, http://www.colonialfilm.org.uk/node/2566.
44. Richard Dyer MacCann, 'Subsidy for the Screen: Grierson and Group 3/1951–1955', *Sight and Sound* vol. 46 no. 3 (1977), p. 168.
45. Harper and Porter, *British Cinema of the 1950s*, p. 188.
46. Simon Popple, 'Group 3: A Lesson in State Intervention', *Film History* vol. 8 no. 2 (1996), p. 138.
47. John Grierson, 'Letter to Richard Wright', 2 October 1950, quoted in Hazel Rowley, *Richard Wright: The Life and Times* (Chicago, IL: Chicago University Press, 2008), p. 579.
48. Cyril Frankel, 'Personal Interview with Cyril Frankel', conducted by Martin Stollery, London, 16 August 2008.
49. Anon, 'Memorandum 1: Attitude to the African in *The Kigezi Story*', John Grierson Papers, Special Collections, University of Stirling (hereafter GP), G6:21:6, undated.
50. Ibid.
51. Frankel, 'Personal Interview with Cyril Frankel'.
52. Montagu Slater, *This Way to the New Country/The Kigezi Story* (script) 2/5 March 1952, BFI Special Collections.
53. Rachel O. Moore, *Savage Theory: Cinema as Modern Magic* (Durham, NC: Duke University Press, 2000).
54. Even Grierson's paper at the January 1948 conference, replete as it was with reference to colonial development, was initially entitled 'The Film and Primitive Peoples'.
55. For the technical difficulties involved, see Isobel Pargiter, 'Letter to John Baxter', GP G6:21:5, 27 November 1952.
56. Anon, 'Memorandum 2: The Use of the Flashback Technique in *The Kigezi Story*', GP G6:21:7, undated.
57. Anon, 'Untitled document relating to *Man of Africa*', GP G6:21:8, undated.
58. Cyril Frankel to John Baxter, GP G6:36:227, 1 September 1953.
59. The pioneering text in these debates is Manthia Diawara, 'Oral Literature and African Film: Narratology in *Wend Kuuni*', in Jim Pines and Paul Willemen (eds), *Questions of Third Cinema* (London: BFI, 1989).
60. Anon, 'Memorandum 1', GP G6:21:6.
61. For a discussion of Cameron's casting in this film, see Martin Stollery, '"Scarred by a Cheated Ending"/"Not Suitable for Audiences in This Colony": The Film Adaptation of Graham Greene's *The Heart of the Matter* in Metropolitan and Colonial Contexts', *Literature/Film Quarterly* vol. 40 no. 3 (July 2012).

62. Frederick Cooper, *Decolonization and African Society: The Labor Question in French and British Africa* (Cambridge: Cambridge University Press, 1996), pp. 205, 206.

63. Grierson, 'The Film in British Colonial Development', p. 3.

64. Ernest Bevin, '4 October 1947 Memorandum', quoted in Cooper, *Decolonization and African Society*, p. 205.

65. Slater, *This Way to the New Country*, revisions following discussion of 16 December 1952, 19 December 1952; Anon, Untitled document relating to *Man of Africa*, GP G6:21:8.

66. Aitken, *Film and Reform*.

67. Tom Rice, *Man of Africa*, October 2009, http://www.colonialfilm.org.uk/node/237.

68. Grierson, 'Making *Man of Africa*', p. 14.

69. Gérard Genette, *Paratexts: Thresholds of Interpretation* (Cambridge: Cambridge University Press, 1997), p. 136.

70. Richard Griffith, 'Letter to John Grierson', GP G6:21:14, undated.

71. See Grace Carswell, *Cultivating Success in Uganda: Kigezi Farmers and Colonial Policies* (Oxford: James Currey, 2007).

72. Aitken, *Film and Reform*, p. 7.

73. John Grierson, 'Letter to Charles Crandall', GP G6:36:33, 20 May 1953.

74. James Lawrie, 'Letter to to John Grierson', GP G6:36:160, 21 July 1953.

75. Frankel, 'Personal Interview with Cyril Frankel'.

76. Simon Featherstone, *Postcolonial Cultures* (Edinburgh: Edinburgh University Press, 2005), p. 53. Despite the lorry driver's request, 'Nora' is not actually played in *The Boy Kumasenu*, presumably due to the cost of securing the rights.

77. Henry Swanzy, 'Quarterly Notes', *African Affairs* vol. 51 no. 205 (October 1952), p. 279; Rice, *The Boy Kumasenu*.

78. Anon, 'Memorandum 1'.

79. *This Wonderful World* script, GP G8:21:14, (episode 141, tx. 26 January 1961).

80. Wendy Webster, 'Mumbo-jumbo, Magic and Modernity: Africa in British Cinema, 1946–65', in Grieveson and MacCabe, *Film and the End of Empire*, p. 239.

81. Cyril Frankel, *Eye to Eye: A Memoir* (London: Bank House Books, 2010), p. 58.

82. Frankel, 'Personal Interview with Cyril Frankel'.

83. Marjorie Bilbow, 'End of Exile for Frankel's *Man of Africa*', *Screen International*, 15 November 1986, p. 21.

84. M.M.W., *Man of Africa*, *To-Day's Cinema* vol. 85 no. 7404 (25 November 1955), p. 6.

85. John Grierson, '*Man of Africa*', *Monthly Film Bulletin* vol. 23 no. 264 (January 1956), p. 3.

86. John Grierson, 'First Principles of Documentary [1932]', in Hardy, *Grierson on Documentary*, p. 35.

87. *This Wonderful World* script.

88. Grierson, 'Making *Man of Africa*', p. 14.

89. *This Wonderful World* script.

90. Kevin C. Dunn, *Imagining the Congo: The International Relations of Identity* (New York: Palgrave Macmillan, 2003), p. 102.

91. Patrice Lumumba, Speech at the Proclamation of Congolese Independence, 30th June 1960', in Alan P. Merriam (ed.), *Congo, Background of Conflict* (Chicago, IL: Northwestern University Press, 1961), pp. 354, 352.

# REFERENCES

Aitken, Ian, *Film and Reform: John Grierson and the Documentary Film Movement* (London: Routledge, 1990).

Allman, Jean, '"Let Your Fashion Be in Line with Our Ghanaian Costume": Nation, Gender, and the Politics of Clothing in Nkrumah's Ghana', in Jean Allman (ed.), *Fashioning Africa: Power and the Politics of Dress* (Bloomington: Indiana University Press, 2004).

Anon, 'Memorandum 1: Attitude to the African in *The Kigezi Story*', John Grierson Papers, Special Collections, University of Stirling (hereafter GP), G6:21:6, undated.

Anon, 'Memorandum 2: The Use of the Flashback Technique in *The Kigezi Story*', GP G6:21:7, undated.

Anon, Untitled document relating to *Man of Africa*, GP G6:21:8, undated.

Anon, 'Feature Film from the Gold Coast', *The Times*, 3 January 1952.

Baëta, A. R., 'The Two Worlds', *Sight and Sound* vol. 17 no. 65 (Spring 1948), pp. 5–7.

Bilbow, Marjorie, 'End of Exile for Frankel's *Man of Africa*', *Screen International*, 15 November 1986, p. 21.

Blackburne, K. W., 'Financial Problems and Future Policy in British Colonies', *The Film in Colonial Development: A Report of a Conference* (London, 1948), pp. 33–7.

Blaylock, Jennifer, 'An Interview with a Former Cinema Van Commentator', posted 26 January 2011, https://cinemaintransit.wordpress.com/2011/01/26/an-interview-with-a-former-cinema-van-commentator/.

Bloom, Peter and Kate Skinner, 'Modernity and Danger: *The Boy Kumasenu* and the Work of the Gold Coast Film Unit', *Ghana Studies* no. 12 (2009), pp. 121–53.

Carswell, Grace, *Cultivating Success in Uganda: Kigezi Farmers and Colonial Policies* (Oxford: James Currey, 2007).

Catalogue of Films: Ghana Central Film Library 1971–72 (Accra, n.d), http://archive.org/details/CatalogueOfFilmsGhanaCentralFilmLibrary1971-72.

Cooper, Frederick, *Decolonization and African Society: The Labor Question in French and British Africa* (Cambridge: Cambridge University Press, 1996).

Diawara, Manthia, *African Cinema: Politics and Culture* (Bloomington: Indiana University Press, 1992).

Diawara, Manthia, 'Oral Literature and African Film: Narratology in Wend Kuuni', in Jim Pines and Paul Willemen (eds), *Questions of Third Cinema* (London: BFI, 1989), pp. 199–211.

Dunn, Kevin C., *Imagining the Congo: The International Relations of Identity* (New York: Palgrave Macmillan, 2003).

Ellis, Jack C., *John Grierson: Life, Contributions, Influence* (Carbondale and Edwardsville: Southern Illinois University Press, 2000).

Featherstone, Simon, *Postcolonial Cultures* (Edinburgh: Edinburgh University Press, 2005).

Fox, Jo, 'John Grierson, His "Documentary Boys" and the British Ministry of Information, 1939–1942', *Historical Journal of Film, Radio and Television* vol. 25 no. 3 (2005), pp. 345–6.

Frankel, Cyril, 'Personal Interview with Cyril Frankel', conducted by Martin Stollery, London, 16 August 2008.

Frankel, Cyril, *Eye to Eye: A Memoir* (London: Bank House Books, 2010).

Genette, Gérard, *Paratexts: Thresholds of Interpretation* (Cambridge: Cambridge University Press, 1997).

Graham, Sean, *A Surfeit of Sun* [1964] (London: Panther, 1967).

Grierson, John, 'First Principles of Documentary [1932]', in Forsyth Hardy (ed.), *Grierson on Documentary* (London: Faber and Faber, 1966), pp. 39–42.

Grierson, John, 'The GPO Gets Sound', *Cinema Quarterly* vol. 2 (1934), p. 216.

Grierson, John, 'The Film in British Colonial Development', *Sight and Sound* vol. 17 no. 65 (Spring 1948), pp. 2–4.

Grierson, John, 'Progress and Prospect' [1949], in Forsyth Hardy (ed.), *Grierson on Documentary* (London: Faber and Faber, 1966), pp. 349–57.

Grierson, John, 'Letter to Charles Crandall', 20 May 1953, GP G6: 36:33.

Grierson, John, 'Making *Man of Africa*', *Films and Filming* vol. 1 no. 2 (October 1954), p. 14.

Grierson, John, '*Man of Africa*', *Monthly Film Bulletin* vol. 23 no. 264 (January 1956), p. 3.

Griffith, Richard, 'Letter to John Grierson', GP G6:21:14, undated.

Hardy, Forsyth, *John Grierson: A Documentary Biography* (London: Faber and Faber, 1979).

Harper, Sue and Vincent Porter, *British Cinema of the 1950s: The Decline of Deference* (London and New York: Oxford University Press, 2003).

Hesse, Chris, 'Personal Interview with Chris Hesse', conducted by Kate Skinner, Accra, 23 June 2010.

Higson, Andrew, 'Review of Ian Aitken, *Film and Reform* and Paul Swann, *The British Documentary Film Movement, 1926–1946*', *Screen* vol. 32 no. 3 (Autumn 1991), pp. 350–6.

Jones, Phillip W. with David Coleman, *The United Nations and Education* (London: Routledge, 2005).

Larkin, Brian, *Signal and Noise: Media, Infrastructure, and Urban Culture in Nigeria* (Durham, NC: Duke University Press, 2008).

Lawrie, James, 'Letter to John Grierson', GP G6:36:160, 21 July 1953.

Lumumba, Patrice, 'Speech at the Proclamation of Congolese Independence, 30th June 1960', in Alan P. Merriam (ed.), *Congo, Background of Conflict* (Chicago, IL: Northwestern University Press, 1961), pp. 352–4.

MacCann, Richard Dyer, 'Subsidy for the Screen: Grierson and Group 3/1951–1955', *Sight and Sound* vol. 46 no. 3 (1977), pp. 168–73.

M.M.W., '*Man of Africa*', *To-Day's Cinema* vol. 85 no. 7404 (25 November 1955), p. 6.

Moore, Rachel O., *Savage Theory: Cinema as Modern Magic* (Durham, NC: Duke University Press, 2000).

Noble, George, 'Cameraman on the Gold Coast', *Colonial Cinema* vol. 10 no. 2 (1952), quoted in Jennifer Blaylock, 'African Agency in the Gold Coast Film Unit', posted 27 October 2010, https://cinemaintransit.wordpress.com/2010/10/27/african-agency-in-the-gold-coast-film-unit/.

Pargiter, Isobel, 'Letter to John Baxter', GP G6:21:5, 27 November 1952.

Popple, Simon, 'Group 3: A Lesson in State Intervention', *Film History* vol. 8 no. 2 (1996), pp. 131–42.

Pratt, Mary Louise, *Imperial Eyes: Travel Writing and Transculturation* (London: Routledge, 1992).

Rice, Tom, *Progress at Kojokrom*, April 2008, http://www.colonialfilm.org.uk/node/2566.

Rice, Tom, *The Boy Kumasenu*, May 2008, http://www.colonialfilm.org.uk/node/332.

Rice, Tom, 'From the Inside: The Colonial Film Unit and the Beginning of the End', in Lee Grieveson and Colin MacCabe (eds), *Film and the End of Empire* (London: BFI, 2011), pp. 135–53.

Rice, Tom, *Man of Africa*, October 2009, http://www.colonialfilm.org.uk/node/237.

Rowley, Hazel, *Richard Wright: The Life and Times* (Chicago, IL: University of Chicago Press, 2008).

Sandon, Emma, Tom Rice and Peter Bloom, 'Changing the World: Sean Graham', *Journal of British Cinema and Television* vol. 10 no. 3 (2013), pp. 524–36.

Slater, Montagu, *This Way to the New Country/The Kigezi Story* (script) 2/5 March 1952 (BFI Special Collections).

Smyth, Rosaleen, 'The Post-war Career of the Colonial Film Unit in Africa; 1946–1955', *Historical Journal of Film, Radio and Television* vol. 12 no. 2 (1992), pp. 163–77.

Stollery, Martin, *Alternative Empires: European Modernist Cinemas and Cultures of Imperialism* (Exeter and Chicago, IL: Exeter University Press, 2000).

Stollery, Martin, 'From *Storm over Asia* to *Dawn over Africa*: Transnationalism and Imperialism in British Intellectual Film Culture of the Late 1920s and 1930s', *Transnational Cinemas* vol. 2 no. 1 (2011), pp. 93–111.

Stollery, Martin, 'Voiceover/Commentary', in Scott Anthony and James Mansell (eds), *The Projection of Britain: A History of the GPO Film Unit* (London: BFI, 2011), pp. 168–78.

Stollery, Martin, 'The Last Roll of the Dice: *Morning, Noon and Night*, Empire and the Historiography of the Crown Film Unit', in Lee Grieveson and Colin MacCabe (eds), *Film and the End of Empire* (London: BFI, 2011), pp. 35–54.

Stollery, Martin, '"Scarred by a Cheated Ending"/"Not Suitable for Audiences in This Colony": The Film Adaptation of Graham Greene's *The Heart of the Matter* in Metropolitan and Colonial Contexts', *Literature/Film Quarterly* vol. 40 no. 3 (July 2012), pp. 216–32.

Swanzy, Henry, 'Quarterly Notes', *African Affairs* vol. 51 no. 205 (October 1952), pp. 267–305.

*This Wonderful World* script (episode 141, tx. 26 January 1961), GP G8:21:14.

Webster, Wendy, 'Mumbo-jumbo, Magic and Modernity: Africa in British Cinema, 1946–65', in Lee Grieveson and Colin MacCabe (eds), *Film and the End of Empire* (London: BFI, 2011), pp. 237–50.

Williams, Raymond, 'A Lecture on Realism', *Screen* vol. 18 no. 1 (Spring 1977), pp. 61–74.

# 13

# Grierson, Afrikaner Nationalism and South Africa

*Keyan G. Tomaselli*

South Africa's greatest immediate concern is the misunderstanding of it on the part of other nations ... no one in his senses will expect, by simple formula, to liquidate the host of misunderstandings and prejudices which, coming from the depths of 19th Century political formulae, now surround the considerations of South African problems. Much can, of course, be done by direct attack; for the major facets of South African development in all the spheres of technical and sociological achievement have not yet been commandingly presented.[1]

Though his and the apartheid government's political philosophies were very different, Grierson was impressed with the development he observed in South Africa, especially in comparison to other African territories. Grierson shared with Afrikaners a sense of historical loss at the hands of the English. In the Dutch Reformed Church (DRC) he found familiar Calvinist doctrines taught it by the Church of Scotland. Grierson identified English expatriates as 'pampered Whites': these 'lost and conceited children' of the empire embodied 'a sort of decadent evaluation of the imperial idea in which privilege is accepted without any appropriate sense of leadership and guidance'. Afrikaners, he admitted, had wrested from them the nettle of political leadership. Where Afrikaner means 'of Africa', Grierson wrote that English speakers' 'only basic bond with Africa is in the escape it offered from British taxation and the cutting down of their class privileges'.[2] Liberalism, he indicated, had little or no role to play in South Africa. Grierson's proposal for the establishment of a national film board was nevertheless predicated upon liberal ideals.

Grierson had arrived in South Africa in the wake of another influential Scotsman, Lord John Reith. Reith's[3] proposals had formed the basis in 1936 of the South African Broadcasting Corporation (SABC), modelled on the British Broadcasting Corporation (BBC). Both men stressed the idea of public-service media. Both however mistakenly assumed a linguistically, ideologically and culturally homogeneous society; and both fundamentally misunderstood the nature of the South African political economy.[4] Their respective media proposals thus neglected the black majority. However, Grierson was careful to note that a state film service should, in contrast to radio as an entertainment medium, be restricted to public observation and information. Co-operation with the trade, cinemas, was his suggestion.[5]

South Africa was divided by language – English and Afrikaans, spoken by the white and coloured descendants of the original Dutch, British and European colonisers. The National Party (NP) government understood 'culture' to be race-, language- and

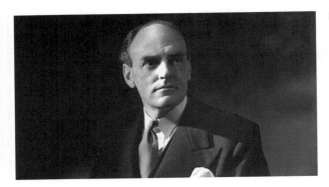
Lord John Reith

location-specific, and was the prime mechanism used by the NP to legitimise apartheid. Afrikaner cultural organisations and the DRC argued that film offered a key channel for the shaping of social and racial relations. The historical connections between the state and capital, cultural production and ideology, thus should have provided Grierson the terrain for an analysis of cultural protectionism. The deliberations of this discursive field were available in two reports, both issued well before Grierson's (1954) report.

## INITIAL DELIBERATIONS

The Cilliers Film Committee (1943), aimed to stimulate the growth of a specifically white Afrikaans cinema, by requiring exhibitors to screen Afrikaans-language shorts at every performance (Cilliers Film Committee, 1943). English-speakers demonised Cilliers as 'a lifelong nationalist' educated in Germany.[6] A growing Afrikaner nationalism found resonance in statements like 'rich national life', 'spread of national Culture', 'spiritual content', bilingualism, 'cultural protection' and so on. Cultural and amateur film-making organisations aimed to appropriate the English-dominated economy and transform it into a *volkskapitalisme* (an [Afrikaner] capitalism).

The Cilliers report was not enacted, but it did legitimise Afrikaner cultural affirmations. Individuals, argued the committee, formed the 'foundation' of culture, while the emergence and maintenance of 'a high standard of culture' is conditional upon 'the supplementation and augmentation of individual effort by the organised and organising power of the whole – ... the state'. The state, in turn, is responsible for 'cultural functions' that are 'beyond the powers of private initiative, whether individual or collective'. In other words, the state was directed to manage the social organisation of discourse.

Grierson envisaged a 'vivid machinery', a strong central direction of the state, in administering co-ordination and production. State control was not his intention. Public debate, for him, was the prime condition for democracy.[7] Cilliers argued that cinema offers a 'healing and formative influence' to mediating cultural and language barriers that divided English- and Afrikaans-speakers. While aware that the private industry would resist state attempts at intervention, the committee hoped that capitalist common sense would persuade the industry – totally owned by English South African capital – 'to agree in the national interest'.

Cilliers recommended the establishment of a national film board to produce documentaries aimed 'at presenting essential industries, ways of living and environment of normal people in such a way that the appeal is no less dramatic than that of the fiction film, in which life is often reconstructed in an exaggerated way'.[8] The board was to provide an ideological portrayal of life in terms of the reciprocal relationship between 'national culture' and the economy, since white documentary film-makers were seen as 'trustees of the native and other non-European races', who needed 'to make the public aware of the world it lives in, to show up the romance and dramatic quality of reality, and thus make the real experience of one the imaginary experience of all'.[9]

Against the background of the Voortrekker Centenary Celebrations held in 1838, the Cilliers report was explosive. This was a period when a neo-fascist interpretation of South African history by a number of films in the 1930s had been made directly or indirectly with state involvement. It also coincided with the internment by the British-supporting United Party (UP) government of many Afrikaner Nazi sympathisers during World War II, some of whom were aspiring film-makers, and some of whom were politicians with whom Grierson may have interacted during 1949.[10]

The UP government then appointed the Smith Committee.[11] Its proposals suggested a consolidation of the various government film units into a board concerned with the 'production, distribution and exhibition of educational, instructional, informative and publicity films which were not normally intended for exhibition in commercial cinemas'. Smith's recommendations were less sectional than the Cilliers report and served the needs of the national economy rather than merely the Afrikaner cultural constituency. The UP government, however, failed to enact Smith's recommendations.

## THE GRIERSON REPORT

In May 1949, less than a year after the NP had won parliament from the UP, the cabinet invited Grierson to conduct an enquiry into the scope and adequacy of the state's film services. A National Film Advisory Committee framed the terms of reference. Grierson was to report to the state information officer.[12] Grierson met editors, film executives, officials of state-owned enterprises and private companies, captains of industry, members of the Natal Indian Congress and both black and white academics.

Grierson aimed to open up 'the screen on the real world' where 'Documentary would photograph the living scene and the living story.'[13] Afrikaans-speaking film-makers and cultural theorists had fine-tuned their techniques through a technicist reading of Eisenstein's theory of film, which they mistakingly assumed was similar to that of Grierson. KARFO, the Afrikaner Calvinist Film-making Organisation, in particular, believed cinema had a duty to enable the urban socialisation of hundreds of thousands of displaced Afrikaners who had migrated to the cities between 1903–40. This migration was caused by the British army wrecking Boer farms in the

Transvaal during the Anglo-Boer War (1899–1902). The defeated, known as 'poor whites', now laboured for the enemy – British imperialism – in unskilled mining jobs under skilled black supervisors. This humiliation was a defining moment in the postwar Afrikaner struggle. Apartheid became the mechanism by which Afrikaners almost half a century later successfully turned the tables on their class, cultural and language subordination.

Both Grierson and KARFO substituted fantasy for reality. However, neither was aware that the realities they wished to depict were constituted by very specific ideological discourses. Grierson's idea of realism was to provide the individual with information which s/he could use to more effectively participate in democratic social processes. This view implies choice, but choice is relative to what the state will allow. Thus, both KARFO and Grierson wanted to use film. KARFO's more literal interpretation, although appearing to offer choice, does not in fact do so. For it, realism was a simple correspondence between prescription – socialisation of Afrikaner into a Christian urban society – and the image that Afrikaner nationalism was. In this regard, the KARFO report to Grierson stated:

> The ... cinema should adhere to the conditions of real life. If the 'variety of situations' which it depicts digresses from reality to any extent it will become clear that it may be more confusing than helpful to whoever may look upon the cinema as a source of information through which he can come to a better understanding of his own environment. The types of problems and situations dramatized must be more or less the same type of problem and situation for which modes of conduct and behaviour are sought ... otherwise we can only expect the cinema to add to the confusion and bewilderment which we face in life today.[14]

KARFO promulgated a strategy of adaptation, while also providing support to those members of the (white Afrikaner) *volk* who were succumbing to English cultural imperialism. KARFO thus aimed to mediate the interests of Afrikaner-dominated capital as it sought to prepare the depastoralising society for its role in the city, the new site for the struggle against a now English South African-controlled economy. That KARFO took its twin theoretical cues from a Briton, Grierson, and the Communist, Eisenstein, both from enemy nations, is explained by its selective reading, which highlighting only what would be useful to its own project. It never occurred to KARFO that Grierson's propositions were very different to Eisenstein's dialectic. The difference lies in Grierson's remark that 'Cinema has a sensational capacity for enhancing movement which tradition has formed or time worn smooth.'[15] Eisenstein, in contrast, never 'enhanced'; he displaced and manipulated in the name of realism. Eisenstein's 'nature', corresponded to Grierson's 'real world'. Technical resources, particularly editing, fundamental to Eisenstein's theories of montage, removed film from the 'real' world, reordering it through cutting. Grierson criticised Eisenstein for this. However, the Marxist base of Eisenstein's approach demanded a displacement of the 'real' world, itself a construction of bourgeois ideology. It was, of course, the bourgeois class to which Afrikaners were aspiring. A further implication – though not then clearly articulated – was the need to subordinate non-whites (blacks, coloureds, Asians).

Grierson remarked that key NP politicians are:

worth hearing, even when their solutions are desperate, and to have a full sense of their case one has to appreciate, too, a background of hurt in relation to both political and economic developments of the past. Theirs has been a battle of the have-nots.[16]

Proposing a film board structure designed to counter international criticism of South Africa's racial policies, Grierson argued:

Its problems, seen in closeup, may seem frustrating, are the best earnest of dramas (sic) in the making and a destiny to be revealed. Its vistas, both technological and human, are not only national-wide but also Africa-wide and, in many respects, world-wide. South Africa, moreover, has the eyes of the world upon it. It has, therefore, everything to gain by giving them reality to look upon.[17]

Grierson asserted that South Africa's high political profile needed to be complemented by more than 'one of the poorest places in the distribution channels of the world'. The strategy that he suggested was:

a) a conviction in high quarters that the film can and ought to be developed as an instrument of national policy;
b) an objective appreciation – free from mere film interest and film enthusiasm – of the relationship of the film to the larger and deeper processes of public information;
c) a plan of action which will, (i) serve departments in an orderly and long-term fashion; (ii) serve to inculcate patriotism, unity and drive in the Nation as a whole; (iii) present South Africa abroad in the most powerful and penetrating way and on all valuable levels of interest, and provide a direct service to the officers of External Affairs; (iv) bring into the service of the union and co-ordinate in common interest, all possible forces, other than governmental, which can contribute to the articulate presentation of the national image; not least the forces in the film industry; of the churches, and of the public relations departments of industry and commerce, with, of course, all due regard for the preservation of their free and independent initiation and development; (v) mobilize and encourage creative, technical and administrative talents to these ends.[18]

Grierson's plan exhibits little sense of the ideology or economic process which 'the articulate presentation of the national image' would seek to obscure. A potential result of these recommendations was that film would help to mystify the emergent apartheid base of the 'Nation' in which 'patriotism', 'unity' and 'drive' would need to be inculcated. Grierson's 'Instrument' misunderstood the nature of emergent Afrikaner national socialism. This was because Grierson never considered the state as part of the class system. Rather, he understood the state as 'the machinery by which the best interests of the people are secured'.[19] For Grierson, politics and economics were dependent upon the policies of the party in power, rather than a structural process condoned by the hegemonic socio-economic bloc. He therefore falsely distinguishes between the state and the government. Due weight was not given to the consideration that the party in power is, in fact, part of the mechanism of the state. Grierson assumed a benign and non-partisan nature of the state in the constitution and execution of its policies. He thus imbues the liberal view of the state as a neutral institution external to class.

Grierson's strategy served Afrikaner nationalists well, notwithstanding his realisation that blacks would ultimately impose the 'whip hand'.[20] Nevertheless, Grierson separated the 'real world' from state propaganda. The latter, or in Grierson's words, the 'seeping powers as (sic) the media possesses' were to be tempered by a 'progressively knowledgeable review on Ministerial level and subject to parliamentary discussion'.[21] This faith in the Westminster system is at the core of Grierson's uncritical acceptance of the NP's position. (The few representatives of colour in parliament in the late 1940s were removed by the NP after 1948). The starting point for Grierson stemmed from Walter Lippmann's (1922) pessimism about democracy (see Stephen Charbonneau's chapter in this book). In contrast, Grierson argued that ordinary voters could make informed judgments given relevant information. Grierson wanted to shock the average citizen out of blissful ignorance.[22]

Unlike KARFO, Grierson wanted to involve everyone in the democratic process. He lauded the fast progress of Africans in South Africa, and the higher expenditure on black education than any other country in Africa, while also lamenting the 'tragic pictures' of shanty towns and the 'emptyness' of the 'tribal code'. Grierson accepted the Colonial Service's 'splendid and liberal and realistic concern for the future of Africa', as he did white custodianship of a people not yet ready for full citizenship. Industrialisation, argued Grierson, would in time bring blacks to political maturity, a fact accepted, he revealed, by 'a not unimportant Nationalist'.[23]

The South African report clears up Williams's indecision as to Grierson's perception of the relationship between 'social purposes' and 'aesthetic questions'.[24] Of the South African context, Grierson argued that 'Effective distribution results are the proper measure of justified production; and no double talk – aesthetic or other – should be allowed to confuse the issue.'[25] However, Grierson does reveal confidence in imaginative talent. Experimentation was expected to act as checks and balances in helping South African film-makers under the auspices of the board to destroy, as in the case of Canada, a culture 'rotted with spiritual colonialism; measuring itself at every turn against the examples of Europe and the United States'.[26] The angry and heated political and racial arguments that were rife with English and Afrikaner pitted as antagonists, again deceived Grierson into believing that an intrinsic social value of benefit to all in South Africa would emerge from these conflicts:

> The deflated and deflational atmosphere of many countries today is not only lacking in the spirit of 'audace'; and it is the presence of this quality in South African political discussion which is so striking and refreshing to the observer. South Africa can lose nothing and can only gain if it comes to invest the wider field of national expression. If South Africa has a message, this is probably it.[27]

The remainder of Grierson's report is devoted to 'Shaping a South African Film Instrument'. This was aimed at stimulating an informed public participation in the process of democracy. Grierson proposed a board accountable to parliament chaired by cabinet ministers. His recommendations were geared to maintaining the maximum flexibility and operational independence for the board. His dual experience as film-maker and administrator had clearly alerted him to the dangers of allowing the institution to become clogged by bureaucracy, excessive equipment and, as a result of these, an ever expanding staff. The hallmark of his programme was that documentary encoded the ideas of intellectuals which coincided with the interests of some state and large-scale private organisations, a convergence which sprang from the common belief of the need for some form of rationalised mass society.[28]

The report revealed Grierson's scepticism for 'self-appointed experts' and 'medium enthusiasts', whether amateur or professional. He argued that 'no forces have hurt and frustrated the national use of films as much as those who have brought it into discredit by irresponsibility in the use of public funds'. Furthermore, these individuals 'get in the way of the purpose of the Information Service'.[29] He insisted that film-makers:

> were primarily civil servants; routineers with periodical raises and a pension to come; efficient enough no doubt but within the limits of theme and story determined by men who were not film makers, not artists and would, to do them justice, make no claim to creative power over events.[30]

Grierson's visit had been motivated by KARFO, which had hoped thereby to secure state assistance. Ironically, the medium enthusiasts to which Grierson was referring comprised KARFO itself. Admitting KARFO's 'especial position', Grierson recognised its access to large numbers of halls, their availability for cultural and social purposes, and its access to capital. He therefore suggested that KARFO facilitate distribution of the proposed board's films. He suggested that KARFO's distribution infrastructure be government-subsidised, rather than its production facilities.[31]

Grierson viewed KARFO members as 'ordinary citizens' making 'amateur judgements'. These kinds of judgments were considered by Grierson to be the responsibility of the State.[32] KARFO's close relationship with the NP, the NP-administered state and the DRC, however, would have led it to believe that it had purchase on state funding. Grierson, however, was adamant that funds be administered by the proposed board and not compete with the trade. KARFO responded by dismantling its production unit.

Nothing came of Grierson's 1954 proposals. The NP was able to enforce its hegemony through state and other agencies, applying a host of other economic, repressive and political policies.

## AFTER GRIERSON

A National Film Board (NFB) was established in 1964, but its structure differed in crucial ways from Grierson's original proposals. As constituted, the NFB subverted Grierson's democratic assumptions and, until its dissolution in 1979, functioned as a production and distribution facility for NP propaganda. In 1955, the Minister of Finance appointed another commission of enquiry to report on the production and distribution of films for state departments.[33] Chairman of the NFB De Villiers concentrated on films produced and distributed by state departments. This commission's recommendations, rather than Grierson's, were finally accepted. The idea that one of the NFB's aims was 'the promotion of the development of the cinematograph film industry' was to prove contentious, along with proposals that the NFB be given a censorship role as well as the administration of film subsidies.[34]

De Villiers specified two problems: the one internal (national), the other external (international). First, state departments were either replicating production facilities or were approaching the State Information Office to make films on their behalf, though the office lacked a production unit.[35] Second, the NP's racial policies were drawing adverse criticism internationally, driven by international television exposure.[36] Where Grierson promoted film as part of a detached, self-conscious and 'democratic' debate on political principles, De Villiers was more interested in producing films to justify the government's race policies, both at home and abroad.[37] De Villiers's assumption was that it was the 'representation' of 'population removals' that caused the PR damage rather than the actual removals.

Where Grierson had argued that national interest would best be served by a National Film Board, De Villiers proposed a 'South African Film Corporation' (modelled on SABC). Both reports recognised the need for effective distribution. Here, however, their proposals differed radically: Grierson had posited that parliament appropriate funds annually to the board, thus enabling wide-ranging non-commercial distribution of the state's titles. This confirmed the practice at the time whereby the budget of the Department of Education, Arts and Science (DEAC) included an annual provision for the making of films by its Film Service, supplied at no charge to other state departments. De Villiers, conversely, argued that while the corporation should be subsidised for the first five years, it should become self-sustaining through charges for services rendered. Each department would budget for its requirements separately and negotiate with independent producers, if necessary, via the SAFC.[38] This procedure was instituted (without the subsidy). This arrangement was, however, contested by the industry and led to the collapse of the NFB in 1979.

The trade would provide additional distribution channels in exchange for access to some of the board's technical services. The formulation of the De Villiers Report in this regard was incorporated almost verbatim into the National Film Board Act (1963), which reads:

> The objects for which the board is established are (a) the co-ordination of the activities of the State relating to cinematograph films and photographs; and (b) the promotion of the development of the cinematograph film industry and of photography in the Republic.[39]

These two aims appeared entirely worthy ones but proved, in fact, to be irreconcilable and led to some of the most acrimonious debates on the NFB.

In view of the NFB's later history, two areas of disagreement in the respective reports warrant discussion. The first concerns Grierson's insistence that the board be attached to the Minister of the Interior rather than the DEAC. It is worth quoting Grierson's comments in full:

> In particular, it is the strong view of those closer to the development of Public Information that the logical portfolio in a modern state is not the Ministry of Education, because of its lack of functional contact with the larger processes of technological, economic and public development outside the sphere of formal education. With this view I concur. It may even be that the scholastic or schoolman's point of view is an obstacle to the larger development of the mass media in the highly complex and informal world in which they are bound to operate.

The key to the matter is that the film in the service of the Nation is something more than an instrument of instruction and something more than an instrument of culture and art. It is not just a mirror held up to nature; it is a hammer helping to shape the future. We are dealing, to be plain, with a process which reaches out beyond the schools and the academies to the whole life of the nation and neither the pedagogic nor the aesthetic aspect of its work represents the more effective reaches of its influence.[40]

Grierson is possibly thinking here of his distinction between 'propaganda with a political meaning' and 'propaganda as social information', a distinction he made in Paul Rotha's (1936) book, where he attempts to distinguish between propaganda as a public service and as a political and ideological tool as well as expressing his belief that documentary film is an exploratory and formative medium. For De Villiers, however, 'political meaning' and 'social information' were virtually synonymous, although he was aware of the dangers of 'mere propaganda films'. De Villiers implies that 'education' comes down to grasping and promoting the 'official version' of the condition of one's culture.[41]

Grierson had suggested that the board work under the Minister of the Interior. The De Villiers Report does not specify a portfolio; it merely states that production cannot be left in the hands of private enterprise as this will expose the country to the risks of serious misrepresentation both locally and abroad and that the cabinet should appoint a minister to act as a link between parliament and the SAFC.[42] An anonymous memorandum on the Grierson Report, however, put a strong case for making the NFB the responsibility of the Minister of Education. This was effected in 1963, though the minister had earlier mentioned, when the matter of the relationship between the state archives and film board was raised, that the Minister of Information could be responsible.[43]

An incidental disagreement in the two reports was to flare in the 1970s; the expansion of the NFB's microfilm operation was to affect its structure and operations dramatically. Grierson proposed that the scope of the board's work should not include microfilm as such services could be best dealt with by the State Information Department and State Archives; the De Villiers Report specifies that SAFC should confine its microfilm operations to state departments.[44] Microfilming did not seem a major issue in the 1950s, but both Grierson and De Villiers took it for granted (as did the NFB) that the eventual introduction of television services to South Africa would provide a tremendous impetus for the state's film services. Contrary to all expectations, the board did not become a major supplier to SABC-TV when it started broadcasting in January 1976.

The legislation introduced by DEAC was based on the De Villiers Report, with the exclusion of the clauses on censorship and subsidy, but with the addition of a clause empowering the NFB to undertake archival activities.[45] It would be the NFB's task to co-ordinate the purchase, production, exhibition and distribution of state films 'of an informative nature',[46] which would contribute to the development of the industry by passing on some of the board's work to the trade rather than offering the film industry direct financial assistance.

At no stage of the NFB's sixteen-year existence, however, did industry accept the board. The board was unable to allocate work externally as it was not financed by a parliamentary appropriation (Grierson's proposal) or an initial five-year subsidy (De Villiers) but by interest-bearing loans from the state. This made the NFB the only statutory body to receive no government subsidy; the Film Institute (i.e. archives), however, did receive a grant from 1969 onwards.

## LEGITIMATION

The board's administrative structure differed in two significant ways from Grierson's original proposals. The first was that the Minister of the Interior was the chairman rather than the Minister of Education. The Department of the Interior, however, was unsuited to the task. Its administrative function was to regulate and register people, their race classifications, group areas, movements, births, deaths, domicile – a sort of human book-keeping function. The board was consequently placed under Education. From the state's point of view, this department offered an ideal home as the educational institution is the foremost apparatus through which ideological discourse is disseminated. This agency was not interested in the democratic assumptions permeating Grierson's thesis but in socialising individuals into accepting as natural and desirable apartheid-based practices. (Indeed, future prime minister Hendrik Verwoerd's infamous statement that: 'There is no place for [the Bantu] in the European community above the level of certain forms of labour',[47] was made in the same year that Grierson submitted his final report to the government.)

The second recommendation not enacted was the Experimental Production Fund. Grierson had argued that: 'In the case of a young country, this special measure of latitude encourages the discovery of new talent in a medium which is not yet highly developed from a professional point of view.'[48] Despite representations, the state remained unyielding, for experimentation tend to articulate counter-ideological discourses.

Apart from co-ordinating state activities in film-making, the NFB was entrusted with the 'acquisition, production, exhibition, distribution' of films and photographs 'intended for dissemination, in the Republic or elsewhere, of information regarding Southern Africa, its peoples, their way of life, culture, traditions, economic conditions and problems'. It was also to give 'information regarding the problems of and social evils present in the Republic and the services available and developments taking place in the Republic'. Clearly framed within the apartheid doubletalk, the NFB's function was to legitimise the government's racial policies. In the absence of broadcast television, the NFB had to assume a direct responsibility for cultural production as far as short and documentary films were concerned. The board was eventually to enter production on a large scale, competing with the 'trade' as Grierson called it – earning the wrath of commercial producers. Whereas until 1966 about 60 per cent of the private documentary market consisted of government-commissioned films, by 1972 the proportion had dropped to 30 per cent. The introduction of television in 1976, however, heralded the dissolution of the board in 1978, for many of its propaganda tasks could now be carried out much more effectively by the national broadcast television services.

## CONCLUSION

Grierson had little impact on South Africa. He himself remarked on the lack of debate over aesthetics. The fact that no university film courses existed until the early 1970s contributed to this neglect. When Grierson was discussed, usually by the odd cinephile, and usually in the context of European film theory, his visit to South Africa was never mentioned. These anecdotes reveal something about the isolation of South Africa from international influences during the apartheid years.

## ACKNOWLEDGMENTS

This chapter acknowledges 'The National Film Board of South Africa: A Short History' by Edwin Hees, in *Annale* no. 1 (1991), University of Stellenbosch, Stellenbosch, South Africa.

## NOTES

1. John Grierson, 'Union of South Africa: The Grierson Report', second draft, 1954. Although a third draft was written, its whereabouts are unknown. Reprinted in *Screening the Past* no. 7 (1999), p. 2, http://www.latrobe.edu.au/screeningthepast/classics/cl0799/JG1cl7a.pdf.
2. John Grierson, 'In the Heart of the Country', unpublished, undated notes held in the Grierson Archives, Mimeo. G:4:19:21, Grierson Archives, Stirling University, pp. 19, 21.
3. The role of Reith in South Africa is discussed more fully in R. E. Tomaselli and G. Hayman, *Broadcasting in South Africa* (London: James Currey, 1989).
4. Ibid.
5. Grierson Report, 'Arguments', Item 9 (G5:6:35), incomplete version held at the Grierson Archives (see Grierson Report 1954).
6. *Union Review*, 'Let's Go to the Cinema ... and See a Government Film (in Afrikaans)', August 1944, p. 38.
7. John Grierson, 'The Artist in Public Service', in I. Lockerbie (ed.), *Eyes of Documentary* (Stirling: John Grierson Archives, 1990), p. 12.
8. Cilliers Film Committee Union of South Africa (July 1943) 'The Cilliers Film Committee', unpublished (and unlisted) report.
9. Cilliers Film Committee Union of South Africa, p. 84.
10. K. G. Tomaselli and M. Eckhardt, 'Brown-red Shadows: The Influence of Third Reich and Soviet Cinema on Afrikaans Film, 1940–45', in R. van Winkel and D. Welsh (eds), *Cinema and the Swastika: The International Expansion of Third Reich Cinema* (London: Palgrave, 2011).
11. Union of South Africa, *Report of the Inter-Departmental Committee Appointed to Consider the Reports of the Committee on State Publicity and the Film Committee and Other Relevant Matters* 14 December 1944, Government Printer, 1954, p. 9.
12. Memorandum to the Minister of the Interior from the National Film Advisory Committee attached to copy of Final Draft of Grierson Report at National Film Archives in Pretoria.
13. C. Williams (ed.), *Realism and the Cinema* (London: Routledge and Kegan Paul, 1980), p. 27.

14. H. Du Preez, KARFO Report to John Grierson, Mimeo, undated, *c.* 1954.
15. Williams, *Realism and the Cinema*, p. 17.
16. Grierson, 'In the Heart of the Country'.
17. Grierson, 'Union of South Africa'.
18. Ibid.
19. A. Lovell and J. Hillier, *Studies in Documentary* (London: Secker and Warburg, 1972), p. 19.
20. Grierson, 'In the Heart of the Country'.
21. Grierson, 'Union of South Africa', p. 7.
22. Grierson, 'In the Heart of the Country'.
23. Grierson, 'Union of South Africa'.
24. Williams, *Realism and the Cinema*, pp. 17–18.
25. Grierson, 'Union of South Africa.', p. 3.
26. Ibid.
27. Ibid., p. 4.
28. Lovell and Hillier, *Studies in Documentary*, p. 31.
29. Grierson, 'Union of South Africa', p. 4.
30. Grierson, 'The Artist in Public Service', pp. 12, 38, 39–40.
31. Grierson Report, 'Arguments'.
32. Grierson, 'The Artist in Public Service', p. 14.
33. De Villiers Report (1956), Union of South Africa, unpublished, National Film, Video and Sound Archives, Pretoria, 1956.
34. Ibid., pp. 24–5.
35. Ibid., p. 10.
36. Ibid., p. 4.
37. Ibid., pp. 7–8.
38. Ibid., pp. 20–2.
39. National Film Board Act, 1963.
40. Grierson, 'Union of South Africa', pp. 16–17.
41. De Villiers Report, pp. 5, 8.
42. Ibid., pp. 23–4.
43. Hansard, 1962.
44. Grierson, 'Union of South Africa'; De Villiers Report, p. 20.
45. National Film Board Bill, n/d.
46. Hansard, 1963.
47. Grierson, 'Union of South Africa', pp. 2595–622.
48. Ibid., p. 15.

## REFERENCES

Althusser, Louis, *Lenin, Philosophy and Other Essays* (London: New Left Books, 1971).
Cilliers Film Committee Union of South Africa (July 1943) The Cilliers Film Committee. Unpublished (and unlisted) report.
De Villiers Report, Union of South Africa, unpublished, National Film, Video and Sound Archives, Pretoria, 1976, pp. 24–5
Du Preez, H., KARFO Report to John Grierson, Mimeo, undated, *c.* 1954.

Grierson, John, 'The Artist in Public Service', in I. Lockerbie (ed.), *Eyes of Documentary* (Stirling: John Grierson Archives, 1941, reprinted in 1990), pp. 12, 38, 39–40.

Grierson, John (1954), 'Union of South Africa. The Grierson Report', second draft. Reprinted in *Screening the Past* no. 7 (1999), http://www.latrobe.edu.au/screeningthepast/classics/cl0799/JG1cl7a.pdf.

Grierson Report, 'Arguments', Item 9, incomplete version held in the Grierson Archives (G5:6:35) (see Grierson Report 1954).

Grierson, John, 'In the Heart of the Country', unpublished, undated notes, Mimeo, G:4:19:21, Stirling: Grierson Archives, undated).

*Hansard*, col. 5186, 8 May 1962.

*Hansard*, col. 70623, 3 June 1963.

Hayman, G. and R. E. Tomaselli, 'Ideology and Technology in the Growth of South African Broadcasting, 1924–1971', in R. E. Tomaselli, K. G. Tomaselli and J. Muller (eds), *Broadcasting in South Africa* (London: James Currey, 1989).

Hees, E., 'The National Film Board of South Africa: A Short History', *Annale* no. 1 (1991), University of Stellenbosch, Stellenbosch, South Africa.

Lippmann, W., 'Public Opinion', in D. A. Graber (ed.), *Mass Media and American Politics*, 5th edn (Washington, DC: Congressional Quarterly, 1997).

Lockerbie, I. (ed.), *John Grierson: Eyes of Democracy* (Stirling: John Grierson Archive, 1941), reprinted in 1990.

Lovell, A. and J. Hillier, *Studies in Documentary* (London: Secker and Warburg, 1972).

National Film Board Act No. 73 of 1963, Section 9..........1963

National Film Board Bill (As adopted at Report Stage), Clause 9(e). n/d

Rotha, P., *Movie Parade* (London: Studio, ld./New York: Studio Publications, 1936).

Smith Committee, Union of South Africa, 14 December 1944: *Report of the Inter-Departmental Committee Appointed to Consider the Reports of the Committee on State Publicity and the Film Committee and Other Relevant Matters*. Government Printer, 3pp.

Tomaselli, K.G. 'Grierson in South Africa: Culture, State and Nationalist Ideology in the South African Film Industry: 1940–1981,' *Cinema Canada* no. 122 (1985), pp. 24–7.

Tomaselli, K.G., *Ideology and Cultural Production in South African Cinema*, unpublished PhD thesis, University of Witwatersrand, 1984.

Tomaselli, K.G. and M. Eckhardt, 'Brown-red Shadows: The Influence of Third Reich and Soviet Cinema on Afrikaans Film, 1940–45', in R. van Winkel and D. Welsh (eds), *Cinema and the Swastika: The International Expansion of Third Reich Cinema* (London: Palgrave, 2011).

Tomaselli, K.G. and E. Hees, 'John Grierson in South Africa: Afrikaner Nationalism and the National Film Board', *Screening the Past* no. 7 (1999), latrobe.edu.au/www/screeningthepast/index.

Tomaselli, R.E. and G. Hayman, *Broadcasting in South Africa* (London: James Currey, 1989).

*Union Review*, 'Let's Go to the Cinema ... and See a Government Film (in Afrikaans)', August 1944, p. 38.

Union of South Africa, *Report of the Inter-Departmental Committee Appointed to Consider the Reports of the Committee on State Publicity and the Film Committee and Other Relevant Matters*, 14 December 1944, Government Printer.

Union of South Africa, *Senate Debates*, Second Session, 7–11 June 1954, cols 2595–622.

Williams, C. (ed.), *Realism and the Cinema* (London: Routledge and Kegan Paul, 1980).

# 14
# Grierson and Latin America: Encounters, Dialogues and Legacies

*Mariano Mestman and María Luisa Ortega*

I will never forget the moment when John Grierson saw the films by Manuel Chambi at the First Meeting of Latin American Filmmakers in Montevideo in 1958. The documentary master's surprise and fascination with the images brought in from the *altiplano* celebrations in Peru led Grierson to travel there on a meticulous expedition, though unfortunately, without a camera.

Nelson Pereira dos Santos

In May 1958, Montevideo (Uruguay) hosted the third International Documentary and Experimental Film Festival. Organised by SODRE (Uruguay's national broadcast radio station), it was the first film festival in Latin America to specialise in documentaries. In terms of the way cinema developed in the region, the 1958 festival is considered a turning point. Two important and oft-mentioned facts about these editions reveal its interest: the presence of John Grierson, invited that year as the honorary president, and the First Latin American Meeting of Independent Film-makers, held in conjunction with the festival. The convergence of these events helped film-makers become aware of the shared problems they were facing and assisted them in mapping out the future for a cinema that could help Latin America take on 'the inevitable task of protecting its education, culture, history, tradition and working for the spiritual elevation of the population', as stated in the resolutions adopted by the 'delegates' from different countries. These delegates, who also founded the Asociación Latinoamericana de Cineístas Independientes (ALACI), included Simón Feldman, Leopoldo Torres Nilsson and Fernando Birri (Argentina), Jorge Ruiz (Bolivia), Nelson Pereira dos Santos (Brazil), Patricio Kaulen (Chile), Manuel Chambi (Peru) and Danilo Trelles and Roberto Gardiol (Uruguay), among others.

It is possible, as Julianne Burton noted, that Grierson's visit had a 'largely ceremonial function'[1] but it was an opportune moment for the encounter and dialogue with the Scottish master. Latin American cinema found itself in a period marked by explorations and definitions, in which there was a need to direct the winds of renewal that had begun to blow and to channel the film-makers' desires for action and creation. In this regard, the documentary emerged as an important mechanism in changing the course and development of the new national cinemas. As Paulo Antonio Paranaguá has noted, these independent documentaries which began to be produced in Latin America in the 1950s were a radical novelty in the region, one that marked the break with classic cinema and a transition towards the independent films of the 60s.[2] That

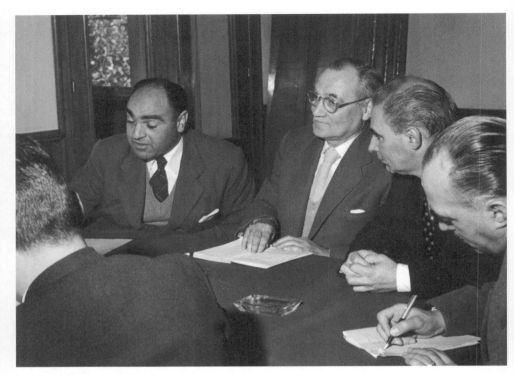

Hugo Rocha, John Grierson and Danilo Trelles, at the Documentary and Experimental Film Festival of the SODRE, Montevideo, 1958 (Courtesy Juan José Mugni, Archivo Nacional de la Imagen, Montevideo)

transition was based on a broad set of experiences and influences, with neo-realism and the Griersonian documentary as their cardinal points.

These experiences and influences were assisted by a proliferation of film clubs and societies across Latin America at the beginning of the 1950s, featuring some of the most renowned film-makers of the period. Young film enthusiasts enjoyed diverse programmes thanks to the involvement of consulates and embassies, organisms such as UNESCO and SODRE itself. Films from different eras and from all across the world were shown, from institutional documentaries to some of the masterpieces of world cinema, many of which had previously been difficult to access in the region. This is how films from the British documentary movement and from the National Film Board of Canada reached the young people at the sessions organised by the cinema club *Gente de Cine* (in Argentina), the Montevideo film societies and the Cinema Club of the Chilean Student Federation, founded by Pedro Chaskel. In some cases, as the film-maker Mario Handler recalls, the cinema clubs were also places where the Uruguayans of the time tried their hand at amateur film-making as part of 'lightning contests' occasionally sponsored by the film societies, a kind of movie-making marathon.[3] In this context, several new film-making schools were born and nurtured by universities. Two of these schools explicitly acknowledged John Grierson as a source of inspiration: the Documentary Film-making School of Santa Fe at the Universidad del Litoral

*The Grierson Effect*

(Argentina, founded by Fernando Birri) and the Centre of Experimental Cinema at the Universidad de Chile (founded by Sergio Bravo). During his visit, Grierson entered into dialogue with film-makers from both of these schools.

In the work of the film-makers who made documentaries at that time, it is difficult to identify specific international influences (at least, not in their 'pure' state). These directors' views – as with the programmes of the film societies – were influenced by a variety of factors, such as the Griersonian documentary, and film-makers like Eisenstein, Flaherty and Zavattini. In all of these experiences and in the desire for renewal, however, a network of mimetic and original expressions gave way to a peculiar exchange of gestures between Grierson and the Latin American film-makers in 1958.

Without a doubt, the South American film-makers who gathered in Montevideo were proud to be recognised by John Grierson, an internationally prestigious figure. However, they also sought out the guidance and advice of the man who had shown an extraordinary gift for promoting films that expressed national identity by depicting a social and cultural reality that had eluded commercial cinema. If the film-makers who gathered for this 1958 conference had one thing in common, it was the will to create a truly national cinema to counter film-making which was no more than an imitation of Hollywood models. This new cinema would represent and rethink the social, historical and cultural reality of Latin America for the first time, with documentary films one of the major avenues in this regard. At the 1958 SODRE festival, the film-makers discovered that their documentaries, made on their own and with little contact between each other, expressed a common search, revealing facets of a shared Latin American social reality never before captured on screen.

For Grierson, the trip to Uruguay may have been just one of his many incursions to regions across the planet in search of material for *This Wonderful World*, a programme which had aired for the first time on Scottish television on 11 October 1957. Grierson had a tight travel agenda which led him to Paris and Brussels in May 1958 for the Experimental Film Festival and then to Montevideo on 25 May. His meeting with the pioneers who would go on to create the New Latin American Cinema was not limited to his days at the SODRE, because he went on to visit Argentina, Chile, Bolivia and Peru; he remembered the trips to the latter two countries as a 'great journey and in a way, the most beautiful I had ever made'.[4] The trip led to encounters that have not received enough attention from researchers, but which reveal a dialogue with South America that is interesting to explore, which we attempt to do in this chapter.

## EXCHANGING VIEWS IN THE 'SWITZERLAND OF AMERICA'

The history of the SODRE, the institution which hosted the meeting, can explain how it became a centre of attraction and a meeting point for film-makers in a country that was considered the Switzerland of America, as it was as advanced culturally as in other spheres of life. Many elements connect the identity of the festival's project with the Griersonian concept of cinema

The art-cinema department of the SODRE, founded at the end of 1943 by Danilo Trelles, would expand after the inauguration of the festival. During the first edition (in 1954), 112 films from eighteen countries were screened. Held every two years until

1962 (and later in 1965, 1967 and 1971), a selection of the films featured would go on to be screened in the country's cinema clubs after each festival.

From the beginning, the festival presented itself as a supporter of the documentary as the main battering ram of active cinema, one with social and educational aims: 'There is no doubt', states the catalogue of the first edition,

> that filmic document allows us to get to know, understand and assess the degree of culture and serve as a coming attraction of the world surrounding us … . Thanks to the power of suggestion and its infinite possibilities, documentary cinema sows rich, fertile images, and will surely be the best way to educate the men of the future.

The first festival had included a selection of films by Norman McLaren and productions by the National Film Board; and midway through 1954, during the tenth season of SODRE cinema, films such as *North Sea*, *Song of Ceylon* and *Night Mail* would be shown. Two years later, in the presentation of the 1956 festival catalogue, the Scottish master would be mentioned as the guiding light of the project and of the fields of interest of the SODRE. In fact, the national cinema competitions organised by the SODRE before the festivals have been considered, in retrospect, in line with 'the best British documentary school', particularly because they 'created a collective awareness of how cinema collaborated with citizens and countries'.[5]

In this way, Grierson's arrival confirmed that he had become a reference point within the SODRE, revealing an almost programmatic orientation based on Griersonian principles. However, the 1958 edition was exceptional in terms of the quantity and quality of the Latin American films presented; over time, some of these films went on to become historical milestones within the new national cinemas of the region and raised the profile of their directors correspondingly.

The Montevideo press concurred with Grierson on the best films and Latin American film-makers. In a long article assessing the festival, the works of the Peruvian film-maker Manuel Chambi, the Bolivian Jorge Ruiz and the Brazilian Nelson Pereira dos Santos were all praised for authentically expressing national character through folklore, tradition, religion and landscape.[6]

The attendance of these directors and other 'celebrities' at the film-makers meeting was promising indeed, claimed the same source. The debates at the event emphasise the importance of cinema as a cultural medium for expression, insisting that Latin Americans had a right to their own cinematographic production and eschewing the 'desire for profits' as an incentive. Within this framework, the difficulties of producing and distributing independent films were discussed, along with obstacles to regional exchange and co-operation, the ties with the still emerging medium of television, as well as issues such as legislation, unions and training. Those in attendance demanded measures such as the incorporation of cinema into a common Latin American market as a 'true medium for mutual knowledge and understanding'. The market would involve a customs policy without obstacles and, if possible, a preferential one; the necessary government support and protection, particularly for independent cinema; special assistance for short films, in order for them to be seen both nationally and regionally; and support for schools that would provide professional training for cinema technicians and grants for exchanges.

The affinity between these ideas and the Griersonian ideology was evident to those who heard Grierson speak at the press conferences or at the informal talks he gave at the Boston café in Montevideo. It was also clear to those who accompanied him on his excursions throughout the city, on his visit to the port and in his talks with people. Grierson was always carrying a small notebook that he consulted or jotted notes down in from time to time. In his feverish day-to-day activities, in both public and private, Grierson expressed his opinions on the urban architecture, his interest in steaks and soccer, his astonishment at the talent of the boys and young men playing soccer on the streets, his curiosity about different types of cheese or about the types of cattle or bulls that Uruguay had once imported from Scotland, and other subjects. He was remarkably vital for his age, according to the locals, and his unremitting interest in all things local during his sojourn made him popular with all.

Hugo Alfaro, in the pages of the legendary weekly *Marcha*, for example, emphasised how Grierson

> took by storm the press conferences, the ministry offices, the receptions, the café-music bars, the street corners and even the stadium locker rooms … . With his passionate words, a mixture of humor, feeling and imagination, he shook people free of their boredom or their curtness as if he himself were a source of work and life, as if he were a 35-millimeter prophet.[7]

The well-known critic Homero Alsina Thevenet published an 'interminable series' (as he himself called it) of articles on the visit, including coverage of Grierson's public and daily activities along with long texts on his career and his 'extraordinary' personality. The admiration and fondness for Grierson expressed by this critic in the pages of the daily *El país* are also reflected in other media sources, like the weekly *Marcha* (cited above) and in the daily *La mañana*. The press identified with Grierson in the same way as the film-makers and audiences packing auditoriums to hear him speak; it was the same recognition granted in the homages organised by the groups Cine Club [Cinema Club] and Cine Universitario [University Cinema], which screened films by Grierson (or his collaborators) and published lengthy screeds about the film-maker and his work.

Grierson's pronouncements during his days in Montevideo may have included some 'capricious opinions' or 'hurried statements' – according to certain media sources[8] – that could have been accused of *pintoresquismo* or 'exoticism' in some cases.[9] However, from the beginning it was clear that the Scotsman would not waste his time doing the tourist circuit or gathering images 'for export'; instead, he took a critical viewpoint that belied an interest in the everyday, such as the severe contrasts between the city's rich and poor. It was a respectful dialogue, one based on a commitment and a desire to collaborate with Uruguayan film-making.

In this regard, with a language 'caustic and filled with naivety' or with his 'strength of character' or 'stimulating insolence' – to quote the Montevideo press – the Scotsman conveyed a series of ideas and even made reference to a possible 'plan'.[10] He spoke of how the Uruguayan film sector needed protection – a protection he considered 'essential' in a country as small as Uruguay – and of the creation of a film bank (or a national film board) to finance movies. In Grierson's view, this entity would distribute a percentage of ticket sales of the most popular national films to finance

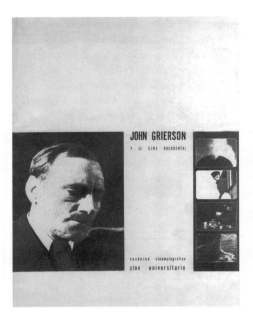

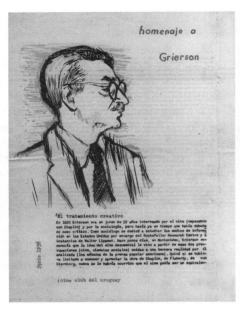

Homage organised by the group Cine Universitario (University Cinema) during Grierson visit to Montevideo (Courtesy Eduardo Correa, Centro de Documentación Cinematográfica, Cinemateca Uruguaya)

Homage and screening organised by the group Cine Club during Grierson's visit to Montevideo (Drawing by Antonio Pezzino, member of the Taller Joaquín Torres García. Courtesy Eduardo Correa, Centro de Documentación Cinematográfica, Cinemateca Uruguaya)

documentaries (six per year initially) and initiate a small fund for experimental films 'without regard for their immediate usefulness'. He added that documentaries and newsreels produced nationally – for which television would become an extraordinary field[11] – should be screened at every cinema (ten minutes of each programme). This plan also reflected other ideas that arose from the film-makers meeting, such as team work, co-operation between countries in terms of production and distribution; a common agreement to acquire the rights to international films; and support for film schools.

Although Grierson supported a programme that would combine active government policies with protection for the expressive and creative freedom of film-makers, the idea of 'independence' supported by the film-makers meeting and the interests of public or private support did create some conflicts.[12] At *El país*, Thevenet underlined what the paper considered a 'complex debate', since in practice, government used film productions for political ends while companies opted for 'direct advertising', to promote their own goals through film. And when confronted with these requirements, '(Latin)American filmmakers may differ socially with industries that could be deemed oppressive or imperialist', in the critic's view. But at the same time, Thevenet referred to Grierson's words in recalling his own experience, pointing out that 'during the height of the British documentary, Flaherty, Cavalcanti, Auden and he himself [Grierson] had been trustworthy public servants without ever abandoning their role as filmmakers'. Grierson's experience in the 1930s could also be applied to his 1958 Montevideo proposal of 'reducing the issues between the state and the artist', a goal that could be achieved by creating an 'intermediate entity that makes governments understand the issues related to artistic creation while allowing artists to understand the real needs of the state. The struggle will continue as long as necessary.' It was a struggle that could only be resolved by striking a certain balance.

At one of his last events in Montevideo, the closing ceremony of the festival, Grierson gave a talk. The Argentine film-maker Fernando Birri would later remember that at a certain point Grierson pointed to the exhibition of photo-documentaries of Birri's Institute as exemplary work, referring to the 'photo-documentaries'[13] made at the Santa Fe Documentary School. These photo-documentaries would later give way to the middle-length documentary *Tire-dié* (1958–60), one of the founding works of the New Latin American Cinema. Founded by Birri in 1956 after returning from his studies in Rome at the Centro Sperimentale di Cinematografia, the Santa Fe Documentary School (Argentina) explicitly acknowledged its roots in both Italian neo-realism and the British documentary movement. In *Escuela documental inglesa/The British Documentary School*, the first book published by the Santa Fe School, the author Manuel Horacio Giménez provides an overview of British and Canadian documentary film-making and the Griersonian principles (with quotes from the classic work by Hardy). The book's backcover showed a photo of the master engrossed in the photo-documentaries presented in Montevideo.[14] It was a true sign of the Grierson effect and of the meaning attributed to his visit.

Although Grierson did not travel to the city of Santa Fe, he did cross Río de la Plata after his stay in Montevideo to visit Buenos Aires, as the invited guest of Argentina's National Institute of Cinematography. According to *El Heraldo*, it was rumoured that the institute could offer Grierson a position 'as the director or organizer of the Experimental Filmmaking Center (for training)' to be created under the new film-making law. What can be said with certainty about Grierson's visit is that on the day he arrived (9 June), he gave a press conference at the Claridge Hotel, attended by well-known members of Argentina's film-making community. 'Vivacious, dynamic, quick, perceptive', were the terms used by the daily *La Prensa* to refer to his interventions; 'likeable', 'sure of himself' and 'precise and clear' in his dialogues, noted the film critic of the newspaper *La Nación*. During his time in Buenos Aires, Grierson returned to the same themes he had brought up in Montevideo: state support for cultural cinema and a concern for authenticity when depicting national and Latin American realities. In addition, the Scotsman had taken the time to read the new law of Argentine film-making – a law which he considered 'very precise' – and he mentioned the intention to legislate on the quality of films. The last part of his address dealt with his wish to see cinema incorporated into television and the differences and similarities between the two mediums. Although some criticised his approach to this topic, he noted the importance of both mediums in terms of developing educational cinema and disseminating cultural expression, in comments clearly informed by the programme he was directing for Scottish television at the time.[15]

# A PARALLEL STORYLINE: CAVALCANTI AND BRAZILIAN CINEMA

Two of the best films at SODRE '58 were *Rio, 40 gráus/Rio, 100 Degres F.* (1955) and *Rio Zona Norte/Rio, Northern Zone* (1957), the first feature-length films by Nelson Pereira dos Santos, the spiritual father of the Brazilian *Cinema Novo* movement that would burst out in the following decade. They were also paradigmatic films in terms of appropriating Italian neo-realism along the path towards true national cinema. However, any work on Brazilian cinema must make reference to Alberto Cavalcanti, a man who returned to his country in 1950 after being asked to head the recently founded Companhia Cinematográfica Vera Cruz in San Pablo, Brazil. The company had accepted the proposal of Grierson's old collaborator to produce two documentaries for every feature film it released, an ambitious objective, for which Cavalcanti had hired Henry E. 'Chick' Fowle, Rex Endsleigh and John Waterhouse. However, the project fell through because the company failed to fulfil its side of the agreement: this – in addition to the firm's financial crisis – led Cavalcanti to abandon the scheme and Vera Cruz closed its doors in 1953.[16] Had the project not failed, it could have proved an exceptional laboratory for documentary creation during the period, one where the experiences of the core members of the British documentary movement would have converged with the Brazilian cinematographic tradition. It would have been fruitful ground for developing the concept of 'neo-realism' that the Brazilian had favoured over the label 'documentary' in his early debates with Grierson.[17]

However, Brazil found its 'Grierson' in the figure of Humberto Mauro,[18] who would not be discovered by the Latin American film-makers of this generation until later, when Glauber Rocha called him the precursor of *Cinema Novo*, in a family tree in which Mauro's name was associated with the likes of Jean Vigo and Robert Flaherty. Rocha put Mauro on a map of international cinema in the 1930s in which Grierson and the British documentary movement that attracted Cavalcanti played an important role.[19] In an independent, contemporary way, Humberto Mauro had designed and partially completed, in his series *Brasilianas* (1945–54), a programme for national film development in which the documentary was considered the cinema of the future due to its artistic possibilities and low cost: it did not imitate foreign models yet had the potential to be commercialised abroad. In addition, the project's platform was a state entity, the National Institute of Educational Cinema (INCE), founded in 1936. Thus Mauro came up with an idea for propaganda cinema that reflected the international context of his time. It would be a cinema supported by the state, one with its own language and artistic expression, though its projects and films would not become known until some time later. By that time, the model – like perhaps the similar Griersonian one – had become obsolete in terms of the new challenges of Latin American cinema.[20]

## GRIERSON AND THE ANDEAN WORLD

Grierson's intelligent and perceptive perspective during the days of the SODRE led him to the documentaries whose cameras had focused on one previously invisible reality, that of the indigenous populations. The films by the Peruvian film-maker Manuel Chambi and the Bolivian Jorge Ruiz sparked the master's interest in the Andean region and its 'creative energy'. Grierson praised these films while vehemently criticising the paternalist, condescending viewpoint of other foreign productions about these countries.

In 1957, José María Arguedas, then the director of the Contemporary Art Institute of Lima, had become enthralled with the short documentary films being made in the Cuzco region. He went on to 'discover' them for the audiences in the Peruvian capital. The news of these films reached the SODRE organisers and Manuel Chambi was invited to present the films seen by Grierson at the festival: *Corpus del Cuzco/Body of Cuzco* (1955), *Corrida de toros y cóndores/Bullfighters and condors* (1956), *Las piedras/The Stones* (1956), *Carnaval de Kanas/Carnival of Kanas* (1956) and *Lucero de nieve/Light of Snow* (1957). After studying architecture in Buenos Aires, where he had his first contact with cinema, Chambi founded the Cusco Cine Club after returning to Peru in 1955. Chambi made these first films with his brother Victor and the photographer Eulogio Nishiyama; later, Luis Figueroa would join the collaboration. This formed the core of the 'École de Cuzco', as Georges Sadoul called the group at the Karlovy Vary Festival in 1964 after the 'discovery' of the first feature film made in this context, *Kukuli* (1960), directed by César Villanueva, Eulogio Mishiyama and Luis Figueroa.[21]

As in the black-and-white photographs by the renowned Martin Chambi, Manuel's father, Nishiyama's colour cinematography in these films eludes the use of an artistic construction that artificially extols the dignity of the indigenous people, an emphasis common in the *indigenist* artistic expressions of the period. As opposed to calculated staging, these films opted for a direct record capitalising on the visual strength of filmed reality. Similarly, the documentaries depart from the educational exposition of ethnographic cinema: most of the first films forego the support of a guiding commentary to make the Andean rural dweller and indigenous culture (mixed with colonial culture) the unquestionable stars. These films present the complexity and richness of the rites and festivals of the Quechua communities with naturalistic beauty and simplicity.

For this reason, it is likely that Grierson found in these films extraordinary raw material for his programme *This Wonderful World*; they were images freed from exoticising, paternalistic viewpoints and did not attempt to hide the poverty of the residents. 'These people of the *Alto Plano*', said Grierson on the programme,

> however poor, have created in their *fiestas* such spectaculars of mask and dance that I doubt if there has been the like at any time, anywhere, from a peasant people. I don't suppose that will disappear, but what will certainly disappear, and perhaps better so, is the bitter irony of one of the poorest and saddest peoples of the world, putting up for compensation the very richest and most joyous demonstration of their innate pride.[22]

These words closely reflect the tone of Chambi's documentaries, far from the *salvage ethnography* and the threat of a culture in danger of extinction; these films speak in terms that reveal no signs of accusation or the tension between tradition and modernity (or modernisation) so common in other documentaries.

In Bolivia, Grierson discovered a reality quite different from that of the rites and festivals of Peru. He established a much more intense and productive relationship with Jorge Ruiz; the two would make a ten-day trip by jeep from La Paz to the altiplano.[23] Jorge Ruiz[24] was the South American film-maker most in touch with the Anglo-American documentary-makers through collaboration on different projects, mainly documentaries sponsored by entities like the United Nations, International Development Agency or British and North American television networks. In 1956, for example, Ruiz was responsible for the cinematography for *Renace un pueblo/The Forgotten Indians* (Bolivia–Great Britain, 1956–7), directed by Anthony de Lothbiniere, with commentary by Paul Rotha. The programme was produced by the BBC in collaboration with Telecine, a small Bolivian production film company where Ruiz worked. In 1956, he co-directed *Miles como María/People like Maria* (1958) with Harry Watt, a documentary for the World Health Organisation that would win the television film award at the 1959 Venice Film Festival.

These projects were clearly aligned with the work that Ruiz had done since 1957 as a film-maker and director at the Bolivian Cinematographic Institute (ICB). Founded by the new government that took power after the 1952 revolution – an administration that would be the first to stake a claim for including the indigenous element in the construction of national identity – the ICB was a symbol of the country's modernisation and a model in the use of cinema as an instrument to promote state programmes of reform.[25]

The propaganda documentaries produced at the ICB by Waldo Cerruto (the institute's first director, 1953–7) and Jorge Ruiz reveal a rich and extensive repertoire of film resources (narrative, rhetorical and expository), where the construction of a visual and discursive imagery of the rural indigenous world is combined without apparent tension with images associated with modernisation and programmes for economic development and infrastructure (the majority financed and sponsored by the US). However, it was the film *Vuelve Sebastiana/Come Back, Sebastiana* (1953, a prizewinner at the 1956 SODRE) that witnessed Jorge Ruiz finding his own voice as a film-maker representing the Andean world. 'This is one of the six most important documentary filmmakers in the world', said Grierson after seeing the film.[26] The other Ruiz films shown during the 1958 SODRE festival would also represent the type of film that the Scotsman liked. While *Voces de la tierra/Voices of the Earth* (1956) – a 'continuous visual delight', to quote the press – presented the cultural world of the altiplano, *La vertiente/The Source* (1958),[27] an epic about community work, was reflective of the Griersonian tradition.

## OTHER DIALOGUES WITH THE LATIN AMERICAN DOCUMENTARY IN THE 1950S

The cinematographic and institutional career developed by Ruiz exemplifies how certain South American film-makers met and dialogued with Grierson. He promoted the creation of institutional spheres where documentaries could be developed to construct national identity and serve as a tool for promoting political, modernising reforms. But his career also reveals the breadth of documentary modes of representation, encompassing storytelling, dramatisation and the use of native actors. *Vuelve Sebastiana* is one of the best examples of this.

However, the documentaries of Jorge Ruiz also reveal how other dialogues and influences converged in the modes and aesthetics of representation. Ruiz himself stated that he 'felt like a disciple of Robert Flaherty and John Grierson' when he made *Virgen India/Virgin India* (1947), one of his first documentaries. When asked about his influences, he did mention the British school and the American Willard Van Dyke, but he also pointed out the pleasant impact of a Mexican, *El Indio* Fernández, director of *Flor Silvestre/Wildflower* (1943) and *La candelaria/María Candelaria* (1943).[28]

Ruiz had mentioned the first two films resulting from the intense, productive collaboration between director Emilio Fernández and photographer Gabriel Figueroa, two Mexicans who would play critical roles in configuring the national cinema of the period. Together they constructed powerful narrative and visual imagery in the idealised, hieratic, sculptural representation of the 'Indian' and the indigenous world, the product of a conscious appropriation and reinvention in a nationalistic tone of the legacy left by Sergei M. Eisentein during his visit to Mexico in 1931. The Soviet master had left without completing the project that had taken him to Mexico, *Qué viva México/Thunder over Mexico*, a film cited by John Grierson in 'First Principles of Documentary'. According to the Scotsman, the 'posturing or contemplative symbolic figures' of the film are a feature of one of the three methods of documentary film-making, which tended to be contemplative and poetic.[29] Footage from the Soviet's film, edited on different occasions and by different hands, would leave an indelible mark on Latin American cinema in the 1940s and 50s, a mark that would be especially visible in the artistic composition of the poetic documentary. In addition to Eisenstein's influence, Paul Strand also had an effect on regional cinema after serving as the director of photography on another mythic film for Latin American cinematography, *Redes/Fisherman's Nets* (1934). *Redes* was a realist drama filmed with native actors whose revolutionary calling was perfectly clear. Sponsored by the Fine Arts Department at the Secretary of Education, *Redes* would become a model for a cinema that attempted to serve as more than spectacle and entertainment, one based on state sponsorship aimed at establishing a national cinema and in which the borders between propaganda and the education of citizens often become blurred. *Redes* was also a model in terms of its aesthetic and discursive forms, with Flaherty and Eisenstein merging with Strand's characteristic stamp and that of his fellows at the Workers' Film and Photo League and Nykino.

In a film like *Láminas de Almahue/Sheets of Almahue* (1962), the most experimental of the works by Chilean film-maker Sergio Bravo, we can find hints of the cinematography of Strand, Ralph Steiner and Leo Hurwitz, though Bravo is one of the documentary film-makers who explicitly acknowledged Grierson's influence and who had met the Scotsman in person during his 1958 visit. After his stay in Montevideo that year, Grierson had also travelled to Chile where, as in the Uruguayan capital, 'he appeared right from the first as the Apostle of a resurgence of the national industry'. Once again, Grierson put together an intense agenda in Chile and continued his incisive discourse in support of an authentic regard for everyday reality and institutional support for cinema.[30] At the Experimental Cinema Centre founded by Bravo in Santiago in 1957, Grierson became excited after seeing the Chilean documentary-maker's first films, *Trilla/Threshing* (1957) and *Mimbre/Wicker* (1958), two paradigmatic examples of the poetic Latin American documentary during the period.[31] In works such as these, Grierson may have noted a model different from the ethnographic naturalism of Chambi or Ruiz's narrative. We can assume that he viewed Bravo's work as a singular development, one culturally rooted in the path he had sketched out in 'First Principles of Documentary', where dramatic construction gave way to a visual, lyrical and poetic treatment. This model would reach its apotheosis in Latin American production a short time later with Margot Benacerraf's *Araya* (1959). Eisenstein's shadow was once again visible, while the film also had recourse to postwar European documentaries for source material. In addition, Benacerraf's work reveals a new connection to the British documentary movement: the Shell Film Unit, founded in 1952 under the direction of Lionel Cole, collaborated on the production of *Araya*. Although film historians acknowledge *Araya* as a milestone in Venezuelan cinema, it was to have few repercussions on Latin American film-making at the time. This is probably owing to the fact that it was a swan song of an aesthetic-discursive model that would soon become obsolete.

## CONCLUSIONS

Jorge Ruiz would later reflect on what the film-makers he cited as influential (Grierson, Watt, Van Dyke, Fernandez) had actually given him:

> They convinced me that cinema could go hand in hand with social development. And I am not put off by the idea of being considered a propagandist. I have always been in favor of audiovisual persuasion. The influential figures to whom I am indebted made a true discovery: a cinema with proposals can be more useful than a cinema of protest.[32]

During the transition from the 1950s to the 60s, Latin American documentary film-makers were convinced of the power of audiovisual persuasion. The proposals would soon give way to protest, to open sociopolitical denunciation, and propaganda was thus necessarily conceived of in terms of counter-information and agitation. Perhaps the time had passed for documentaries imbued with the will to reform and transform society within the parameters of modernity and democracy (the bases of the programme drafted by John Grierson during the interwar period).[33] The call to arms was now aimed at overthrowing dictatorships in the region or fighting imperialism, and the film language, as expressed in the naturalist, dramatic and poetic modes of the Latin American documentary, would prove insufficient and soon be replaced by other aesthetics and other more radical politics.

Grierson's visit to South America in 1958 took place at an opportune time for dialogue and exchange, and it was important for the consolidation of previous influences and the creation of legacies for the future. Although it would be shortlived, the inspiration provided by his programme of social intervention through documentary – in a way perhaps similar to what occurred with Italian neo-realism in Latin America – can be seen both before and after his visit, in the propagandistic and creative trends of documentary cinema. These trends can be seen to some extent in certain types of cinema newsreels and documentaries from the 1940s and 50s; they are also present in certain manifestos and projects from the 60s where, although the languages were undergoing a full transformation (among other reasons, due to the arrival of Direct Cinema), the Griersonian legacy, in some cases, persisted.

## NOTES

1. Julianne Burton, *The Social Documentary in Latin America* (Pittsburgh, PA: University of Pittsburgh Press, 1990), p. 18.
2. Paulo Antonio Paranaguá, 'Orígenes, evolución y problemas', in Paulo Antonio Paranaguá (ed.), *El cine documental en América Latina* (Madrid: Cátedra, 2003), pp. 39–45. The memory of the Brazilian film-maker Pereira dos Santos cited in the epigraph come from his preface to this book. See also Paranaguá, *Tradición y modernidad en el cine de América Latina* (Madrid: Fondo de Cultura Económica, 2003), pp. 200–20.
3. The context was evocative of the European cinema clubs at the end of the 1920s, such as the London Film Society, where Grierson had recruited a few of the members who would participate in the British documentary movement. See Mario Handler, 'Starting from Scratch: Artisanship and Agritprop', in Julianne Burton (ed.), *Cinema and Social Change in Latin America: Conversations with Filmmakers* (Austin: University of Texas Press, 1986), p. 16.
4. He would discuss his experiences in the *altiplano* in his programme *This Wonderful World* on 29 January 1959, 9 February 1959 and 16 December 1966. See Forsyth Hardy, *John Grierson: A Documentary Biography* (London: Faber and Faber, 1979), pp. 209–10. Hardy's work is the only book on Grierson that focuses at length on his trip to Latin America.
5. Juan José Mugni and Mario Raimondo, 'El Archivo Nacional de la Imagen', in *SODRE: 70 ANIVERSARIO* (Montevideo: SODRE, 2000), pp. 155–67. See also the important dossier edited by Mariana Amieva, 'Volver a las fuentes: El Festival Internacional de Cine Documental y Experimental, 1954–1971', in *33 Cines* vol. 2 (2010), pp. 6–47. We would like to express our sincere thanks to Juan José Mugni (Director of the Archivo Nacional de la Imagen-Sodre, Montevideo) and to Eduardo Correa (Centro de Documentación Cinematográfica, Cinemateca Uruguaya) who let us view important documents for this research. We are also grateful to Adrián Muoyo, Octavio Morelli, Alejandro Intrieri and Julio Artucio (Biblioteca, Centro de Documentación y Archivo, INCAA, Buenos Aires).
6. Hugo R. Alfaro (member of the jury of the international section of the festival), in *Marcha*, 27 June 1958, p. 19. According to the Uruguayan press, Grierson also expressed interest in other films made in the same country such as *Makiritare*, by Roberto Gardiol and *Cantegriles*, by Alberto Miller.
7. Ibid.
8. *La mañana*, 6 June 1958.
9. *La mañana*, 6 June 1958; *Marcha*, 30 May and 6 June 1958.
10. Homero Alsina Thevenet, 'Grierson explica cosas', *El país*, 7 June 1958.
11. On 19 May, Grierson gave a talk entitled 'Perspectives for Cinematographic Art with the Advance of Television'.
12. See *La mañana*, 28 May 1958; *El país*, 28 May 1958; *Marcha*, 30 May 1958.
13. Photo reports, generally on social problems, made with a camera and tape recorder and then exhibited with captions.

14. Manuel Horacio Giménez, *Escuela documental inglesa* (Santa Fe: Editorial Documento del Instituto de Cinematografía de la Universidad del Litoral, 1961). Besides the photograph, the backcover featured an excerpt from the letter sent by the Scotsman to the school's students:

> I want to tell you how highly I thought of your exhibition in Montevideo. It is a splendid and exemplary teaching method and it is the first I have seen that contributes so simply and so well to learning how to make a film. You get to the very root of this matter, capturing the essential images and obliging them to hand over their content through the captions. This is a notably simple but profound contribution, and I would like to congratulate you and wish you further success.

15. *El Heraldo*, 18 June 1958; *La prensa*, 10 June 1958; *La Nación*, 10 June 1958.
16. It also discussed his project to create a National Cinema Institute in Brazil that would give priority to documentaries. See Paranaguá, 'Orígenes, evolución y problemas', p. 39.
17. Elizabeth Sussex, 'Cavalcanti in England', *Sight and Sound*, Autumn 1975. Reprinted in Kevin Macdonald and Mark Cousins (eds), *Imagining Reality: The Faber Book of Documentary* (London: Faber and Faber, 1996), pp. 116–17.
18. Amir Labaki would give the following title to a section of his book on Brazilian documentary focused on Mauro: 'Grierson à la brasileria', Labaki, *Introduçao ao documentário brasileiro* (Sao Paulo: Editora Francis, 2006).
19. Glauber Rocha, *Revisión crítica del cine brasileño* (Madrid: Editorial Fundamento, 1971), p. 26.
20. On the projects of Humberto Mauro, see the analyses in Paranaguá, *El cine documental en América Latina* and *Tradición y modernidad en el cine de América Latina*.
21. Carlos Bedoya, *100 años de cine en el Perú: una historia crítica* (Lima: Universidad de Lima/ICI, 1995), pp. 181 and 143. See also the interviews with the members of the group in Giancarlo Carbone (ed.), *El cine en el Perú: 1950–1972. Testimonios* (Lima: Universidad de Lima, 1993).
22. *This Wonderful World*, 16 December 1966, quoted in Hardy, *John Grierson*, p. 221.
23. As Ruiz himself recalls in José Antonio Valdivia, *Testigo de la realidad. Jorge Ruiz: memorias del cine documental boliviano* (Huelva: Festival de Cine Iberoamericano de Huelva, 1998, 2nd edn, 2003), pp. 67–8.
24. On the trajectory of Ruiz, see also Alfonso Gumucio-Dagron, 'Jorge Ruiz', in Paranaguá, *El cine documental en América Latina*, pp. 141–9.
25. A post he would hold until 1964. On the the productions of the ICB, see Mikel Luis Rodríguez, 'ICB: el primer organismo institucional en Bolivia (1952–1967)', *Secuencias. Revista de Historia del Cine* vol. 10 (1999), pp. 23–37.
26. Ruiz would do an English-language version of the film for Grierson to screen at Edinburgh. See Valdivia, *Testigo de la realidad*, p. 59.
27. A fictional full-length feature that used local residents as actors, this film recounted the collective efforts of the village of Rurenabaque (Beni) to construct a pipeline for drinking water.
28. Valdivia, *Testigo de la realidad*, p. 37.
29. John Grierson, 'First Principles of Documentary' (1932), in Ian Aitken (ed.), *The Documentary Film Movement: An Anthology* (Edinburgh: Edinburgh University Press, 1998), pp. 81–93.

30. Raúl Aicardi, 'John Grierson, el sorprendente', *Pomaire* vol. 13 (1958), p. 16, quoted in Claudio Salinas Muñoz and Hans Stange Marcus, *Historia del Cine Experimental en la Universidad de Chile, 1957–1973* (Santiago de Chile: Uqbar editores, 2008), pp. 70–1. Also the magazine *Ecran* vol. 1430 (24 May 1958), quoted in Alicia Vega, *Itinerario del cine documental chileno, 1900–1990* (Santiago de Chile: Universidad Alberto Hurtado, 2006), pp. 165–6.

31. Alicia Vega remembers that the three films that Bravo did between 1956 and 1958 (*Mimbre, Imágenes antárticas* and *Trilla*) were analysed in a seminar scheduled as part of Grierson's visit. (See Vega, *Itinerario del cine documental chileno, 1900–1990*, p. 165.) Grierson was so enthusiastic about these films that he recommended Bravo and his group to the Cultural Outreach Department at the University of Chile, thus forging institutional relations between the centre and the university (Muñoz and Marcus, *Historia del Cine Experimental en la Universidad de Chile, 1957–1973*, p. 35). On this period of Chilean cinema, see also the classical works of Jacqueline Mouesca and the recent book by Pablo Corro *et al.*, *Teorías del cine documental chileno 1957–1973* (Santiago de Chile: Pontificia Universidad Católica de Chile, 2007).

32. Valdivia, *Testigo de la realidad*, p. 37.

33. See Ian Aitken, *Film and Reform: John Grierson and the British Documentary Film Movement* (London: Routledge, 1990).


## REFERENCES

Aicardi, Raúl, 'John Grierson, el sorprendente', *Pomaire* vol. 13 (1958), p. 16.

Aitken, Ian, *Film and Reform: John Grierson and the British Documentary Film Movement* (London: Routledge, 1990).

Alfaro, Hugo R., 'La vuelta al mundo en 40 días. Festival Cinematográfico del SODRE memorias de un jurado', *Marcha*, 27 June 1958, p. 19.

Amieva, Mariana, 'Volver a las fuentes: El Festival Internacional de Cine Documental y Experimental, 1954–1971', *33 Cines* vol. 2 (2010), pp. 6–47.

Bedoya, Carlos, *100 años de cine en el Perú: una historia crítica* (Lima: Universidad de Lima/ICI, 1995).

Burton, Julianne, *The Social Documentary in Latin America* (Pittsburgh, PA: University of Pittsburgh Press, 1990).

Carbone, Giancarlo (ed.), *El cine en el Perú: 1950–1972. Testimonios* (Lima: Universidad de Lima, 1993).

Corro, Pablo *et al.*, *Teorías del cine documental chileno 1957–1973* (Santiago de Chile: Pontificia Universidad Católica de Chile, 2007).

'De Problemas de Cine habla J. Grierson', *La prensa*, 10 June 1958.

Giménez, Manuel Horacio, *Escuela documental inglesa* (Santa Fe: Editorial Documento del Instituto de Cinematografía de la Universidad del Litoral, 1961).

'Grierson se va y el Festival sigue', *La mañana*, 6 June 1958.

Grierson, John, 'First Principles of Documentary' (1932), in Ian Aitken (ed.), *The Documentary Film Movement: An Anthology* (Edinburgh: Edinburgh University Press, 1998), pp. 81–93.

Grierson, John, 'Perspectives for Cinematographic Art with the Advance of Television', Sodre International Festival, Montevideo, 19 May 1958.

Gumucio-Dagron, Alfonso, 'Jorge Ruiz', in Paulo Antonio Paranaguá (ed.), *El cine documental en América Latina* (Madrid: Cátedra, 2003), pp. 141–9.

Handler, Mario, 'Starting from Scratch: Artisanship and Agritprop', in Julianne Burton (ed.), *Cinema and Social Change in Latin America. Conversations with Filmmakers* (Austin: University of Texas Press, 1986), pp. 13–24.

Hardy, Forsyth, *John Grierson: A Documentary Biography* (London: Faber and Faber, 1979).

J.G.F., 'Con humorismo Grierson supo decir importantes verdades', *La manana*, 28 May 1958.

'John Grierson in Bs.As. ¿Oferta del Instituto?' *El Heraldo*, 18 June 1958.

Labaki, Amir, 'Grierson à la brasileria', in *Introduçao ao documentário brasileiro* (Sao Paulo: Editora Francis, 2006), pp. 37–57.

Mouesca, Jacqueline, *Plano secuencia de la memoria en Chile* (Madrid: Editorial del Litoral, 1988).

Mouesca, Jacqueline, *El documental chileno* (Santiago de Chile: LOM Ediciones, 2005).

Mugni, Juan José and Mario Raimondo, 'El Archivo Nacional de la Imagen', in *SODRE: 70 ANIVERSARIO* (Montevideo: SODRE, 2000), pp. 155–67.

Muñoz, Claudio Salinas and Hans Stange Marcus, *Historia del Cine Experimental en la Universidad de Chile, 1957–1973* (Santiago de Chile: Uqbar editores, 2008).

M.T., 'Algo más que un cineísta: John Grierson vino, vió y ojalá venza', *Marcha*, 30 May 1958.

Paranaguá, Paulo Antonio (ed.), *El cine documental en América Latina* (Madrid: Cátedra, 2003).

Paranaguá, Paulo Antonio, *Tradición y modernidad en el cine de América Latina* (Madrid: Fondo de Cultura Económica, 2003).

'Presencia de Grierson', *La Nación*, 10 June 1958.

Rocha, Glauber, *Revisión crítica del cine brasileño* (Madrid: Editorial Fundamento, 1971).

Rodríguez, Mikel Luis, 'ICB: el primer organismo institucional en Bolivia (1952–1967)', *Secuencias. Revista de Historia del Cine* vol. 10 (1999), pp. 23–37.

Sussex, Elizabeth, 'Cavalcanti in England', *Sight and Sound*, Autumn 1975. Reprinted in Kevin Macdonald and Mark Cousins (eds), *Imagining Reality: The Faber Book of Documentary* (London: Faber and Faber, 1996), pp. 116–17.

Thevenet, Homero Alsina, 'Le hablan, Señor Ministro', *El país*, 28 May 1958.

Thevenet, Homero Alsina, 'Grierson explica cosas', *El país*, 7 June 1958.

Valdivia, José Antonio, *Testigo de la realidad. Jorge Ruiz: memorias del cine documental boliviano* (Huelva: Festival de Cine Iberoamericano de Huelva, 1998), second edition 2003.

Vega, Alicia, *Itinerario del cine documental chileno, 1900–1990* (Santiago de Chile: Universidad Alberto Hurtado, 2006).

# Select Bibliography

Aitken, Ian, 'John Grierson, Idealism and the Inter-war Period', *Historical Journal of Film, Radio and Television* vol. 9 no. 3 (1989), pp. 247–58.

Aitken, Ian, *Film and Reform: John Grierson and the Documentary Film Movement* (London: Routledge, 1990).

Aitken, Ian, (ed.), *The Documentary Film Movement: An Anthology* (Edinburgh: Edinburgh University Press, 1998).

Aitken, Ian, 'The Development of Official Film-Making in Hong-Kong', *Historical Journal of Film, Radio and Television* vol. 2 no. 4 (2012), pp. 589–609.

Amieva, Mariana (ed.), 'Volver a las fuentes: El Festival Internacional de Cine Documental y Experimental, 1954–1971', *33 Cines* vol. 2 (2010), pp. 6–47.

Anstey, Edgar, 'The Early Days of Documentary', *Cine-Technician* vol. 7 (September–October 1941), pp. 102–4.

Anstey, Edgar, 'The Living Story: E.M.B.-G.P.O.', *Sight and Sound* vol. 21 no. 4 (April–June 1952), p. 176.

Anstey, Edgar, Stuart Hood, Claire Johnston and Ivor Montagu, 'The Grierson Influence', *Undercut* vol. 9 (Summer 1983), p. 17.

Anthony, Scott and James Mansell (eds), *The Projection of Britain: A History of the GPO Film Unit* (London: BFI, 2011).

Bertrand, Ina, 'Theory into Practice: Stanley Hawes and the Commonwealth Film Unit', *Screening the Past*, special issue: 'After Grierson', edited by Ina Bertrand, 1999, http://tlweb.latrobe.edu.au/humanities/screeningthepast/firstrelease/fr0799/ibfr7d.htm.

Bertrand, Ina and Diane Collins, *Government and Film in Australia* (Sydney: Currency Press/Australian Film Institute, 1981).

Beveridge, James, *John Grierson: Film Master* (New York: Macmillan, 1978).

Beveridge, James, 'Grierson and Distribution', in *John Grierson and the NFB*, proceedings of a conference held at McGill University, 29–31 October 1981 (Toronto: ECW Press, 1984), pp. 29–41.

Chittock, John (ed.), *Researchers Guide to John Grierson: Films, Reference Sources, Collections, Data* (London: Grierson Memorial Trust, 1990).

*Cinéma d'aujourd'hui*, issue devoted to the British documentary, vol. 11 (February–March 1977).

Colls, Robert and Philip Dodd, 'Representing the Nation – British Documentary Film, 1930–1945', *Screen* vol. 26 no. 1 (1985), pp. 21–33.

Cronin, Mike, 'Selling Irish Bacon: The Empire Marketing Board and Artists of the Free State', *Éire-Ireland* vol. 39 nos 3–4 (2004), pp. 132–43.

Dahl, Rasmus, 'A National, Historical Perspective on Documentary in Denmark', *Screening the Past*, special issue: 'After Grierson', http://tlweb.latrobe.edu.au/humanities/screeningthepast/firstrelease/fr0799/rdfr7c.htm.

Dawson, Jonathan, 'The Grierson Tradition', in Ross Lansell and Peter Beilby (eds), *The Documentary Film in Australia* (Melbourne: Cinema Papers/Film Victoria, 1981).

Druick, Zoë, *Projecting Canada: Government Policy and Documentary Film at the National Film Board* (Montreal and Kingston: McGill-Queen's University Press, 2007).

Druick, Zoë, 'Visualising the World: The British Documentary at UNESCO', in Scott Anthony and James G. Mansell (eds), *The Projection of Britain: A History of the GPO Film Unit* (London: BFI, 2011), pp. 272–80.

Ellis, Jack, 'The Young Grierson in America, 1924–1927', *Cinema Journal* vol. 8 (Fall 1968), pp. 12–21.

Ellis, Jack, 'John Grierson's First Years at the National Film Board', *Cinema Journal* vol. 10 (Fall 1970), pp. 2–14.

Ellis, Jack, 'John Grierson's Relation with British Documentary during World War Two', in *John Grierson and the NFB*, proceedings of a conference held at McGill University, 29–31 October 1981 (Toronto: ECW Press, 1984), pp. 62–76.

Ellis, Jack, 'The Final Years of the British Documentary Movement as the Grierson Movement', *Journal of Film and Video* vol. 36 (Fall 1984), pp. 41–9.

Ellis, Jack, *John Grierson: Life, Contributions, Influence* (Carbondale and Edwardsville: Southern Illinois University Press, 2000).

Evans, Gary, *John Grierson and the National Film Board: The Politics of Wartime Propaganda* (Toronto: University of Toronto Press, 1984).

Evans, Gary, *In the National Interest: A Chronicle of the National Film Board of Canada from 1949 to 1989* (Toronto: University of Toronto Press, 1991).

Evans, Gary, *John Grierson: Trailblazer of Documentary* (Montreal: XYZ Publishing, 2005).

'The Film in Colonial Development Conference', London, British Film Institute, 1948.

Film Enquiry Committee, *Report of the Film Enquiry Committee* (New Delhi: Government of India Press, 1951).

Fox, Jo, 'John Grierson, His "Documentary Boys" and the British Ministry of Information, 1939–42', *Historical Journal of Film, Radio and Television* vol. 25 no. 3 (2005), pp. 345–6.

Grierson, John, 'Flaherty's Poetic *Moana*', *New York Sun*, 8 February 1926. Reprinted in Lewis Jacobs (ed.), *The Documentary Tradition*, 2nd edn (New York: Norton and Co., 1979), pp. 25–6.

Grierson, John, 'The Film in British Colonial Development', *Sight and Sound* vol. 17 no. 65 (Spring 1948).

Grierson, John, 'Union of South Africa: The Grierson Report', 2nd draft, 1954. Reprinted in *Screening the Past* no. 7 (1999), http://tlweb.latrobe.edu.au/humanities/screeningthepast/classics/cl0799/JG1cl7a.pdf.

Grierson, John, 'O These Problems, These Priorities', in Jag Mohan (ed.), *Four Times Five* (Bombay: Films Division, Ministry of Information and Broadcasting, 1969), pp. 7–8.

Grierson, John, 'Memorandum to the Right Honourable, the Prime Minister', in Albert Moran and Tom O'Regan (eds), *An Australian Film Reader* (Sydney: Currency Press, 1985), pp. 72–8.

Grierson, John, 'A Film Policy for Canada', in Douglas Fetherling (ed.), *Documents in Canadian Film* (Peterborough: Broadview, 1988), pp. 51–67.

Grieveson, Lee and Colin MacCabe (eds), *Film and the End of Empire* (London: BFI, 2011).

Hardy, Forsyth, *John Grierson: A Documentary Biography* (London: Faber and Faber, 1979).

Hardy, Forsyth (ed. and comp.), *Grierson on Documentary* (London: Faber and Faber, 1966).

Hardy, Forsyth (ed.), *Grierson on the Movies* (London: Faber and Faber, 1981).

Hardy, H. Forsyth, 'Democracy as a Fighting Faith', in *John Grierson and the NFB*, proceedings of a conference held at McGill University, 29–31 October 1981 (Toronto: ECW Press, 1984), pp. 86–94.

Hawes, Stanley, 'Grierson in Australia', in Albert Moran and Tom O'Regan (eds), *Australian Film Reader* (Sydney: Currency Press, 1985), pp. 79–84.

Hees, E., *The National Film Board of South Africa: A Short History*, University of Stellenbosch Annale, no. 1 (1991).

Higson, Andrew, 'Britain's Outstanding Contribution to Film', in Charles Barr (ed.), *All Our Yesterdays: Ninety Years of British Cinema* (London: BFI, 1986), pp. 72–97.

*Historical Journal of Film, Radio and Television* vol. 9 no. 3 (1989), special issue: 'John Grierson: A Critical Retrospective', edited by Ian Jarvie and Nicholas Pronay.

Hogenkamp, Bert, 'The British Documentary Movement in Perspective', in Willem De Greef and Willem Hesling (eds), *Image, Reality, Spectator: Essays on Documentary Film and Television* (Louvain: Acco, 1989).

Hood, Stuart, 'John Grierson and the Documentary Film Movement', *Sight and Sound* vol. 17 no. 65 (Spring 1948), pp. 44–5.

Jarvie, Ian and Robert L. Macmillan, 'John Grierson on Hollywood's Success', *Historical Journal of Film, Radio and Television* vol. 9 no. 3 (1989), pp. 309–26.

'John Grierson Archive', *Historical Journal of Film, Radio and Television* vol. 9 no. 3 (1989), p. 327.

*John Grierson and the NFB*, proceedings of a conference held at McGill University, 29–31 October 1981 (Toronto: ECW Press, 1984).

Jones, D. B., *Movies and Memoranda: An Interpretive History of the National Film Board of Canada* (Ottawa: Canadian Film Institute, 1981).

Jones, D. B., 'Assessing the National Film Board, Crediting Grierson', *Historical Journal of Film, Radio and Television* vol. 9 no. 3 (1989), pp. 301–8.

Lee, Rohama, *Master of the Film Medium: John Grierson Pioneered the Documentary Film in Britain and Canada* (Ames: American Archives of Factual Film, Iowa State University, 1984).

Lockerbie, Ian, 'Grierson and Realism', in *John Grierson and the NFB*, proceedings of a conference held at McGill University, 29–31 October 1981 (Toronto: ECW Press, 1984), pp. 86–101.

Lockerbie, Ian (ed.), *John Grierson: Eyes of Democracy* (Stirling: John Grierson Archive, 1990).

Lovell, A. and Hillier, J., *Studies in Documentary* (London: Secker and Warburg, 1972).

Low, Colin, 'Grierson and "Challenge for Change"', in *John Grierson and the NFB*, proceedings of a conference held at McGill University, 29–31 October 1981 (Toronto: ECW Press, 1984), pp. 95–103.

MacDonald, Richard, 'Evasive Enlightenment: *World without End* and the Internationalism of Postwar Documentary', *Journal of British Cinema and Television* vol. 10 no. 3 (2013), pp. 452–74.

MacPherson, Don and Paul Willemen (eds), *Traditions of Independence: British Cinema in the Thirties* (London: BFI, 1979).

McInnes, Graham, *One Man's Documentary: A Memoir of the Early Days of the National Film Board* (Winnipeg: University of Manitoba Press, 2004).

Mohan, Jag (ed.), *Two Decades of the Films Division* (Bombay: Ministry of Information and Broadcasting, 1969).

Mohan, Jag (ed.), *Documentary Films and Indian Awakening* (New Delhi: Publications Division, Ministry of Information and Broadcasting, 1990).

Moran, Albert, *Projecting Australia: Government Film since 1945* (Sydney: Currency Press, 1991).

Moran, Albert and Tom O'Regan, 'Two Discourses of Australian Film', *Australian Journal of Screen Theory* vol. 15 no. 16 (1983), pp. 163–73.

Morris, Peter, 'Backwards to the Future: John Grierson's Film Policy for Canada', in Gene Walz (ed.), *Flashback: People and Institutions in Canadian Film History* (Montreal: Médiatexte, 1986), pp. 17–35.

Morris, Peter, 'Re-thinking Grierson: The Ideology of John Grierson', in Pierre Vérnonneau, Michael Dorland and Seth Feldman (eds), *Dialogue: Cinéma canadienne et québécois / Canadian and Quebec Cinema* (Montreal: Médiatexte, 1987), pp. 21–56.

Morris, Peter, '"Praxis into process": John Grierson and the National Film Board of Canada', *Historical Journal of Film, Radio and Television* vol. 9 no. 3 (1989), pp. 269–82.

Mugni, Juan José and Mario Raimondo, 'El Archivo Nacional de la Imagen', in *SODRE: 70 ANIVERSARIO* (Montevideo: SODRE, 2000), pp. 155–67.

*National Film Board: Survey of Organization and Business Administration*, Canadian Parliamentary Papers, 1950.

Nelson, Joyce, *The Colonized Eye: Rethinking the Grierson Legend* (Toronto: Between the Lines, 1988).

Nichols, Bill, 'Documentary Film and the Modernist Avant-Garde', *Critical Inquiry* vol. 27 no. 4 (2001), pp. 580–610.

Pronay, Nicholas, 'John Grierson and the Documentary – 60 Years On', *Historical Journal of Film, Radio and Television* vol. 9 no. 3 (1989), pp. 227–46.

Rice, Tom, 'Distant Voices of Malaya, Still Colonial Lives', *Journal of British Cinema and Television* vol. 10 no. 3 (2013), pp. 430–51.

Roger, Andrew, 'Some Factors Contributing to the Formation of the National Film Board of Canada', *Historical Journal of Film, Radio and Television* vol. 9 no. 3 (1989), pp. 259–68.

Rotha, Paul, *Documentary Film* (London: Faber and Faber, 1935).

Rotha, Paul, *Documentary Diary: An Informal History of the British Documentary Film, 1928–1939* (New York: Hill & Wang, 1973).

*Screening the Past*, special issue: 'After Grierson', edited by Ina Bertrand (1999), http://tlweb. latrobe.edu.au/humanities/screeningthepast/current/cc47.html.

Sellars, William, 'Making Films in and for the Colonies', *Journal of the Royal Society of the Arts* vol. 1-1 no. 4910 (16 October 1953), pp. 828–37.

Smyth, Rosaleen, 'The Central African Film Unit's Images of Empire, 1948–1963', *Historical Journal of Film, Radio and Television* vol. 3 no. 2 (1983), pp. 131–47.

Smyth, Rosaleen, 'The Post-war Career of the Colonial Film Unit in Africa; 1946–1955', *Historical Journal of Film, Radio and Television* vol. 12 no. 2 (1992), pp. 163–77.

Smyth, Rosaleen, 'Grierson, the British Documentary Movement, and Colonial Cinema in British Colonial Africa', *Film History: An International Journal* vol. 25 no. 2 (2013), pp. 82–113.

Stollery, Martin, *Alternative Empires: European Modernist Cinemas and Cultures of Imperialism* (Exeter: Exeter University Press, 2000).

Stollery, Martin, 'From *Storm over Asia* to *Dawn over Africa*: Transnationalism and Imperialism in British Intellectual Film Culture of the late 1920s and 1930s', *Transnational Cinemas* vol. 2 no. 1 (2011), pp. 93–111.

Sussex, Elizabeth, 'The Golden Years of Grierson', *Sight and Sound* vol. 41 no. 3 (Summer 1972), pp. 1449–53.

Sussex, Elizabeth, *The Rise and Fall of British Documentary: The Story of the Film Movement Founded by John Grierson* (Berkeley and Los Angeles: University of California Press, 1975).

Swann, Paul, 'John Grierson and the G.P.O. Film Unit 1933–1939', *Historical Journal of Film, Radio and Television* vol. 1 no. 1 (1983), pp. 19–32.

Swann, Paul, 'The Selling of the Empire: The EMB Film Unit', *Studies in Visual Communication* vol. 9 no. 3 (1983), pp. 15–24.

Swann, Paul, *The British Documentary Film Movement, 1926–1946* (Cambridge: Cambridge University Press, 1989).

Tallents, Sir Stephen, 'The First Days of Documentary', *Documentary News Letter* vol. 6 no. 55 (January–February 1947), pp. 76–7.

Tallents, Sir Stephen, *British Documentary* (London: Film Centre, 1968).

Tallents, Sir Stephen, 'The Birth of British Documentary', *Journal of the University Film Association* vol. 20 nos 1–3 (1968), n.p.

Tomaselli, K. G, 'Grierson in South Africa: Culture, State and Nationalist Ideology in the South African Film Industry: 1940–1981', *Cinema Canada* vol. 122 (1985), pp. 24–7.

Tomaselli, K. G. and Hees, E. 'John Grierson in South Africa: Afrikaner Nationalism and the National Film Board', *Screening the Past* vol. 7 (1999), latrobe.edu.au/www/screeningthepast/index.

Tudor, Andrew, 'The Problem of Context: John Grierson', in *Theories of Film* (New York: Viking, 1974), pp. 59–76.

UNESCO, *Report of the Commission on Technical Needs in Press, Radio, Film, Following the Survey in Twelve War-devastated Countries* (Paris: UNESCO, 1947).

Waugh, Thomas, Michael Brendan Baker and Ezra Winton (eds), *Challenge for Change: Activist Documentary at the National Film Board of Canada* (Montreal/Kingston: McGill-Queen's University Press, 2010).

Williams, Deane, 'Between Empire and Nation: Grierson in Australia', *Screening the Past*, special issue: 'After Grierson', edited by Ina Bertrand (1999), http://tlweb.latrobe.edu.au/humanities/screeningthepast/current/cc47.html.

Williams, Deane, *Australian Post-war Documentary Films: An Arc of Mirrors* (Bristol and Chicago, IL: Intellect, 2008).

Winston, Brian, 'Great Artist or Fly on the Wall: Accommodation and Its Destruction?', in Jay Ruby and Martin Taureg (eds), *Visual Explorations of the World: Selected Papers from the International Conference on Visual Communication* (Aachen: Herodet in Rader Verlag, 1987), pp. 190–204.

Winston, Brian, *Claiming the Real: The Griersonian Documentary and Its Legitimations* (London: BFI, 1995).

Woods, D. L., 'John Grierson: Documentary Film Pioneer', *Quarterly Journal of Speech* vol. 57 (1971), pp. 221–8.

Woods, Philip, 'From Shaw to Shantaram: The Film Advisory Board and the Making of British Propaganda Films in India, 1940–1943', *Historical Journal of Film, Radio and Television* vol. 21 no. 3 (2001), pp. 293–308.

Wright, Basil, 'The Progress of the Factual Film: 1. Grierson the Pioneer', in *Public's Progress* (London: Contact, 1948), pp. 64–71.

Wright, Basil, 'Documentary To-day', *Penguin Film Review* vol. 2 (January 1947), pp. 37–44.

Wright, Basil, 'Documentary: Flesh, Fowl or …?', *Sight and Sound* vol. 19 (March 1950), pp. 43–7.

Wright, Basil, *The Long View* (London: Secker & Warburg, 1974).

# Appendix: John Grierson Biographical Timeline

- **26 April 1898**
  John Grierson born, Deanston, Scotland.
- **1915**
  Grierson attends Glasgow University.
- **1917**
  Enlists in Royal Naval Volunteer Reserve.
- **1919**
  Returns to Glasgow University.
- **1923**
  Receives an MA from Glasgow University with distinctions in English and Moral Philosophy.
- **1924**
  Takes up post at University of Chicago as a visiting postgraduate scholar on a Rockefeller Research Fellowship in Social Science. This where Grierson's interest in film and in theories of public opinion, such as expressed by Walter Lippmann, commenced. Spends time in Chicago, New York and Los Angeles. During this period also becomes film reviewer for newspapers such as *New York Sun*, where the term 'documentary' was first used in a review of Robert Flaherty's *Moana* published 8 February 1926 under the pseudonym 'the Moviegoer'. Helps John S. Cohen Jr compile the titles for the US premiere of Sergei Eisenstein's *Battleship Potemkin*.
- **1926**
  Researches Famous Players–Lasky records in Hollywood and publishes findings in *Motion Picture News* in November and December. Also meets directors such as Erich von Stroheim, Harry Landon, Charles Chaplin, King Vidor, F. W. Murnau and Ernst Lubitsch.
- **1927**
  Leaves the US and joins Stephen Tallents at the Empire Marketing Board in proposing that film study, screening and production could 'bring the Empire alive' to its peoples and could be 'a medium of education and persuasion'.[1]
- **1929**
  Completes *Drifters*, his first film for the EMB.
- **1929–30**
  Hires J. D. Davison, Basil Wright, John Taylor, Paul Rotha, Evelyn Spice, Donald Taylor, Arthur Elton, Edgar Anstey and Stuart Legg for the EMB Film Unit.

- **1933**

  *Industrial Britan* released as part of the Imperial Six. Other films in this package were Basil Wright's *The Country Come to Town*, Arthur Elton's *Upstream*, Wright's *O'er Hill and Dale*, Elton's *Shadow on the Mountain* and Wright's *Lumber*.

- **1933**

  EMB Film Unit and Stephen Tallents move to the General Post Office Film Unit and are joined, for various periods of time, by Alberto Cavalcanti, Harry Watt, Raymond Spottiswoode, Humphrey Jennings, Alan Shaw, Len Lye, Benjamin Britten, and W. H. Auden.

  Some of the most famous films of the British documentary movement were made by the GPO Film Unit, including *Song of Ceylon*, *Pett and Pott* (1934), *Night Mail*, *The Savings of Bill Blewitt*, *Housing Problems*, *North Sea* and *Target for Tonight* (1941).

- **1934**

  Grierson continued speaking and writing on documentary film. His engagements included a series of ten lectures at the University of Leicester entitled 'The Arts of Cinema and Its Social Relationships' as well as lectures to the Glasgow Film Society and the Scottish Educational Cinema Society, Independent Film-makers Association, Manchester Film Institute, British Film Institute.

- **1937**

  Established Film Centre, 'not to produce or distribute films ... but to advise sponsors, supervise production, make arrangements for distribution, undertake scenarios work and research, open up new markets, and in general stimulate and guide the development of the [documentary] movement in general'.[2]

- **May 1938**

  Visits Canada as film consultant on behalf of the Imperial Relations Trust.

- **14 October 1939**

  Appointed Canadian Government Film Commissioner.

- **January 1940**

  Leaves Canada to visit Australia and New Zealand as a continuation of his role as film consultant for the IRT.

- **December 1940**

  Returns to Ottawa and Canadian NFB.

- **August 1945**

  Resigns from Canadian NFB.

- **1945**

  Establishes International Film Associates, a documentary production and distribution network alongside Robert Flaherty, Stuart Legg, Raymond Spottiswoode, Jena Benoit-Lévy and Margaret Ann Adamson.

- **May 1946**

  Sets up *The World Today*, to produce shorts for theatrical release.

- **February 1947**

  Appointed advisor to UNESCO.

- **1948**

  Joined Films Division of the Central Office of Information, which included the Crown Film Unit and the Colonial Film Unit as well as commercial units such as Basic Films, Greenpark Productions, Paul Rotha Productions and Realist Film Unit.

- **1949**
  Visits South Africa to advise the government on setting up of a national film board.
- **1950**
  Appointed executive producer of Group 3, a government-backed studio intended to produce feature films for the purpose of training film-makers.
- **October 1957**
  *This Wonderful Life*, produced and presented by Grierson, is aired on Scottish television and runs for nine years.
- **January 1969**
  Visiting Lecturer at McGill University, Montreal.
- **April 1970**
  Visits India with the Canadian International Development Agency to advise on methods of communication and education pertaining to birth control. Later invited to review the production of the government's Films Division.
- **19 February 1972**
  Dies Bath, England.

## NOTES

1. Jack Ellis, *John Grierson: Life, Contributions, Influence* (Carbondale and Edwardsville: Southern Illinois University Press, 2000, pp. 38–9.
2. Ibid., p. 111.

## REFERENCES

Aitken, Ian, *Film and Reform: John Grierson and the Documentary Film Movement* (London and New York: Routledge, 1990).

Beveridge, James, *John Grierson: Film Master* (New York and London: Macmillan/Collier Macmillan, 1978).

Ellis, Jack, *John Grierson: Life, Contributions, Influence* (Carbondale and Edwardsville: Southern Illinois University Press, 2000).

# Index

**Notes:** Page numbers in **bold** indicate detailed analysis. Those in *italic* refer to illustrations. Foreign-language films are indexed under their English titles (where these are given), with country of origin.

*n* = endnote.

## LIST OF ILLUSTRATIONS

While considerable effort has been made to correctly identify the copyright holders, this has not been possible in all cases. We apologise for any apparent negligence and any omissions or corrections brought to our attention will be remedied in any future editions.